Understanding Vietnam

A

Philip E. Lilienthal

Book

The Philip E. Lilienthal imprint
honors special books
in commemoration of a man whose work
at the University of California Press from 1954 to 1979
was marked by dedication to young authors
and to high standards in the field of Asian Studies.
Friends, family, authors, and foundations have together
endowed the Lilienthal Fund, which enables the Press
to publish under this imprint selected books
in a way that reflects the taste and judgment
of a great and beloved editor.

Understanding Vietnam

NEIL L. JAMIESON

University of California Press

BERKELEY   LOS ANGELES   LONDON

University of California Press
Berkeley and Los Angeles, California

University of California Press, Ltd.
London, England

First Paperback Printing 1995

Library of Congress Cataloging-in-Publication Data

Jamieson, Neil L.
    Understanding Vietnam / Neil L. Jamieson.
      p.   cm.
    "A Philip E. Lilienthal book."
    Includes bibliographical references and index.
    ISBN 0-520-20157-4
    1. Vietnam—History—1858–1945.   2. Vietnam—History—
20th century.   I. Title.
DS556.8.J36   1993
959.7—dc20   92-20978
                                                                      CIP

Printed in the United States of America
9 8 7 6 5 4 3 2

To my wife, Virginia Winstead Jamieson,
and to the memory of my parents,
Neil Livingston Jamieson, Jr., and Alice Williamson Jamieson

Contents

Preface

Over two and a half million Americans went to Vietnam, and over 55,000 of us died there. We spent many billions of dollars in a losing cause that divided us as a nation, battered our self-esteem, and eroded our confidence in both the morality and the effectiveness of our foreign policy. Yet our understanding of this tragic episode remains superficial and, I believe, in many respects simply wrong. We have failed to understand our experience because, then and now, we have ignored the perspectives of the people most deeply concerned with the war in which we became involved: The Vietnamese, both our friends and our foes, as well as those who wished to be neither.

To no insignificant extent the war became defined in Washington, distorted in Washington, and finally lost in Washington through a process that was out of touch with any realistic understanding of what was in the much-touted "hearts and minds" of the people. The images of Vietnam about which controversy swirled in the United States arose from our own culture, not from Vietnamese realities or perceptions. Yet the ways in which the Vietnamese themselves perceived the war, including our role in it, were always at the heart of the matter. The war was, after all, in Vietnam; and it was fought mainly by Vietnamese against other Vietnamese—over the nature of Vietnamese society.

Even in retrospect, as a people we have learned very little about Vietnam or the Vietnamese. The films and books about the war in Vietnam that have appeared in the United States are almost entirely limited to the experience of being an American in Vietnam. The Vietnamese, when they appear at all in these works, are shadowy cardboard figures, merely one-dimensional stage props for the inner workings of the American psyche.

Lost in our own visions, we have never really grasped the passionate commitment with which Vietnamese clung to and fought over their own competing and incompatible visions of what Vietnam was and what it might and should become. But so long as we compulsively look inward, focused upon our reactions to the war as individual Americans, our experiences will never make sense as part of any larger whole. We simply cannot make sense of our experience in Vietnam by further brooding upon what we as Americans felt, or saw, or thought we were trying to do. In isolation, whatever our bias, this experience makes no sense.

To better understand ourselves, we must understand the Vietnam War. To understand the war, we must understand the Vietnamese. We must learn more about Vietnamese culture and Vietnamese paradigms in order to untangle the muddled debates about our own. Realizing that we must do this is the first and most important lesson of Vietnam. And it is one we Americans have been exasperatingly slow to learn. We remain far too ready to assume that other people are, or want to be, or should be, like us.

My fascination with Vietnamese culture and society began in 1959 with a small incident that revealed my ignorance of Southeast Asia and spurred a period of reading about French Indochina. With a fresh M.A. in folklore, I was attracted to Vietnam as a place to collect folklore in its social context, in a culture very different from the Indo-European tradition with which I was familiar.

I was neither for nor against American policies in Vietnam, and my knowledge of political issues in that part of the world was very superficial. When I attended language school after enlisting in the U.S. Army, I leaped at the chance to study Vietnamese.

After nearly a year of intensive study of Vietnamese, however, I was sent not to Vietnam but to the Philippines, where I traveled widely in rural areas during my free time and learned to appreciate the beauty, wit, and generosity—and the poverty—to be found in rural Asian villages. When my three years of military service ended, I looked around for some way to get to spend time in rural Vietnam as a civilian. The driving force was still primarily intellectual curiosity, along with a desire to improve my language ability in a non-Western language and some vague idea of doing folkloristic or literary studies in the future. But by now I was also very sympathetic to the effort to stave off a Communist takeover of South Vietnam.

In January 1963 I went to work as a provincial representative of the U.S. Agency for International Development in its new Office of Rural Affairs in Vietnam. I spent two years in the field and another three months in Saigon as a staff officer. During my time in the field I met frequently with Vietnamese officials, both civilian and military, in provincial and district offices, discussing problems and opportunities for improvement in agriculture, animal husbandry, public health, and education. I also spent much time in rural villages, usually alone, walking about and chatting with whomever I encountered. People often invited me into their homes for a cup of tea, and we talked of many things.

I also traveled around the countryside inspecting projects paid for with American dollars. Among many other things, we paid for food and housing for defectors from the insurgency while they were processed back into civilian life, and I often stopped by to check the quality of the detainees' meals and housing. More often than my official duties required, I lingered for talks with them about their lives as insurgents and the background of their recruitment into the movement.

In all of my activities, both professional and social, because I spoke Vietnamese I had often found myself explaining the Americans to the Vietnamese and the Vietnamese to the Americans. The number and scope of misunderstandings were incredible. Having taken one anthropology course in college and read perhaps five or six books, I was being pushed by events into practicing anthropology on a regular basis. Also, my efforts to read Vietnamese literature were often foundering on my ignorance of Vietnamese literary conventions and classical language and allusions. At the same time, my desire to learn more about Vietnam's literary heritage was increasing as people I met in my travels kept telling me about this poem or that novel that I must read to really understand the answer to some question I had posed. To a degree that would be astonishing in the United States, Vietnamese in all walks of life could recite long passages from poems, recount folktales and legends, and discuss novels thirty years old as if the characters lived next door. I wanted to read much more of this literature that lived so vividly in people's minds. After twenty-seven months in Vietnam (from early 1963 until mid-1965), I resigned to go back to graduate school. Although I was increasingly unhappy about the way we Americans were going about things in Vietnam, I quit not in protest but to seek the intellectual skills and tools I needed to understand a whole new set of questions.

In fall 1965 I went to the University of Washington, where Nguyen Dinh Hoa (a noted specialist of Vietnamese language, literature, and culture) was then a visiting professor. I studied Chinese, Sino-Vietnamese, Vietnamese literature, and anthropology. The academic work was a pleasure, but the debates over American involvement in Vietnam troubled me. I did not recognize the Vietnam that either the "hawks" or the "doves" were talking about. Nor did I recognize the America they talked about. America now seemed to me as exotic a culture as Vietnam. In the four years I had spent in Southeast Asia, I had changed, and so had the people back home. And I could not communicate effectively about these differences in perception. I talked to a wide range of people, everyone from the John Birch Society to radical leftists. But we all talked right past each other.

Over the next ten years I spent two more years in Vietnam during six trips. I left for what I thought would be the last time on April 29, 1975, the evening of the "final day." In between these trips, which were mostly research trips (the last one was purely personal), I pursued graduate studies at the University of Washington and then at the University of Hawaii. I took classes on Southeast Asia, China, and Japan, and I read everything I could get my hands on about Vietnam. Eventually these studies culminated in a Ph.D. in anthropology.

During my travels I collected a small library of Vietnamese-language books. In conversations with Vietnamese I often asked people questions about books they had read, stories they remembered being told as children. I asked students what they were assigned to read in school. And when in Saigon, I sometimes stood in bookstores and watched what books people bought. I read hundreds of poems, short stories, folktales, essays, and novels. I had no rigid sampling plan, but I tried to read the books that many people had mentioned in conversation, books commonly used in high school classes or introductory college classes in Vietnamese literature.

Originally, I intended to publish a book on Vietnamese literature. Between 1970 and 1972, with the help of a grant from the National Endowment for the Humanities, I began translating some of this literature. But under the impetus of the strident positions taken on the war by Americans, and my growing feelings that both hawks and doves were somehow missing the point, what was originally a straightforward idea became more complicated. I wanted to convey to Americans some deeper understanding of Vietnamese culture and society.

Although I have conducted a lot of research in Vietnam and about Vietnam, this book is not really a report on that research. It is an attempt to convey to readers what I learned over the past thirty years in all of my reading and experience, and what it led me to believe about the Vietnamese and the nature of social change. Much of what I learned was serendipitous, caught out of the corner of my eye while waiting for something quite different to happen, shaped by happenstance, by personal values, and by the materials to which I had (or did not have) access. And more than anything else, my experience of Vietnam has been shaped and colored by people.

The several thousand villagers with whom I have chatted, a dozen or so very close friends, several dozen other friends, teachers, colleagues, several hundred other acquaintances, co-workers, counterparts, research assistants, neighbors, maids, and drivers—many Vietnamese taught me about their culture. So did many people who served as "informants" in structured research. But formal interviews gave me only facts and opinions, mere information. Almost everything truly important was gained from spontaneous experience "recollected in tranquility," to borrow Wordsworth's dictum on poetry. I learned from being around, and being open to, people going about their daily lives.

Being open to people was not always easy in the 1960s and early 1970s. The Vietnam War involved misunderstandings and conflict between cultures. But it also involved conflict arising from different ways of looking at the world—different metaphors, models, or paradigms through which people perceive, organize, and interpret their experiences—within both Vietnamese and American cultures. At the most basic level, I came increasingly to believe, the Vietnam War was fought over competing and incompatible paradigms in Vietnamese society. But it also involved, and exacerbated, similar paradigmatic conflict in American society. It became virtually impossible for anyone to sort out the paradigmatic discourse within cultures from misperceptions and miscommunication across cultures.

This assessment led me to focus increasingly on the debates in twentieth-century Vietnam, the ways in which images of Vietnamese history and culture and society were contested and redescribed in the decades preceding American involvement. I was trying to place the war in a broader context of social change as it evolved and was perceived and expressed by the Vietnamese themselves. This effort led to the 1981 doctoral dissertation, a comprehensive analysis of continuity and change in Vietnam from ancient to modern times. The book that follows is a distillation, revision, and updating of that manuscript, rewritten to share what I have learned with a larger audience in the hope that, by providing new perspectives on old events and issues, it may contribute to an understanding of a complex, divisive, and painful period that continues to plague us.

Acknowledgments

Many people and institutions have helped me in many ways over the years I spent researching, writing, and revising this book. I can mention only a few of them here. It was Francis Lee Utley of Ohio State University who stimulated me to begin thinking about the process of cultural change. I first studied Vietnamese at the U.S. Army Language School at Monterey. Later, at the University of Washington, Nguyen Dinh Hoa guided me to a deeper understanding of Vietnamese language and literature and Nguyen Ngoc Quyen subsequently provided further help and encouragement, while Charles Keyes and Melville Jacobs opened new doors of anthropological thought to me.

At Human Sciences Research Corporation (HSR), where I worked off and on for several years, my interest in Vietnam was indulged and stimulated by many people: M. Dean Havron, Peter G. Nordlie, Herbert H. Vreeland, E. Frederick Bairdain, Herbert White, Martin Sternin, A. Terry Rambo, Jerry Tinker, John Lenoir, Carol Hayward, Gary Murfin, Edith Bairdain, Robert Silano, Janice Hopper, and Bruce Allnutt.

In 1969 a grant from the Southeast Asian Development Group (SEADAG) enabled me to do field research in the Mekong Delta. In 1970 I began some of the translations in this book under a grant from the National Endowment for the Humanities. In 1972 I did fieldwork in Vietnam as part of a study by the National Academy of Sciences to assess the effects of the use of herbicides in Vietnam.

Alexander Leighton and Jane Murphy have been sources of insight and encouragement ever since, and I learned much from other team members: A. Terry Rambo, Gary Murfin, and Jeary Glenn.

Much of this book comes from my doctoral dissertation at the University of Hawaii, where I benefited greatly from the comments of my graduate committee: Alice Dewey, Alan Howard, Philip Jenner, Nguyen Dang Liem, and, especially, Takie S. Lebra, who chaired the committee with great skill and patience. Many other faculty members and graduate students also made significant contributions. And I would not have survived the process without the support of a wonderful office staff, especially Ethel Okamura and Irene Takata, and the typing and editing skills of Freda Hellinger.

A. Terry Rambo and Gerald C. Hickey deserve special thanks for many years of intellectual colleagueship, practical help, and valued friendship. Le Thi Que, also a good friend and colleague, has contributed immeasurably to this manuscript in many ways, especially through help with and advice on some of the translations.

The dozens of Vietnamese who helped me gather data in the field shall remain anonymous, although my gratitude to them is immense, but Pham Hung Dung deserves special thanks for providing me with many useful books, articles, and comments over the years.

Alexander Leighton, Reuel Denney, and especially Samuel Popkin provided help and encouragement in getting this work published. Herbert Vreeland, Thomas Kirsch, and Hue Tam Ho Tai have provided many useful suggestions in the revision process. Nona M. Sanford made useful comments on earlier versions and indexed this volume as a labor of love. I am grateful for both her help and her friendship over the years. At the University of California Press I was fortunate to work with Sheila Levine, whose competent and supportive help carried me through many difficult times.

Above all, my family has always been a vital source of support and encouragement. The patience and unfaltering love of my parents were truly special. For many years my wife Ginnie held a demanding job while keeping our household going. In addition to the support of her love and friendship, she helped substantially with editing, typing, and useful criticism. Ruth, Jim, and Joe tolerated my parental inadequacies with patience and affection.

Despite all the help I had, many errors and deficiencies may remain in the following pages; for these I alone am responsible.

1 How the Vietnamese See the World

It is not actions but opinions about actions that disturb men.

Epictetus

Throughout the twentieth century the Vietnamese have been in upheaval, wracked by conflicting images of the past, the present, and the future. For more than six decades now, the emphasis has been on change, even revolution. During the 1930s many debates in Vietnam were expressed in terms of "the old" versus "the new." Modes of social interaction, claims to status, dress styles, marriage customs, literature, religious practices, medical treatment, even haircuts, were polarized around this dichotomy. A Western-educated, urban middle class had developed, producing a vital new publishing industry to voice its aspirations and to serve as an arena where conflicting visions of the future would compete for influence. Many young writers argued that a sentimental attachment to traditional culture was a major obstacle to progress.

The Communists, a tiny minority in the 1930s, had, of course, a blueprint that purported to provide them with insight into the future. But most young intellectuals in Vietnam before World War II simply knew they were dissatisfied with the way things were and that Vietnam had to discover, or create, a viable modern identity. As Nhat Linh, the editor of a popular Vietnamese-language newspaper, argued in 1932: "When the old civilization is brought out and put into practice before our very eyes, we are dissatisfied with the results. We can only continue to hope in Western civilization. Where that civilization will lead us to we not know, but our destiny is to travel into the unknown, to keep changing and to progress" (*Mores* [Phong Hoa], 20 October). But change to what? To become what kind of people? What kind of society? This is what the subsequent decades of fighting were fundamentally about. Competing

1

ideologies concerned with the issue of modernization abounded. People were divided in their opinions, even within families. To complicate things further, there was considerable regional variation in Vietnam, dating back to earlier times.

Both regional variation and debates between advocates of competing ideologies in Vietnam are best understood, I believe, as specific outgrowths of, or reactions to, the dominant traditional culture. All major changes and variations are responses to particular circumstances (environmental, political, social) with which the old culture was not designed to cope. Despite all the variability and all the change, the culture of nineteenth-century Vietnam is within— and often constitutes an important part of—the various twentieth-century innovations, just as in its fullest development it contained all of its predecessors. Memories of the past remain an important part of all contemporary Vietnamese sociocultural systems—from the politburo in Hanoi to Little Saigon in Los Angeles to Saigon-sur-Seine in Paris.

"Traditional Vietnam" in the following pages refers to this generalized picture of what has existed in the minds of more recent generations. It is a broad portrait gleaned mainly from widely known literature, commonly used school textbooks, popularized historical and biographical writings, thousands of conversations with Vietnamese of diverse backgrounds, reminiscences exchanged over teacups or beer, in a village home or in the back of a jeep, in a temple, a church, or a Saigon nightspot, in offices and classrooms and refugee camps.

We must learn what people had in mind when they spoke of "the old" before we can understand their debates over "the new" that would replace it. All Vietnamese people are today still, as they were fifty years ago, interacting with that past in the process of shaping their future. And so, in a sense, are we.

Our experience in Vietnam is now part of us; and we are part of Vietnam. We cannot forget Vietnam, but neither can we fit what we "know" about it into our sense of self and country. A grinding tension persists, generated by the discrepancy between our memories and our views of who we are and our proper place in the world. We have tried to resolve this tension by revising our views of ourselves, our society, and the larger world, or by suppressing these memories or denying their importance. But the dissonance remains, and our functioning as individuals and as a people is still impaired.

By putting our old and partial perceptions into a new and broader context, we may transform them. By working to understand the competing Vietnamese paradigms, we may clarify the muddled debates about our involvement in Vietnam, and perhaps in the process transform the lingering pain and doubt into more positive insights. In trying to understand the Vietnamese, we may learn something important about ourselves.

The Land of Vietnam: Ecology as History

The Socialist Republic of Vietnam is the twelfth most populous nation in the world. Although it has one of the world's largest and most battle-hardened armies, it is also one of the poorest nations in the world. The territory of Vietnam is slightly smaller than the state of California, but its population, about seventy million, is more than a quarter as large as that of the United States. Vietnam is elongated along a north-south axis that extends from China to the Gulf of Siam. It is evident that Vietnam is a crowded country, and the population is stretched along a fairly narrow band of land. But the topography of Vietnam exaggerates this phenomenon. Most of the people live in a relatively small portion of the land area (see map on p. 4).

Only about a quarter of Vietnamese territory is good farmland (i.e., suitable for wet rice cultivation), and that is where most of the ethnic Vietnamese, who make up roughly 85 percent of the population, live. Wet ricefields, people, and political power have always been associated and concentrated in relatively small core areas. Even today, most of the paddy fields, most of the people, most of the wealth, most of the industry, and most of the economic, political, and cultural activity are in one of two core areas. One core area consists of the Red River delta and the City of Hanoi in the north; the other consists of the Mekong River delta and Ho Chi Minh City (formerly Saigon) in the south. These two concentrations of people are joined by a long thin band of coastal plains along the South China Sea. The bulk of the central portion of Vietnam is mountainous and has been traditionally inhabited by ethnic minorities, tribal peoples who have been seen by almost all Vietnamese as "backward."

Ecological and historical factors have combined to produce very significant regional differences between the two core areas that dominate the country.[1] The Red River is subject to rapid and extreme variation in water level, and both flood and drought have

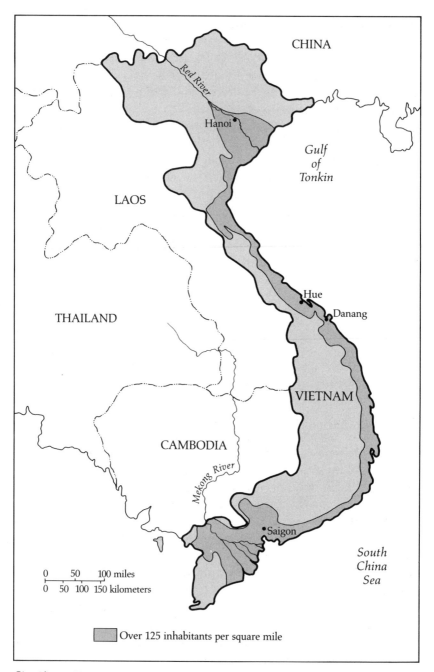

CHINA

Red River

Hanoi

Gulf
of
Tonkin

LAOS

THAILAND

Hue

Danang

VIETNAM

CAMBODIA

Mekong River

Saigon

South
China
Sea

| 0 | 50 | 100 miles |
| 0 | 50 100 | 150 kilometers |

Over 125 inhabitants per square mile

Significant Vietnamese settlement areas, early twentieth century always occurred with ominous regularity. Epidemics and pest infestation have also been common. The Red River delta has simultaneously been one of the most densely populated and least safe regions in the world. In an uncertain and dangerous environment, hunger and social unrest have been constant threats. As a result, the local culture has emphasized the subordination of the individual to collective discipline of family and village. Both the family and the village have been relatively closed, corporate entities, self-reliant, and responsible for the action of their individual members.

In the south, the flow of the Mekong River is regulated by its link to the Tonle Sap, a large inland lake in Cambodia, which absorbs any excess flow of water and supplements a reduction in flow from its large reserve storage. The Mekong environment is more predictable and more benign than that of the Red River. These ecological differences between the Red River and the Mekong delta have been of immense significance in generating differences in cultural emphases and social organization between the two core regions of Vietnam. But historical factors have exacerbated these differences. The Mekong delta has been the recent frontier area. Not until the seventeenth century did Vietnamese seriously begin to settle the southern delta region, and the lower Mekong delta was not heavily settled until the nineteenth century.

Life has been easier and more secure in the southern third of Vietnam, and the harsh discipline found in the north has always been considerably moderated there. Southern villages have always been more open, less corporate, more tolerant of individual initiative and cultural heterodoxy. Then, under the French, who began colonizing Vietnam in 1859, the southern third of Vietnam, known as Cochinchina, was the first part to be colonized, and it was directly administered by the French authorities as a colony. The south thus experienced relatively greater Western influence and more political freedom than did the rest of the country, which was administered as "protectorates" (Annam in central Vietnam and Tonkin in the north). The protectorates came under French rule later and were administered indirectly, through local Vietnamese administrators.

There are, then, two common ways of talking about Vietnamese geography. We think of the north and the south, divided by the seventeenth parallel. This makes sense in recent political terms. It also makes sense historically, because Vietnam was divided not too differently for most of the seventeenth and eighteenth centuries.

But Vietnamese have more commonly spoken of their country in terms of three sections: north, central, and south. And this makes some sense culturally and linguistically, although all Vietnamese share a core culture, have a common historical heritage, and speak mutually understandable dialects of the same language.

The point to be emphasized here is that "traditional" Vietnam refers primarily to the Red River delta and the central coastal plains regions, mainly as they existed in the nineteenth century. The discussion does not always apply directly to the villages of the Mekong delta. In fact, when the French arrived only a small percentage of the Vietnamese population lived in the Mekong delta. The French opened much of the Mekong delta for settlement with massive engineering projects that drained swampland to make it arable. The later chapters of the book will examine southern Vietnam as a variant development of Vietnamese culture.

The People of Vietnam

The story of the Vietnamese—of all Vietnamese—began in the north.[2] Many millennia ago Austronesians, remote relatives of the peoples of the islands of Southeast Asia and the Pacific, were an important part of the population of this area. Then, some four or five thousand years ago, people, languages, and cultures flowed out of what is now southern China into Southeast Asia, where they interacted with indigenous peoples and cultures. The Vietnamese people, southern and northern, their culture and their language, are a rich mixture of these and other influences. The Vietnamese language is basically Mon-Khmer, related to Cambodian. But Tai influence (which produced the Thai and Laotian languages of today) is reflected in the tonal quality of Vietnamese and in many vocabulary items.[3]

Early Vietnamese shared many traits with their Southeast Asian neighbors. Chinese influence has been extremely important, but more recent. When genes and languages and cultures began interacting and intermixing and developing intensively in what is now northern Indochina, some five thousand years ago, much of what is now the Red River delta was still under water; the elevated sea level that had covered it for millennia had not yet receded completely.[4] And as the sea withdrew much of the newly exposed plain was swampy. It was in the midlands, on the foothills and surrounding valleys of the Red River delta, about three or four thousand years ago, that a distinctive culture began to emerge that can be traced to the people who now call themselves Vietnamese. Vietnamese archeologists have come a long way in tracing the descent of these people down onto the emerging plain and into historical time.

Sometime in about the seventh century B.C. in and around the area where the Red River descends from the mountains and enters the plain, the kingdom of Van Lang came into being, ruled by the Hung kings.[5] This tiny kingdom that existed over 2,500 years ago is an important part of contemporary Vietnam's living past. The ancient site from which the Hung kings ruled, only recently discovered by Vietnamese archeologists (the French dismissed Van Lang as a fairy tale), is now a national park, like our Independence Hall or Valley Forge, but more than two thousand years older in significance.

According to ancient myth the Vietnamese are descended from dragons and fairies. When the Dragon Lord of the Lac fathered a hundred children by a mountain princess of fairy blood named Au Co, he returned to the sea with half their offspring while she settled in the midlands of the Red River with the other half. One of these children became the first king of the Vietnamese people, the first of the eighteen Hung kings featured in so many myths and legends and venerated in village shrines into the twentieth century.[6] The last Hung king is said to have committed suicide in 257 B.C. after being defeated by a neighboring chieftain to the north; this led to the creation of the new kingdom of Au Lac. With the aid of a Golden Turtle spirit, the new king, An Duong, built a magnificent citadel at Co Loa, near present-day Hanoi.

Early Vietnamese rulers were often powerful mediators with the spirit world, high priests whose claim to office was based on a privileged relationship with a powerful spirit who could be persuaded to serve a supernatural protector of the realm. The Dragon Lord of the Lac served as protector of the kingdom under the Hung kings, as the Golden Turtle spirit guarded the realm of Au Lac. As these potent leaders and other major cultural heroes joined the spirit world after death, they too became powerful spirits whose aid and sympathy could be evoked by subsequent generations in time of need. The historical memory of the Hung kings and King An Duong was transmitted over centuries not only in myth and legend but through the physical presence of hundreds of village shrines and altars. Before these visible emblems of ancient glory, rituals periodically bound the people to their shared past and to each other.

In 208 B.C. a new kingdom appeared in south coastal China, Nan Yueh in Chinese, Nam Viet in Vietnamese. Au Lac was soon conquered by Nam Viet, and the Red River delta and northern coastal plain of what is now Vietnam was incorporated into Nam Viet. Then the great Han dynasty unified China, and in 111 B.C. Nam Viet fell under its control. The plains of northern Vietnam became a colonial province of China, although indigenous cultural patterns remained essentially intact and local leadership was little disturbed.

In the first century A.D. this indigenous authority structure came into sharp conflict with more rigid demands for conformity as Chinese administrators from the north became more numerous and more assertive. One dauntless young woman sparked the leap from protest to revolt. Trung Trach was a member of the indigenous elite class through both birth and marriage. Her father and her husband were Lac Lords, hereditary district chiefs. With her sister, Trung Nhi, Trung Trach prayed at a shrine on Hung Mountain, where her ancestors once ruled in the name of the Dragon Lord, invoking their blessing upon rebellion. In A.D. 40 Trung Trach was proclaimed queen after her rebel army forced the Chinese officials to flee to Canton. As an expeditionary force recaptured the Red River delta for the Han dynasty in A.D. 43 the Trung sisters are said to have committed suicide. They became immortalized in song and story and today are still held up as exemplars of traditional Vietnamese values.

In the decades and centuries that followed, the population of the Red River delta and northern coastal plain was gradually Sinicized in many ways; ethnic Chinese in the region were also heavily influenced by local custom and regional perspectives. Genes and cultures mingled to produce a new Sino-Vietnamese elite. For seven hundred years this region would be Giao Chau, a province of China. But a distinctive local identity was retained.

Revolts broke out periodically, producing new culture heroes, more shrines, and more legends. During the ninth century rebellions grew more frequent and a renaissance in local cultural traditions emerged. With China plunged into weakness and disorder under the crumbling Tang dynasty, the Vietnamese gained independence in A.D. 939. During the early years of independence, no monarch could integrate the land firmly. Leadership in Vietnam rested ambiguously on two separate concepts of political legitimacy: indigenous tradition and a heavily Sinicized system of politics and administration that had been assimilated during a thousand years of Chinese rule. Most early monarchs were soldiers whose leadership was based largely on personal prowess. In this milieu, Buddhism played a vital role in stabilizing Vietnamese society.

Not until the Ly dynasty (1009–1225) did the development of what we now think of as traditional Vietnam begin to take shape. Shortly after taking the throne, the first Ly king moved the capital to what is now Hanoi, which he named Rising Dragon (Thang Long). In 1048 an agrarian cult was established, with the construction of a temple to the gods of soil and grain, formalizing the role of the king as a national high priest of agriculture. The Ly kings bore a dragon tattoo, signifying spiritual succession from the illustrious Dragon Lord of the Lac and the Hung kings. In fact, the greatness of the Ly dynasty rested to no small degree on a foundation of unprecedented moral force that was built by calling forth these spirits of past culture heroes to bolster the efficacy and legitimacy of their rule;[7] this same kind of moral force has been significant in the rise to power of many Vietnamese leaders up to the present day.

Buddhism flourished. Many Ly kings spent part of their lives in a monastery, and one was leader of a major sect. The ideological viewpoint of the Ly court, as revealed in the extant poetry of the time, was strongly Buddhist in tone and content, with a marked Zen influence emphasizing insight and awakening rather than scriptures or good works. Noninvolvement, detachment, and paradoxical mysticism were pervasive values.[8]

But a modest rejuvenation of Confucian studies was also encouraged after a century of relative neglect. In 1070 a Temple of Literature dedicated to Confucius was constructed in Rising Dragon (its remains can be viewed today in Hanoi). In 1075 national examinations were held for the first time under independent Vietnamese rule, and in 1076 a national university was created. Confucianism began to revive under the Ly.

The Ly dynasty was succeeded by another great dynasty, the Tran (1225–1400). Vietnam slowly continued to expand in population and territory. The army, the bureaucracy, and the examination system were further developed. But the early Tran kings spent much of their energy in foreign affairs and national defense, fighting off threats from the north. In 1284 Vietnam seemed doomed to fall to Chinese forces, but under the inspired leadership of Tran Hung Dao, the invaders were driven from the land.

During the Tran dynasty the Confucian element in official ideology continued to develop while Buddhism remained important. Then, late in the fourteenth century, in the midst of economic crisis and peasant revolts, a powerful court councillor seized the throne. Under this unpopular new ruler, Vietnam once again fell under Chinese rule in 1407. For a time Ming dynasty administrators from China vigorously regulated village government, religious ceremonies, hair styles, modes of dress, the writing and distribution of literature, and virtually everything else of cultural, economic, or political significance. Both the Ming and the Vietnamese ruler they displaced encouraged the spread of Neo-Confucian doctrines.[9]

Under Le Loi, the Chinese invaders were expelled and the Le dynasty was established in 1428. Neo-Confucianism, based on Chu Hsi's reinterpretation of the classics in eleventh-century China, became a vital influence on Vietnamese thought. During the thirty-seven-year reign (1460–1497) of the great king Le Thanh Tong, Neo-Confucianism became a dominant element in Vietnamese ideology. But the Le dynasty then quickly fell into decline. For nearly three centuries internal conflict sapped the wealth and energy of the Vietnamese. Few heroes, little great literature, and only modest cultural innovations emerged until the second half of the eighteenth century, when cultural ferment was expressed in a lively body of literature in the Vietnamese language. One important element in this resurgence was the expansion and standardization of the writing system employed for transcribing Vietnamese (*nom*).[10]

The later decades of the eighteenth century were dominated by the Tay Son rebellion, which began as a peasant uprising against what were perceived to be unsatisfactory conditions. By 1786 rebel leaders controlled all of Vietnam. The Tay Son era is controversial and poorly understood. This revolutionary movement expressed deep-rooted discontent in rural Vietnamese society; but it also involved new commercial interests, overseas Chinese intrigues, religious heterodoxies, and a resurgence of indigenous tradition at the expense of borrowed elements in Vietnamese culture, especially Neo-Confucianism. *Nom*, the demotic Vietnamese script, replaced Chinese as the official writing system. The Trung sisters were revitalized as culture heroes of the first order.

But by 1802 the Nguyen dynasty held power, declaring the Tay Son reforms null and void. Perceiving recent Vietnamese history as characterized by decadence and disorganization, the Nguyen rulers strenuously sought to make Neo-Confucianism the foundation of the national culture. Under the Nguyen, traditional Vietnamese culture assumed its final form, the one that would persist into the twentieth century to interact with Western influences.[11]

The Traditional Vietnamese View of the World

Over many centuries, Taoism, Buddhism, and Confucianism had become intertwined, simplified, and Vietnamized to constitute—along with vestiges of earlier animistic beliefs—a Vietnamese folk religion shared to some extent by all Vietnamese.[12] But over time, beginning in the late fifteenth century and becoming most extreme in the nineteenth century, Neo-Confucianism came to be a dominant influence.[13] Neo-Confucianism focused on proper social relationships, but ideas about the proper form of social relationships were based on a wider set of ideas regarding the nature of reality.

The traditional Vietnamese worldview constituted an all-encompassing cosmological scheme based on *yin* and *yang*, conceived as two primordial forces from which everything else in the universe was created. This root paradigm, through which one of the oldest and most fundamental elements of Sinitic influence eventually became a basic part of the way Vietnamese viewed the world, ran right through the entire system, from the family to the state. It suffused the entire world with a coherent system of meaning. Everything was a model, an icon, of everything else.[14] Based on the assumption of a unified and orderly universe, this model provided Vietnamese with a sense of insight into—and a means of dealing with—the intrinsic structure of the universe.

In all things, when a proper balance was maintained between *yin* and *yang*, harmony was maintained and beneficent outcomes were assured. This was equally true in the individual human body, in families, in villages, and in nations. For example, the treatment of illness consisted primarily of restoring the balance between *yin* and *yang*, both within a person and between the person and the external world. According to traditional folk thought, all foods were believed to have an "essential nature," to be hot, warm, cool, or cold. "Hot" and "warm" foods were *yang*, "cool" and "cold" foods were *yin*. Diet could thus disrupt or restore harmony between *yin* and *yang*.[15]

Exactly as the human body was perceived to be a microcosm of the natural world, so too was the family viewed as a microcosm of the social world. And just as the proper balance between *yin* and *yang* in the human body—and between the human being and his or her environment—produced good health in people, so would proper relationships between categories and groups of people produce social harmony, creating happy and prosperous families, villages, and nations. Both formal education and family socialization emphasized teaching children proper behavior within this framework, which formed the basis of a social system that served Vietnamese society well for hundreds of years.

The ancient paradigm of *yin* and *yang* can readily be interpreted as a metaphorical expression of cybernetic theory.[16] Modern cybernetics, or systems theory, has provided us with considerable insight into how such a dynamic equilibrium system must work.[17] Society is neither an organism nor a machine; it is—like organisms and machines—a system. It is composed of components that are related in such a way that the whole is greater than, and essentially different from, the sum of the parts. This is so because relations between the parts are maintained by mechanisms of communication and control that depend on the flow of information, on "feedback," for effective operation.

Cybernetic theory informs social analysis in a variety of ways: by focusing attention on system properties such as entropy and redundancy and on the values that function as operating rules; by emphasizing the extent to which the meaning and function of any part of the system is determined by context; and so on. Above all else, it reminds us that *it is the context*—a set of relationships, rather than any single component in isolation—*that evolves*.[18] The focus of this book is on the evolving context of ideas in twentieth-century Vietnam.

Vietnamese Society as a System of Yin and Yang

In traditional Vietnamese culture we can find, in every domain of society, two different sets of operating principles, or values. These two sets can be used as the basis for a model of society and culture. One set can be seen as *yang* in nature; the other, as *yin*. *Yang* is defined by a tendency toward male dominance, high redundancy, low entropy, complex and rigid hierarchy, competition, and strict orthodoxy focused on rules for behavior based on social roles. *Yin* is defined by a tendency toward greater egalitarianism and flexibility, more female participation, mechanisms to dampen competition and conflict, high entropy, low redundancy, and more emphasis on feeling, empathy, and spontaneity.

Much of traditional Vietnamese culture, social organization, and behavior expressed the balanced opposition between *yin* and *yang* as interlocking sets of ideas (including values, conceptual categories, operating rules, etc.). At a high level of abstraction, a great deal of persistence may be detected in the system over time. At the level of specific cultural content, much change has taken place. The dozens of anecdotes and literary and ethnographic examples embedded in this narrative will serve to make these abstractions meaningful. Suffice it to say here that *yin* and *yang* coexist, that *yang* is normally dominant, but that when the *yang* system becomes too extremely dominant the stage is set for a *yin* reaction in the social system, and social change takes place.

The relationship between actual social systems and systems of ideas is real and important, but it is essentially metaphorical. The observable world of behavior and artifacts and the imagined or culturally construed world of concepts and categories continue to reproduce and reshape each other, maintaining the essential integrity of their relationships, more or less imperfectly, throughout a process of change. As these two worlds coevolve over time, each is built into the other. Thus the particular form and content of either category or both may change considerably over time while the symbiotic relationship persists at the abstract level of functional complementarity through logical opposition.

There is, I believe, great heuristic value in looking at Vietnamese history, into the twentieth century, as a case of patterned oscillation around a point of balance between *yin* and *yang*. The sages of antiquity asserted this to be the nature of reality, a universal process, the Tao. The *yin* and *yang* components of traditional Vietnamese society—from the family through literature to religion to economic structures to political systems—contained within themselves logically opposed but functionally complementary components that had a characteristic structure to them. These may be thought of as being separate subsystems at work within any given part of the total social system. When one or the other became disproportionately strong, the imbalance generated stress and strain in the social system, and a reaction set in as discomfited individuals and institutions sought a more comfortable social milieu. Gregory Bateson has likened this process to the setting of a thermostat.[19] He suggested that the most significant points in history are "the moments when attitudes are changed. These are moments when people are hurt because of their former values." What is truly important, for individuals and entire peoples, he insisted, is a change in the "bias" or "setting" of the "thermostat" that regulates social behavior.[20]

Because human attempts to maximize values entail choice under conditions of uncertainty and competition, they give rise to a certain amount of conflict and tension, not only within groups, but sometimes within individuals. In men and women, and in societies, there are thresholds of tolerance for tension which, when approached, lead to some sort of remedial action. The result may be cultural or social change, including revolution. Twentieth-century Vietnam represents an extreme case of social conflict over the setting of the social thermostat. It has been a time and a place when new attitudes have arisen and millions of people have been badly hurt because of their former values.

The true social analogy to Bateson's metaphor of the social thermostat is the entire ensemble of values held and acted upon by individuals who interact and communicate with one another as they include the results of their own action and that of others in the new information by which they modify their subsequent behaviors. Sometimes, as in twentieth-century Vietnam, this process leads people to seek to change the codes of behavior by which they and others are expected to generate future interaction, to change the social thermostat by achieving patterned change in the distribution of values of the entire society. It seems to me that this process is readily amenable to description and analysis in terms of the conceptual categories of *yin* and *yang*.

For convenience, *yin* and *yang* and their associated values will often be referred to as "systems" or "domains" throughout the book. The social organization of traditional Vietnam can be seen as being achieved and maintained through the interaction of these two conceptually distinct systems. Going beyond normal Vietnamese usage, I have extended the domains by applying the abstract principles in what the Vietnamese thought of as *yin* and *yang* to situations and events in ways they never dreamed of doing. In other words, in this book I use *yin* and *yang* as metaphors.

The following section describes the state of the Vietnamese sociocultural system as it existed when French colonial influences began to exert pressure on it, in the nineteenth and early twentieth centuries—the point at which the part of the Vietnamese story told in this book begins.

Traditional Vietnamese Values and Institutions

Traditional Vietnamese culture was much more complex, and much more widely shared in all its richness, than many recent commentators would lead one to believe. In the brief survey that follows, I necessarily present an oversimplified, somewhat idealized, and highly selective portrait of traditional Vietnam, even allowing for the qualifications that it applies primarily to northern and central lowland villages in the nineteenth and early twentieth centuries, that it focuses on culture rather than behavior, and that it emphasizes the norm while skipping over much variability. The actual nature of traditional Vietnamese society is controversial. Again somewhat oversimplifying, let me say that two main schools of thought may be discerned.

To many observers, especially to many early French scholars who began studying Vietnam after acquiring a thorough grounding in Chinese studies, what I call the *yang* subsystem, especially that which was Neo-Confucian, "was" the traditional cultural system. Much of what I call the *yin* subsystem, although well known to them, was perceived to be (in the terms of cybernetic theory) "noise" in the system, "flaws" or "irregularities" that led to tension, confusion, and malfunction in "the system" as they understood it.[21]

Another view, more recent and currently more fashionable, essentially sees what I call the *yin* subsystem, especially Buddhism and the more egalitarian village institutions, as the "real" Vietnam, as somehow more authentically Vietnamese and representative of the "actual culture" of the majority of the people. From this perspective, what I call the *yang* subsystem and categorize as "dominant" is perceived as an elitist view, historically recent and culturally superficial. This model, it is argued, is something which the "ruling class" attempted, generally unsuccessfully, to impose upon "the people" as a tool of exploitation, which has been popularized by self-serving writings of that elite class and foreign scholars who have identified with the elite minority instead of with "the people."[22]

My own view differs sharply from both these perspectives, as I understand them. I believe that the *yin* and the *yang* were complementary dimensions of a single cultural system that was essentially shared by all Vietnamese. The Neo-Confucian *yang* and the Buddhist, Taoist, and animist *yin* elements coevolved to constitute a single system, best thought of as Vietnamese folk religion, that pervaded all aspects of Vietnamese life. There were *yin* elements and *yang* elements in families, in villages, in religion and economics, and so on.[23]

Neither was more "authentic" or "legitimate" than the other. Without either, Vietnamese culture, and Vietnamese social organization, would have been something altogether different. Individuals, families, society itself, oscillated between these two ideological poles I have labeled *yin* and *yang*. Within this framework and in response to history and circumstances, there developed a core of values that formed the heart of traditional Vietnamese culture, the "window" through which Vietnamese viewed the world and interpreted what they experienced. The related ways of thinking and doing were inculcated into children from birth and were reaffirmed and reinforced in myriad ways through life and dominated Vietnamese beliefs of what the world was like and what correct behavior should be. In the story that follows this portrait, the story of "what happened" when the culture of Vietnam and Western cultures encountered each other, many of the events make no sense without frequent reference to these values, which are described briefly here (and are included in the glossary for convenience of reference).

REASON (*LY*) The world, and everything in it, was perceived to have a characteristic structure. Based on this natural order, rationality, or "reason" (*ly*), consisted of conformity to the structural principles that governed the universe. *Ly* came to mean "the nature of things." It was an overarching principle, based on observation and experience, intended to provide harmony in the system by specifying the proper form of all relationships. The concept of *ly* rationalized and legitimated the hierarchical order of society and of nations, making hierarchy itself part of the intrinsic structure of the universe, a state of affairs that was both "natural" and unalterable.

FILIAL PIETY (*HIEU*) and moral debt (*ON*) Family relationships were models for social organization. Both child-rearing practices and formal education emphasized learning to behave properly toward other family members. First and foremost, children were taught filial piety (*hieu*), to obey and respect and honor their parents. Children were made to feel keenly that they owed parents a moral debt (*on*) so immense as to be unpayable. A child was supposed to try to please his or her parents all the time and in every way, to increase their comfort, to accede to all their wishes, to fulfill their aspirations, to lighten their burden of work and of worry, and to comply with their wishes in all matters, great and small. From everyday life and from several thousand years of history, youngsters were bombarded with exemplars of children who "knew *hieu*." The parent-child relationship was at the very core of Vietnamese culture, dominating everything else.

THE RELATIONSHIP BETWEEN BROTHERS (*DE*): A MODEL FOR SOCIETAL ROLES Next in importance was the relationship between brothers. An older brother was supposed to teach, nurture, and protect his younger brother. Younger brothers were supposed to respect, obey, and support older brothers. The proper relationship between older and younger brothers (*de*) is elaborated in hundreds of maxims and folktales. Fraternal ties are often sharply opposed to conjugal ties in these stories, with unambiguous advocacy of the former. Brothers, this corpus of literature asserts, should never let anything or anyone, especially women, come between them. Many well-known stories reinforce the ideological primacy of blood ties, implicitly illustrating that going against family obligations was contrary to a natural order in the world. And to oppose the natural order was futile and dangerous.

Unlike most Western children, children growing up in traditional Vietnamese families learned dependence and nurturance, not independence. They learned the importance of hierarchy, not equality. They learned the rewards of submission to those of senior status, not assertiveness. The paradigmatic example for extending this basic family model to society was *de*. One was supposed to behave toward those senior to one, or of higher rank, or older, as if they were older brothers.

Younger brothers were supposed to be self-denying and docile in their relationships with older brothers. Yet in Vietnamese folktales younger brothers prosper despite their meekness. They triumph precisely because they are true to the prescribed role behavior appropriate to their situation. They were supposed to be meek and compliant toward older brothers, as toward parents, despite all provocation. In submitting even to unreasonable demands from an older brother, they were earning merit. Never does a younger brother triumph because of boldness or cleverness or assertiveness. The ideal role model provided by school and family and folklore is one of compliance with the wishes of superordinate figures in a social hierarchy: child to parents, younger brother to older brother, and wife to husband.

GENDER ROLES Women came in for a large share of ideological pressure to perform their roles as daughters, wives, and mothers in a nondisruptive manner. The role of women was a source of tension in society. There was often a grating disjuncture between ideological ideals and sociological reality. Vietnamese myth, legend, and history are filled with stories of strong, intelligent, and decisive women. In all but the uppermost strata of society, men and women often worked side by side. Women performed many arduous physical tasks, ran small businesses, and were skilled artisans.

Yet ideologically men were *yang*; women, *yin*. Women were subordinate to men in the nature of things. Like children and younger brothers, they were supposed to be submissive, supportive, compliant toward their husbands. Husbands were supposed to teach and control their wives as they did their younger brothers and their children.

There was a persistent tendency, rooted in the pervasive *yin-yang* notion of hierarchy, to denigrate the status of females and subjugate them to at least nominal male dominance. A woman was supposed to be submissive to her father when young, to her husband when married, and to her oldest son when widowed. The notion of intrinsic male superiority was incessantly reinforced. "One boy, that's something; ten girls, that's nothing."[24] "A hundred girls aren't worth a single testicle."[25] Little girls were loved and nurtured, but boys were obviously preferred.

Boys also received more attention, got their own way more frequently, and were permitted to roam more freely. Girls were kept closer to home, supervised more closely, and given more responsibilities for helping with chores. If money was tight, all of it went to the boy's education while the girl stayed at home. If a girl ever asked "Why can brother do that but I can't?" she would simply be told "Because he is a boy!" No further explanation was felt to be necessary.[26]

After marriage, a wife typically went to live with, or at least near, her husband's family. So a family had to groom girls for export, so to speak, and to bind boys emotionally to the family in which they would remain for the rest of their life. The boys' mothers in particular were getting a headstart in competing with their future daughters-in-law for their sons' primary allegiance in coming decades.

THE RIGHTEOUS PATH (*NGHIA*) These role-based behavioral ideals, with *hieu* and *de* at the core and combined with the concept of *on*, instilled in Vietnamese a rigid code of conduct and a strong sense of duty, often laced with no small amount of guilt. Other values functioned in support of these core *yang* values. Wisdom, or learning (*tri*), propriety (*le*), and sincerity or truthfulness (*tin*), along with courage (*dung*) and perseverence (*chi*), were all primarily valued as they served to support and implement the primary social obligations inherent in *hieu* and *de*, extended to guide one's relations within wider social groups. Loyalty (*trung*) was an extension of *hieu* to the relationship of a subject to his lord.

The primacy of social obligation was summarized by the value of *nghia*, perhaps best translated as "righteousness." *Nghia* implies duty, justice, and obligation. It inculcates the willingness to do what one must do to fulfill one's social obligations, to repay *on*, to meet the demands of *hieu* and *de*. *Nghia* demands calm rationality within the structure of *ly*, the nature of things, and that one live scrupulously by an unbending set of rules, regardless of circumstances, regardless of individual preferences, regardless of the apparent consequences. The concept of *nghia* was based entirely on behavior in key social roles. It dictated, for example, how a son should behave to a father, how a younger brother should behave toward an older brother, how a subject should behave toward a king, and so on. It ignored relationships and behaviors that did not pertain to strategic social roles.

SPONTANEITY AND FEELING (*TINH* AND *NHAN*) At the core of the rigid *yang* framework were the value-laden and emotionally charged concepts of *ly*, *hieu*, *de*, and *on*. This social framework was strongly Neo-Confucian, male-oriented, focused on roles rather than on people, concerned with the welfare of the collectivity (family, village, nation) rather than with the feelings, desires, or problems of the individual. While it achieved a position of structural dominance, especially among the elite, and was most powerful in the northern and central portions of Vietnam, its very strength and its narrowness put it in dynamic opposition to a wide range of alternative values and concepts. *Yin* and *yang* were logically contradictory but functionally complementary domains. When one became too strong vis-à-vis the other, certain functions became impaired.

The *yang* domain, with its rigid insistence on orthodoxy and its denigration of that which was heterodox or female, and with its emphasis on role behavior at the expense of the whole person and on the group at the expense of the individual, was a constraining influence that often failed to meet individual needs. Some critics have called it a "straitjacket" and concluded that it led to "maladjustments."[27] Buddhism, Taoism, indigenous tradition, and elements of earlier Confucian thought provided a broad array of values, institutions, and practices that constituted a *yin* counterbalance to the *yang* superstructure of society. One of the broadest and most fundamental oppositions in Vietnamese culture—indeed, in Vietnamese life—has long been that between *nghia* and *tinh*. While *nghia* is about morality, ethics, and duty, *tinh* is about feelings. *Tinh* is spontaneous, subjective, intuitive, unpredictable, emotional. *Tinh* is often used to refer to "love," but it is also used to signify passion, sentimentality, desire, or emotionalism, what we might call the dictates of the heart. *Tinh* was always subordinated to *nghia*, however, in folklore and in literature; and families and school primers both asserted that this was as it should be.

Another overlapping but somewhat more restricted value standing in opposition to *nghia* was *nhan*, the Confucian virtue of compassion, charity, benevolence, humanity, love for one's fellow human beings. *Nhan*, like *tinh*, involves spontaneity and feeling. It entails going beyond the rules to do good because one has empathy and compassion in one's heart. In practice, *nhan* merged with Buddhist teachings to remind people to be nice to one another, to be kind, to be generous. *Tinh* and *nhan* provided an emotional balance to the rationality of righteousness embodied in *nghia*.

RELATIVE VERSUS ABSOLUTE HARMONY: *LY* AND *DIEU* Another source of dynamic tension between *yin* and *yang* values entailed two different ways of viewing harmony, two different ways of being "reasonable." Harmony was a core concept, valued in both the *yin* and the *yang* sphere. And in both, being reasonable was a prerequisite for achieving harmony. But the harmony of the *yang* domain always referred back to the concept of *ly*, that pervasive notion of a natural order that included the physical, social, and natural worlds. *Ly* was a constant, a given to which individuals and societies had to conform. This cosmological belief buttressed the entire *yang* domain. There was one right answer, one right way of doing things, and harmony resulted from conformity to what was "right," what was in accord with *ly*.

But there is another sense of the English word "reasonable" that functioned in the *yin* domain. In Vietnam this was the value of *dieu*. This word is used in compounds that refer to mixing colors, to harmonizing in music, to reconciling diverse opinions, to arbitration in a dispute. *Dieu* always refers to interaction and dictates a willingness to adapt or modify one's position or actions to fit a concrete situation, to "get in tune," so to speak, to moderate one's stance in the interest of social harmony. *Ly* implies an absolute standard or frame of reference, while relativism is the essence of *dieu*. *Dieu* as a value means "reasonable" in the sense of being moderate, of not being excessive. People who do not know moderation—who are too greedy or too rigid or too assertive— bring about their own downfall. Finding the proper balance between *yin* and *yang*, between duty and feeling, made the constructing of a proper life a form of art, entailing conflict and judgment.

ABSTENTION VERSUS PARTICIPATION   Another major dimension of this tension was the opposition between active participation in society and abstention or withdrawal from society. In Chinese Buddhist thought "participation in worldly affairs" and "abstention from worldly affairs" were separate, irreconcilable categories. But many Vietnamese strove for a dynamic combination of these two modes in their lives and in society.[28] Neo-Confucianism, the entire *yang* domain, encouraged activism and tended to generate competition. Public service especially was portrayed as both an honor and a duty. Buddhist and Taoist elements, however, glorified meditation and passivity while denigrating or even ridiculing the futile struggle to impose one's will upon a reality that is indifferent to it.

The concept of *on* made this dichotomy between participation and abstention extraordinarily dynamic and often poignant in Vietnam. A cultivated man properly longed to retreat from the polluting and disturbing turmoil of the world, hoped to withdraw from social competition to pursue detachment, tranquillity, and self-cultivation. But one did not always have the right to do this.

Debts had to be repaid, obligations fulfilled; when duty called, an honorable person had to respond to the dictates of *nghia*.

On the other hand, sometimes, when the world was out of joint, when that which was right and proper was unattainable under prevailing conditions, an honorable man or woman withdrew from the world as a means of reaffirming higher values, rather than perverting them by participating in a context that distorted them. Such people, in withdrawal, waited to "meet their time." With a view of time as cyclical, they were awaiting the inevitable return of a properly constituted social order in which they might participate with dignity and honor.

THE POWER OF THE NATURAL ORDER The return of a "proper" state of affairs was guaranteed by a process of moral justice that operated in the universe. Virtually all Vietnamese believed that time was cyclical, that deviation from the natural order of things could not long survive. The natural and proper order would inevitably reassert itself. Family teachings, primary education, folktales and proverbs, and popular literature instilled in children an implicit belief in the workings of this principle of order. Children absorbed a cosmological view that posited a cause-and-effect relationship between virtuous behavior and good luck. People and institutions that were "reasonable," in accord with the natural order of things, were rewarded; those who violated the natural order invited disaster. Significantly, they invited disaster not just upon themselves but also upon their families; and to harm one's family was the ultimate sin.

THE FAMILY: THE NATURAL ORDER IN MICROCOSM The Vietnamese family was a small world unto itself. What Westerners consider "nuclear families" were embedded in extended families and patrilineages, and the sense of family included the deceased and those not yet born in a single fabric of spiritual unity and material well-being.[29]

First and foremost, children were taught *hieu*, the cardinal virtue of society. Anxiety over repayment of *on* to parents and ancestors was a powerful force for both virtue and achievement. Through their efforts and their sacrifices, and through their virtue, one's ancestors had accumulated merit—a veritable account with the gods—that was part of the family heritage.

You were, simply by being alive, in debt to your family—no matter how much you might have accomplished, no matter how wretched you might be. You still had to thank them for the food you ate, the house you lived in, your spouse, your land, your membership in the village, most of all for life itself. You benefited from the merit accumulated by other family members over time, and from the family reputation. Success only increased the debt; it could never serve to repay it fully. Every family had to work hard constantly to maintain its relationship with the neighborhood, the lane, the rest of the village. This network of relationships, too, you held in trust for your family. Obligations extended in both directions, to those not yet born as well as to those who had passed away. The primary obligation was to the family itself as an eternal corporation.

The cultural ideal was an extended family household functioning as a single, well-integrated unit, hierarchically structured. Full authority and ownership of all property rested with the parents, whose wishes had to be obeyed. Any blatant breach of filial piety was, in fact, illegal and would be severely punished by the authorities should it come to their attention. Even worse, to be found guilty of such behavior in the court of public opinion would give one a heavy burden of shame to be borne the rest of one's life.

Ancestor worship tended to reinforce and transmit the potency of this body of precepts, perpetually reproducing a powerful sense of family solidarity. It was at the very heart of the familialism that was so dominant a characteristic of traditional Vietnamese society. One's membership and position in one's family was the primary element in one's personal and social identity. Ritual life in the households of traditional Vietnam was rich and varied, but to a singular degree ancestor worship periodically generated important and solemn rituals in which many people participated with deep emotional involvement. Each year on the death anniversary of each departed ancestor within a certain degree of genealogical proximity, a formal offering was made. Depending on the relative closeness and status of the ancestor and the size and wealth of a patrilineage, a moderate to large crowd would participate in such events. In the words of Le Thi Que:

> One has to attend one of these family gatherings to understand the intense emotional attachment the Vietnamese feel for their families. In this atmosphere composed of memories, traditions, and habits, of common points of reference, family hierarchy is strictly observed. A member, whatever his social status, finds his place in front of the ancestral altar and at the

feasting table determined on the one hand by the place he occupies in order of generation, and on the other by the order number he holds in his own family. In this ambience, the individual loses himself and feels at ease and is really at ease there only. It is also there, in this community of life and thought, that he finds the strength of the group to which he belongs. The person would not exchange his place in this group for any other, however exalted the new one might be.[30]

A large and well-to-do patrilineage might have at least several dozen such get-togethers a year, and almost every family would have at least several. But the number of people involved, the elaborateness of the ritual, and the amount and quality of food and drink consumed would vary greatly. Ideally, each family had a special category of land set aside to subsidize such events. Known as "incense and fire land," the sanctity of such property was protected both by law and by custom. These rituals were part of a powerful socialization process, intended to induce certain moods and attitudes in the minds of all participants. Bringing families together and reminding them of their shared roots, death anniversary celebrations built family unity and helped to create a family mentality. Within such families the living, the dead, and those not yet born were joined in an intimate relationship of mutual dependence.

Ancestors remained active participants in family life, sharing in joy and sorrow, admonishing wickedness, chiding deviation from propriety. They worked from the nether world to contribute to the well-being of the family, watching over and assisting their descendants. When faced with a momentous decision, some Vietnamese would talk with deceased family members, often reporting flashes of insight or clarity of thought arising from such discussions. Ancestors could assist, advise, and sometimes punish their descendants, always for the good of the family.

Although ideally a family was as self-sufficient as possible, social competition rather than isolation was expected. Competition between families took place within an open, consensus-based "class system" that arrayed families along a prestige hierarchy in which public opinion was the final arbiter. Villagers placed their own subjective judgments into the formal status equations and modified a family's standing according to the behavior of its members. Wealth, education, status, and prestige were correlated, but in no deterministic fashion.

People noticed shortcomings, and they talked about them. People feared ridicule and gossip. High status was both constraining and expensive. In particular, the many ritual interactions between a family and the village community were occasions on which conspicuous public generosity was expected to match claims to status, somewhat taking family resources into account.

When a boy's name was placed upon the village rolls, ceremonies had to be performed, and gifts given. Deaths were even more expensive. Elaborate mourning ceremonies and funeral extravaganzas were expected of the well-to-do. Marriages were complex and expensive affairs. A close look at marriage reveals much about traditional culture and the way Vietnamese society worked, especially for the elite and the socially ambitious.

MARRIAGE   Marriage was seen primarily as a transaction between two families, so spouses were chosen not by individuals but by parents, often with the active participation of other senior family members.[31] The bride, often living with or at least near her husband's parents, was expected to honor them even above her own parents. She would often enter her husband's home as a virtual stranger and would have to please not just her husband but his entire family, especially his mother.

For all parties, a direct approach was difficult. The important thing was to avoid exposing the family to a humiliating loss of face through direct public rejection, so intermediaries were often used. Shrewd estimates would be made of economic resources, moral character, reputation, influence, and future financial expectations of the prospective spouses and their families.

Local tradition tended to simplify the selection phases of this process (dropping or simplifying a more complex Sinitic tradition) while emphasizing the engagement phase. Here transactions shifted to the public realm, becoming more distinctively Vietnamese, and more expensive. The engagement ceremony was built on a formal presentation, acceptance, and redistribution of gifts from the groom's family to the girl's family.

The wedding ceremony itself was commonly called *ruoc dau*. *Ruoc* means "to welcome," "to greet," or "to escort." *Dau* has the double meaning of "bride" and "daughter-in-law." Vietnamese speak of "taking a wife" or "establishing a family," but never in conjunction with the wedding ceremony. Nor does one ever hear the wedding procession referred to as "welcoming a wife." It is always called "welcoming a daughter-in-law." The bride's role as daughter-in-law is given social and cultural emphasis, linguistically expressed, equal to or greater than her new role as wife. By far the most significant element in the transaction is her movement from membership in one family to membership in another. It is her integration into her new family that is of cardinal importance.

The wedding ceremony involved the symbolic and physical transfer of the bride from her home to the groom's home. The groom, accompanied by his family and friends, would march in procession to the bride's house to claim her and escort her home. This sometimes involved travel between villages. Girls especially liked to marry within the village, but an appropriate spouse could not always be found there. Many villages, hamlets, lanes, and even some lineages exacted a fee from anyone who took a bride from their midst, stretching a string across the road to block the procession until the fee was paid. When the groom finally reached the bride's home, he might find his progress blocked yet again, with the bride's younger siblings requesting money to "open the gate." These various "gate-blocking" encounters expressed the strong sense of corporate identity that typified these groups. At the bride's house the groom prostrated himself before the family altars, replicating a set of rituals he had performed for his own ancestors before leaving home. Finally refreshments would be served, and soon the procession would depart.

The bride, surrounded by her own helpers and other relatives and friends, was also symbolically protected by various devices to ward off evil spirits along the road, especially if travel was between villages. Family and village were the culturally constituted enclaves in which one was a meaningful part of ordered society. The bride was no longer a daughter, nor was she yet a daughter-in-law or a wife. Passing between families, perhaps between villages, the bride was outside of culture, exposed to the dangerous natural world as an isolated and therefore an impotent and vulnerable individual.

At the groom's house she would perform a series of rituals that were a mirror image of those the groom had performed at her house. Only then would bride and groom perform a brief ritual that would make them man and wife. Next would come a wedding feast, the best the family could afford. After the guests had departed, the couple would retire to a nuptial chamber. Often this was their first chance to get acquainted. It would often be difficult for the new bride to partake fully of the rich emotional life that bound her husband, his parents and siblings, and perhaps grandparents, aunts, and uncles, into a tightly knit household. The house would often be very crowded, and she and her husband would have little privacy in which to build intimacy.

Only gradually would she be affectively integrated into her new family. Only over the years—as she bore and raised children, nursed the sick, earned money, which she contributed to the common treasury, and demonstrated her total loyalty and devotion to her new family—might she begin to regain some measure of emotional support. Like children to parents and younger brothers to older brothers, wives/daughters-in-law were expected to be supportive and compliant.

Vietnamese folklore often dramatizes the ideal of a wife's total devotion to her husband. However, if a wife deceives or betrays or disobeys her husband in folktales, retribution and disaster often follow, and many tales stress that a headstrong woman causes problems. But women are seldom portrayed as incompetent, gullible, or easily manipulated. In some tales, in fact, a shrewd and forbearing wife supports a bumbling husband.

Bound by a behavioral code and internalized values that stress the maintenance of face, public generosity, and a preoccupation with lofty affairs, in folklore and in daily life Vietnamese men often appear to be less adept than their womenfolk in practical economic matters. Each family is like a small nation. The husband is nominal head of state and in charge of foreign relations; the wife is minister of the interior and controls the treasury. There is a formal division of labor, and somewhat different sets of values are inherent in the different roles.

A "good" woman was self-sacrificing, frugal, industrious, chaste, and totally devoted to her husband. She was "bad" if she so much as looked at another man. Vietnamese were second to none in having a double standard for judging the sexual conduct of men and women. But this entire constellation of beliefs, values, attitudes, and norms regarding sexual behavior was intimately related to their overriding concept of family and was reinforced by the value of *hieu*.

A primary obligation of *hieu* was to provide male descendants to perpetuate the cult of the ancestors. Less than total certainty as to the actual paternity of one's children was a source of intolerable anxiety. Motherhood, of course, could not be in question. The sexual double standard arose ineluctably from structural differences between a man and his family and a woman and her two families, one by birth and the other by marriage. The needs of the family bent both men and women to serve as required, but the requirements were quite different for the two sexes. Few questioned the axiomatic basis of social life that firmly placed the welfare of the family above individual wishes and desires.

TET: THE ANNUAL FAMILY RITUAL OF RENEWAL   The coming of the new year produced abundant symbols of integration. People planned for the new year well in advance with an air of pleasurable anticipation. The ancestors were coming for a visit, and the entire family would be reunited. The new year had to be greeted with one's family in front of the ancestral altar. This was the quintessential celebration of the family as a living entity. It is difficult for Americans to grasp how important Tet was, and is, to Vietnamese. Tet was Christmas, Easter, New Year's Eve, Thanksgiving, and the Fourth of July all rolled into one celebration. Celebrating Tet with one's family was an essential part of what it meant to be Vietnamese, to be a complete human being. As the new year arrived a crescendo of firecrackers and pealing bells washed over the land. The entire nation cried out joyfully—to one another and to the ancestors and the gods, with resounding voices of communion and hope—uniting the Vietnamese as one people around the very core of their culture.

THE TRADITIONAL VIETNAMESE VILLAGE   The village and the nation were in a sense larger families—as the family itself was a small nation or village. In northern and central Vietnam (but not in the more recently settled and less densely populated southern region) villages were closed and corporate communities with a relatively high degree of autonomy.[32] Not only were most villages separated from others by an expanse of paddy land, village houses tended to be tightly clustered together within a dense bamboo hedge that totally surrounded them, physically and symbolically setting the community apart from the adjacent countryside as well as from other communities. The residential portion of the village could be entered only through an ornate, well-guarded, and highly symbolic gate, which was closed and locked at night. This gate was the face the village presented to the world, an outward sign of identity and emblem of corporate self-respect. Inside was the *dinh*, the heart of the village. The *dinh* was at once ritual center and town hall. Here the fusion of politics and religion in village life was evident.

Ritual life at the *dinh* revolved around veneration of the guardian spirit of the village, a powerful spirit appointed by the king as a symbol that this community had attained the formal status of a village, a semiautonomous administrative unit. The cult of the guardian spirit provided a focal point for village identity and symbolized "the history, customs, ethics, legal code, and common aspirations of the entire village."[33] The *dinh* was also a place for feasting, for public and private worship, for all public ceremonies, both secular and sacred.

Each year the village held several major rituals to offer special sacrifices to the guardian spirit with an air of great solemnity. These ceremonies were performed by the community, as a community, for the community, making manifest the shared values, needs, and concerns of the group as a whole in meaningful symbols. Focused on the cult of the guardian spirit, village ceremonial activity at the *dinh* served to symbolize the dependence of all members of the village not just upon one another but upon powerful external forces—natural, supernatural, and social—which could be adequately manipulated and controlled only by the corporate group, not by its individual members. The cult of the guardian spirit replicated for the village as a whole the functions performed by the cult of the ancestors for Vietnamese families.

Not all who lived in a village were members of the village as a legal corporate entity nor members of the "congregation" of the cult of the guardian spirit. Both privileges and obligations were associated with village membership, and membership was not to be had by anyone for the asking. The most basic distinction in the village was between members and nonmembers. Membership was formally restricted to males, with a strong tendency to limit eligibility to men born and raised within the village.

As a legal corporate entity, the village itself was an important landowner. While the proportion of land that was corporately owned varied, such communal ownership was an important characteristic of the traditional Vietnamese closed corporate village. Village land was reallocated every three years, providing subsistence for the very poor and reimbursement to those who rendered service to the village. Some land was rented to other villagers at a substantial fee, generating revenue. This land tenure system supported village solidarity. No one outside the village either owned or worked village land. Villagers might quarrel among themselves, but they stuck together against outsiders. The village was corporately responsible for payment of taxes to higher authority, to provide military conscripts and corvée labor. So long as it met its obligations, the village was left alone. Outsiders, even the central government, dealt with the village, not with individual members. Only through the village could one be a fully participating member of society.

THE VILLAGE STATUS HIERARCHY: SOLIDARITY AND COMPETITION Village members were ranked in a strict hierarchy corresponding to named social statuses. The upper strata of this hierarchy were known collectively as the Council of Notables. Although the particular status and the criteria for recruitment varied, all villages had a status hierarchy and a body of notables at the top. Directly beneath the notables were the village elders, and beneath the elders came other adult members of the village. Within these broad categories were many finer distinctions. These statuses were explicitly rank-ordered positions, and all affairs of the *dinh* involved an elaborate protocol in which this rank order was scrupulously observed and symbolically expressed. On formal occasions no two men could be completely equal.

It was precisely within the explicit context of symbolic relationships at the *dinh* that village solidarity was most profoundly and forcefully expressed and competition became most fierce. The shared hierarchy and the ritual activity associated with it promoted solidarity and provided a sense of identity in the village as in the family. But in the village, unlike the family, status was achieved rather than ascribed by birth.

The village status hierarchy was not an administrative body. The notables dominated village affairs, but not as an executive body. Village functionaries executed the will of the council. To become a village official often meant hard work and heavy responsibility with little real power and little pay. But it permitted one to rise in the status hierarchy, providing entrée to the council of notables where real power and prestige lay.

STATUS HIERARCHY AND THE "PRESTIGE" ECONOMY A "prestige" economy was deeply embedded in the status hierarchy expressed in the cult of the guardian spirit. This was a very competitive and rigidly structured domain. Relative position within this status hierarchy was very important to villagers. They ardently competed to "eat above" and "sit before" each other at village feasts in the *dinh*. After all important sacrifices a high feast would be organized at the *dinh* for all village members. These feasts located one in village society, as the feasts associated with the cult of the ancestors located one in one's family and patrilineage. Seating arrangements and the distribution of portions at such feasts were prescribed down to the smallest detail in accord with relative position in the hierarchy. Status was manifested by who sat at which table, how many men would share a tray of food, who received which cut of meat. Details varied, but all villages had some such distinctions.

Nguyen Khac Vien tells us that in his village: "After the ceremonies honoring the village guardian spirit, the head, beak and crown of the sacrificial rooster had to be set aside for the highest ranking notables. Heaven help anyone else who took a piece for himself! Notables were known to commit crimes just to get the crown of a rooster." No gastronomic considerations impelled men to such competitive extremes. "Each notable competed with the others to bring home the head of the sacrificial chicken from the ceremony because in the eyes of his wife, children, and neighbors this would be irrefutable proof that he was the most honored man in the village."[34]

Traditional Vietnamese accepted the principle of social hierarchy and cared passionately about face and relative status. Any claims to elevated status were met by one's fellow villagers with elevated expectations about behavior. A serious breach of propriety could send a family's reputation plummeting. In effect, the village population exacted a "tax" on prestige, consisting of persistent social and economic demands. The price of status, prestige, and respect was constant vigilance, conformity to village norms, and conspicuous generosity. If people did not act in accord with their status pretensions, respect behavior would be withdrawn.

Every family had periodic expenses, such as the placing of children on the village rolls, funerals, marriages. One could organize such events either cheaply or lavishly, but each public transaction was a statement about relative status and prestige. In aggregate such behavior summarized the prestige of individuals, and especially of families. For those with a reputation and a social position to protect, or for those trying to rise in the status hierarchy, there was little choice.

Although these rank-ordered positions were achieved statuses, village custom still insisted upon public validation. To rise significantly in the hierarchy required sponsoring a series of feasts, "celebration offerings" (*le khao vong*). Whenever a member met the criteria for an elevation in status, he had to organize an offering at the *dinh* and a subsequent feast. This could mean hosting a party for the entire village membership at his own—that is, his family's—expense. If the status were a high one, these could be costly affairs.

This concern with face, status, and prestige expressed in celebration offerings, rites of passage, and other such semipublic occasions reflected a more general ethic that infused village life, one that enjoined villagers to lead lives of public generosity and private frugality. Dozens of village customs revealed this ethic in operation. Details varied; the principle did not. It was incumbent upon the more well-to-do, and the socially ambitious, to give more freely than did most other families. Families cared what their fellow villagers thought and said about them. They also believed in luck, and that generosity would bring good luck. And so, with the eyes of the village upon them, they spent freely when local custom expected it of them.

Concern with face and honor not only operated to impel those who had a surplus to part with some portion of it, it also made those in need reluctant to reveal the true extent of their poverty. People did not accept charity lightly. They lived as frugally as possible and tried to maintain the appearance of normalcy.[35] Everyone was expected to be self-reliant and self-sacrificing. Those who were not quickly became aware of the censure of their neighbors. The same principle that guided the conduct of families applied to villages as well. As corporate entities concerned with their own face, entire villages exhibited the same self-reliant, self-sacrificing behavior. Inhabitants of a village would endure considerable hardship rather than lose face by asking for outside assistance.[36]

The deep-seated concern for face and the desire to gain prestige and to have it publicly acknowledged, combined with the belief that good deeds brought good luck, made village welfare mechanisms self-generating and self-regulating to some significant extent. Those villagers with a surplus were psychologically and sociologically impelled to exchange some portion of it for prestige, while those in need found it difficult to accept charity and did so only when and to the extent that it was absolutely necessary.

The basic principle of redistribution might be summarized as "from each according to his desire for face, to each according to his willingness to lose face." Both need and ability to pay were self-assessed, regulated by powerful psychosocial predispositions. Because they were extremely sensitive to nuances of disapproval or disrespect, many Vietnamese were vulnerable to public opinion as expressed in gossip, ridicule, or satire.

THE SUBSISTENCE ECONOMY   Within the village there were many organizations and activities that exhibited a pattern quite different from that discussed above. Traditional Vietnamese were highly social creatures, and villages had a remarkable variety of social groups. There were, for example, clubs for everything from kite flying to raising songbirds, clubs for old soldiers, for people born in the same year, for students of the same teacher.[37] Despite their great heterogeneity—and entropy was high in the *yin* system—many different kinds of groups shared certain key characteristics that make them unmistakably *yin* in nature.

In sharp contrast to the well-defined and highly redundant *yang* domain of family and village—marked by high internal differentiation and status competition—*yin* groups were much more loosely structured and egalitarian. All were strictly voluntary and informal groups, all emphasized cooperation and solidarity, and all had mechanisms to reduce competition and dampen potential conflict. Internal differentiation was minimal. Leadership was often rotating or based on seniority. The expenses of membership were prescribed and equal. Also, many of these groups were for females. Finally, while the *yang* domain was the focal point of state attention, including the legal code, these *yin* groups tended to arise spontaneously and were a matter of complete indifference to the state. None were prescribed by law or by culture.

Villagers lived in discrete neighborhoods within the village, and at the entrance to each the gateway marked a sociological boundary. Each neighborhood had its own membership rolls and its own elected chief to serve as intermediary between the neighborhood and village authorities. Some neighborhoods had shrines of their own, built with their own resources, to worship a cult figure of their own choosing. Neighborhoods had no legal status, however, and membership was relatively open. One could, and often did, belong to a neighborhood without qualifying for village membership. Even lanes within a neighborhood sometimes had their own membership rolls, their own chief, and their own meetings and ritual activities. Lanes, even more than neighborhoods, were face-to-face groups, where everyone knew everyone else well and mutual aid was commonplace and informal. Such informal mutual aid was characteristic of a subsistence economy that paralleled the prestige economy discussed above.

Most villages had a place set aside for an outdoor market, usually located outside the bamboo hedge that defined the village proper. This symbolized the low status of commerce, which was usually reserved for women and foreigners. The bustling markets involved transactions on a very small scale, primarily the redistribution of local goods. Women supplemented the family income by buying oil or sugar in small amounts and reselling them in smaller increments, by making foodstuff for sale, or by selling a temporary surplus from the home garden. Profits were usually miniscule.

Virtually every family was engaged in the exploitation of the ricefields that surrounded most villages. Most occupations, even the growing of most other crops, were things to be done when one could not be profitably engaged in growing rice. Everyone—carpenters, blacksmiths, barbers—tried to farm if it were at all possible. The specter of hunger was familiar and lurked close at hand. There could never be too much rice, and growing rice was never too much work. But many families could not make a living farming, and most villagers were perpetually short of cash. Village industries provided a means of using extra time to earn additional money. These were almost exclusively family enterprises. Labor was not considered to be a cost. An entire family would work hard all day for a very small profit.

There was an extraordinarily high degree of village specialization.[38] Instead of each village having its own blacksmith, carpenter, and so on, each village tended to specialize in one task. In some villages many adult males were skilled silversmiths, barbers, masons, tinkers, or herbalists. Other villages were devoted to making paper, parasols, pots, fishnets, or hats. Even greater specialization existed within these categories. The manufacture of a single product often involved the work of several villages, each with a monopoly over some aspect of production, a formula, a technique, or a raw material. This again was both cause and effect of village solidarity. Those artisans or craftsmen engaged in the same kind of work within a village would often organize themselves into a guild. Such groups shared knowledge within the group, but guarded it from outsiders. They also served as mutual aid societies. When an emergency arose, one could usually count on group assistance.

Guilds were only one form of the mutual aid societies found in traditional Vietnam. There were funeral and burial societies, special groups for almost any occasion that called for a sudden outlay of cash. There were even groups for celebrating the new year. Each household would contribute a small amount of money each month, and at the end of the year various expensive delicacies would be bought and distributed in small portions to the members. A common kind of organization with mutual aid functions was the *giap*.[39] A *giap* might have been organized on the basis of a lineage or a common surname, membership in the same neighborhood or hamlet, worship of a particular spirit, or any other common bond. The *giap* was a corporate entity with its own property, its own ritual life, and its own status hierarchy. But rank order in the *giap* was based solely on the order in which names were registered on the village rolls. Regardless of wealth or status, seniority would enable one to sit above and eat before all those who joined the *giap* at a later date. Although there were expenses associated with *giap* membership, these were always shared in prescribed and equal amounts. No gain or loss of prestige was involved; therefore, expensive competition was precluded. This was true of all mutual aid groups. It was true of the subsistence economy as a whole, and of what I call the *yin* domain of village life.

THE POLITICAL ECONOMY OF *YIN* AND *YANG*   The prestige economy, associated with the cult of the guardian spirit, exacted a "tax" on status and prestige. This realm was characterized by extreme formality and vigorous competition. The elements of this system were relatively closed and tended to be highly differentiated. Reciprocity was unbalanced. Various mechanisms and local customs exacted a price for status and prestige. This constituted a self-regulating village welfare system, one that kept the "free-rider problem" within reasonable bounds. There was, however, no glorification of shared poverty and no intention to achieve equality. True equality was perceived to be destabilizing, to be contrary to the natural order of the world. Village insurance functions, on the other hand, were provided within the context of a subsistence economy that paralleled and complemented the functioning of the prestige economy. As we have seen, the subsistence economy involved a completely different set of institutions, based on quite different principles.

Working in tandem, the subsistence economy and the prestige economy—like *yin* and *yang*—were integral parts of a single complex system that contributed to the viability of the village in its uncertain and dangerous environment. Logically contradictory principles—competition and cooperation, hierarchy and egalitarianism, conflict and solidarity—were functionally complementary parts of the political economy. This duality of structure characterized the ideology and the society of traditional Vietnam.

THE *YIN* DIMENSION OF RELIGION IN THE VILLAGE   While the cult of the ancestors in the family and the cult of the guardian spirit in the village were *yang*—male dominated, culturally prescribed, hierarchical, formal, and often competitive—the *yin* domain of religion involved a high level of female activity and was culturally optional, more egalitarian, more informal, more cooperative, and much less competitive.

Each family elaborated the content and rhythm of its ritual life according to its own preferences, needs, and capacities. Any house might have many altars, or few, or none. One might find in people's homes dozens of different kinds of altars to spirits from the pantheons of Taoism, Buddhism, popular mythology, Vietnamese history, and local legend. Altars were used to beseech support from a particular spirit, often for a specific purpose. The spirits of fierce generals were believed to be potent defenders of the home against evil spirits. The Goddess of Mercy, Quan Am, helped women and children especially and was believed to be of particular assistance against the dangers of childbirth.

Some women felt called to the service of a female patron deity, such as the Dark Maiden of the Ninth Heaven or the Jade Queen of the Immortals. Illness and misfortune befell women who did not respond to such a call. But if worshipped faithfully, the possessing spirit would bring health and good fortune. Shamanistic cults often sprang up around such phenomena. These cults too might combine religious events with social activity, such as an annual banquet.[40]

Buddhism was a conspicuous part of *yin* religion. Pagodas were common in traditional Vietnam, but they had no "congregation" in the strict sense of the term. Attendance was arbitrary and irregular for most "believers." As a systematic body of beliefs and ideas,

Buddhism has long been a pervasive influence in Vietnam, but the institution of Buddhism, especially the role and influence of the Buddhist clergy, has waxed and waned. The monk qua monk had no real place in village social structure and little or no influence in village affairs, although individual monks of talent and virtue could become very influential. The pagoda had its greatest attraction for, and received much of its support from, older women, often widows. A Buddhist women's association existed in most villages, with leadership rotating annually. Many of these groups would organize a ceremony once a year and indulge in a banquet.[41]

NATIONAL INTEGRATION   The rulers in the Nguyen dynasty that ascended the throne in 1802 had an unusually strong *yang* bias, in reaction to the conditions that preceded their rule. They sought to construct a more orderly, more orthodox, more homogeneous, and more tightly organized society. They mandated the use of Chinese as the official language, adopted a harsher legal code, which placed women in a more subordinate position than ever before, restricted Buddhism, and propagated Neo-Confucian doctrines in dozens of ways that ritually and symbolically socialized both villagers and officials to more orthodox role behavior and greater social solidarity in accord with *ly* and *nghia*.

The Nguyen kings constructed a court in Hue that was carefully modeled upon the Chinese court in Peking. The hierarchical principles of society were expressed in the design of the palace and its grounds. The architecture and landscaping promoted harmony with the natural order by structuring interaction and organizing ritual behavior.[42] The Vietnamese king was leader of four ritual cults: of Heaven, of his own ancestors, of Confucius, and of agriculture. His kingly role emphasized ritual leadership over executive and legislative functions. His ritual actions combined and integrated his dual role as indigenous king and Sinified emperor.

In 1808 a special edifice was built just outside the new imperial city of Hue for sacrifices to Heaven and Earth. This site, carefully modeled after a similar one in China, consisted of a large circular platform (*yang*) for sacrifices to Heaven and a smaller square one (*yin*) for sacrifices to Earth. Only the king or his official representatives could participate in the cult of Heaven, thus symbolizing his unique role in society as the sole representative to natural and supernatural forces.

The cult of the ancestors was also carefully observed within the imperial city. The king was extraordinarily scrupulous in his observance of filial piety, both to perfect his own balance of merit and as exemplar and teacher for his people. A national agricultural cult focused on a square outdoor altar (*yin*) at which sacrifices were offered to the gods of soil and grain and the four seasons. The king himself presented a ritual offering here every spring, then commanded a high official to plow a furrow to symbolize the proper beginning of another agricultural cycle. At the same time, this ritual was being performed in each province by a representative of the king.

There was also a temple of Confucius in the capital and in every province. Twice a year, in spring and fall, Confucius was ritually honored. The king presided over these rites in the capital as provincial officials imitated his actions throughout the land. There were similar shrines in many cantons and some villages where local scholars replicated these rites.

The entire nation was meticulously organized in a hierarchically ascending series of replications of the same ritual patterns, these patterns themselves a replication of the natural order of the universe. Homologies of symbolic and ritual action promoted social solidarity within and between levels. The Nguyen kings were keenly aware that dutiful sons made loyal ministers. State laws punished violations of mourning customs and rewarded any family that managed to assemble five generations under a single roof. Family customs were consciously adopted for the bureaucracy to strengthen and integrate it by enhancing the feeling among its members of belonging to one great family.

An intricate network of metaphorical relationships—father to son, and older brother to younger brother—bound the nation and its component elements together in ties of mutual obligation. Each family was like a small nation. The village was the family writ large. The national bureaucracy was organized around the metaphor of family. Each of these structures expressed the root paradigm of *yin* and *yang*, and each took its shape in accord with *ly*, the cultural model of universal natural order. At the apex of these structures the king became, as a fusion of indigenous mythology with Taoist and Neo-Confucian thought, a personification of the moral order in Vietnamese society. His primary responsibility was to exert spiritual leadership through ritual and through personal example.

This same burden of moral leadership fell to some degree upon the mandarinate, upon village elites, and upon family heads. They were all supposed to teach and to lead by virtuous example, like fathers, like older brothers. The head of any administrative unit was supposed to bring harmony and prosperity to his domain by means of the virtue of his life and of his rule. So a district, a prefecture, or a province was also considered to be in some ways like a family.

Beyond the eye-catching pomp and ceremony and imposing symbolic barriers that shielded the scholar-officials and the court from the masses, a relatively simple and inexpensive apparatus stood between the king and his subject. The Vietnamese state achieved this cost-effective operation by governing through "powers of verification and eventual repression, but not of execution."[43] This state propagated ideals through many channels, monitored behavior and punished deviation from the orthodox ideological model, and strove to uphold harmony with the natural order through assiduous ritual action. The key ministry of this government was not the Ministry of Justice or of Finance or Defense. It was the Ministry of Rites.[44]

This lean apparatus was possible because the state did not deal directly with individuals, families, lineages, hamlets, or any of the thousands of local organizations. State officialdom dealt with villages; and the village itself directed, coordinated, and controlled the behavior of its inhabitants. And villages themselves dealt with families, not with individuals. The entire family was responsible for the behavior of any of its members.[45] Individuals were closely controlled, not just by family heads but by all family members, especially by anyone senior to themselves. Misbehavior on the part of an individual hurt everyone, and everyone understood this, just as it was understood that the entire family expected to benefit when any family member enjoyed success.

As families regulated the behavior of their members, families in turn were regulated both by village leaders and public opinion to function in ways that increased the viability and prestige of the village as a whole. Both the family and the village were closed corporate communities in which individual interests were submerged in the interests of the collectivity. In this society, what we in the West think of as personal freedom was thoroughly subjugated to what Pierre Gourou called "the complete supervisory control of public opinion over the private life of the individual." Yet this very trait gave impetus to, and imposed discipline upon, various institutional mechanisms of welfare and redistribution. Little coercion was required to maintain this system. People were socialized to behave in these ways, and life in the family and the village could be immensely meaningful and satisfying. Traditional Vietnamese were not socialized to strive for individual independence. They did learn to handle, and to prize, relationships characterized by nurturance, dependency, and mutual obligation. And they took pride in responding to the dictates of *nghia*.

The Success and Failure of the Traditional System

Ultimately it was the widely shared worldview and system of values that made this traditional system workable. Family socialization, formal education, folklore, and the vernacular literature that flourished in the late eighteenth and the nineteenth century and was spread throughout the land by itinerant storytellers and presses that delicately balanced popular taste with government regulations, all converged to reinforce a shared cosmology. The entire social structure rested upon the pervasive notion of natural order.

At the heart of this worldview was the central, unifying proposition that the extent to which conformity to a natural order was maintained in word and deed had profound and inevitable consequences. When serious deviation from proper role behavior occurred, the natural order was violated and compensatory mechanisms—as natural as gravity or moonlight—redressed the balance. Exploitative older brothers, disobedient wives, rapacious priests, and other miscreants brought misfortune upon themselves. But sometimes improper behavior could bring misfortune down upon other members of corporate groups, where blame as well as honor was shared. Conversely, virtuous families, by maintaining the natural order through proper role behavior, by observing *hieu* and *de*, by being loyal and generous, prospered and enjoyed good fortune as a well-deserved gift from the gods.

This shared cosmology, combined with a general desire for prestige, a concern for face, and a sensitivity to criticism, provided a powerful moral dimension to life in traditional Vietnam. Public opinion served as a very real, if sometimes inadequate, constraint upon the exercise of political and economic power. Despite many individual instances of greed and lust and egoism, the society retained a capacity for self-correction. It was in this limited but profound sense a value-oriented, self-correcting, and self-integrating system.

Eventually, this system failed, perhaps in part because of the overblown *yang* emphasis of the Nguyen dynasty. There were many peasant rebellions in the first half of the nineteenth century. Corruption, poverty, and injustice blighted the land. And Vietnam was colonized by France. It has long been fashionable to denigrate the traditional Vietnamese cultural system described above as "feudal," "superstitious," and a tool by which the elite exploited the lower classes. We should not let the failures, nor the many undoubted shortcomings, of the traditional system blind us to the power of its logic or to the extent to which it penetrated and persisted at the deepest levels of Vietnamese culture.

Even today, one cannot attain a very sophisticated understanding of current Vietnamese behaviors without taking the persistence of traditional Vietnamese culture into account. If we want to understand the drama in which we became engulfed in Vietnam from the 1950s into the 1970s, we must begin by seeing twentieth-century Vietnam as a clash between the old and the new, between diverse reactions to the failure of the traditional cultural system and the continuing grip of this cultural heritage on the hearts and minds of the Vietnamese people, including those who called most loudly for its abandonment.

2 Confrontation with the West, 1858–1930

The West Overwhelms Vietnam

For much of Asia the nineteenth century was a traumatic time.[1] A powerfully expanding Western civilization compelled the entire world to participate in an international market economy. This self-amplifying blend of science, industry, and Christianity was driven by competition among its member nations for raw materials and markets and was expanded by force of arms when necessary. Overcommitment to a conservative worldview that saw change as both ephemeral and undesirable blinded Vietnamese to the fundamental nature of the transformations occurring around them. In their certain belief in a natural order of a quite different kind, Vietnamese leaders remained contemptuous of the web of trade, industry, and science that was encircling them. While Western nations experienced massive economic and technological development, Vietnam steadfastly resisted any tendency in that direction.

Yet the portents of externally imposed change had long been visible. Long before the Nguyen had assumed the throne in 1802, the British had been trampling on India's autonomy, the Dutch controlled Java, and the Philippines had been a colony of Spain for centuries. The British had acquired the island of Penang in 1786, added territory on the Malay peninsula in 1800, taken over Singapore in 1819, and wrested Hong Kong from China in 1841.

Throughout the first half of the nineteenth century the Nguyen court had been hostile to the *yin* system. Commerce was discouraged and left in the hands of Chinese immigrants, who were administratively segregated from the Vietnamese population.[2] The legal rights of women were reduced.[3] Buddhism and Taoism were strictly regulated,[4] and after 1830 Catholicism was harshly repressed.[5] Much popular literature was also suppressed.[6] The tendency was clearly to reduce diversity and negative feedback and to make the sociocultural system more tightly linked, homogeneous, and centralized. A more disastrous policy for preparing to cope with change in the external environment can scarcely be imagined.

In 1858 a combined French and Spanish fleet of fourteen ships sailed into this anachronistic world carrying some three thousand troops, who quickly seized a foothold on Vietnamese soil at Danang. Unexpectedly fierce resistance made them abandon their original goal of marching northward to capture Hue; but the Vietnamese court had to be punished for its persecution of Catholics and to be jolted out of its obstinate refusal to permit adequate trade. Furthermore, many Westerners erroneously believed that the Mekong River might provide access to the riches of China. Sustained by this potent combination of piety and greed, the invaders turned south and captured the Saigon area in 1859.[7]

Additional French military victories in 1861 and 1862 forced the Vietnamese court to cede the three provinces of Bien Hoa, Gia Dinh, and Dinh Tuong to the French, and to make numerous other concessions. Catholic missionaries were permitted to propagate the faith freely within Vietnam. France and Spain were granted trading privileges at Danang and several other ports. French ships could sail the Mekong without interference. And, to make matters worse, the Vietnamese had to compensate France for the military expenses incurred in exacting and enforcing this treaty; this imposed a crushing debt on the treasury in Hue.[8] Despite their overwhelming numerical superiority and deeply felt outrage at the impertinence of the "white-skinned barbarians," the Vietnamese troops were no match for their European opponents. The better-armed and better-trained Westerners slaughtered the Vietnamese with pitiless volleys. No amount of heroism could withstand the disciplined use of such superior fire power.[9]

When Vietnamese soil was ceded to France in 1862, the horrible reality of the threat to their civilization struck the complacent Vietnamese intelligentsia like a thunderbolt. When the entire Mekong delta fell under French control in 1867, the nation became obsessed with the problem of determining the appropriate response to the challenge of an aggressive Western civilization. For many Vietnamese, especially those of elite status, the dictates of *nghia* required total resistance. When the treaty of 1862 was signed, resistance flared up throughout the southern region. Dozens of local patriots led uprisings, rallying thousands of ardent spirits to their cause as "soldiers of *nghia*." The royal court did not support this activity, in the belief that it could not succeed and might provoke further French aggression. But royal disclaimers went unheeded, and the king and the mandarins who had signed the hateful treaty were pilloried in verse and song.[10]

Local partisan groups formed under a variety of banners, such as "Pacify the French; Wipe Out Heresy," "Royalist National Salvation," and "People's Self-Defense." The Mekong delta provided heroism in abundance, but lacked the economic and technological means of constructing a viable military opposition. And few Vietnamese had any realistic understanding of the wealth, power, and ideology hidden behind the thin line of French troops that visibly opposed them.

A torrent of protest literature appeared almost overnight. The most famous and articulate advocate of resistance was Nguyen Dinh Chieu (1822–1888), who heaped scorn upon those who did not fight the French and despised those who cooperated with them. Those few Vietnamese who seemed to wish to imitate the French were beyond his comprehension. He himself refused all contact with anything of Western origin, even soap powder. It is said he even refused to walk on a paved road, and he forbade his children to learn the romanized alphabet.[11]

His seething verse made a major contribution to the resistance movement. Contemporary events were unambiguously polarized in terms of conformity to or betrayal of traditional values:

> The way of Heaven is not at all remote,
> Wash a human heart and out it comes.
> How can a man of *nghia* betray his country?
> How can a man of *nghia* reject family feelings?
> The path to choose is as always that of *trung* and *hieu*.
> Our books distinguish clearly between truth and heresy.[12]

He poured out his scorn upon less fervent countrymen in verse that was copied and recopied in painstaking brushstrokes and was spread by crumpled manuscript and word of mouth throughout the land:

Our people are infatuated with Western religion.

. . . .

And if one isn't anesthetized with faith,
There is always opium to smoke.
Some clutch their pipes day and night,
Eating opium to suppress rebellion.[13]

By 1867 the futility of continued armed resistance became so obvious that many of those dedicated to traditional values either left the south or simply stayed at home and eked out a living from the land, or became schoolteachers or herbalists. But the Vietnamese were soon to have a brief respite. In 1870 the French were defeated by the Prussians in a war that lasted only seven weeks and ended with Napoleon III himself being taken prisoner. Coming immediately after foreign policy disasters in Mexico and elsewhere, this humiliation left the French badly shaken and with little energy or enthusiasm for overseas adventures.

Yet the Vietnamese were still incapable of capitalizing on France's political weakness. Vietnamese decision-makers had no mechanisms for obtaining timely and reliable information about the outside world, nor for analyzing and interpreting the odd bits of information that filtered into the court as third- or fourth-hand accounts. They had no diplomatic corps in any modern sense of the term, no embassies or consulates in other countries, no organized group of specialists trained in diplomacy and foreign languages.

Nor could the king and his court give foreign affairs their full attention. The land was rife with bureaucratic intrigues, palace plots, peasant rebellions, and organized banditry, and there were floods, droughts, epidemics, locust plagues, tax protests, and tribal uprisings. The reign of Tu Duc (1847–1883) was a nightmare from beginning to end. Monarchy as a concept was still popular, but he was not, and he knew it. Challenged even from within his own family, he was forced to execute his older brother in 1854 and then to execute most of his brother's family in 1866 to preserve his own hold on the throne.[14]

But Tu Duc was neither a fool nor a monster. He represented, not a degeneracy of the traditional monarchy, but rather its logical conclusion, almost its *reductio ad absurdum*. He and his immediate predecessors and successors were trapped by their own principles. Both psychologically and politically overcommitted to a strict Neo-Confucian orthodoxy that was inevitably grounded upon a rigid and disproportionately weighty *yang* subsystem, the Nguyen kings were alienated from the resilient *yin* dimension of their cultural heritage by continuing overreaction to the Tay Son episode, which had exposed the (to them) terrifying existence of powerful heterodox forces within Vietnamese society, forces that seemingly could not adequately be encompassed within nor contained by the traditional paradigm of Vietnamese society.

When the French gained control of the entire Mekong delta, armed resistance quickly tapered off, and most of the educated elite left the southern region to live elsewhere.[15] Some still fought, of course, and some decided to cooperate with the French. But from 1867 on, increasing numbers of Vietnamese, especially the intellectual elite, would choose abstention, harking back to an eremitic tradition best exemplified by Nguyen Binh Khiem, the renowned sixteenth-century seer and poet.

Phan Thanh Gian, grand councillor, one of the most brilliant and dedicated mandarins in the realm, provided a shining example to many of his countrymen. He was one of the primary negotiators of the unpopular treaty of 1862. For performing this necessary but unpleasant duty, he and his colleagues had been vilified in folksongs and unfairly rebuked by King Tu Duc himself: "How painful it is! . . . You are not only criminals in the eyes of the court but also in the eyes of the whole generation."[16]

Yet Tu Duc wisely selected Gian to lead a diplomatic delegation to France in an attempt to regain the lost territory through direct negotiation with the highest French authorities. The mission was ultimately unsuccessful, but as a man who had known the inner circles of power under three Vietnamese monarchs and who possessed firsthand knowledge of the military and political situation in the countryside, Gian was in a unique position to appreciate fully the significance of his experiences in France. He saw little hope in either negotiation or armed resistance, yet the fateful consequences of surrender were equally clear to him. In France he had marveled at the roads cutting across rivers and through mountains, the incredible distances covered by a train in a single day, the amazing superiority of gas lights over the oil lamps of Vietnam. On his return from France, Gian reported to King Tuc Duc that "their wealth and strength are beyond description."[17]

Tu Duc's response was to appoint Gian viceroy of the remaining southern provinces with vague assurance that everything would work out if one were confident and righteous. Tu Duc responded to Gian's realistic assessments with platitudes:

If faithfulness and sincerity are expressed
Fierce tigers pass by,
Terrifying crocodiles swim away
Everyone listens to *nghia*.[18]

Burdened with full responsibility for a disaster he could foresee but could not avoid, Phan Than Gian chose the ultimate withdrawal. He permitted himself to be lured from his headquarters at a crucial moment, enabling the French to achieve a bloodless takeover of the lower Mekong delta region while his troops stood by awaiting orders that never arrived. What they finally received instead of battle orders was a letter of explanation.

> The empire of our king is antiquated. Our gratitude to our kings has always been profound and fresh and we cannot forget them. But now the French have come. . . . We are too weak for them. Our leaders and our soldiers have been defeated. Each fight brings more misery.
> The French have enormous warships, groups of well-armed soldiers, and heavy cannons. No one can resist them. . . . You, mandarins and people, can live under French rule. They are only terrible in war. But their flag may not be allowed to fly above the fortress while Phan Thanh Gian is still alive.[19]

Gian then submitted to his king the last and bleakest report of a long career, personally accepting full responsibility for the loss of territory. With it he returned all badges of office and the twenty-three royal awards acquired in a lifetime of distinguished service. Then, after fasting for fifteen days, he finally resorted to poison to achieve complete abstention from a situation in which he could not resolve the conflict between honor and conscience, between *nhan* and *nghia*. On his deathbed he enjoined his children to accept no employment and no honors from the French, urging them to earn their living as simple farmers.[20]

Meanwhile, the situation in northern Vietnam was getting out of hand as peasant unrest, organized brigandage, tribal rebellions, and Le restoration movements simultaneously threatened the social order. Amidst all this, a French merchant, eager to use the Red River to trade with Chinese troops in Yunnan, became embroiled in a heated controversy with Vietnamese officials in Hanoi. In 1873, with the agreement of the Vietnamese court, French authorities in Saigon sent a small force to Hanoi to settle the dispute.

What happened next, and why, is murky, but the outcome was decisive.

On November 20, 1873, in just one hour two hundred well-armed men under the command of the impetuous French officer dispatched from Saigon, supported by naval artillery, overran a citadel defended by seven thousand Vietnamese troops. Astonishingly, the French force suffered only one man killed and two wounded while among the defenders eighty were killed and three hundred wounded. Flushed with so dramatic a victory, the French troops then overran four major provinces in the Red River delta.[21]

In 1874 a new Franco-Vietnamese treaty was signed, which formalized French sovereignty over the entire Mekong delta and reaffirmed and extended French rights to trade and proselytize throughout all of Vietnam. Among the discouraged and disgusted population of the Red River delta, all semblance of public order disappeared. Soldiers of *nghia*, bandits, rebels, Catholics, French and royal troops swarmed across the countryside in violent confusion.[22] Villages closed themselves off from a hostile and unpredictable world. The social contract by which men lived existed only within the village hedge.

As chaos enveloped his disintegrating realm, King Tu Duc made overtures to China for military assistance. Fearful of losing the initiative, in 1882 the French once again launched an attack on the citadel of Hanoi. This time the defense was better prepared and stronger than before, but still it could not withstand the sustained shelling of naval artillery. The citadel rocked as its own reserves of gunpowder exploded. As the surviving defenders scrambled to escape the imminent collapse, General Hoang Dieu, the commanding officer, calmly composed his final report to the king and hung himself from a tree.

Regular troops from the Ch'ing army had already entered Vietnam, and the Black Flag outlaws had reached a new zenith of power. Captain Henri Rivière, leader of French troops in the north, planned a surprise thrust up the Red River valley, but the forewarned Black Flags repeated their successful ambush of Captain Garnier and were soon parading through delta villages with Captain Rivière's head displayed upon a pikestaff. With the full weight of an inflamed public opinion in France as well as in colonial society now firmly behind them as a result of this "outrage," at long last French military and business leaders were enabled to pursue their long-cherished goal of overthrowing the obstructionist court in Hue once and for all.[23]

In 1883 French troops poured ashore near Hue and threatened to take the capital. Tu Duc had died only a month before, and the court was plagued with dissension and intrigue. Tu Duc's immediate successor was dethroned and imprisoned after ruling for only one day. Four months later the next king was driven to commit suicide. The third of Tu Duc's hapless successors died of unknown causes after only six months on the throne. Finally a twelve-year-old was named to reign as King Ham Nghi. In the midst of this turmoil the French had exacted a treaty making them virtual masters of all Vietnam. Southern Vietnam was French territory, and central and northern Vietnam were each separate French "protectorates."[24]

In 1885 Ham Nghi fled to the mountainous hinterlands of the central region. Calling for all Vietnamese to rise up against the French, he likened to "disguised animals" those of his subjects who failed to respond to his call to live and die for *nghia*. As in the south twenty years earlier, "soldiers of *nghia*" arose in numerous localized rebellions. And as before, these uprisings were foredoomed exercises in futility. Thousands died in vain as the French smashed these poorly coordinated revolts one by one. The deadly French volleys did more than shatter rebel strongholds and slay the bravest champions of traditional values; they delivered a mortal blow to the fundamental belief in a just natural order on which those values had been based. Ham Nghi was captured in 1888 and exiled to Algeria. The "Son of Heaven" was to the French just another unruly teenager to be "instructed" if that were possible and disciplined if it were not.[25]

After the scandalous turnover of monarchs following the death of Tu Duc, and the infamous treaties of 1884 and 1885, which made any further claim by the court in Hue to actually rule Vietnam appear ridiculous, the number of those who chose to abstain from public life grew dramatically. As resistance faded, first in the central region and then in the north following a brief but disastrous spate of activity between 1885 and 1888, abstention from worldly affairs became a significant mode of response among Vietnam's educated elite.

Nguyen Khuyen (1835–1909) and Tran Te Xuong (1870–1907) illustrate this state of mind.[26] Through superb poetry these two men satirized the age in which they lived: the French, their compatriots, and themselves. To them the final decades of the nineteenth century were a period when "water flowed upward." It was an "unnatural" time, one that defied the natural order of *ly*.

Three centuries earlier, Nguyen Binh Khiem had deftly captured the essence of harmony with nature in these lines:

> I eat bamboo shoots in fall, bean sprouts in winter;
> Bathe in the lotus pond in spring, swim in the lake in summer.

In shocking contrast, Tran Te Xuong now observed that many of his contemporaries acted in an "unnatural" and outrageously silly way:

> In winter they use feather fans;
> In summer they wear socks.[27]

Nguyen Khuyen was from northern Vietnam and his great-great grandfather had been a high official in the Le court. He himself held a number of responsible offices during the troubled first decade of Tu Duc's reign and under his ill-fated successors. But when Vietnamese sovereignty over northern and central Vietnam was ceded to the French in 1884, he pleaded severe eye trouble and retired at the age of forty-nine, forsaking a promising career. For the rest of his life he feigned ill health and spurned all public activity. When invited to return to active life in the colonial administration, he revealed no flicker of interest, often declining in scathing verse that quickly passed into the popular lore of the region.[28]

In a *yin* tradition reminiscent of so many earlier poems of protest or personal anguish, Nguyen Khuyen once expressed his feelings through the words of a woman in a poem entitled "The Words of a Widow":

> Doesn't he realize I'm a widow,
> Sad and lonely, lacking food and clothing?
> He really has outdone himself, this fine matchmaker,
> Who would mate me with the vigor of youth.
>
> A young man seldom tires in his pursuit of pleasure.
> An old widow like me lacks that kind of stamina.
> How could I possibly satisfy all of his desires?
> The match looks promising, but it could never last.
>
> Marry a mere boy for rice and a tunic?
> Even in hunger and rags one still knows shame.
> My parents taught me long ago,
> A girl who runs after boys brings ridicule upon herself.
>
> Is this the regard in which you hold me, my matchmaking
>   friend?

I'm glad you are concerned, but I do not care for your plan.
If you love me, loan me cloth or loan me rice.
This old lady declines to remarry![29]

The overall tone of Nguyen Khuyen's poetry was wistful rather than vicious, but he was capable of writing status-leveling rebukes to the more corrupt or servile of his former colleagues, and sometimes he chided his contemporaries for their lack of dignity in defeat. One good example of the mordant wit for which he is justly famous is a poem he wrote about the celebration of Bastille Day:

Firecrackers are resounding. It's Bastille Day!
So many waving banners, so many lanterns hung.
With bulging eyes officials' wives gape at a boat race.
A funny skit meanwhile attracts all of the very young.
Many girls cling to swings in a tight embrace,
While greedy guys pursue their goal of climbing up the well-
   greased pole.
Whoever organized these games has done a splendid job.
Yet the more fun that these folks have, the greater the
   disgrace![30]

A friend of Nguyen Khuyen's had declined to accept appointment to an official post, claiming he was deaf. So Khuyen composed a poem to tease the man, express admiration for him, and publicize this patriotic act to increase its effect. The poem is known as "The Man Who Feigns Deafness":

There's a man who pretends to be deaf.
"Huh? Huh? What say?" he stupidly asks.
Little does one suspect he stops and starts his ears like they
   were plow buffaloes.
I'd certainly like to be deaf like that.
Amidst a chattering crowd he sits dumb as a block of wood.
But late at night and all alone he's lively as a monkey.
In the back garden, to the front pond, enjoy a pipe, then a
   chew of betel,
Six or seven cups of tea while playing with some lines from
   Kieu.
Who wouldn't want to be deaf like that?
But do you think it's easy?
Just ask him. "What say?" he'll reply.[31]

Scholar-officials like Nguyen Khuyen, and this man who pretended to be deaf, were doing much more than merely withholding their services from an administration of which they did not approve. They were communicating this disapproval in a highly effective way.

Yet Nguyen Khuyen also delicately expressed a deep melancholy, which he shared with many contemporary traditional scholars. His poetry conveys the feelings of alienation and impotence with which these men watched the rapid demise of the world they knew and cherished. Little was left of this world at the end of the century except fading memories and a few treasured friendships. Many of Nguyen Khuyen's finest poems treat the subject of friendship with great sensitivity.

One by one the friends disappeared. On the death of a close friend in 1902 Nguyen Khuyen wrote a long poem of mourning that expresses the enormity of his loss, not just of a friend, but of a way of life that had been perpetuated only through the friendship:

> Fine wine, but no good friends,
> So I buy none though I have the money.
> A poem comes to mind, but I choose not to write it down.
> If it were written, to whom would I give it?
> The spare bed hangs upon the wall in cold indifference.
> I pluck the lute, but it just doesn't sound right.[32]

By the end of the nineteenth century the traditional Vietnamese scholars realized full well that their accustomed world was gone forever. But another generation was maturing amid the pathos and confusion of a crumbling sociocultural system that provided few certain guides to either morality or efficacy.

Tran Te Xuong, who was younger and much less successful than Nguyen Khuyen, had a more acerbic wit. He too came from a family of scholars in the north, but he failed in his examinations several times. In 1894 he finally achieved the lower-level baccalaureate degree, but then in 1897 he failed once more in trying for the higher level. The examination system was still thriving in the 1890s, especially in the north. In 1897 over fifteen thousand anxious candidates waited in Nam Dinh for almost six weeks while the nitpicking examiners laboriously graded and tallied the test results. Since most candidates were accompanied by servants or relatives and Nam Dinh was already a fairly large town, this crowd was of a size seldom to be seen in Vietnam.

The French, having just experienced an abortive coup d'état in 1896, were justly apprehensive. Two French gunboats stood in the river. And a curfew was imposed. Yet, eager to impress so large a captive audience, French authorities decided that the awards ceremony should be organized with greater pomp and ceremony than usual. In addition to the normal array of high mandarins and the time-hallowed paraphernalia of ritual, this long-awaited awards ceremony was further dignified by columns of troops, a brass band, and the presence of the newly arrived French governor-general for all of Indochina and his wife, M. and Mme Paul Doumer.[33]

The official party was carried onto the field in sedan chairs while the band blared. As the name of each successful candidate was announced, the chosen few detached themselves from the crowd and assembled at one side of the field. There each young man was presented with an outfit of new clothes appropriate to his new status. One of the most important pieces of this regalia was a special hat. This "dragon hat" was traditionally regarded as "something very valuable and noble; the mark of an intellectual."

Meanwhile the official party waited on a high platform to congratulate the successful candidates and receive their bows of gratitude. M. and Mme Doumer, unremitting in their performance of duty, had brought a gift for each graduate. The austere dignity of this traditional Sino-Vietnamese ceremony was to be enlivened by a touch of Gallic conviviality. Each candidate in turn reached up to the platform and received a turnip-shaped pocketwatch and a handshake from the Doumers. As Madame Doumer, whose mere presence at such an event was a shocking incongruity, kept bending over to shake hands and pass out watches, Tran Te Xuong, who was standing among the disappointed spectators, conceived a poem, "Teasing the Successful Candidates":

> A flock of those who flunked stood looking on instead.
> How happy they would have been to receive a pass.
> Up on the podium, madame waggled her duck-like ass.
> Down in the yard each new B.A. raised his dragon head.

The image of Madame Doumer's ample derriere towering above the upturned heads of those proud young men in their dragon caps achieves a rare symbolic resonance. Among the many political, racial, and even obscene dimensions to this image, it was the *yin-yang* implications that provided much of its shock value for contemporary readers and integrated multiple interpretations.

In this solemn ritual, which conveyed the very essence of the

tem, no woman should ever have been elevated above a
alone a man possessed of the dragon symbol. Only a
....an would have placed a woman in such a position, and
only a Frenchwoman would have assumed it so blithely. That Vietnamese dignitaries were willing to participate in such a farce was
eloquent testimony to their state of impotent subjugation. As for
those successful examination candidates who so proudly donned
their dragon caps and anticipated wielding power and influence in
their land and moving to the head of the table in their villages on
the basis of this emblem of royal favor, Tran Te Xuong delivered
them a sharp reduction in status by referring to them as a "flock."
They fancied themselves to be dragons, but in fact they were mere
ducklings, dominated by that strange mother duck, Mme Paul
Doumer.

To Tran Te Xuong this ceremony was a disgusting spectacle.
Everyone present was playing the fool and was too obtuse to realize it. Yet they were all successful while he stood rejected on the
fringes of the crowd. To make matters worse, he could not help en-
vying them! Who, he often asked himself, was the bigger fool? This
sense of isolation arising from a detached and sensitized awareness
of his social environment is made vividly explicit in several well-
known poems.

Like many young men of his generation, Tran Te Xuong was
dissatisfied with himself and the world in which he lived. He ridiculed unmercifully the things he desired and could not get and
mocked himself for wanting them. He launched vicious attacks on
those who succeeded where he had failed, and then poured equal
scorn upon himself for his failure. Despite having a wife and a
growing number of children, Xuong led a life of self-indulgence,
and his poetry defiantly paraded all his faults for the world to see
and laugh at. He readily joined in their laughter, feeling, one sup-
poses, that as they joined him in laughing at himself they were unwittingly laughing with him at their own foibles and the absurdity
of the society they represented. This element of self-deprecation is
evident in the poem "Laughing at Myself":

> There's a clay statue on Brown Street,
> With staring eyes and a pasty face.
> He strokes his beard, and flatters his wife as "my sweet,"
> Furrows his brow and frowns at life, such is his conceit.
> When I was young I was number one at gambling and at
> chess.

And gulping wine? Sipping tea? Chasing girls? Oh, yes!
I guess I always thought that I was so darned clever.
I could breeze through my studies, and just play forever.[34]

Xuong's failure to master the canons of classical studies may not have been the sole cause of his repeated failure in examinations. Many influential officials were humiliated by vicious portraits in Xuong's verse. No one, in fact, was immune from his biting wit. When a Buddhist monk was arrested on suspicion of robbery, Xuong mockingly offered a poem of condolence and advice to "The Monk in Jail":

All that compassion and still you land in jail!
Surely you didn't stray from the path of monastic life?
You've chanted prayers of salvation from over three hundred
    books.
Maybe you were so busy you forgot the right amulet.[35]

After cleverly sketching the imposing appearance of some local male shamans who claimed to be possessed by the spirits of heroes, Xuong concluded:

If you shamans are so clever, why haven't you come to the aid
    of your nation?
You wouldn't be afraid of cannons, would you?[36]

Despite his failure and poverty Xuong resolutely persisted in the traditional path of examination in the Chinese classics, although he made fun of it and himself at the same time:

What good are Chinese characters?
All those Ph.D.'s are out of work.
Much better to be a clerk for the French:
You get milk in the morning and champagne at night.[37]

Yet he refused to attend the school in Hanoi that trained interpreters and clerks to go to work for the French.

As the nineteenth century drew to a close, almost the entire leadership of Vietnam's "soldiers of *nghia*" had passed from the scene.[38] Then with the death of Tran Te Xuong in 1907 and of Nguyen Khuyen in 1909, the poetic tradition they represented also became moribund. The next generation seemed to contain no one capable of breathing life into the time-honored genres of Vietnamese poetry. Within a single decade both the soldiers and the bards of tradition had largely disappeared, not to be replaced. Both armed resistance and righteous abstention had become meaningless responses to the French colonial takeover. The worldview on which both resistance and withdrawal had been based was shattering under the continuous assault of demonstrated French military and technological superiority.

Under Paul Doumer the French instituted a frenzied program of building highways, bridges, and railroads. In a country that had never even known extensive stagecoach service, French officials sped about their business in powerful automobiles, appearing to the Vietnamese as "disguised genies, . . . half-gods in their flying chariots."[39] The mighty Red River itself was conquered by French technology. Even their most faithful supporters had advised the French not to attempt to build a bridge across the Red River. Others merely smiled. The dragon who lived in the river would never permit such a thing to happen. In response the French built the greatest bridge in Asia. Its pilings extended over a hundred feet beneath the surface, plunging into the heart of the dragon! Over a mile long, it was named for Doumer. Many Vietnamese were impressed, and also resentful.[40]

By 1900 the French were congratulating themselves that the conquest and reorganization of Vietnam had been brought to a satisfactory conclusion. In 1901 Governor-General Paul Doumer complacently reported that not a single one of the colonial troops in French Indochina had been killed since 1897.[41] While the French pleasurably anticipated the stability and profit that had long eluded them, many Vietnamese were experiencing a nadir of despair and self-doubt. After forty years of painful but futile effort, the Vietnamese felt like total failures. "What contempt our ancestors must have for us!" one poet cried in anguish.[42] As Vietnamese burned with shame at their growing sense of inferiority, French arrogance stung all the more sharply.

Growing numbers of people were forced to conclude that only by mastering Western culture and its secrets could the nations of the East become the equal of Western nations. Up to this point, merely to express such views would have been tantamount to heresy or treason. To many people this was still so. But in the first decade of the twentieth century such sentiments were uttered in public for the first time by men whose scholarly and patriotic credentials were beyond question.

At the turn of the century Chinese reformist writings began to trickle into Vietnamese intellectual circles from Shanghai, where they had stirred up much excitement in 1898. By 1903 and 1904 a few Vietnamese were avidly circulating such materials and discussing them in small private groups. Some literati became acquainted with recent Chinese publications that discussed basic issues of modernization. And Chinese translations of Western classics coming out of the "self-strengthening" movement introduced significant numbers of Vietnamese intellectuals to the best of Western thought for the very first time. The ideas of Rousseau, Voltaire, Montesquieu, Darwin, and Herbert Spencer invigorated a new generation of activist scholars in Vietnam. A new era began in Vietnam with the founding of an Association for the Modernization of Vietnam in 1904.[43]

Early in 1905 one of the leaders of this organization, Phan Boi Chau (1867–1940), went to Japan to seek outside support for revolutionary activity and to investigate at first hand the results of a modernization program in Japan that had incorporated Western ideas and institutions into its traditional sociocultural system. As he traveled Japan stunned the world by achieving a decisive victory over Russia. While this news of an Asian triumph over a Western power greatly revitalized the flagging hopes of the demoralized Vietnamese and tremendously increased their interest in the "new learning," an exhilarated Phan Boi Chau returned to Vietnam in August 1905 and urged his compatriots to go observe "the miracle of the rising sun" for themselves. Phan Boi Chau was a paragon of Neo-Confucian virtue, so his advocacy of the new learning and new values commanded a respectful hearing.[44]

Chau was invaluable as a fund-raiser, recruiter, and inspirational leader, but he was still committed to violence and armed rebellion as the primary means of struggle, and he still looked to a strong and independent monarchy as its proper goal. He had even selected his own candidate for the throne, Prince Cuong De, a direct descendant of Gia Long. Cuong De was a dapper young man who read books about George Washington, Abraham Lincoln, and other heroes of both East and West. In Japan Phan Boi Chau enjoyed intimate discussions with prominent Chinese exiles as well as sympathetic Japanese "liberals." All advised him to be more patient and to concentrate on education at home and public relations abroad.[45]

In early 1906 Chau was back in Japan accompanied by Prince Cuong De and a scholar activist named Phan Chu Trinh. Cuong De was enrolled in the Shimbu Military Academy, while Chau gave

Trinh a guided tour through the miracles of modern Japan. Trinh, however, saw the strength and prosperity of Japan as confirmation of his own belief that only through a general and modern education could any lasting progress be made. Trinh favored nonviolent reform, emphasis on education, and gradual progress toward independence as a democratic republic. To him, Chau's penchant for violence and his preference for monarchy were shortsighted responses to the challenge of the modern world.

This disagreement between Phan Boi Chau and Phan Chu Trinh was reflected throughout the larger intellectual community.[46] The activists in the Association for the Modernization of Vietnam could agree on only one thing: the urgent need of the Vietnamese people to acquire greater knowledge of the sources of Western power in order to improve their own position in the world. After 1905 the example of Japan made the advantages of this approach irrefutable.

The initial result of the new enthusiasm for modern education was a movement known as "Travel East." Under the personal direction of Phan Boi Chau a network of fund-raisers and guides was organized to help young Vietnamese get out of the country and travel to Japan, where they joined students who had been arriving from China over the previous several years. By 1907 there were an estimated thirteen thousand self-exiled Chinese students in Japan, and Vietnamese students set out to join them.[47]

In March 1907 a new school was opened in Hanoi, largely under the influence of Phan Chu Trinh. This was a private school, which charged no tuition and was open to young and old, male and female, rich and poor, advanced students and beginners. The Dong Kinh Nghia Thuc was inspired by the Keio Gijuke (later to become the prestigious Keio University), a tuition-free school that Trinh had seen as the cradle of the Japanese drive for modernization. The school was staffed with volunteer teachers and created much of its own instructional material. Many lessons and texts were reproduced in the school's own primitive printing facility. Courses were developed in mathematics, science, geography, physical education, hygiene, political history and economics, French, and Chinese. But the primary emphasis was placed on popularizing the use of the romanized alphabet for Vietnamese in place of both Chinese and *nom*. *Quoc ngu*, the romanized system for transcribing Vietnamese, was still only marginally respectable and not widely known, especially in the northern and central regions.[48]

The Dong Kinh Nghia Thuc referred not merely to the modest school in Hanoi but to a larger movement for mass education. Books were printed and distributed to other schools and bookstores free of charge. Attempts were made to open classes elsewhere. And lecturers went out on the first and fifteenth of every lunar month to carry the message of the school to a wider audience. Phan Chu Trinh was the most popular public speaker.

Phan Chu Trinh symbolized the forward-looking, reformist element in Vietnamese society. He went to considerable trouble and expense to acquire a wardrobe that was stylish in contemporary Western good taste but was made in Vietnam of local materials. Trinh had been a success in the court examinations of 1901 and had acquired and then resigned a coveted appointment in the Ministry of Rites. He self-consciously started some business enterprises, a shockingly déclassé act for one of his high status, as a means of demonstrating that commercial activity was respectable. Trinh was not a profound thinker, nor was he successful as an organizer or as a businessman. His prominence in the reform movement rested on his talent for reasoned debate and on his mastery of the symbolic gesture.

Phan Chu Trinh and Phan Boi Chau were leaders of the group of progressive scholars who in just a few years completely shifted the equation between such emotion-laden terms as independence, colonialism, tradition, patriotism, heresy, and *nghia*. These two men in their different ways convinced large numbers of Vietnamese that it had become the duty of the patriotic and the virtuous to put aside the old ways rather than to defend them. They forced many people to contemplate for the first time the possibility that at least some of the "new ways" of the West might be worthy of imitation.

One evening Phan Chu Trinh was giving a speech at the Dong Kinh Nghia Thuc school in Hanoi. He very carefully built up to his climax and ended with his voice ringing in exultation:

> Several thousand years ago our people cut off their hair and tattooed themselves. Only when Chao T'o took over our country did we become infected with Chinese customs, but even then only a few people in urban centers followed them. It was not until the Ming invaders came in and . . . compelled us to imitate them that our men began to let their hair grow and wore it in a bun, that our women began wearing trousers, and we became Chinese. But today . . . fortunately,

Heaven has opened our minds. We have awakened, and the
entire nation is modernizing. So go out and cut your hair!
Don't leave any more land for that stupid gang of parasites to
colonize on top of your heads, from which they can suck your
blood! Wouldn't it feel wonderful to be rid of them? Don't
you think so? Don't you?[49]

The lecture hall resounded with laughter and applause. In one
skillful thrust Trinh had linked the revered Sinitic tradition with
colonialism and had vividly underlined the parasitic nature of
colonialism—Chinese or French—with the metaphor of lice. At the
same time he offered a new symbol for modernity and freedom:
the haircut. Within a few weeks an anonymous "Haircutting
Chant" was spreading from the streets of Hanoi to the rest of the
land:

> Comb in the left hand,
> Scissors in the right.
> Clip away! Clip away!
> Easy, easy, do it right.
> Off with stupidity!
> Off with foolishness!
> Today we snip,
> Tomorrow we shave![50]

Patriots took to the streets and lanes with scissors, giving haircuts
to all who wanted them, and to many who did not. The French
were rightly suspicious of the political implications of this activity.
They were also exasperated at being put in a position where they
either had to ignore revolutionary agitation or appear ridiculous by
objecting to haircuts exactly like their own. Finally, despite the
snickers it aroused, an official investigation was launched into
what was called "Le Mouvement de la Tonsure."[51]

The symbolic significance of a haircut went far beyond mere
questions of style or habit. The male chignon was capable of arousing passionate emotions because as a custom it was deeply embedded in the primary traditional values of *on* and *hieu*, moral debt and
filial piety. To cut one's hair was to sully a body one possessed as a
gift from one's parents and ancestors. To willfully "mar" this product of their loins was a clear breach of filial piety and a failure to
acknowledge one's moral debt to one's progenitors. In his last major work the blind poet of the resistance, Nguyen Dinh Chieu, had

summed up the prevailing Neo-Confucian position on this subject precisely in terms of the relationship between patriotism and adherence to traditional values:

> I would rather face eternal darkness
> Than see the face of traitors.
> . . . .
> Being blind but knowing how to uphold family virtues
> Is better than having eyes but neglecting one's ancestors
> . . . .
> Being blind and keeping one's body and mind intact
> Is better than having eyes but having to cut hair and trim the beard.[52]

Against this background the haircut became a potent symbol. During the year 1907 progressive Vietnamese scholars achieved results beyond their expectations, and guarded optimism began to replace the despair of the previous decade. Over a thousand students were enrolled in classes at the Dong Kinh Nghia Thuc school in Hanoi, and similar classes in the "new learning" were beginning elsewhere in Vietnam. Meanwhile over a hundred young Vietnamese were in Japan with Phan Boi Chau and Prince Cuong De, and an equal number were on their way to join them. An enthusiastic public response and generous donations from a wide spectrum of Vietnamese offered attractive prospects for expansion of all these educational programs. Disturbed by the way in which this rapidly growing demand for modern educational opportunity was being exploited by dangerously independent private groups, the French opened a government-sponsored school in Hanoi to compete with the Dong Kinh Nghia Thuc and even created a University of Hanoi in a belated attempt to regain control over the educational process.

The political implications of this new outburst of activity, especially the "haircut movement," had been made all too clear. One popular poem was quite explicit:

> Now is the time to shave our heads and become monks,
> To chant the prayer of Independence in the temple of
>   Modernity.
> To pray, to supplicate tirelessly, day and night,
> For the benefit of the nation, for the benefit of the people.
> Become monks to open the minds of the people,
> Become monks to help make our country rich and strong.[53]

ong Kinh Nghia Thuc school was closed down after less
ear of operation. Although the Dong Kinh Nghia Thuc
ealized that the closing of the school was partly justified in
political terms by a genuine strain of sedition within some of the
school's activities (this had been a source of controversy within the
group's own inner councils),[54] French repression of the school
served to confirm what many people already suspected: France
wanted to keep the Vietnamese people ignorant and weak, and the
"mission civilisatrice" dimension of French policy was a cruel hoax.
The year 1908 brought even more active protest and even more
vigorous repression. The new educational programs inaugurated
by the French were inadequate, but they far exceeded what had
been available. In the spring of 1908 demands for educational
reform were surpassed by even more strident demands for tax
reform.

Paul Doumer, determined to achieve a basic transformation of
French Indochina within his five-year (1897–1902) appointment as
governor-general, relentlessly pursued an ambitious development
plan greatly in excess of the region's needs and capacities. There
was a uniform tendency to overestimate the advantages of a project
and to underestimate its actual cost. The burden of these miscal-
culations was borne by the Vietnamese people in the form of
ruinous taxes and enormous demands for corvée labor. Soon, the
Vietnamese joked, there would be a tax on bowel movements.
Everything else, it seemed, was taxed already. Through a combination of ignorance and cynicism, French policies at the turn of the
century had reduced large numbers of Vietnamese to unendurable
depths of poverty.[55]

Although the possession of opium was a criminal offense in
France, the French administration purchased raw opium in India
and Yunnan, brought it to Saigon for processing, and then sold it
at official outlets at a profit of 400 to 500 percent. With sardonic
humor, Vietnamese observed that the French at least granted them
freedom to poison themselves, a liberty denied the inhabitants of
the mother country.[56] But indirect taxation through state monopo-
lies took other and even more invidious forms. The state alcohol
monopoly was bitterly resented. Rice whiskey was an essential
part of the many feast days celebrated by each family and each village during the course of the year. Not only did the Vietnamese
have to pay more money for an inferior product, they were also

forced to purchase it in carefully stamped official bottles, which raised the actual cost by about 900 percent.[57]

Predictably, the opium monopoly was threatened by extensive smuggling activity, and the alcohol monopoly resulted in much illicit distilling. The French response was direct, brutal, and effective in the short run. Networks of secret agents and informers were organized, and the law was changed to permit unregulated entry, search, and seizure in private homes in a manner never before tolerated under either French or Vietnamese law. While the use of opium was only encouraged, the purchase of alcohol was made compulsory. Quota systems were established whereby a province was obliged to purchase a certain amount of whiskey each month, based on "normal usage." Then within each province every village had to buy a certain quantity of whiskey or face harsh punishment on the charge that illicit distilling was being condoned. The evils produced by these techniques of enforcement generated even more resentment than the indirect taxes themselves.[58]

Although the French opium policies were racist and exploitive, and the alcohol monopoly forced the Vietnamese to purchase a beverage they did not like in bottles they did not need at a price they could not afford, the salt monopoly was even worse. Salt was essential to existence. And although the price of salt in 1907 was five times what it had been in 1897, both production and distribution had been so disrupted by ruinous costs and bureaucratic meddling that sometimes there was no salt available at any price. A salt worker had to sell to the colonial government every last grain of salt he produced and then repurchase the salt required for his household use at six to eight times the price he had just received for it.[59]

On top of the dizzying spiral of direct and indirect taxes between 1897 and 1907, Doumer's grandiose public works program generated an insatiable demand for corvée labor. This often arbitrarily requisitioned labor was frequently a physical and emotional ordeal from which some workers did not return and others never recovered.[60]

Against this background of crushing taxes, forced labor, and oppressive law enforcement, three consecutive years of poor crops (1903, 1904, and 1905) combined with a drop in the value of the piaster to drive many rural Vietnamese to the verge of hysteria. During March and April of 1908 large groups of peasants in central

Vietnam went on a rampage—refusing to pay taxes, seizing district and prefect officials and clerks (sometimes giving them haircuts), and laying siege to administrative offices with demands for reduced corvée labor and taxes.[61]

Several dozen demonstrators were killed and over a hundred were wounded in the suppression of these incidents. At least nine people were captured and summarily executed. Thousands were arrested and over a hundred were shipped off to the penal colony of Poulo Condore. Although the Dong Kinh Nghia Thuc leaders apparently had not been directly involved in the riots nor even encouraged them, they were singled out for especially harsh punishment. Phan Boi Chau, still in Japan, was sentenced to death in absentia. Phan Chu Trinh—who had pleaded with both the French and the Vietnamese to avoid violence—was arrested and sentenced to death, but through the intervention of French liberals he was given a last-minute reprieve and sent to Poulo Condore instead.[62]

In September 1907 King Thanh Thai was declared insane and transported to Reunion Island off the coast of Africa to spend his life in obscure exile. The young monarch, attired in the finest clothing Western fashion could provide and affecting a jaunty walking stick, had proven to be a disappointment to both the French and the Vietnamese. During the sacred sacrifices to Heaven and Earth, feeling ludicrous, he had laughed openly at himself and at those Vietnamese who watched him with awe and devotion. In addition to his painful awareness of the fraudulent nature of his role as disbelieving priest and impotent ruler of a subjugated and "backward" people, King Thanh Thai had been forced to endure the further indignity of becoming a "tourist exhibit" for important visitors to the colony. Grotesque outbursts became commonplace, and rumors circulated about sadistic orgies conducted in private chambers.[63]

Upsetting as this behavior was to the French, to the handful of traditional monarchists remaining in the court at Hue it was an even greater source of frustration. The king's disregard for decorum thwarted their efforts to maintain the sacrosanct nature of his office. Foremost among these outraged monarchists who were struggling to preserve the prerogatives of the throne even against the king's own wishes was Ngo Dinh Kha, minister of rites, grand chamberlain, and keeper of the eunuchs. When Thanh Thai was exiled, Minister Kha resigned in chagrin and retired. Sequestered in the family estate, Kha brooded in isolation, indulging his morbid sense of self-righteousness and wrestling with a gnawing ache of shame and failure. His bleak presence cast a pall over the entire household, affecting none perhaps more strongly than young Ngo Dinh Diem, his six-year-old son.[64]

Minister Kha had made a lasting impact on the future of his country, however, by establishing a "national school," the Quoc Hoc Academy in Hue, where outstanding students, including his own children, could receive an education that combined Western and Vietnamese studies, taught from a Vietnamese rather than from a French point of view. Many boys left the classrooms of the Quoc Hoc Academy to shape Vietnamese history. Meanwhile, under diplomatic pressure from France, and with a quid pro quo French acquiescence to their own colonial designs on the mainland of Asia, the Japanese Ministry of the Interior mounted a campaign against the Vietnamese students. By early 1909 only twenty of them remained. In March 1909 Phan Boi Chau and Prince Cuong De were deported.[65]

By the end of the first decade of the twentieth century most prominent leaders of the Association for the Modernization of Vietnam were dead, imprisoned, or scattered in exile. A more docile king was on the throne. The private schools for modern education and the fledgling commercial enterprises that contributed to their support had been closed down. The University of Hanoi had been abolished without completing a single semester of instruction. In just a few years Vietnamese intellectuals had passed from despair through naive optimism to reach at last a more realistic assessment of how difficult it would be for Vietnam to become a modern, prosperous, and independent nation. As chastened spirits readjusted their efforts toward more modest goals, a new and even more complicated phase of reaction to colonialism began.

The Fermentation of Vietnamese Culture, 1908–1932

A new and unlikely figure came to the forefront of Vietnamese intellectual life during the second decade of the twentieth century. Nguyen Van Vinh (1882–1936) came from a humble peasant family living in the Red River delta. Vinh did not possess the flashing wit, the talent for impromptu poetry, nor the passionate patriotism of men like Nguyen Khuyen or Tran Te Xuong. He was no larger-than-life hero like Phan Boi Chau, no audacious reformer or brilliant debater like Phan Chu Trinh. Nguyen Van Vinh was, in fact, just the sort of person Phan Boi Chau was always railing against and whom Khuyen and Xuong ridiculed in their poetry.

As a teenager, Vinh had jumped at the chance to attend the very school (Collège des Interprètes) that Xuong had spurned at about the same time. He graduated from that school and took pride in becoming one of the "milk in the morning and champagne at night" fellows whom Xuong held in such contempt. Vinh attended Bastille Day celebrations and had a thoroughly good time. He worked as a clerk and interpreter for the French, and he was an exceptionally good employee—competent, bright, reliable, hardworking, polite, eager to learn. As a reward he was selected to travel to France in 1906 as part of a team to work the "Tonkinese" pavilion at an exposition being held at Marseilles.

Vinh was only twenty-four years old when he went to France, a junior clerk in the colonial administration with but a mediocre education. How dazzled he was by his experiences on this journey! It was not merely the imposing buildings, the automobiles, the overwhelming sense of material prosperity that captured his attention. He fell in love with French art and literature, with French philosophy, with the ideals of democracy and personal freedom. And, most of all, he became enamored of the lively and exciting world of journalism.

At the Marseilles Exposition, the Tonkinese pavilion was directly beside one sponsored by a regional French newspaper, *Le Petit Marseille*. The enterprising publisher of the paper had moved his entire operation into the exhibition grounds as a publicity stunt. The complete workings of a fair-sized modern newspaper were put on display. File clerks, reporters, copy boys, editors, typesetters, printers—all performed their daily tasks next door to the pavilion where Vinh was working. "Every day I watched that scene of activity with hungry eyes, the humming presses, reporters dashing off to gather news. I became infatuated with the newspaper business. All day long I'd be over there asking one question after another. The publisher patiently explained everything to me in a very kindly manner."[66] And thus a dream was born. Nguyen Van Vinh now had no doubt about his goals in life. He wanted to become a pioneering Vietnamese journalist who would lead his people in a cultural revolution, turning them away from what he perceived to be the "backwardness" and "superstition" of their "ossified" Asian heritage.

Vinh was still in France when the idea for founding the Dong

Kinh Nghia Thuc was presented at a meeting of the Association for the Modernization of Vietnam by Phan Chu Trinh. But shortly after his return to Hanoi Nguyen Van Vinh agreed to file the application papers necessary for obtaining permission to open the school.[67] The French, uncertain of the intended symbolic linkage between the *nghia* in Nghia Thuc and that in "soldiers of *nghia*," investigated and pondered for two months before finally issuing a permit for the school's operation. When official permission was received there was an enthusiastic outburst of activity, and Nguyen Van Vinh was one of the principal participants. He took charge of the French-language classes, and urged the establishment of a sports and physical education program that was singularly unsuccessful in attracting either students or instructors. Vinh was also one of the lecturers who gave fortnightly public speeches advocating modernization and popularizing new ideas.[68]

But this was only a small part of Nguyen Van Vinh's ambitious campaign. Shortly after his return to Hanoi he had opened a translation bureau and printing house. His first publication was a *quoc ngu* (romanized alphabet) edition of *Kieu*, the epic poem widely acknowledged as the masterpiece of Vietnamese literature, and this was quickly followed by a *quoc ngu* edition of that perennially popular Chinese novel, *Romance of the Three Kingdoms*. Vinh always placed the highest priority upon popularizing the use of *quoc ngu*. In an introduction to one of his earliest editions, Vinh wrote: "The condition of our nation in the future, good or bad, depends on *quoc ngu*." Phan Chu Trinh shared this opinion, saying, "Without the overthrow of Chinese characters, we cannot save Vietnam."[69]

But Vinh never neglected his primary goal of establishing a *quoc ngu* newspaper to provide a forum for popularizing Western culture to lead his people out of their benighted state of cultural stagnation. The situation was not promising. For many Vietnamese, especially the intellectual elite of the northern and central regions, the use of *quoc ngu* had been tainted by its associations with Catholicism, colonialism, and the unorthodoxy and crudity of southern frontier society.

Two Hanoi newspapers at this time were published half in Chinese and half in *quoc ngu*, and Vinh edited the *quoc ngu* portion of one of them. Both papers were linked to the Dong Kinh Nghia Thuc through overlapping personnel, and both gave it much favorable publicity. Although these papers failed to survive, they helped to remove the stigma from *quoc ngu* journalism and to mediate be-

tween the haughty cultural conservatism of the north and the earlier development of journalism, *quoc ngu*, and Western influence in
the south. Nguyen Van Vinh played a major role in incorporating
earlier initiatives in Saigon into an effective modernization campaign in Hanoi.[70]

The first newspaper ever to appear in Vietnam was the *Gia Dinh
Journal*, which appeared in Saigon in April 1865. It began as a modest monthly publication of the French colonial administration in
Cochinchina, consisting of only four pages containing mainly official announcements and decrees and some national news items. In
1869, however, its content became more varied. Historical essays,
poems, legends, and other cultural materials became increasingly
important. It was then published twice a month instead of monthly
and eventually came out three times a week.[71]

The motives of the French colonial authorities in sponsoring this
landmark publication were clearly articulated by the French governor of Cochinchina, M. Roze, in 1865:

> This journal is intended to disseminate among the indigenous
> population all the news worthy of their attention and to pro-
> vide them with some knowledge of current cultural matters
> and of developments in agriculture. The inspectors of native
> affairs have informed me that the *Gia Dinh Journal* has the en-
> thusiastic support of the population, and in many localities
> small children who are literate in *quoc ngu* have been reading
> the paper aloud to their parents. This monthly publication
> will be of irrefutable usefulness, and it will contribute to the
> replacement of our language and of Chinese characters,
> which are understood only by a minority of officials.[72]

In 1866 the director of internal affairs at the colonial headquarters in Cochinchina wrote to a colleague:

> From the very outset it has been recognized that the Chinese
> writing system has been a major barrier between the natives
> and ourselves. We must avoid giving instruction by means of
> ideographic characters. This kind of writing presents nothing
> but difficulties in transmitting to the population those diverse
> ideas which are necessary at the level of their new commercial
> and political situation. We are obliged as a consequence to
> follow the traditions of our own educational system. It is the
> only way which has the power to effect a reconciliation be-
> tween ourselves and the Annamites of the colony, to incul-
> cate them with the principles of European civilization, and to
> isolate them from the hostile influences of their neighbors.[73]

The *Gia Dinh Journal* consistently stressed the advantages of *quoc ngu*, as in the issue of April 15, 1867:

> The clerk or secretary who is wise and conscientious will exert himself to learn *quoc ngu*. There are only twenty-seven letters and they enable one to write tens of thousands of things. One can write down any word at all. It is not like Chinese characters. One can study them until old age and then still encounter strange words and not know how they are written. . . . *Quoc ngu* isn't difficult at all. With a few months of effort you can learn it perfectly.[74]

Opinion within the French community in Cochinchina was divided on the merits of *quoc ngu*. Many preferred to concentrate on teaching the Vietnamese French. Even some Vietnamese who were sympathetic to the goals of the French authorities criticized *quoc ngu* on various grounds. Many educated Vietnamese vigorously resisted all attempts to introduce a "Western-style" alphabet to replace the characters then in use. But two Vietnamese whose careers were associated with the *Gia Dinh Journal* had already developed *quoc ngu* writing and demonstrated its adequacy for expressing any kind of feeling or idea. These two men, Truong Vinh (Petrus) Ky and Huynh Tinh (Paulus) Cua, were southerners and devout Catholics.[75] Huynh Tinh Cua (1834–1907) was well educated in both Chinese and French. It was he who established and operated the *Gia Dinh Journal* in 1865, and he held the post of editor for many years. But Ky achieved greater influence.

Truong Vinh Ky (1837–1898) was the son of a military commander who died when Ky was only eight years old. A Catholic priest who had once been sheltered from persecution by Ky's father offered to adopt the boy and provide for his education, and this offer was gratefully accepted. Young Ky impressed the missionaries with whom he studied. They sent him to a Catholic school in Cambodia and then to a seminary in Penang, where he acquired a firm grounding in both Asian and Western civilization and reputedly learned fourteen languages. He was twenty-one years old and had just returned to Vietnam when the French expeditionary force swarmed ashore at Danang in 1858.

In 1863 Ky accompanied Phan Thanh Gian and his delegation to Paris as official interpreter for their negotiations with the French government. On his return to Saigon he was appointed a teacher at the newly opened school for interpreters, and he served as director of the school from 1866 to 1868. In 1868 he was named editor in chief of the *Gia Dinh Journal*, becoming the supervisor and collaborator of Huynh Tinh Cua in the task of expanding the role of the paper and improving its quality.

Over the next three decades not only did Ky and Cua develop *quoc ngu* into a standardized and effective medium of communication, they contributed greatly to the development of a modern Vietnamese language and literature, to the preservation in writing of traditional Vietnamese culture, and to the promotion of mutual understanding between East and West. Ky was a pioneer in producing textbooks for the Vietnamese to learn French and for the French to learn Vietnamese. He also wrote textbooks for teaching many other foreign languages and produced Vietnamese-French and French-Vietnamese dictionaries. Cua produced a massive and authoritative *quoc ngu* dictionary of the Vietnamese language, the first and for many decades the best of its kind. These two men wrote dozens of books and articles on Vietnamese geography, history, and culture, translated many classics from *nom* (demotic script for transcribing vernacular Vietnamese) and Chinese into *quoc ngu*, and produced four collections of short stories that broke new ground in the evolution of a modern Vietnamese prose style. Among these, *Ancient Tales* (1866) is a valuable collection of folktales garnered from oral tradition and written in a simple colloquial style.

Truong Vinh Ky was one of the first and most dedicated advocates of modernization in Vietnam. His was a unique perspective because during the formative years from age nine until age twenty-one he lived apart from his family and his village. His greatest moral debt was to the priests and missionaries who fed him, housed him, clothed him, and educated him during those years. Yet he remained a Vietnamese, refusing French citizenship when it was offered, despite the many advantages that accrued to "Frenchmen" in that colonial setting.

Truong Vinh Ky was dedicated to effecting basic cultural change in Vietnam. He believed that the development and popularization of *quoc ngu* was a prerequisite to progress. Although he seems to have demonstrated no political ambitions, because of his unique educational background and the moderation of his views he was appointed secretary of the Cholon city council in 1872 and several years later became the first and only Vietnamese member of the Saigon city council. In 1876 he made a fact-finding trip to northern Vietnam for the French authorities. He noted the misery of the people and identified a number of badly needed reforms, but he concluded that "the Hue court is incapable of carrying out these reforms, and only the French are capable of taking on the task of instructing so weak a nation." The French were in Ky's view obviously stronger, more advanced, than the Vietnamese, and so were worthy of imitation rather than hostility. Ky's concept of proper Franco-Vietnamese relations seems very like the traditional idea of *de*. France, the older brother, should be firm in providing guidance but generous and understanding of faults in the Vietnamese. Vietnam, the younger brother, should be respectful, obedient, and ready to learn from one possessed of greater knowledge and experience.

Although many southerners came to a passive acceptance of French domination, and superficial Westernization proceeded at a rapid pace,[76] Truong Vinh Ky and Huynh Tinh Cua nevertheless failed to achieve the progress they confidently expected to arise from their groundbreaking labors. There was no florescence of *quoc ngu* literature in southern Vietnam, partly because French authorities in Cochinchina decided to make French the primary language of instruction in public schools, introducing it into the curriculum at the elementary school level. But Ky and Cua laid the foundations on which Nguyen Van Vinh would build.

After his unsuccessful venture into *quoc ngu* journalism in Hanoi, Vinh established two unsuccessful French-language journals. The actual owner and publisher of all three publications was M. François Henri Schneider. Only a Frenchman could obtain a license to publish a newspaper. M. Schneider owned another, more successful, newspaper in Saigon, *News of the Six Provinces*, and in 1910 Vinh traveled south to assume active management of this venture. After three uneventful years in Saigon, Vinh and Schneider returned to Hanoi in 1913 to establish the *Indochina Journal*, the first of a series of influential publications that would play a vital role in creating and disseminating new patterns of thought in Vietnam. Newspapers would both shape and reflect patterns of change in the distribution of values in Vietnam.[77] The *Indochina Journal* succeeded in 1913 for a variety of reasons. The number of people who could read *quoc ngu* was rapidly increasing. In reaction to the uproar caused in 1907 and 1908 by the Travel East (Dong Du) movement, the Dong Kinh Nghia Thuc movement, and the protests for tax and educational reforms, the French had pressed ahead in developing a fledgling public school system.[78]

By 1909 there were about ten thousand pupils in these new public schools; by 1913, forty thousand.[79] The students in these schools represented well under one-half of one percent of the population. But out of these new classrooms over the next two or three decades would emerge a passionate and energetic generation of men and women, people excited by ideas, people who would fight with and against the French and Japanese and the Americans and most of all each other for a new "setting of the thermostat" in Vietnamese society. Nguyen Van Vinh saw the growing body of students in 1913 as a potential market for a *quoc ngu* newspaper, a network through which he might disseminate his doctrine of co-operation between the French and the Vietnamese in their joint task of transforming Vietnamese society by popularizing Western culture.

But while Vinh and Schneider had both cultural and economic motives, the immediate impetus for them to plunge once more into the newspaper business in Hanoi was primarily political. When Phan Boi Chau and Prince Cuong De were expelled from Japan in 1909, they went to Hong Kong and attempted to salvage the tattered remnants of their revolutionary movement, but with little success. They were isolated, without funds, and lacking in effective lines of communication. Prince Cuong De eventually drifted off to Europe with vague hopes of locating some powerful new patrons. Phan Boi Chau settled down with some other exiled activists in a commune in rural Thailand. For eight months he worked, rather ineptly, as a peasant, and composed patriotic literature in his spare time. But with the success of Sun Yat-sen in sparking revolution in China in late 1911, Chau set off in search of those Chinese revolutionary leaders whom he had gotten to know in Japan.

In February 1912 Chau met with a number of other Vietnamese activists and proposed a new organization to replace the Association for the Modernization of Vietnam, which was by this time virtually defunct. A new group emerged from this meeting known as the Association for the Restoration of Vietnam (Viet Nam Quang Phuc Hoi). A more "republican" program was adopted, in part because Phan Boi Chau had read and been influenced by Chinese translations of Montesquieu and Rousseau, but also with the practical purpose of attracting support from the victorious Chinese revolutionary alliance. Chau's Chinese acquaintances, however, were far too busy consolidating revolutionary power in China and maneuvering against competing influences within their own ranks to give serious consideration to his pleas for concrete assistance in driving the French out of Vietnam. Once again, as in Japan six years earlier, instead of money and munitions, Chau received advice to remain patient and to concentrate on propaganda and training. By now, however, such advice was to go unheeded. Chau required action, and terrorism seemed the only feasible means of beginning his campaign.[80]

An attempt was made in November 1912 to assassinate Governor-General Sarraut. In April 1913 a prefect chief was killed in the Red River delta, and a few weeks later two French officers were murdered in a bombing incident at the Hanoi Hotel. An alarmed French security apparatus arrested over two hundred suspects, and seven of them were summarily sentenced to death. Among both the French and the Vietnamese passions were inflamed. It was in response to this situation, and especially to the poisonous effect it was having on relations between Frenchmen and Vietnamese, that Vinh and Schneider rushed to Hanoi and hastily began publishing the *Indochina Journal*, a weekly newspaper in *quoc ngu*.[81]

The *Indochina Journal* appeared only three weeks after the two officers were killed in Hanoi. The connection between these two events was made explicit in the very first issue: "Our weekly is published in a hurry because of the terrorist activity . . . to bring literature and learning, the blessings of French civilization, and stir them up to drown out the words of rebellion. . . . We must snuff out the fuses on the firecrackers of the rebels to prevent them from going before the bells and drums of civilization." This was intended to be a direct confrontation with Phan Boi Chau and the Association for the Restoration of Vietnam.[82]

Phan Boi Chau was, however, one of the most admired Vietnamese of his generation. Those who disagreed with his methods, even those who rejected his goals, respected him for his courage, intelligence, and integrity. Thus Vinh suffered irreparable harm in important segments of contemporary public opinion by his scathing denunciation of Chau. In addition to criticizing terrorist activity and Chau's ideas, Vinh denigrated Chau as "this petty man who has gone mad, fleeing the country and inciting the people to revolt, sowing disaster and harming the people."[83]

Nguyen Van Vinh was convinced that the Vietnamese were quite inferior to the West in general and to the French in particular, but for cultural rather than racial reasons. By espousing the con-

cept of culture as the variable that best explained differences between the peoples of the world, Vinh was actually adopting a
rather advanced position for the time. This perspective was shared
by Phan Chu Trinh, but Phan Boi Chau sometimes sounded a racist theme of yellow-skinned brothers uniting against an alien
white world. Such themes, combined with Chau's activities in
Japan and China, could be all too provocative to alarmists in the
West who were ever ready to become agitated over the "yellow
peril" that threatened Western civilization from the teeming and
inscrutable Orient.

Vinh believed that Vietnam was too weak to remain independent in the modern world, and that French rule was much to be
preferred over increased Japanese or Chinese influence. Vinh even
maintained that French colonialism was superior to the traditional
elite rule in precolonial times. He asserted that "although the colonial government has not taken us to the apex, still, compared with
the past it has been a hundred times better in giving us a breath of
freedom and a taste of democracy."[84]

To Vinh, Phan Boi Chau posed a grave threat to continued
Franco-Vietnamese cooperation, which was Vietnam's greatest
hope for progressing into a more advanced state of cultural development. If the Vietnamese people listened to Phan Boi Chau,
they might never overcome their cultural inferiority to the West. At
a more personal level, if Chau and his associates succeeded in
poisoning relations between the two peoples, Vinh and people like
him would no longer find a welcome in either French or Vietnamese society. Vinh was eager to be accepted by the French,
whom he so admired, and to be respected by his Vietnamese compatriots. For all his rejection of traditional Vietnamese culture, he
acted very much like a man who wanted to "sit above and eat before" his fellows, if only in a figurative sense.

Vinh was an incongruous and slightly comical figure in the
streets of Hanoi. He was frequently seen racing around town
perched on the seat of his motorcycle, weaving in and out among
rickshaws, horse-drawn carriages, sedan chairs, and an occasional
stately automobile. He was always carefully dressed in a Western
business suit, with his hair neatly trimmed. Vinh was also an in-
veterate joiner of groups. He was the first Vietnamese member of
the League of Human Rights, and he was among the first to sign a
petition circulated by this group in a successful attempt to obtain a
reprieve for Phan Chu Trinh when he was sentenced to death in

1908. Vinh was also a Freemason, another example of his early participation in a predominantly French group. He had been president of a group composed of Vietnamese who were employees of the French colonial administration, and he was among the most active members of another large and progressive scholarly organization.

To cap this penchant for public activity, Vinh had a most satisfactory political career within the prescribed limits of the colonial framework. He was elected to the Hanoi city council at the age of twenty-six and then became a member of the Consultative Assembly for the Northern Region in 1913. He eventually became a member of the General Convention on Finance and the Economy of Indochina, the highest consultative body in the colonial administrative structure. For him this was reaching the head of the table.[85]

Nguyen Van Vinh's own intellectual and emotional predilections were clearly reflected in the *Indochina Journal*. Of particular interest is a series of articles written by Vinh himself entitled "Examining Our Faults." Vietnamese readers were bombarded with a long list of shortcomings, which they were encouraged to overcome. These cultural characteristics were "faults" from a European point of view. Vinh tried to teach his Vietnamese readers to see themselves as the French saw them, to feel embarrassed when they unwittingly violated French standards of "proper" behavior. These sharp critiques of Vietnamese habits probably gained pungency from Vinh's own excruciating embarrassment when his fellow Vietnamese acted in ways that incurred the disapproval of his French friends and superiors. One good example is an article entitled "Laughing At Everything." Vietnamese often smile or laugh, but they frequently intend to convey a meaning quite different from that understood by most Westerners. Many instances of cross-cultural misunderstanding have arisen from a smile that was misinterpreted.

I once saw an American point out to a Vietnamese employee that he had made a rather serious error. The American explained the situation earnestly and with great patience. The Vietnamese listened intently. When the American finished, the Vietnamese grinned from ear to ear and did not say a word. For a moment the American stared at him in amazement, then abruptly lost his temper. "Look at that son-of-a-bitch! He thinks it's funny!" The smile had indicated embarrassment; the silence, agreement and acceptance of fault. The employee had understood the explanation, accepted responsibility for the problem, and would probably have corrected the deficiency at the earliest possible moment. But the American had expected some verbal response: an explanation, a denial, an apology, or even an argument. He interpreted the silence as disinterest and the smile as impertinence.

Actually this Vietnamese employee had respected the American employer until he lost his temper and gave vent to such an emotional outburst. Then the man actually did become sullen and resentful, because the American had not treated him with respect. Ironically, when the man signaled his compliance and respect to the American, it had been viewed as insolence. Each man felt the other had acted in a rude and disrespectful manner, and never again did these two men have the effective working relationship they had enjoyed before this unfortunate exchange.

This incident took place in a matter of seconds, and the damage was done before I could intervene. Yet, while I had not been involved in the conversation, the two men—both acquaintances of mine—each looked to me for some sympathetic response. Although I did later and separately try to explain to each of them what had happened, neither felt that my response at the time was satisfactory. Meanwhile, I remained slightly irritated with both of them for having put me into an uncomfortable situation. I felt that I too had been judged unfairly and found wanting, and I could not help feeling angry and resentful, even though I realized this was irrational.

One should read "Laughing At Everything" in light of the cumulative social and emotional consequences of such cross-cultural events:

> People in our country have the strange habit of laughing at everything. Laughing at praise, laughing at criticism. If it's good, we giggle. If it's bad, we giggle. We twist our mouths, let out one giggle, and the seriousness is gone from everything.
>
> There are people who say we should laugh at everything, that it is the mark of a good-natured person. . . . But upon examination there is often unintentional cruelty in our laughter. There is a kind of insolent contempt for other people in it, some insulting quality to it. It has a meaning of being content to disregard other people's thoughts before hearing all that they have to say. . . .
>
> There is nothing so irritating as having to deal with people who listen to you and give only a laugh in reply. It wouldn't be so bad if they contradicted you. Even someone who

covered his ears and wouldn't listen would not be so
irritating. . . . No word of appreciation for praise, no
argument to criticism, no answer to a question, from beginning to end all that comes out of their mouth is a laugh. Who
wouldn't grow angry?

We should know that when someone talks with us it is to
find out our thoughts and opinions. When someone speaks to
us, we must respond. According to our inclination, if we wish
to reveal our thoughts to others we speak the truth; if we
don't understand, we ask them to repeat their question; and
if we do not wish to reveal our thoughts to others, then we
cleverly find some polite words to let them understand that
their question is violating our privacy. . . . But if someone
asks us a question and we have listened to them, we owe them
a response.[86]

In "Examining Our Faults" Nguyen Van Vinh attacked a broad
spectrum of alleged faults of the Vietnamese people: a weakness
for gambling, awkward modes of conversation, corruption, superstition, a shallow and erroneous concept of learning. Vietnamese
ways were implicitly judged by French standards and assumed to
be inferior. On a less regular basis over a longer period of time,
Vinh wrote some similar columns specifically for women, "Women
Talk," based on an implicit and unfavorable comparison of Vietnamese women with French women. Customs relating to childbirth, child rearing, betel chewing, and even family relationships
were ridiculed as "peculiar," or even "somewhat barbaric." Sha-
manism was characterized as "a disgusting disguise for female
lustfulness."[87]

Between 1913 and 1915 Vinh wrote over a hundred articles and
columns in the *Indochina Journal* that in one way or another denigrated traditional Vietnamese culture and society. He was constantly advocating some change in belief, attitude, value, or behavior, always in the direction of Westernization. The persistence
of respect for the Confucian scholarly tradition was especially ran-
kling to him, but Vinh was careful not to attack the saints and sages
directly. The genuine message of sages like Confucius and Mencius
had been, Vinh insisted, misunderstood and perverted:

Our Confucian scholars . . . did not understand that in every
nation sages come in succession, with those who go before
teaching what they have learned, and those who follow
absorbing that knowledge and adding to it, teaching more in
their turn, with a daily expansion of knowledge. . . . We have

these ancient teachings to use as a ladder that enables us to climb to a better one. If for a thousand years everyone has studied the teachings of the sages and there is not yet anyone who has surpassed them, then it must be recognized that this is precisely what is wrong with Confucianism. . . .

It must be understood that the sages of ancient times were the children of humanity, while the youth of today must become the adults.

The maturity of the entire race must be taken into account, not just the age of an individual. For a race still young knows little, but one which has matured must know more.[88]

Vinh also wrote a series of columns called "Citizenship," which explained the administrative organization of the government, the functions and responsibilities of various government offices, and the rights, privileges, and duties of citizens in the French protectorate of northern Vietnam in their dealings with the government. He did not hesitate to include warnings and advice concerning the rapacity and corruption people could expect to encounter when dealing with the leftover traditional Vietnamese officials with which the bureaucracy was encumbered.

In yet another series of columns written in 1914, Vinh analyzed the critical issues involved in "reorganizing village administration." This was an outgrowth of his experience in the Consultative Assembly for North Vietnam, where village administration was a controversial and hotly debated issue. Vinh's incisive analysis of the traditional Vietnamese village revealed an unusual degree of boldness and insight. He had, after all, been born and raised amidst the poverty of just such a village and narrowly averted the plight of becoming a poor peasant himself.

One could not blame the French for the misery of the Vietnamese people, Vinh argued. The real villain was ignorance, and Vinh's sharpest attacks were reserved for what he looked upon as the complacent and narrow-minded rigidity of parasitic village notables and the foolish mumbo-jumbo of monks and shamans. The best way to improve the lot of the peasants, in Vinh's opinion, was to open up the closed villages in which they lived, to expose them to new ideas and new ways of doing things.[89]

In the early issues of *Indochina Journal* almost everything was written by Vinh. The emphasis was political; the tone, strident. But when Schneider and Vinh established another *quoc ngu* newspaper that specialized in news coverage, the contents of the *Indochina*

Journal became more varied, and other writers contributed regularly. There were more feature articles, editorials, intellectual and scholarly essays, and translations of great literature from both East and West. Two types of writers contributed to the *Indochina Journal*: those with classical educations who were masters of traditional Sino-Vietnamese learning, and those with more modern and more Western educations who read and spoke French with fluency and pleasure. Most of the more important members of the Western-oriented group were, like Vinh himself, graduates of the French school for interpreters in Hanoi.

Tran Trong Kim had graduated from the school for interpreters in 1903. He went to the Marseilles Exposition with Vinh in 1906 and then stayed on in France to earn a bachelor's degree in pedagogy before returning to Vietnam in 1911. He was a regular contributor to the *Journal*, specializing in essays on educational theory and practice, including model lessons in history, grammar, geography, mathematics, and ethics. Pham Duy Ton contributed scholarly essays and humor. He also made some of the first tentative steps toward developing the modern Vietnamese short story.

The staff of the *Indochina Journal* was rounded out by two men who had predominantly traditional educations but wrote in *quoc ngu* with a lively flowing style. Phan Ke Binh wrote voluminously for the *Indochina Journal*, primarily on Vietnamese history and customs. Some of his articles on Vietnamese customs were later collected and published in book form. Nguyen Do Muc translated the works of Confucius and is remembered for his many extremely popular translations of Chinese novels, including *The Romance of the Western Chamber*.[90]

Nguyen Van Vinh himself was a prodigious translator. He produced a French-language version of *Kieu* and published it in the *Indochina Journal* in an attempt to demonstrate to the French community that Vietnam had a rich literary heritage of its own and to provide them with some insight into the Vietnamese worldview. For the rapidly increasing number of people who could read *quoc ngu* but not Chinese, Vinh presented an enchanting translation of *The Red Cliff* by Su Shih, and as early as 1907 he had published a translation of *The Three Kingdoms*. But as one would have expected, Vinh devoted much of his energy to introducing his Vietnamese audience to Western literature, especially popular French classics.

He translated and published—primarily in the *Indochina Journal*—such works as *The Three Musketeers* by Dumas, *Les Misé-*

rables by Victor Hugo, La Fontaine's *Fables*, Perrault's collection of folktales, and many other masterpieces of Western literature. Vinh also translated some French philosophy into Vietnamese, including excerpts from Rousseau's *Social Contract* and *The Spirit of Laws* by Montesquieu.[91]

For its few thousand readers, the *Indochina Journal* opened the doors to new intellectual worlds. During the second decade of the twentieth century, Vietnam was becoming a sharply bifurcated world. The older generation was, by and large, either illiterate or literate only in Chinese and *nom*. But the younger generation now had little incentive to learn thousands of characters. They studied French and *quoc ngu* or nothing. It took years to learn French, and even more years to master Chinese. Without prior mastery of Chinese, it was very difficult to learn *nom*. Yet any reasonably intelligent native speaker of Vietnamese could master *quoc ngu*, which was basically a phonetic system for transcribing spoken Vietnamese, in a manner of months.

For those who learned *quoc ngu*, the *Indochina Journal* offered something new and interesting in almost every issue. For the traditional scholars, it offered a sampling of Western literature and Western thought that was not available in Chinese. For younger, French-educated readers, it provided an access to their own cultural heritage and to East Asian literature and culture that was not available to them in French-language publications. Nguyen Van Vinh was the cultural broker par excellence of early-twentieth-century Vietnam. In the *Indochina Journal* under Vinh's leadership the *quoc ngu* periodical became a major force in the process of sociocultural change in twentieth-century Vietnam.

Only 3,000 villages out of a total of 23,000 had their own school.[92] By 1917 the total number of students had grown to 75,000, and by 1921 the figure would reach 150,000.[93] This was a pitifully small number of students for so large and industrious a population, but these few trailblazers would make history. And the *Indochina Journal* strongly influenced this generation of students, who were to become the leading teachers, writers, poets, and community leaders in subsequent decades.

Tran Trong Kim went on from his days as a staff member of the *Indochina Journal* to become one of the more prominent educators and scholars in the first half of the twentieth century. Basing the works largely on columns written for the *Indochina Journal*, he published *Ethics in Primary Education* in 1914, *The Basics of Pedagogy* in

1916, and in 1920, the best known, *An Outline of Vietnamese History,* in which Tran Trong Kim recounted the major events in Vietnamese history from origin myths concerning the kingdom of Van Lang and the Hung kings to the coming of the French. It was still a best-seller in Saigon during the 1960s and early 1970s, having been republished many times and used in tens of thousands of classrooms. Several generations of Vietnamese schoolchildren were introduced to their historical heritage through this book.[94]

The Basics of Pedagogy was the first and for decades the major attempt to discuss modern educational theory in Vietnamese. Utilizing a rudimentary notion of developmental child psychology, it represents a quantum leap forward from traditional teaching methods that stressed memorization of long and abstract texts by young children who did not wholly understand them. The indirect influence of such a work may have been very important.[95]

Ethics in Primary Education introduced many Western concepts into Vietnamese classrooms. Many words now commonly used first appeared in this book, words like "duty," "responsibility," "conscience," "soul," "patience," "bravery," and "tolerance." This new vocabulary offered a new way of looking at the world, of generating behavior and interpreting events.[96] Its dissemination helped to change the distribution of values in Vietnamese society, to reset the social thermostat. Tran Trong Kim explained "conscience" as "a court of law that sits in your own heart. When you do something good, it rewards you. It makes you feel satisfied and happy. When you do something bad it punishes you. It makes you feel upset and worried." What a new and distinctive idea this was! No mention here of "face" or "reputation," no concern for the ridicule or criticism of other people. This is a bold-faced portrait of a self-directed individual.[97]

In discussing "duty" Kim introduced a shift in orientation only slightly less radical. One had, he taught, duties to oneself: the duty to exercise one's body and to keep it clean. One had duties to other people, to respect their private property, their personal dignity and freedom. One also had duties to one's society: to love one's country, to pay taxes, and so forth. One even had duties to animals. These duties were quite different from the particularistic, role-based obligations of *nghia*. Traditional values were not entirely abandoned, but modified, redefined, and reorganized into an essentially Western framework. Students were taught, for example, that "we worship our ancestors not because we fear that otherwise they will find no place of rest [as traditional belief would have it]. This worship is performed in order to remember our *on* to the forebears who wholeheartedly strove to create our homes and our land for us."[98]

Tran Trong Kim was one of the first thinkers to address the question of reconciling French and Vietnamese values. The naive optimism in *Ethics in Primary Education* eventually yielded to a more somber concern for the flimsy ethical foundations of this jerry-built hybrid value system. During the second decade of the twentieth century he outpaced his fellow reformers in articulating what was to become the dominant intellectual theme in 1917–1930: synthesizing the best elements of Eastern and Western cultures into a new model containing the best of both worlds. The leader of this harmonizing movement was neither Tran Trong Kim nor Nguyen Van Vinh, however, but Pham Quynh, a junior and part-time member of the *Indochina Journal* staff. In 1917 Pham Quynh began publishing *South Wind*, which soon eclipsed the *Indochina Journal*.

Pham Quynh quickly became a dominant figure in Vietnamese intellectual life. Like Truong Vinh Ky and Nguyen Van Vinh, Pham Quynh had an unusual background. He was born in Hanoi in 1892. His father was a poor scholar who achieved a baccalaureate degree but had no official rank or position in the bureaucracy. His mother died while he was still an infant, and his father died when the boy was only nine years old. He was raised by his paternal grandmother, who lived in Hanoi. Although she sent him to pursue a traditional course of study in school, he became interested in Western learning at an early age and managed to pick up enough French to gain admittance to the school for translators in Hanoi, by then known as the Protectorate School, from which he graduated in 1908 at the age of only sixteen. From 1908 until 1917 he worked at the Ecole Française d'Extrême Orient, mostly as a librarian. These years spent at the Ecole provided him with ample time for reading and study, free access to a superb library, and intimate contact with some outstanding scholars.

The erudition and intellectual polish he gained from this situation was rare in a Vietnamese of his generation. By 1917, although only twenty-five years old, he brought a sober authority to *South Wind* that was lacking in the *Indochina Journal*. Nguyen Van Vinh was talented and enthusiastic, but he was largely self-educated and had always been preoccupied with popularizing *quoc ngu* and Western learning. Where Vinh wrote in a lively but simple style and encouraged others to do likewise, Pham Quynh favored a more stately and elevated prose. Vinh was more eclectic and less critical in the materials he introduced in his journal, while Pham Quynh was more selective in what he was willing to accept from both France and China.

The uncritical importation of bourgeois French culture was distasteful to Pham Quynh, who seemed to believe that Rousseau, Confucius, and Mencius were all guilty of overestimating the innate goodness of mankind. To him the greatest problem confronting any society was a universal human tendency to lapse into a Hobbesian world of all against all in a brutish state of nature. In his life and his writings, his political biases and his social philosophy, Pham Quynh stressed discipline and order over freedom, precedent ˙and rules over creativity. He was classical and elitist in orientation, and a very cautious moderate when it came to change of any kind. Pham Quynh was much less certain than Nguyen Van Vinh, Phan Chu Trinh, or Tran Trong Kim that things were improving and would continue to do so. To Pham Quynh the past, while not perfect, was preferable to certain trends he saw emerging.

France and China were decadent and declining cultures, Pham Quynh argued, and there was no need for Vietnamese to imitate their mistakes. The incipient individualism discernible in the writings of Vinh and Tran Trong Kim made Pham Quynh uneasy. Where, he asked, would it lead? Consider, for example, this essay he wrote in 1917, "The Idea of Family":

A distinguished man once remarked that "one's actions in life may be compared to children tossing pebbles into a pond." No sooner has the stone fallen to the water than it is transformed into a small circle, which becomes a larger circle. The circle continues to expand until it has covered the entire pond.

This means that no one lives in isolation. One's acts, no matter how small, always affect someone else, and their influence spreads like the circle in the pond. It is just such a profound relationship that binds people together into groups, jointly shouldering life's burdens.

The smallest, strongest, and most enduring of all such groups is the family. In one house father and child, brother and sister, husband and wife all relate to one another; they live to help, to support, to protect one another. That is why every nation since time immemorial has honored the idea of family.

Today modern science has progressed, the human intellect has expanded, and the human heart and the ways of the world have also very much changed with the times. Some people's hearts thirst for freedom, as if they wish to smash all the established frameworks of previous generations. The family itself is an ancient institution, dating back to the time mankind first came together in society. Can the institution of the family withstand the movement of today? Can it survive any longer? Or is the day of its destruction about to arrive?

. . . In all societies of Europe the family is passing through a crisis. It is being forced to resist the movement for freedom, for liberty. This movement seeks only advantages, prosperity, and happiness for each person, making each and every discrete human being the center of the universe. It is called, in a word, "individualism."

Most of those who are infatuated with individualism are merely followers of fashion, usually people without any foundation of their own, often lacking any moral base. Without any foundation, it is easy for them to follow the times and change. Lacking any moral base, it is easy for them to be selfish and not think about others.

But apart from those people who lead such precariously attuned lives, everyone concerned with a proper way of living knows that the family is a secluded harbor in which we may be saved from the turbulent seas of this period. Religion is now growing weaker day by day; philosophies have no evidential basis; the human heart does not know where to find a port. Without a fixed set of rules, people's hearts are perturbed, society is dangerous.[99]

Only the family, he concluded, was "uniquely capable of preserving society." The family thus had to be protected and maintained at any cost, as a firm island in the midst of disruptive change.

In many of his essays Pham Quynh reasserted the *yang* principles of traditional Vietnamese society, the need to maintain a "natural order" based on hierarchical principles of organization and the subordination of the individual to the group. Like Nguyen Van Vinh, he could look at his fellow Vietnamese and see them as they appeared to the French. He recognized that a certain amount of change was inevitable and that the Vietnamese would have to adapt to it. But he was unwilling to yield to Western standards or modern trends. In Pham Quynh's reforms traditional values were not being abandoned, they were being retooled to serve

more effectively, to survive in a changing world. Phː
tempted to preserve the "essence" of traditional Vi
ture, combining it with selected Western influences
that Cartesian logic, scientific methodology, advanced
the intellectual bases of Western materialism—could
with the traditional religious beliefs, social institutions, and core
values of Vietnamese society. This was "the middle way."

But the reconciliation of many elements of the French and Vietnamese attitude/value systems proved to be a very difficult en-
deavor. How could one justify the Vietnamese *yin-yang* distinction
between male and female roles in society in the face of the egalitarian influence of French culture? In 1917 Pham Quynh was already
addressing a crucial question, in "The Education of Women":

> Why is it that from early times in every country men have
> always been admired while women have been looked down
> on? It is because of the natural principle of strength and
> weakness, which originated when society first was formed
> and has been perpetuated into civilized times. . . .
>
> Not until recent times did European countries declare that
> men and women were equal, thus truly opening a new era in
> the history of mankind. A woman is like a flower that has
> been growing in a dark room and has now been brought out
> into a fresh, bright place. Breathing in the free air of nature,
> she is able to blossom, to grow fragrant, to become a further
> adornment to life on earth.
>
> The world has always belonged to men alone, but now it
> will belong to women as well. Although women have not
> achieved any great deeds, have not transformed the face of
> the globe, their influence in the family, in society, has been
> ever so deep and intimate. Everyone knows that European
> society is both strong and elegant. Its elegance blends with its
> strength to make it supple and calm, to prevent it from be-
> coming a cruel and vulgar force. That strength is the accom-
> plishment of men, men who have invented machines, evolved
> projects, dug rivers, hewed out mountains, crossed oceans,
> and gone into the air. But the elegance is the accomplishment
> of women, women who present poetic and fanciful scenes,
> who manage to create islands of Paradise out of love and the
> abundant pleasures of daily life amidst the sea of competi-
> tive materialism. How could people live with only the noise
> of machinery and the fevered atmosphere of competition?

    •   •   •

Such is the God-given function of women in this world.
The education of women, then, must conform to this natural
function if it is to be sensible and appropriate. What has the
education of women been like in our country?

Although we have not yet attained the level of European
countries where women are treated with deference and nurtured tenderly as if they were flowers or pearls, still, we have
not acted like many half-primitive peoples who manhandle
the weak and gentle sex, viewing them only as baby-making
machines or beasts of burden. Women have always occupied
a respectable position in our society, and they have never betrayed their reputation of being good daughters, gentle
wives, and loving mothers, providing an excellent and long-
standing example of feminine virtue.

Nevertheless, in the past our elders relied too heavily on
the traditional theory of *yin* and *yang,* of weak and strong,
and as a result women were considered to be decidedly inferior to men and incapable of being educated on a level equal
to that of men. Furthermore, there was no need to educate
them, because *yin* is inherently dependent upon *yang,* and
the weak must submit to the strong. Women could not have
self-determination and had to depend on men. As daughters
they followed their fathers; as wives they followed their husbands; as widows, their sons. Their entire lives were circum-
scribed by these three submissions. . . .

. . . In summary, women in our country were not abused,
but they were treated like "minors," and like minors they remained for all their lives, never becoming independent nor
self-sufficient and in no need of much teaching or education. . . . Is such thinking still appropriate today?

Certainly not! Women are certainly not born inferior to
men. Their character and intellect is different, but not inferior. . . . Vietnamese women especially have many fine
traits. They are alert and courageous, patient and wise,
famous for being competent and resourceful in financial matters. Commercial enterprise in this country is mostly in the
hands of women. Perhaps nowhere in the world can a scene
be found that is so worthy of our admiration and respect as in
the home of a traditional scholar where the wife supported
her husband so he could study . . . while she, all by herself,
worked day and night to take care of the entire family, including her husband's parents and a flock of children. . . .

How can a country that has such wonderful women ignore
them and fail to nurture their education and encourage the

full development of their personalities in a manner appropriate to their excellent qualities and their high status in society?

In the past, traditional education was strict in the sphere of morality, and even though women received no formal education they remained virtuous through the influence of their families. Such influence was deep and powerful, and women breathed in such an atmosphere from the moment of their birth. As they grew older they intuitively knew what was the right thing to do, and few people made mistakes. Such was the natural molding of society. The higher the moral level of society remained, the more effective did this molding remain. The coals in a stove must be glowing if the stove is to heat objects outside. A dying fire cannot heat its own container, let alone have any hope of providing warmth to anyone else.

The state of morality among our people today is like a stove with dying embers, growing a little bit cooler day by day. Anyone who observes and reflects must acknowledge that fact. But this cooling effect is ten times more harmful to women than to men. . . .

Alas! When men lack virtue, it is harmful to society; but not so harmful as when women become unsound, because unsound women damage the very roots of society.[100]

Pham Quynh was a staunch conservative who had steeled himself to view realistically the society in which he lived and was forced to adopt a defensive posture. He recognized that the family was the linchpin of Vietnamese society and that maintaining the Vietnamese family system required that women be willing and able to perform the duties and play the roles traditionally assigned to them. Since the social ambience alone was apparently no longer an adequate force to mold Vietnamese women into reliable pillars of family life, some further institutional reinforcement was necessary. Education was to be used as a means of indoctrination to make women want to support the family and as a means of providing them with the skills necessary to perform this function effectively in a society buffeted by new currents of thought and new social forces.

While conceding that women were equal, Pham Quynh stressed that they were different. The "God-given" function of women was to provide elegance to society, to create homes that were "islands of Paradise," and if need be, to support the family financially. Women were to be educated to become stronger supporters of the families of Vietnam, "the very roots of society." Since their education had to "conform to this function if it is to be sensible and appropriate," the equality of women in Pham Quynh's brave new world was largely rhetorical.

Pham Quynh also instructed his Vietnamese readers to preserve the essence of *le* without offending Western sensibilities. The Vietnamese concept of *le* and the Western concept of politeness were to be reconciled through pure technique. No value change is called for in this essay called "Our Way of Politeness." Pham Quynh was, like Nguyen Van Vinh before him, teaching his fellow Vietnamese to see themselves as the French saw them:

> People living in society, when interacting with each other, must have politeness. Whether dealing with someone higher than themselves, their equals, or someone beneath them, people who are wise make appropriate adjustments; but in any case they must be bound by decorum if they are to be considered educated people. But being polite does not mean we have to demean ourselves to respect others. It does not mean that only if we lie down on the ground or bend over until we break in half will it be clear that we respect other people. Such politeness is first of all false, and it is also degrading, both despicable qualities, so much so that it seems that one who was treated with such politeness should be the first to despise it. But if we look at the way in which we are polite, that is largely what it is like.
>
> In dealing with those beneath us we show absolutely no politeness at all, usually treating those who are inferior to us with an atrocious rudeness, while to those above us we are extremely obsequious. Timid, servile, scratching the head, scratching an ear, saying "yes, yes," "right, right," "sir, sir," "honorable, honorable," in such a way that absolutely no one who respected the worth of a human being could debase themselves so much. And in fact such people do not know what it is to be honorable. To be honorable is to have self-respect, respect for one's own dignity. Others are people; we are also people. There is no reason why one person should consider himself to be a worm or a cricket when dealing with another person, no matter how much authority or power the other one might have. Furthermore, if one wishes to demonstrate respect for someone who is superior, it is not necessary to debase oneself in order to be respectful. To debase oneself is to decrease the value of one's respect. Not only that, it actually shows contempt for the other person as well, for it is

as if one uncharitably attributed to others the acceptance of such servile obsequiousness as sincerity.[101]

More than Nguyen Van Vinh, Pham Quynh was willing to confront both the activists and the French in the name of reform, but the "reforms" he advocated were essentially regressive, harking back to the treaty of 1884, when northern Vietnam was administered by a Vietnamese bureaucracy in the name of and at the pleasure of the king. Pham Quynh wanted more autonomy and more freedom for the Vietnamese king and his court, not for the people. A status as a "French protectorate" was desirable as a shield for the throne. As their fair reward for protecting the Vietnamese royal court from all threats to its security, both internal and external, the French would enjoy economic advantages and a military and diplomatic ally.[102]

Nguyen Van Vinh preferred direct French rule over all of Vietnam as an instrument for rapid and unabashed Westernization. To Vinh, the remnants of monarchy and the mandarinate were the major impediments to progress. He was willing, even eager, to have the French remain in Vietnam; but he welcomed them as the best hope for destroying the traditional system once and for all, not as a means of preserving it. From 1930 until 1933 Nguyen Van Vinh and Pham Quynh waged a vitriolic battle in the media over this issue, but by then a new generation was coming to the forefront, concerned with new issues and hearkening to fresh voices.[103]

During the second and third decades of the twentieth century, imitation of the French was widespread in Vietnamese society.[104] The activist resistance movement could not regain its lost momentum. Cautious cultural reform attracted the most support. And as more people learned to read *quoc ngu*, as more original works were written in and foreign works translated into *quoc ngu*, as the print media developed, as the student population increased, and as urban centers grew, a "modernizing middle class" gradually emerged in Vietnamese society.

This was no "class" in the full sense of the word; there was, rather, an inchoate group of people sharing certain objective conditions and intersubjective meanings that set them apart from their own traditions and most of their countrymen. Yet they were not assimilated into either the society or the culture of the French colonialists. Most were young people living in urban centers or provincial towns. Many were civil servants, clerks, schoolteachers, merchants, journalists or writers, or the wives or children of such people. Most knew some French, and all could read and write *quoc ngu*, but few of them knew Chinese or *nom* very well. By traditional Vietnamese standards they were well-to-do, yet very few of them could match the purchasing power of the lowest of the French bureaucrats in Indochina.

These young men and women had very little economic or political power. Few of them had a college education, and many of them had not finished high school. But they read books, poetry, and newspapers and discussed the ideas that the print media presented to them. Such shared identity as these people possessed was based primarily on a common awareness of their liminal position between the glittering prosperity and prestige of Western civilization and the time-honored institutions of traditional village life.

Little by little, some sense of grievances and aspirations as a group began to emerge; and various individuals and factions attempted to transform these feelings into a basis for some sort of concerted action program to achieve modest political or economic reforms, or in some cases to spin off into "revitalization" movements with varying degrees of religious, social, economic, or more broadly cultural emphases. The entire spectrum of Vietnamese society was involved in one way or another, but the emerging middle class was the most important element.

During the 1920s French Indochina experienced a tremendous surge of economic growth and relative prosperity. Overall French investment increased over 600 percent between 1918 and 1930. The area of rubber plantations tripled. Coffee, tea, and sugar plantations also thrived. Although the major thrust of capital investment went into agricultural export crops, mining and industry as well underwent dramatic growth through a sizable influx of capital investment.[105]

The prosperity that accompanied this remarkable economic growth did little or nothing to build a national economy or to improve the living standards of the Vietnamese people. Even "well-to-do" Vietnamese received very little benefit from this lucrative exploitation of Vietnam's agricultural and mineral resources. Among the French themselves the steady flow of capital and goods between France and Indochina was effectively monopolized by a small group of financial syndicates that gorged themselves on handsome profits while incurring very little risk. This was capitalism with a vengeance, but it was neither free nor enterprising.

Almost 90 percent of the capital investment in Vietnam in 1939 belonged to companies controlled by only three financial syndicates. These syndicates, two banks, and a few dozen business firms, all with interlocking management at the very highest levels, controlled the economy of Vietnam as if it were an exclusive club to which only a few carefully selected Frenchmen could hope to be admitted. A mere handful of men exerted near total influence over the entire financial and economic structure of Vietnam.[106]

With the surge of economic development that took place in Vietnam between the end of World War I and 1930, small but highly significant changes occurred in the social structure. The emergence of two new "classes" may be detected: a "working class" and an "urban middle class." In 1930 neither group was large, and neither possessed the cohesiveness and sense of self-awareness and common identity to qualify as genuine "social classes." But even in embryonic form their existence had profound implications for the systematic transformation of Vietnamese culture and society.

In 1930 miners and commercial, industrial, and plantation workers constituted little more than 2 percent of the adult workforce. But such statistics are misleading because of the incredibly high turnover in the labor force. A genuine worker class was a mere fraction of this labor force. Most of these "workers" were peasants who left their families and villages for fairly short periods of time to earn small sums of money.[107]

Little by little, the peasants of the Red River delta were drawn into a more monetary, market-oriented economy, and the closed corporate villages of traditional Vietnam began to be transformed. This transformation was well under way by 1930. As Dao Duy Anh described the early results in 1938, it was a continuously accelerating process:

> In the countryside life has not changed as it has in the city. But farmers used to grow rice to eat, weave clothing to wear, use bamboo from their gardens to build their houses; now they have to take their rice and sell it in order to purchase in turn other things they need which are brought to them from the city by merchants and peddlers. Things that were thought to be very strange fifteen or twenty years ago—like bicycles, flashlights, or thermoses—are now being used by some peo-

ple in the countryside. Soap, matches, and Western tobacco are now to be found everywhere. And for traveling great distances, many people are accustomed to automobiles, trains, and ships. The palankeens, sedan chairs, and horses that were the traditional modes of transportation have either disappeared or become very rare. Rice farming, especially in the southern region, has begun using new techniques from Department of Agriculture experiments. Raisers of silkworms now select varieties distributed by the Department of Agriculture. Weavers purchase thread made in factories, and there are even places that use synthetic fibers. And where there are high ricefields, which were once frequent victims of drought, in many places public irrigation systems administered by the government are in use and crop yields have been multiplied. The number of farmers dealing with government agricultural banks increases day by day. In a few places the government has organized agricultural cooperatives to help the farmers sell their produce. A number of rural youths have gone to the cities to study or work, and on their return have instigated reforms of village customs. There are places that have completely abandoned their numerous costly festival customs and celebrations of promotions, with their attendant wrangling over status and portions. The study of romanized national alphabet has replaced the study of Chinese characters in the countryside; now every three or four villages have a school to teach writing and general knowledge to rural children not yet old enough to work in the ricefields.

From the conditions described above we can see that the attitude of the rural people, or speaking in general, the attitude of the Vietnamese people toward Western culture is now completely different than it was when first encountered.

The rural folk no longer find the French to be a terrifying race of people, nor do they find their artifacts to be miraculous or fantastic any longer. Nor do our scholars still believe that their thought and customs are ridiculous, peculiar, or harmful to moral norms. From now on, the Europeanization of our society shall be even more profound. We cannot yet estimate where the end will be, nor can we anticipate and prevent the difficulties that are going to occur. But there is one thing of which we may be certain, which is that in the new culture of the world that is to come the culture of our nation will be a participant. One cannot say that East is better or West is better, and the hostilities and distinctions between East and West will eventually disappear completely.[108]

By the 1930s life in the traditional villages was changing under the combined influence of an encroaching market economy, administrative and tax reforms, wage labor, technological innovations, and vastly improved transportation and communication facilities. But change in the rural areas of traditional Vietnam was nevertheless a slow, piecemeal, and often grudgingly accepted process prior to World War II. The emerging urban middle class was the major impetus for cultural change. Some young, French-educated city dwellers were coming to reject traditional Vietnamese culture altogether by 1930. Removed from the powerful emotional milieu of family and village, educated in a Western-oriented school system, and economically self-sufficient in their urban employments, these people resented the constraints of traditional culture and blamed that culture for their disadvantaged and humiliating position vis-à-vis the colonial French society with which they came in daily contact.

In the "Preface" to his work *Confucianism* in 1929, Tran Trong Kim expressed his misgivings about the rapidity with which traditional culture was disappearing in Vietnam:

> The majority of our people became accustomed to an attitude of passive acceptance, following a predetermined framework left to them by their ancestors. Any matters of right and wrong, good or bad, were restricted to that framework and no deviation was permitted, so the critical judgment became narrower and narrower, with no realization that there was any other body of thought against which comparisons of better or worse could be made. The result was that we became like a snail, lying contentedly in a rigid shell and not changing at all. . . .
>
> When conditions altered, when new thoughts and different influences suddenly entered the scene, especially when these influences were powerful and active, how could we continue to stand still? At this time it was as if the people in the land had been abruptly wakened from a deep sleep. They were in a daze and did not know how to cope with the situation. At first they kept looking for ways to resist, but they found that the more they thrashed about the more deeply they became overwhelmed. So naturally they were forced to accept the inevitable reshaping. Gradually they became more fully awake and saw that other people had gained imposing prosperity and power, while they had become weaker and weaker. Then they noticed that everyone in the world who had known how

to abandon the old and follow the new was strong and prosperous.

At this point they took the initiative and began imitating other people and changing in every way. Except for a few people with special interests who wanted no change and kept trying to cling to the old shell in order to retain their high position, or some poor and ignorant country folk whose limited vision did not permit them to see what life was all about, everyone else who had the least bit of knowledge beat the drums and sounded the clappers, urging one another on in carrying out various reforms within the country. All of them were satisfied that their old culture was not worth much, and that this was why their society had declined, so the best course was to throw it all out and follow the path of modernization. A movement was formed to get rid of the old and follow the new. This movement became stronger day by day, to the point where in just over the past twenty or thirty years our old culture has already been lost to a very considerable degree. Even those descendants of distinguished families, who previously refused to pursue modern learning, are now themselves criticizing traditional studies even more vehemently than ordinary people.

[As Vietnamese society was buffeted by change] the movement of modern learning sprang up strongly in the world, and everyone began matching wits with everyone else in a competitive way, vying for power and privileges, no longer placing much value on moral considerations, on *nhan* or *nghia*. Our people observed this and thought that they could no longer retain their old attitudes, that they had to follow the times and change. They felt that the old culture was inadequate and wanted to abandon it so they could follow the new culture and keep up with other people. Much of our old culture has been lost for this reason.

When the gentry of the nation was so enthusiastic in their desire to abandon the old and follow the new, the younger generation with a modern education not only saw their fathers and elder brothers criticizing our traditional studies, but at the same time they did not have any clear understanding of the advantages and disadvantages of this learning. They saw nothing but intolerable restrictions, so they came to despise the traditional culture even more, believing it to be outmoded and corrupted, no longer appropriate under current conditions. Moreover, the energies of this group were aroused and focused on their preference for freedom, equality, and so forth.

Any one of these young people who obtained an education became a success. They all gained some position of status, never mind how, sufficient to win the respect of the general public. So anyone in the country who has a son or a younger brother tries to help them get at least a little modern learning to increase their hope of advancing to a higher position. It is recognized that for making one's way in this world it could not be otherwise. . . .

Following the doctrine of Confucius involves working out a very strict hierarchical order. Whoever occupies an exalted upper status has the right to demand respect and obedience from those beneath them in an inferior status. But there is the further condition that those above must possess appropriate talent and virtue and be respected by everyone, so that no matter how severe the hierarchical order may be, no one will complain about it. If the talent and virtue of those above is not sufficient to maintain the respect of others, the more effort that is put into trying to maintain the hierarchy, the more people will feel it is unreasonable and intolerable.

Especially at the present time when people are not completely clear as to how things will work out between the old and the new, many people believe the old hierarchies are an impediment to progress, so they want to abandon them in order to follow new ways, in the hope that perhaps something better will come of them. And this makes the desire for change even stronger. . . .

On careful consideration, it cannot be said that our current abandonment of the old to follow the new is not necessary. But because we are rash and do not let our thoughts mature, we are achieving nothing less than total destruction. As a result of such shortcomings, our faults have not necessarily been abandoned, while we have lost the essence of our society, which kept it stable for thousands of years.

Whenever people wish to discard something old and damaged, they must have something better, something more attractive to take its place. We do not yet have the new, and yet we have hastily abandoned the old; as a result, we have lost everything and have nothing with which to replace it. That is the situation of our country today, no different than a ship that has gone into the middle of the ocean and lost its compass. It does not know which direction to take to keep on course, and just keeps drifting on, in danger of being dashed upon the rock by the wind and the waves and shattered. . . .

Today we find ourselves confused, not knowing which is the right path to take, not knowing what to cling to as a foundation for our ideals, because we have abandoned our beliefs. Once we idolized Confucianism, believing that the policy of this doctrine was the best of all; even though it was not perfect in practice, we interpreted this as a shortcoming of our education. No one thought that the doctrine itself was not good. But now, because the times have changed and Western culture has flowed into our land, ways of behaving and actions have all been completely changed by new influences. Other people have been perceived as being strong, prosperous, and wise in all things, while we are weak and inferior in every way. Especially in a material sense, when we compare ourselves with other people, we see a very great gap between us. We see these things, but we do not examine the source of our inferiority, so we rush to abandon that which we have believed since antiquity and to imitate the new ways of other people.

The trait of imitation is a universal human characteristic, one that is found in all countries, without exception. If we already had a good spirit and just imitated those things that would fortify that spirit, then this imitation would indeed be a very fine thing. Unfortunately we have let our spirit decay and yet we still aspire to imitate the actions of others, so this imitation just makes us worse than ever. What we call imitation is merely imitation of external forms; but as to the spirit within, without expending a long time to imbue ourselves with it and transform it, it will be a very difficult thing to imitate. Consequently, all these many imitations accomplish nothing more than even further disruption of our sentiments, our thoughts, and our customs. There are very many people who erroneously hope that by striving to imitate other people we are performing a useful service for the progress of our race. Little do they suspect that by too hasty an imitation, by not allowing our thoughts to mature, a poison is being formed, which is producing many ills in our society. This is a mistake of many modern scholars at the present time, and it is a mistake that is becoming more widespread every day rather than abating.

Beneath the facade of economic development and political stability during the 1920s, virtually every sector of Vietnamese society was experiencing a deep malaise. The French colonial presence in Vietnam insidiously undermined feelings of self-esteem, self-worth, and self-satisfaction. There were both objective and subjective dimensions to this process. Many people experienced a steady decline in their standard of living, while even those who did not suffer in objective terms developed a strong sense of relative deprivation. For many Vietnamese, there was actually less to eat. Although rice production increased, it could not begin to keep pace with the rate of growth in population, exports, and taxes.[109]

Although the French-sponsored educational system continued to grow and to influence society, it was not able to replace fully the traditional educational system, which the French presence destroyed. Until 1940 there were seldom more than five hundred students enrolled in high school at any one time, and only a small fraction of this educational elite would become university graduates, of whom only a dozen or so were produced each year.[110]

Even those few Vietnamese who did manage to graduate from the University of Hanoi or to acquire a coveted scholarship to study in France remained essentially dissatisfied and unhappy. A brilliant and diligent Vietnamese who earned a doctorate at the University of Paris and returned to become a professor at the University of Hanoi would earn less than the lackadaisical French janitor who maintained the classroom in which he taught. It was one of the firmest principles of French colonialism that "the lowest-ranked representative of France in Indochina must receive a salary superior to that of the highest Indochinese official employed by the colonial administration."[111]

There was an upper level of employment beyond which no Vietnamese was permitted to go. Vietnamese of exceptional ability found themselves denied job opportunities that went to far less competent and less conscientious Frenchmen.[112] The Vietnamese intellectual elite was subjected to constant reminders that as Vietnamese they were second-class citizens and, by implication, second-rate people.[113] With such a keenly developed social sensitivity and high need for public respect, few Vietnamese who came into contact with the French were able to avoid pernicious feelings of inferiority, resentment, and frustration.

Because the Vietnamese had become inextricably enmeshed in the world economy they were dealt a rather heavy blow by the Great Depression of 1929–1930. The price of rice and rubber plummeted. Large firms laid off employees. Small businesses went bankrupt. Many small farmers unable to pay their debts lost their land and possessions through foreclosure.[114]

By the mid-1920s among the comfortable upper-middle-class elements in Saigon, men who had long advocated moderation and Franco-Vietnamese cooperation began to confront the colonial administration with increasingly insistent demands for concrete political reforms. The French were asked to match their actions to their rhetoric and to grant greater freedom of speech and assembly, more freedom of the press, greater access to higher-level jobs for qualified Vietnamese, equal pay for equal work, and greater Vietnamese participation in the political process. A Constitutionalist party, the first political party in Vietnam, was formed in 1917 to work for legal reform along these lines. Several French-language newspapers persistently argued for such reforms. Encouragement and support came from a few liberal-minded Frenchmen in Saigon at the time, including the young André Malraux.[115]

In the northern and central regions, minor bureaucrats, schoolteachers, small businessmen, technicians, journalists, students, and a few professional men were growing equally restive. The Vietnamese Nationalist party (VNQDD) was formed in 1927. Loosely based on the teachings of Sun Yat-sen, this party paid little attention to either legal reform or mass organization, but quickly began covert preparations for an armed uprising. In 1930 elaborate plans for a coordinated series of uprisings misfired, and an abortive mutiny in the military camp of Yen Bay brought the full weight of colonial authority down upon the party, inflicting severe losses and leaving it in disarray.[116]

Meanwhile, the fledgling Indochinese Communist party (ICP) was actively fomenting strikes, work stoppages, and public demonstrations. Ho Chi Minh, known at the time as Nguyen the Patriot (Nguyen Ai Quoc), had been born in Nghe An province in 1890 or 1892. He had listened to Phan Boi Chau as a youngster and had witnessed at first hand the abuses of corvée labor and the brutal repression of the protests of 1908. For a time he had attended the Quoc Hoc Academy in Hue, but at about the age of twenty he shipped out of Vietnam as a galley hand on a freighter and eventually settled in France after several years of travel and odd jobs.

In Paris he got to know Phan Chu Trinh, but eventually drifted into much more leftist circles. A founding member of the French Communist party in 1920, he was sent to Moscow in 1923 to study at the famous University for the Toilers of the East. By 1925 he was in Canton as a Comintern agent. In addition to his other activities there, he laboriously organized a Vietnamese Revolutionary Youth League and almost single-handedly published a small newspaper, *Nien Thanh* (Youth), which appeared in about a hundred copies per issue. In 1930 he succeeded in bringing together various regional Communist factions in the ICP.[117]

In late 1930 under Communist leadership several autonomous rural communes were organized in Nghe An province, defying colonial authorities in the famous Nghe An Soviet Movement, and some six thousand peasants were incited to attack the provincial capital at Vinh. The massive French military retaliation was bloody and effective. Alarmed by the ambition and scope of these VNQDD and Communist activities, French security forces tracked down and jailed thousands of suspected political activists throughout 1930 and 1931. Many were executed or fled the country. By 1932 there were about ten thousand political prisoners. Phan Chu Trinh was dead, and Phan Boi Chau was under house arrest in Hue. Nguyen Thai Hoc, leader of the Nationalist party, had been executed. Ho Chi Minh was imprisoned in Hong Kong by the British. All organized resistance to French rule in Vietnam was effectively suppressed.[118]

In this milieu of economic hardship, political frustration, rapid social change, and cultural disorientation, a chorus of new voices spoke out in 1932 to proclaim the bankruptcy of existing cultural forms and social institutions. There was a heated public debate over the setting of the social thermostat. The years between 1932 and 1939 were rocked by controversy that took myriad forms but revolved around basic value conflicts. Nothing less than the nature of a modern Vietnamese identity was involved in these discussions, and the issues raised in these debates have yet to be resolved for many Vietnamese.

3 The *Yin* of Early Modern Vietnamese Culture Challenges the *Yang* of Tradition, 1932–1939

During the late nineteenth and the early twentieth century the colonized lands of Asia underwent traumatic change under Western influence.[1] The irresistible spread of modern technology and the impersonal rationality associated with the growth of a market economy combined to transform much of Asia into a new and confusingly different place to live for hundreds of millions of people. The development of communication and transportation facilities fostered the diffusion of change, and the growth of urban centers imposed upon a rapidly increasing number of city dwellers a radically different social context for their lives. Population increase alone was sufficient to disrupt many societies. Western-style educational systems introduced by colonial administrators provided a powerful impetus to cultural change. Even in countries that had escaped colonial domination, such as Japan or Thailand, the growth of a public educational system reflecting Western influences was of immense social significance.[2]

The traditional elite of civil servants and wealthy landowners found themselves jostled by those newly made wealthy in modern business enterprises and by a small but growing number of doctors, lawyers, pharmacists, and engineers. They were joined by a new urban class of merchants, clerks and secretaries, technicians, schoolteachers, journalists. Wave after wave of graduates from new schools formed a social force wielding innovative kinds of influence based on new and modern skills. Life was changing for all, but for those who were young and Western-educated and lived in cities life was radically transformed. In urban centers during the early 1930s, especially in Hanoi, there was a sudden and self-conscious rush to replace the old with the new, to Westernize, to be modern. The belief in progress was contagious, but its expression was often superficial, stressing the external trappings of change. Western cosmetics became the rage among some women; for a time the yo-yo was popular. Sports, especially soccer and tennis, became popular, while Western dancing, still frowned upon by many, gained in respectability. A beach resort developed on the South China Sea, and in certain circles it became fashionable to go bathing. Teenagers whose parents went about in carriages or sedan chairs, wearing turbans and loose-fitting tunics, dashed about on bicycles or motor scooters, wearing shorts and brandishing tennis rackets, asserting their membership in the ranks of enlightened youth.[3]

Many young Vietnamese who could afford to do so imitated the latest Paris fashions. Young women responded to a movement aimed at modernizing their clothing. In particular, the traditional tunic became much more form-fitting than before. The leader of this new movement in Vietnamese fashion summed up the transformation in a 1934 newspaper interview: "In the old days people dressed basically to conceal their bodies, so they always presented a baggy appearance. But now one should dress so the body is presented in a natural manner, or sometimes to modify it a bit so it appears more flowing and graceful."[4]

The Indochinese College of Fine Arts, located in Hanoi, graduated its first class in 1930. During the early 1930s the pages of newspapers and magazines were enlivened by radically different forms of illustrations and cartoons. Public exhibitions were held in which these new artists proudly displayed their work to a curious public. One complacent young man wrote:

> Before [the Indochinese College of Fine Arts] opened, there was no one in our nation who could be called an artist. The public had no aesthetic appreciation. The ugly houses, the tasteless furniture, the gaudy paintings of those times are emblems of complete confusion. But when the first graduates of the School of Fine Arts began to appear, the situation began to change completely. The artistic displays and exhibitions made everyone aware of beauty in a more understanding manner. Art has even changed our way of life. We live in a beautiful environment. Our lives are more elegant than before.[5]

Such Vietnamese were so thoroughly cut off from their own traditions that they looked at the artifacts of their own civilization through Western eyes and passed aesthetic judgments derived entirely from Western artistic traditions.

Young urban middle-class Vietnamese enlivened their existence with an unprecedented number and variety of entertainments. At Western-style parties champagne corks popped like firecrackers and confetti filled the air, as if these frivolous French imports were talismans capable of warding off the malaise of the times. Fairs and carnivals were well attended. On Saturday afternoons there were soccer matches. Motion pictures came to Vietnam in 1930, providing yet another means of amusement and opening one more window through which even greater numbers of Vietnamese were to obtain a view, albeit a distorted one, of the way some other peoples lived.[6]

In 1932 eighteen-year-old Bao Dai returned from study in France to assume the role of constitutional monarch. The youthfulness of the cabinet he appointed in May 1933 was another sign that times had changed. Pham Quynh, the successful writer and publisher, now forty years old, was named head of the cabinet and minister of education. The most stirring appointment of all was that of a young province chief only thirty-one years old to become minister of the interior and leader of a special commission for government reform. This was Ngo Dinh Diem, son of the former grand chamberlain Ngo Dinh Kha. Noted for his energy and incorruptibility, Diem took his charge seriously and promptly resigned when he was denied in practice the power he had been promised in principle.[7] Bao Dai soon became disillusioned and drifted into the life of a playboy. Only Pham Quynh ignored the farcical nature of his role and settled for what little power the French saw fit to allow him.

Between 1932 and 1935 there was also an explosion in the publication of newspapers, books, and magazines in *quoc ngu*. In the first half of 1933 alone, twenty-seven permits were granted for the establishment of new publications.[8] New writers, in new publications, presented a barrage of fact and opinion, innovative literature, trenchant editorial comment, and sometimes vicious criticism to a receptive and growing reading audience. Although perhaps less than 5 percent of the population was directly affected by this activity, the indirect effects continued to spread in a variety of ways. This intellectual turmoil reflected, amplified, and became in turn a further cause of conflict and change in Vietnamese society.

The literature that emerged in Vietnam during the 1930s was intimately related to the immediate social context from which it arose. Although the fledgling vernacular literature that already existed and continuing French influence were both important, the new generation of literary artists that came of age in the early 1930s expressed an intensely personal point of view with great passion. They wrote, most of them, for money. They talked about and sometimes honestly aspired to artistic achievement. But their primary motivation was neither art nor profit. This literature was written and read to help solve pressing intellectual and emotional problems. These people wrote to articulate their social and cultural dilemmas, to express powerful feelings, to give vent to the powerful emotional strains that beset them. They wrote to inculcate their own attitudes and values in others, to ridicule and browbeat those who opposed their ideas, to exhort those who agreed with them to greater enthusiasm and commitment. They wrote to transform Vietnamese society, to remake it in their own image.

This was a process of collective reorientation, a quest for some new and urgently needed sense of dignity and self-worth. Imaginary worlds were created and shared to serve as models for structuring and interpreting behavior in the real world, to define and validate a life experience that was disconcertingly fragmented and ambivalent. The new literature functioned as a means by which a certain group of people reassured themselves as to who they were, as to the purpose and meaning of their lives. Within this improvised "village" of readers and writers, these new urban Vietnamese could reaffirm that their essentially detached and alienated lives were indeed worthwhile, that their view of and place in the world had some legitimacy. The writers and poets who had dominated the literary scene during the 1920s rapidly faded from prominence, to be replaced by people who had published little or nothing before 1932. These new literary artists were predominantly middle-class, male, and very young.

This was, however, almost pure *yin* literature, expressing the liminality of the first generation of Vietnamese who, although raised and primarily socialized in traditional Vietnamese families, had been educated exclusively in a French-organized school system. Before 1930 there were few adult Vietnamese who had not added such Western learning as they may have acquired to a prior grounding in the fundamentals of traditional studies. The first step toward Western-oriented public education had been the high school opened in 1908 in reaction to the short-lived Dong Kinh Nghia Thuc movement. By 1909 elementary and primary schools had been added, accommodating about 10,000 students. The student population grew to 40,000 by 1913, to 75,000 by 1917, and to 150,000 by 1921.[9] As the children who attended these schools grew up they became the writers and poets who produced this dramatically new literature, the reading public that supported it, the publishers, the literary critics. By 1932 such people were attaining the critical mass necessary to assert themselves and their tastes in the marketplace. By 1935, though still a small minority of the total population, they had become a potent force for cultural change.

Literature Challenges the "Real World"

Writing or talking about behavior is itself a form of behavior, a culturally significant social act that is often extraordinarily revealing. The fiction of the 1930s provides some profound insights into the turmoil of the past fifty years. The author of fiction is free within broad limits to concoct a plot to suit his or her own purposes. The situational variables that constrain most other forms of behavior—action in the so-called real world—can be controlled and manipulated. Novelists, and their readers, can act out their psychocultural proclivities free of another major constraint on behavior, the need to live with its risks and potential consequences. Literature can thus reveal things about a culture that are not readily discernible from observing behavior, which is generated within the constraints imposed by daily existence.

But fictional behavior is not always typical of the way most people conduct their lives. Even among the literate, urban middle class, life in its essentials continued to conform rather closely to the traditional model. For most people, life still revolved around the family, and families had changed very little. Young people still married mainly to please their parents; and most parents, with other senior family members, felt it to be not only their right but also their duty to exercise control over the younger generation's choice of marriage partners. The marriage ceremonial still consisted of an elaborate set of rites designed to transfer the bride from one family to another more than to join two individuals.[10]

There were tremendous pressures on many young married couples to live with the groom's parents as junior members of an extended family. Even if her husband died, a woman was expected to remain with her husband's family. Should she choose to remarry, not only would her reputation suffer, but her first husband's family would keep the children and retain control of all property from the first marriage. The higher the socioeconomic status of a family, the greater these pressures would be.[11]

Exceptions to these generalizations were rare, yet it was precisely on instances of deviation from the norm that the literature of the period focused. The novels and short stories of the period concentrated on depicting the individual in society. Since these authors were writing about Vietnamese life from a perspective heavily influenced by Western education and by nineteenth-century French literary models,[12] the leading characters in this fiction were unusually individualistic Vietnamese, and society was portrayed as an oppressive force that thwarted their desires and unremittingly pressed upon them to act against both their own enlightened best interests and their higher motivations.

Spontaneous whole-person relationships were almost always positive ones, while role-based part-person relationships were often negative, at the least a source of disappointment and sometimes involving intense conflict. Role-based conflict provided the basis of many short stories and novels during the years 1933–1936 especially and, to a lesser extent, for long afterward.

This literature was a concerted attack upon the *yang* structure of Vietnamese society. The traditional view of the world was upended. Youth was portrayed more favorably than age: younger siblings were superior to their older brothers and sisters; children were wiser than their parents. Wives, once seen as "little sisters" to their husbands, were more enlightened and stronger than their benighted spouses. The declassed or socially detached "nonpersons" of traditional society—such as prostitutes, itinerant singers, street peddlers—were portrayed more favorably than incumbents of traditionally idealized roles. Government officials, parents, and mothers-in-law were commonly cast as villains. Authority figures came under fire as petty tyrants, as ignorant, as misguided. Students, craftsmen, and peasants were more humane and wiser than their higher-status contemporaries, who were, by virtue of their higher status, constricted in thought and action by the rigid confines of narrowly defined roles they had been socialized to accept unquestioningly. A new generation of authors championed the individual in opposition to the social forces that trammeled his or her personal integrity and authentic human impulses, and many did so with a naive optimism that had virtually disappeared in Europe and America after World War I.

The first successful "modern Vietnamese novel" was published in *South Wind* in 1925. *To Tam*, by Hoang Ngoc Phach, is a tragic love story. Its author was born in 1889 and was—like Nguyen Van Vinh, Tran Trong Kim, and Pham Quynh—a graduate of the Protectorate School (formerly the Interpreters School) in Hanoi. Hoang Ngoc Phach was one of a very small number of Vietnamese to have acquired some Western education before the development of the public school system. His heroine, To Tam, was a beautiful girl of twenty who had attained a primary certificate in a French school. She met a fine young man, and gradually acquaintance became friendship, and friendship turned to love. Both she and the young man became pledged by their families in arranged marriages to others. At first To Tam resisted. "I've fallen in love with one person, and I can never love another," she cried. "And if I don't love, I won't marry." But when her dying mother implored her, the weight of *hieu* was too great to withstand. She married according to her mother's wishes, went into a depression, and died of a broken heart. She left a diary for the man she loved and asked him to engrave near her final resting place: "Here lies one ill-fated, who died because of love."[13]

This novel focused on students in an urban area (Hanoi); and its primary source of psychological tension was the conflict between individualism, as symbolized by romantic love, and social obligation, as symbolized by an arranged marriage entered into out of filial piety. It was an updated version of the age-old conflict between spontaneous feelings and the prescribed duty of ideology, between *tinh* and *nghia*, *yin* and *yang*. The story of To Tam was about a young woman painfully torn between love and filial piety. And as in both literature and life in traditional times, the *yang* (*hieu*, *nghia*) ultimately triumphed, while the *yin* (female, spontaneous, wholeperson, non-prescribed role-based elements) resisted by withdrawing, by "dying for love."

When the new literature burst forth during the early 1930s, this conflict between *yin* and *yang*, love and duty, *tinh* and *nghia*, was the dominant and by far the most powerful theme. And it frequently involved the constraints of family ties upon individuals. Romantic love versus arranged marriage was a major plot element in many of the most important novels written during the 1930s, especially during the initial outpouring of pent-up emotions between 1933 and 1936. Plots commonly focused on conflict between two women, usually mother-in-law and daughter-in-law. Male characters were less vividly portrayed and assumed essentially passive roles as their mothers, wives, sisters, and sweethearts engaged in a clash of wills around them.

There were compelling reasons for the grip this basic theme held on the interest of both writers and the reading public. The core of the plot was a parable of the times, embodying elemental truths about the psychological world in which the new urban Vietnamese were living. The *yang* structure of family life was the basic paradigm of Vietnamese social organization. The traditional Vietnamese family remained the primary socializing agent in people's lives in the 1930s. It was still the most powerful of all social institutions. Yet those who read and wrote the *quoc ngu* literature of the 1930s had also undergone another and quite different socializing experience: they had acquired a Western education.

Trained from early childhood to regard the family system as the root metaphor of society, these youths were acutely sensitive to cultural differences between East and West in the area of family relationships; and they discovered at the heart of Western culture a very different concept of family. East Asian civilization had been based on the primacy of moral debt to parents, expressed through myriad injunctions to place filial piety above all other considerations. But Western civilization enjoined its adherents to follow a very different principle, with profound social implications. In Genesis (2:24) it is stated that "a man shall leave father and mother and cling to his wife." This was also the teaching of Jesus as found in the gospels (e.g., Matthew 19:5; Mark 10:7). Here the clash between Eastern and Western cultures was most starkly revealed.

Many urban, Western-educated Vietnamese now believed that if Vietnamese society were to be revitalized, to gain pride and respect in the modern world, to have "face" among nations, the old Vietnamese family system had to be overturned. For people experiencing inner turmoil because of competing claims of incompatible values and the irreconcilable standards of "significant others," to read about such culture conflict in novels written in Vietnamese by Vietnamese for Vietnamese was a moving and sometimes cathartic experience. It also sharpened the awareness of some readers to conflicts and ambiguities they might otherwise have overlooked.

The New Poetry

Another important means of expression for these new urban, Western-educated Vietnamese was vernacular poetry. It is very difficult for Westerners, especially Americans, to apprehend how significant poetry can be as an expressive mechanism in society. For many of us poetry has connotations of elitism, obscurity, impracticality. Few of us read poetry, and fewer still have a real appreciation of it. But in Vietnam this is not the case. Many Vietnamese read poetry with enjoyment, commit it to memory, and recite poems to each other with unfeigned enthusiasm. Everyday speech is liberally sprinkled with poetic allusions. Even the poor and the illiterate imbibe deeply of a rich oral tradition that has incorporated much that originated in the written literature of the educated elite. Poetry has been and remains much more popular and important in Vietnam than in the United States.[14]

Poetry in Vietnam was traditionally written by and for the Establishment, the educated upper class. Up to the eighteenth century, most of the vast corpus of Vietnamese literature that survived was written by kings, generals, court officials, or mandarins in the national bureaucracy. These men produced much of this poetry in conjunction with their official roles, often to achieve a practical and specific purpose. Their work almost always supported or at least implicitly accepted the official view of the world.

Traditional poetry was basically ethical and didactic in nature, deeply imbued with Neo-Confucian ideology after the fifteenth century. Many of the most famous works of the early centuries of Vietnamese literature were occasional pieces: poems, speeches, or proclamations written for a particular occasion. Both poetry and doggeral were used as mechanisms of social control at all levels of society throughout traditional times. Although many works may properly be labeled "protest poetry," this was usually protest against deviation from orthodox ideology, not against the ideology itself.

Beginning in the mid-eighteenth century and continuing into the nineteenth century, however, some anti-Establishment undertones began to creep into Vietnamese poetry, and there was an increased tendency to write for personal instead of official reasons. This alteration of the content and purpose of poetry was intimately connected to a shift from Chinese to Vietnamese as the primary vehicle of poetic expression. But personal emotions remained veiled, and the content of poetry was still predominantly ethical and social in nature.

Apart from the further development of the "tale told in verse," which was written in *nom* employing a prosodic scheme distinctly Vietnamese, Vietnamese poets continued into the twentieth century to write in traditional Chinese forms. They scrupulously adhered to poetic conventions that had developed in China in the eighth and ninth centuries—conventions with constraints that far exceeded those of the English sonnet. Then during the 1930s Vietnamese poetry was rapidly transformed and rejuvenated. Out of an intellectual and artistic upheaval centered in but not limited to Hanoi and Saigon, both the content and the form of Vietnamese poetry abruptly shifted from traditional modes to much more modern ones based on Western models. The new poems ignored the old prosodic conventions.

The "new poetry movement" began with the publication of "Old Love" by Phan Khoi on March 10, 1932. Phan Khoi, born in 1887, was one of the older, Confucian-trained generation. He earned a baccalaureate degree in the examinations of 1905. He participated in the Dong Kinh Nghia Thuc movement, then traveled to central Vietnam, where he was involved in the protests of 1908. Because of this activity he spent the years between 1908 and 1914 in prison. When Pham Quynh's journal *South Wind* appeared in 1917, Phan Khoi became an early member of the staff, but after two years he resigned and traveled south to Saigon, where he went to work for another paper. During the 1920s he shuttled back and forth between Saigon and Hanoi, working for a number of different newspapers and journals. By the time "Old Love" appeared, Phan Khoi was already a very well-known and controversial figure. In the course of a long career he was involved in many disputes in the fields of literature, philosophy, politics, and education; and one of his favorite and most controversial themes had been the disparagement of Confucianism.[15]

In his effort to "seek new ground" in his poetry, Phan Khoi chose to describe the lingering memory of an old romantic attachment that had been disrupted by the custom of arranged marriage:

> Twenty-four years ago
> On a windy, rainy night,
> By dim lamplight in a tiny house,
> Two ebony heads huddled together
> Lamenting their plight.

"Oh, woe is us! Our love is strong,
Yet we can never marry.
Rather than let love lead to tragedy,
Should we not dare to make a quick break
Rather than linger in pain?
Yet how can we speak such cruel words,
How bear to let each other go?

Let us settle, then, for the love we have had,
And let it go at that.
Hasn't Heaven forced this to be?
We are sweethearts, not husband and wife,
To be bound by loyalty."

Twenty four years later . . .
A chance encounter far away . . .
Both heads had turned to silver;
Had they not known each other well,
Might they not have passed unknown?
An old affair was recalled, no more.
It was just a glance in passing!

. . . There still are corners to the eyes.[16]

The first significant response to the publication of "Old Love"
came from a young man only twenty-one years old. Luu Trong Lu,
using a pseudonym, wrote a letter to Phan Khoi commending his
effort but complaining that since its publication neither Phan Khoi
nor anyone else had written any additional works in the new style.
Attached to the letter were two poems, both by Luu Trong Lu.[17]
Other young poets soon followed with more new poems. In June
1934 Luu Trong Lu gave a speech in Qui Nhon in central Vietnam
in which he attempted to articulate the mood of his generation:

As external conditions are altered, the human soul changes
as well. Our pain and sadness, happiness and pleasure, love
and hatred are no longer the same as the pain and sadness,
happiness and pleasure, love and hatred of our forefathers.
Our ancestors led lives that were simple and tranquil: life was
easy, there was little contact with the outside, so their souls
were simple, impoverished, torpid, atrophied, just like their
lives. And in addition to that, Chinese culture engulfed them,
bringing to them the stern and narrow discipline of Confucianism. The totalitarian political rule also had a great impact on poetry and writing, because our ancient poets were
all devoted Confucians who had buried their noses in books

for ten years only out of eagerness to embark upon a public career at some future date. Their poetry was an aristocratic, majestic, public type of poetry, with well-established forms, used to make toasts to each other or to sing the praises of contemporary power figures, the honors and exploits of both others and themselves. And if these Confucians were so unfortunate as to lose out on their opportunities . . . they were capable of no more than chanting a cliché: "The flowers wilt, the clouds pass, life is a sea of misery."

In fact, their disillusionment was as commonplace and as meager as their love of life. With such commonplace and paltry sentiments, what need did they have for a broader, more flexible framework?[18]

But, he continued, after a period of contact with Western culture, in a more complex age where thoughts were in competition and where people had been forced to think about life and reexamine concepts, souls were no longer so simple, and sentiments had come into being that did not exist before. It was, he said, "only natural to have the movement for a new poetry in today's literature."

Traditional forms were for Luu Trong Lu and many others no longer capable of conveying "the actual thoughts that are in the bottom of our hearts." In part this was because older genres and techniques were no longer appropriate to the new conditions. But it was also because these young people were out of touch with these traditions. Their education had provided them with different skills, a different body of knowledge, a different style, different tastes. And it had embued them with a different set of values, in conflict with those on which the traditional models were based.

A New Paradigm: Individualism

The new poetry was emphatically personal. The focus of literature had shifted from the general to the specific, from the objective to the subjective, from reason (*ly*) and ethics (*nghia*) to emotions (*tinh*), from society to the individual. What men in general should think or do seemed suddenly less important than what "I feel." The favorite topic of the new poets was their own emotional lives. They were at their best, and most popular, when writing about themselves.

All social institutions and ethical and moral conventions were now subject to review. The entire panoply of civilization and culture was open to question in light of the individual human being's right to the pursuit of personal happiness. This quest for personal fulfillment was a direct challenge to the traditional priorities of loyalty and moral debt to family, village, and state—that is, the established social order. Other contrasts in both form and content between the old and the new poetry all derived from this single crucial point. What was new, startlingly and abruptly new, was, in a word, individualism.

The word "individualism" first appeared in the English language as a translation of a neologism created by Alexis de Tocqueville in *Democracy in America* (1835) to describe what he perceived to be a novel state of affairs. The concept of individualism dramatically circled the globe in little more than a hundred years. Yet its apparent simplicity and universality were illusory: even individualism ultimately must submit to definition in terms of its relationship to other elements in the particular sociocultural system of which it is a part.

The individualism expressed in Vietnam's new poetry was a romantic nineteenth-century individualism scarcely touched by the doubts that had arisen in the West.[19] This vigorous doctrine of individualism was being espoused by young Vietnamese at the very time when in the United States it was announced by John Dewey to be a mere "echo of the past," a concept whose "bankruptcy" rendered it a source of bewilderment and confusion to those "lost individuals" who continued to espouse it. As Dewey pointed out, individualism had flourished in the West as part of a larger intellectual synthesis that had been eroded in the aftermath of the industrial revolution. The United States was suffering an intellectual crisis, according to Dewey, because "the older mental equipment remained after its causes and foundations had disappeared."[20] Americans were hampered, Dewey argued, by a habit of thinking that "treats individualism as if it were something static, having a uniform content."[21] But individualism, he observed,

> is a unique manner of acting in and with a world of objects and persons. It is not something complete in itself, like a closet in a house or a secret drawer in a desk, filled with treasures that are waiting to be bestowed on the world. Since individuality is a distinctive way of feeling the impacts of the world and of showing a preferential bias in response to these impacts, it develops into shape and form only through

interaction with actual conditions; it is no more complete in itself than is a painter's tube of paint.[22]

Many Vietnamese intellectuals found themselves in desperate need to create a dynamic and authentically Vietnamese form of individualism that could articulate more satisfactorily with the world in which they lived, a world shaped by family, by tradition, and by the stifling reality of colonial domination. Western education had created a desire, in some cases a need, for economic and emotional independence in a generation of Vietnamese who lacked both the emotional and the social base for sustaining an autonomous existence, as well as any viable economic or political means for exercising it in a positive and efficacious manner. Both the excitement and the despair of individualism in Vietnam were expressed in poetry that tells us about the emotional consequences of going from Rousseau to Camus in a single lifetime.

In the forefront of those advocating the new over the old was a new journal, *Mores*, published in Hanoi by Nguyen Tuong Tam and a small band of collaborators. They pioneered in the introduction of new poetry, new clothing styles, crossword puzzles, and numerous other ideas and fashions. But it was with their novels and short stories that these men had their greatest impact.

Tam's own family background was one of Confucian scholarship and traditional morality. He was one of seven children; his father died when Tam was only twelve years old. He missed several years of school because of family financial difficulties. Yet, with his mother's encouragement and self-sacrifice, he managed to obtain a high school diploma by 1923. He then went to work as a clerk in a government finance office, but he was unhappy and dissatisfied there. He may have been describing his own feelings in a short story written in 1926, called "The Dream of Tu Lam":

> I was just coming home from the office, brooding upon how miserable I was and sad over the state of the world. As I went to my job each morning and afternoon, the more I worked the more bored I became. How very insipid my life seemed. . . . Here I was with a job that was not of the slightest benefit to anyone, bowing my way in and out with no means of escape.[23]

In 1925 Tam quit his bureaucratic post to enter medical school. There he was still unhappy, so he transferred to the newly opened program in fine arts. He was developing into a promising young painter, and in 1926 he got married. Still he felt vaguely unfulfilled. In his first novel, *Tradition of Confucian Scholarship*, which appeared in 1926, traditional values were implicit and unquestioned from beginning to end.

Soon Tam moved to Saigon. He was one of the crowd of young men who flocked to Phan Chu Trinh's funeral there. At last, in 1927, at the age of twenty-one he went to France. In three incredibly active years he earned a bachelor of science degree and devoted his spare hours to spirited investigations into French politics, newspapers, literature, painting, the theater, and the printing industry. In 1930 he returned to Vietnam, his mind churning with ambitious schemes. Then, in September of 1932, he took control of *Mores*. At last his immense store of energy, ambition, and idealism had an adequate outlet. He worked day and night writing editorials, short stories, and novels; drawing illustrations; making staff assignments; arranging layout, design, advertisements; soliciting manuscripts; calculating precarious financial projections.[24]

Tam quickly assembled a talented staff of like-minded individuals, with the core group composed mostly of personal friends and family, including three younger brothers. Nguyen Tuong Long, known by his pen name, Hoang Dao, was chief theoretician, polemical essayist, and Tam's intimate confidante. Nguyen Tuong Bach and Nguyen Tuong Lan (only twenty-three years old, known by the pen name Thach Lam) contributed some editorials, short stories, and poems.

To provide a more cohesive organization to his rapidly expanding literary and publishing interests, Tam founded the Self-Strength Literary Movement. In March 1933 a policy statement was issued for the newly formed group. Members pledged themselves to enrich the stock of literature within Vietnam by writing and translating books of social significance, to promote a philosophy of popularism, and to use a clear and simple prose style that was distinctly Vietnamese. They vowed to be always "new, young, full of life," to believe in and to struggle for progress. They also agreed to introduce Western scientific concepts into their writing, and to make people aware that Confucianism was no longer an appropriate philosophy. Further, they would strive to create a popularistic love of country, to avoid bourgeois and aristocratic tendencies, and to respect the freedom of the individual.[25]

The Lu, an early addition to Tam's team, was widely acknowledged to be the new poet par excellence. Born in 1907, he was in his late twenties at the height of his creativity and influence, a bit older than Luu Trong Lu and most of the other new poets. The poems that The Lu published in *Mores* from 1933 through 1936 won the admiration of all but the most obstinate opponents of the new poetry. A poem called "The Lute of Ten Thousand Tones" expresses the spirit of this pioneering work:

. . . .

I love life with all its misery,
With its heartache, its horror, or its gracefulness,
With its brilliance, its love, or its ferocity.

You may say that my character is fickle,
Without purpose, without ideology—but what need have I?

. . . .

Borrowing a lute of a thousand frets, I sing.
Depicting beauty that is sombre, full of passion, or innocent;
Depicting as well the grand and elevated beauty
Of the nation, of poetry, of imagination,
The charm and grace of beautiful women,
The vibrant radiance of spring sunshine,
Painting the profound grief of days of wind and rain,
Scenes of magnificence, waves that tilt the heavens, waterfalls
    with a thousand crashing streams,
Delicate features, indistinct glimpses of fluttering flower petals,
Sights of cold and hunger, the stagnant waters of a swamp,
The exquisite pleasure of a vision,
A will ardent to compete against the turmoil of life:
At once I am in love with, in search of, and intoxicated by life.

. . . .

With the Muse of Poetry, I have a lute of ten thousand tones.
With the Muse of Poetry, I have a brush of ten thousand colors.
I want to be an artist who works miracles,
Taking the voices and beauties of this world as my material.[26]

In a "Self-Portrait" The Lu presents himself as a man very much committed to individualism, and he makes explicit the link between his individualism and his poetry:

The Lu is a strange chap;
He lives today and does not know there will be a tomorrow.

. . . .

A clumsy and silent person, not well liked,
With so many bad habits he has no intention of abandoning,
Sloppy and disheveled in dress,
He arrived in Hanoi clad in a pair of shorts
And a pair of white cloth shoes, which he wore both summer
    and winter
With a yellow leather cap, shapeless and soiled,
Worn in rain and sunshine from the north to the south.
No matter how much criticism his life incurred, he ignored it
And went his way, with his face turned up to look at the sky,
To all appearances as happy as a person who never knew
    misery.
His close friends felt sorry for him and often gave advice:
"What's the matter with you? Why waste so much time?
Listen to us and come here.
You have talent and intelligence; join the crowd and show what
    you can do.
What pleasure is there in your lonely life?
Come here and struggle, compete,
Get for yourself a little fame and fortune."
The Lu thought for three days before replying:
"Oh, you're right!" So here in Hanoi
He was active, he dreamed;
As confused as a savage acting like a lord,
All dressed up in a very fashionable outfit.
He learned to weigh his words, to be moderate and reserved,
To jostle his way in the crowd—he grew up!
But he was never able to get rid of his strange temperament.
He thought everyone in the world was good,
But in this life extreme sincerity is stupidity.
He did not suspect that no number of virtues
Could ever equal cleverness, that being crafty was everything!
So today, suddenly, with a sad face,
With his fashionable clothes thrown over his shoulder,
He came to say:
"Your road to fame and fortune has no savor.
Ask me no more questions, and give me no more advice.
Leave me alone, to lead my own private life.
A simple life of wandering, but a happy one,
Alone, with the Muse of Poetry as my friend.
I'm tired of all this bustling happiness."
He cast off his disguise, which had produced no poetry,
And returned to the cap he had put away, and his white cloth
    shoes,

And his shirt all faded from sunshine and dew,
And he went away, went in search of the Muse,
Who has been hiding someplace for quite a while now.[27]

A good Vietnamese was supposed to prize his reputation, to be extremely sensitive to the opinions of other people, to conform to public standards of dress and speech and behavior, to be eager to compete with his neighbors. Above all else, he was supposed to keep his individuality immersed in the communal life of family and village. Yet The Lu portrayed himself as a man who was happiest going his own way, ignoring all criticism, disregarding conventions, unwilling to compete, uninterested in reputation, and with no desire to abandon his many bad habits: the very antithesis of a good, traditional Vietnamese.

But the traditional Vietnamese traits rejected by The Lu were virtues within the context of the closed corporate families and communities of an organic agricultural society. In Hanoi The Lu found serious discrepancies between the ends and means of social action. Beneath the patina of fashionable clothes and guarded speech, the new city people were confused. The Lu's adaptation to city life had been superficial, merely a disguise. Beneath it all he had been as out of place as a savage cast in the role of a lord. His happiness, his virtue, and his poetry required him to set himself apart from that society, to live in the natural world of rain and sunshine and dew, outside of the social structure. This poetry resembles that of Western romantics who wrote a hundred years earlier, at a time when their own societies were undergoing mechanization, urbanization, and impersonal regimentation.

The Battle of the Novels

A MORAL INDIVIDUALISM: *IN THE MIDST OF SPRING*   In March 1933 a new serialized novel, *In the Midst of Spring*, began appearing in *Mores*. The author, Khai Hung (Tran Khanh Giu), was a key member of the *Mores* staff and a close friend and collaborator of Nguyen Tuong Tam. Khai Hung was already well known to the reading public through the success of his early short stories and his first novel. *In the Midst of Spring* was one of the first works to be produced by the Self-Strength Literary Movement, and it provided an auspicious beginning. Khai Hung was one of the most popular members of the group, a well-liked teacher, known for his skeptical nature and gentle prodding of students, with a keen sense of humor. Khai Hung had begun writing for *Mores* much earlier, and was serving as editor when Tam took over. The two men worked well together, and it was Tam who had urged Khai Hung to concentrate on writing fiction.[28]

The conflict between the old and the new, between traditional Vietnamese and modern Western values, formed the basis of the plot for *In the Midst of Spring*. But Khai Hung chose not to dwell upon the conflict itself. He concentrated on how the conflict was handled by the main character, Mai, a young woman who illustrates the capacity of the human spirit for courage, self-sacrifice, and perseverance in the face of adversity. Mai views the world in human terms, not ideological ones. She is an individualist who is not strictly bound by tradition; hers is a moral individualism, concerned with personal integrity rather than with self-gratification. Aware of herself as a person, Mai knows how to respect the rights and feelings of others.

As the novel begins Mai is desperately trying to help her younger brother, Huy, stay in school to finish his high school education. With both parents dead, Mai decided to sell the family estate to pay the expense of her younger brother's room and board at school. While trying to dispose of the modest family holdings, Mai fell into the clutches of an unscrupulous local squire. The squire was depicted as a sly, ignorant, greedy, lecherous, and overbearing man. His character represented the decadence of traditional rural society. He lusted after Mai's body and her property. Then Mai met a childhood friend, the only son of a deceased provincial judge. Loc had recognized Mai from the days when he, as a pupil of her father, had grown fond of his teacher's pretty little girl. Mai was shy and somewhat aloof, but Loc actively tried to renew their former innocent friendship. When Loc learned about her predicament, he resolved to help her in any way possible. Eventually he persuaded Mai to move to Hanoi. He paid the rent for her and took care of Huy's educational expenses. It was a noble and romantic gesture. He asked nothing in return. For the sake of her younger brother, Mai accepted Loc's assistance. She believed in his sincerity and thought him to be a man of extraordinary compassion and generosity.

There was a beautiful innocence and selflessness to their relationship. But in Hanoi the mutual admiration and respect between them was gently and unexpectedly transformed into love. Loc told his mother all about Mai. Mai was beautiful, courageous, virtuous. He wanted to marry her.

Unfortunately, Mai was the perfect girl only to Loc. As far as Mrs. Judge was concerned, Mai was a miserable little creature, uneducated, a mere child, and from the lower classes— scarcely someone worthy to become the wife of a man who was a government official holding the position of head clerk. Mrs. Judge did not let her son's eulogy penetrate her ears. She thought her young son was still naive. He had been taken in by some sweet-talking little adventuress.

"If she's so agreeable to you, how do you know that she's not just as agreeable to other men? You've got to realize that for a wife to be something precious, she has to be someone your parents have selected for you, with proper engagement gifts and wedding ceremonial. This creature is just some wildflower you've picked up from the side of the road. Do you actually think you're going to bring her home and dirty my house with her?"

Loc's spirited defense of Mai only enraged his mother.

Mrs. Judge pounded the table and screeched: "I told you I don't agree, and that's that! I don't agree! If you think you're so smart, go ahead and take her. But I've requested a province chief's daughter for you and her family has accepted. I'm talking about adults having already discussed this matter. You can't bring in all this kid-stuff now."

When he heard his mother refer to the province chief's daughter, Loc frowned. "Mother, ma'am," he responded, "I asked you not to make that request for me. I'm not satisfied with that match."

"Oh ho, you're trotting out your civilization on me, are you? It's freedom in marriage, is it? You're not satisfied, but I am satisfied. You must know that in marriage it's essential to look for a house of equal status. Do you intend to force me into a relationship with a bunch of country bumpkins? With rural trash? You want to take away all of my face, to lose all the honor of our ancestors. You're a boy without *hieu*, do you hear me!"

His education and sense of self-respect compelled Loc to be true to his love and his convictions. And yet he loved and respected his mother too. He was not capable of defying her authority. "Loc had always been a boy who knew *hieu*."

Caught between Mai's innocent expectations and his mother's strong will, between the dictates of *tinh* and *nghia*, Loc resorted to deceit. Saying he needed a quiet spot to live alone and study for an advanced degree, Loc moved out of his mother's house with her permission. He then staged a scene in which Mai was led to believe that she had met Mrs. Judge and been accepted as a daughter-in-law. Mai thought that she and Loc were married, with his family's blessing. The whole thing was, however, a complete sham. Unwilling either to give up Mai or to defy his mother, Loc was simply trying to postpone a showdown until he could find some way of reconciling his mother to the situation.

For nine idyllic months Loc and Mai and Huy lived together in a blissful family atmosphere. Loc chose to let the situation drift on in deceit rather than risk disrupting a situation in which everyone was so happy. But actually no one else was quite as happy as Loc thought they were. One day by chance young Huy learned that the woman whom Loc had introduced to him and Mai as his mother, Mrs. Judge, was in fact an imposter. Mai forced the story out of Huy and pledged him to silence before he had a chance to confront Loc with this deception. Mrs. Judge also had her suspicions, but she too bided her time.

Then one day while Mai, Loc, and Huy were off on a holiday picnic in the countryside, Mai broke the news to Loc that she was pregnant. Loc was stunned; and he was, all too obviously, not pleased by this revelation. He finally stammered out a weak explanation of his unsatisfactory reaction to Mai's important announcement.

"It's just that I don't want my child, your child . . . our child to be born at a time when . . ." Loc trailed off into silence. Mai pretended not to understand and asked: "At a time when what?"

"Let me go back over the whole story for you. That's the only way you'll be able to get a clear understanding of things. I am the son of a mandarin. My father was the son of a mandarin. My mother was a mandarin's daughter." "And I," Mai chuckled, "am the child of ordinary people." "You shouldn't mock this, and please don't interrupt me. If I go rambling on like this, it isn't to be bragging. Ever since I was a little boy, I've followed a Western education, my mind is imbued with Western thought. I understand the value of individual rights, the freedom of the individual. I love it. I respect it. . . . And

I haven't accepted any Confucian influence. So I've never made any class distinctions. I've never differentiated between the children of mandarins and the children of ordinary people. . . .

"But my mother. . . . Don't misunderstand! If you knew my mother you'd have to like her and respect her, because my mother is a very admirable woman. . . . But that mass of Confucian ethics and ritual propriety doesn't just flit across her intellect; with my mother that's all something that has eaten deeply into her brain, it's something in her blood, like some eternal spirit which is a sacred inheritance. I'm not exaggerating. I myself, who have accepted the influence of my education, of the Western spirit, ever since I was small, even I often find my thoughts are restricted within the boundaries of Confucianism. There's no need to look far for examples. Right now, just because of that one word *hieu* I don't dare enjoy the happiness of love with you openly and completely. I have to follow ritual propriety. I have to put the word *tinh* beneath the word *hieu*, even though we often have only the vaguest notions about what these words really mean or we force ourselves to try to understand them."

Mai began to cry. She realized full well the implications of his inability to be completely forthright. A dark shadow fell over their relationship. Loc grew sick with worry, and finally tried to talk to his mother.

Mrs. Judge was pretty sure she knew what was bothering her son, but she pretended ignorance. "What's the matter, my child?"

"Mother, you'll have to forgive me in advance, or I won't dare speak of it to you." "Go on, tell me." Loc bent his head down and whispered: "Miss Mai . . ." As he paused, his mother broke in to ask: "Has that little country girl led you astray? Did she seduce you?" Loc smiled. "It might be more accurate to say that I seduced her." "Indeed. And why is that?"

"Mother, ma'am, she's been living with me, and she . . ." Mrs. Judge was on her feet, waggling her finger in Loc's face. "Oh, you're a clever one, you are," she scolded. "A head clerk yourself and the son of a judge, and still you let yourself get mixed up in such sordid goings-on. What if his excellency the province chief and his family learned of this? What would you tell them? Huh? Tell me that, you young scalawag!"

When Loc stood silent, it only enraged his mother even

more. "If you want to live to see tomorrow, you're moving back home with me," she shouted. "I must have been crazy to let you go off on your own. As for that little girl, I'll contact the police and have her put in a whorehouse where she belongs."

Loc's cheeks burned red and his eyes flashed. "Mother! She is my wife." Mrs. Judge slammed her hand down. "Your wife! And who asked her to be your wife?

"Oh, you're so smart, you are! You can overstep your parents' authority. You no longer know anything about the five moral obligations or the five cardinal virtues. Oh, no! That's right, you're civilized, you are. You're free to marry as you please. Well, let me tell you, young man, you still have to get my permission first!" "Mother, ma'am, I tried to ask your permission, but you wouldn't agree."

"Oh, you knew I didn't agree so you just went ahead and did it anyway, is that right?"

Loc moved nearer his mother and said soothingly: "Mother, ma'am, I think that taking a wife is something very important in a person's life and that people should have the right to choose for themselves someone who is compatible both in the head and in the heart. Then the family can be happy and harmonious. In selecting a wife-to-be for me, you and father always thought only of picking a house that was at least the equal of our own."

Mrs. Judge chuckled. "And of course there has never been any other family that was happy or harmonious, has there? You kids nowadays think you have to go to school and learn to speak French before you can know anything about picking a wife, and we old folks make nothing but foolish decisions, isn't that right?"

"No, mother, that isn't so. You folks are selective, yes, but you only choose among your status equals. For example, a mandarin's child has to marry the child of another mandarin. And you say that other families have been happy and peaceful, but that's only because it was forced on them, just because of ritual propriety. It wasn't because husbands and wives had dispositions suited to each other. Ritual propriety made wives submissive. Whatever the husband said, the wife had to agree. Even if she were oppressed, she dared not open her mouth. Under those conditions, how could it not have been peaceful?"

Mrs. Judge laughed scornfully. "And still it works. Isn't that better than dragging home any whore you happen to run across and elevating her to be your wife! But never mind. I don't need to say much. If you still want to see my face again, you've got to kick that slut out right away and come back here to live with me."

In a trembling voice, Loc replied. "Mother, ma'am, I can't obey you in this matter. Kill me if you want to, and I'll accept it, because she is pregnant with my child."

Mrs. Judge was brimming with anger, but she sat quietly, thinking. She had noted the determination in Loc's voice, and she realized it would be very difficult to carry off a display of authority over her son at this point. So she immediately revised her strategy. She would sow doubts in her son's heart.

Mrs. Judge finally succeeded in making Loc doubt Mai's faithfulness. She then went to see Mai and, pointing out how unhappy Loc had become, begged Mai to give him his freedom. Mai thought that Mrs. Judge was speaking for her son, saying only what Loc himself lacked the nerve to tell her directly. So she left the house at once, taking Huy, who was in poor health, with her. She was pregnant, without any source of income, and she had very little money.

Thus began a time of unspeakable hardship and humiliation for Mai. She and Huy lived in the slums, encountering both scorn and charity as they struggled to rebuild their lives. Eventually Huy graduated from school and got a teaching job in the provinces. Mai, her son, and Huy lived a simple and tranquil life in a remote area. Loc had obediently married the province chief's daughter, but he was never able to forget Mai. At last he learns the whole truth of her disappearance and subsequent hardships. He seeks her out to beg her forgiveness and to ask her to come back to him. Five years have passed. Mai still loves Loc and she has completely forgiven him, yet she steadfastly refuses to renew their relationship despite his pleading. But Loc persists:

"We'll go away, go someplace very far away, any place at all; we'll rebuild our family, rebuild our happiness."

"We can't. Please let me finish talking before you say any more. . . . There are three options. . . . The first is, I could be your concubine, couldn't I?" "But . . ." "Let me finish. The answer is, no, I couldn't. I myself have sometimes thought that if we loved each other that was sufficient, being the main wife or a secondary wife wouldn't be important. But it can't be that way. I love you, so I'd always be nervous and fearful of your first wife, and I'd always keep thinking about sharing your love with someone else. That would be ten times more painful than being separated. And there's another point to be considered. When you abandoned me and married your wife, I felt like someone had robbed me of my husband. But now the situation is turned around. Now our positions are exactly reversed. If I agree to be your concubine, I'd be stealing someone else's husband. Because if what you say is true, and I do feel certain that it is, then you would give me all your attention and neglect your first wife."

"Mai, darling . . ." "Let me speak first. I don't want that. That's the first option. The second option is that you don't have to distinguish between a first wife and a concubine. Just think about you and me. We could set up a household here, your second family . . ." "My true family," Loc said happily. Mai chuckled.

"And your other family is a false one, is it? No, that won't do. We can't expect to enjoy any happiness hiding out like that. If we want to enjoy happiness we would have to love each other openly. . . ."

Trying very hard to remain cool, Loc asked: "And the third option?" "We could run away together." Loc was delighted. He stared at Mai ardently. But she continued: "Actually that idea occurred to me as soon as I realized that you loved me like before. . . . And let me confess to you that during these past five long years, not a single day has gone by when I didn't think of you, when I didn't think of the time when . . ."

Mai halted. Loc was waiting with his entire being intent upon the completion of her sentence. But Mai sighed and continued: "Never mind. What's the sense in dredging up love stories from days gone by? What's happened in the past is one thing; today is different. Now you have a family that you have to love, that you have to take care of. And as for me, I have my family too, and I can look upon it as a consolation for the disappointment in my life.". . .

"Why disappointment? . . . But you haven't finished talking about the third option. Those words 'run away together' are still ringing in my ears." Mai sighed. "It's no good. You shouldn't think that way. Just imagine what things would be like a week later. Think of what an uproar our running away would have caused. . . . A day would come when you would remember your mother; you'd remember your wife, and your children; and even if you didn't love them any more, you still couldn't help but feel upset, hurt, and miserable. And . . . I would be aware then that I was the one who had upset you, the one who had hurt you, the one who was making you miserable. So I'd feel even worse than you."

Loc sighed and bowed his head. . . . Little did he realize that all Mai's carefully measured words had been rehearsed many, many times as she whispered to herself during countless long nights. . . .

Softly, Loc told Mai, "You're too much of a debater." "No, I'm no debater," Mai replied with a smile. "I'm just discussing all the right and wrong of this matter with you. We shouldn't be afraid of right and wrong. Just think about it. Right now only two people are unhappy: you and I. If we run away we won't be any less miserable, we might even be more so, and we might spread our unhappiness to lots of other people. On your side there's your mother, your wife, your children; and for me there is Huy. Shouldn't we sacrifice our love as well as our happiness for the sake of others?"

When it appeared, *In the Midst of Spring* was the best-written and most widely read novel in the small but rapidly growing corpus of modern Vietnamese fiction. Khai Hung, Nguyen Tuong Tam, The Lu, and other colleagues at *Mores* acknowledged the reality of human frailty and social evils, but they emphasized the capacity of the individual human being for love and courage, for self-sacrifice and dedication. They portrayed the beauty of nature, the warmth of friendship, the satisfaction of achievement, the possibility of progress through individual initiative. They advocated the virtues of self-reliance, optimism, and an unwavering love of life. With these ideals, they were a dominant force from 1932 until 1937 and their strong influence continued long thereafter. But they were constantly beleaguered: artistically, commercially, and philosophically.

CLASS CONSCIOUSNESS: *GOLDEN BRANCHES, LEAVES OF JADE*
Many other writers were beginning to paint a much bleaker picture of the human condition in general and of contemporary Vietnamese society in particular. Reflecting earlier tendencies in Western literature toward "realism" and "naturalism," some major competitors of the Self-Strength Literary Movement depicted human beings who were more heavily pressed upon both by inner compulsions and by external social forces. Both Freudian notions of libido and Marxist conceptions of culture and society can be

detected in nascent form. But in the early to mid-1930s the focus of the new novels was on concrete social issues, not formal ideology.

Within the ranks of those who disagreed with the worldview espoused by the staff of *Mores* was a critic and novelist named Nguyen Cong Hoan. Hoan was one of the earliest writers of the distinctly new fiction, and from the early 1930s until 1945 he was one of the most prominent and most prolific authors in Vietnam. He also wrote much criticism of contemporary literature, including some biting attacks on Nguyen Tuong Tam and the Self-Strength Literary Movement.[29]

Born into a well-to-do family of civil servants, Hoan received a Western education and became a schoolteacher, then a career educator in the civil service. Not until he was well established as a successful writer did he stop teaching and turn to fiction as a full-time vocation. The strands of realism and naturalism are strong in his work, with echoes of Freud and Marx clearly present. Hoan saw the individual in society as far more vulnerable and less efficacious than did Tam or Khai Hung.

During the 1930s over a hundred short stories and more than a dozen novels flowed from Hoan's pen to satisfy an avid reading public. Writing against numerous deadlines for serialized publication in newspapers, he kept his plots simple. His characters tended to be one-dimensional, yet they often came alive with a recognizable touch of humanity. His flair for drama and his exquisite sense of irony more than compensated his readers for a somewhat pedestrian and cliché-ridden style.

The title *Golden Branches, Leaves of Jade* (1934) is a metaphorical allusion to upper-class families, families much like Hoan's own. This novel is about one such family, headed by a haughty and stern prefecture chief, a passionate defender of traditional morality. His wife, from an illustrious family, is as much a snob as her husband, if less rigid in her thinking. They are doting parents of an only child, their daughter, Nga. Mr. Prefecture also has a married younger brother, head clerk in a government office in Hanoi. Mr. and Mrs. Prefecture have thoroughly traditional educations; but Mr. Head Clerk, being younger, has received some Western education, speaks French, and is more receptive to new ideas.

One day while Nga was out walking, a student from a poor family rescued her from a vicious dog. This was the beginning of a friendship that turned to love. But both knew that Nga's parents would never allow their daughter to have anything to do with a boy from a family whose status was so far inferior to their own. Nga loved and pitied Chi, a bright and talented young man who was struggling to acquire a good education and carve out a career for himself; and she resented the strict orthodoxy of her parents. When Chi stopped seeing Nga because he realized their relationship could lead only to heartbreak, she went out of her mind with frustration and grief.

Nga's uncle, Mr. Head Clerk, arranged for a French psychiatrist to visit Nga. Mr. Prefecture had misgivings, but when the Frenchman arrived Mr. Prefecture greeted him obsequiously, grasping the man's outstretched hand in both of his own and bowing low. After examining Nga and learning the background to her illness, the psychiatrist paused as he left the house to speak to Mr. Prefecture.

"You'll have to humor her. It's difficult to treat an illness like this. . . . So I want to speak with you very frankly about something."

While Mr. Head Clerk interpreted the doctor's words, Mr. Prefecture nodded as he listened. "Yes, sir."

"According to your younger brother, at first your daughter had heart trouble, which was then complicated by a disappointment in love. Unfortunately, the weather became hot and muggy, making it easier for mental illness to develop. And develop it did, quite rapidly. Nothing is so good in treating an illness like this as humoring the patient. So you and your wife should give in to her whims."

"Yes, certainly. Whatever Your Excellency suggests, we will obey."

"This means you have to make her feel contented. You must permit her loved one to visit her here. That way her illness will gradually subside, and eventually disappear altogether."

"Yes, sir. It will be done."

"I know that you and your wife consider this to be immoral, because your brother has discussed with me quite clearly your family position and the stern character of those who belong to such noble families."

"Sir, whatever your instructions may be, we shall certainly follow them."

"Very good. I'm happy if you understand this. I can guarantee a successful cure. I've found the Vietnamese are often too inflexible. Westerners, now, they don't mind if a child from a rich and influential family marries a child of a lowly family. The main thing is that the two young people love each other."

"Yes, sir."

"So you go ahead and let your daughter's loved one come to visit her. And while she's recovering, if she asks anything of you, don't go against her wishes. If frustrated, she may have a relapse and become sick again. That would be very dangerous."

"Yes, sir. As you say."

After a few more minutes of conversation, the doctor bid them a cheery farewell and got up to leave. Mr. Prefecture accompanied him all the way out to the sidewalk. He clasped the doctor's hand between both of his own and bowed low to bid him farewell in a very respectful manner. But as soon as the car pulled away, Mr. Prefecture whirled around and stomped into the house ahead of everyone else, flushed with anger. He called his wife and Mr. and Mrs. Head Clerk to come to him.

"The old geezer can say what he wants, there's no call to let that jerk come around here to visit." Everyone stared at him in amazement. Mr. Prefecture continued: "When I heard that fellow use the word 'loved one,' it made me angry enough to bust a gut! . . . But never mind. I'm taking Nga back to my prefecture headquarters."

Mr. Head Clerk pleaded for Nga to be left in Hanoi. Finally, the Prefecture Chief agreed, but with one condition. "You're not to let that doctor talk you into anything foolish."

"Brother, I believe that if the illness is psychological, the treatment should be psychological."

"Aghh, no more psychological this and psychological that! What about the moral teachings of our forefathers? Do you intend to throw them all out?"

"No, brother, but I do believe that morals are appropriate to a particular era, because they are made up by the people who belong to that era. So morality should be appropriate to the times. What's more, morals are for those who are rich and comfortable. They're designed so that the common people can never follow them because of the difficulties involved. Their purpose is to set apart the lifestyles of the upper and lower classes. So there are times when our moral teachings differ from those of the West, and there are times when the morality of previous generations is harmful to the present one."

His face empurpled, Mr. Prefecture pounded the table.

"Don't you preach sophistry to me! If Nga dies, she dies. There must be no more of this outrageous behavior!" The entire household fell silent. Everyone trembled in fear.

The weather grew even warmer and Nga's condition grew even worse, but Mr. Prefecture insisted that the doctor's advice was to be ignored. Nga was to have no treatment except traditional Vietnamese medicine. Mr. Head Clerk was very worried about his niece's chances for recovery.

Once, in frustration, he remarked to his wife: "Niece Nga's situation can be very dangerous if we're not careful. And whatever happens to her, she'll be a victim of her ancestry."

"How so?"

"If she were the child of an ordinary family, the treatment of this illness would be a very simple matter. Or even if she were our own child, we could expect a successful cure. The problem is that older brother and sister are too old-fashioned, that's what makes everything so difficult. Really, being born into a good family is a hardship."

Mr. Head Clerk recounted to his wife the entire story he had pieced together of Nga's innocent and tragic relationship with Chi. She asked him:

"So have you told the doctor about all these complications?"

"Yes, I have."

"That's why he talked to older brother and sister that way, isn't it?"

"That was his way of getting the idea across. He told me quite frankly that we should get Chi over here to visit Nga. Her sickness comes from being frustrated in love, so love must be used in the treatment."

"Then we have to let those two get married?"

"What do you think? And why not? Chi's a person, too, isn't he?" "Yes, but—"

"Women are always so silly and obstinate."

"Not at all. It's all right for them to get married. After all, if Chi succeeds in his studies, he'll probably become a man of substance, won't he? So, once he has succeeded, then go ahead and get married; but what will it look like if they get married right now?"

Mr. Head Clerk burst out laughing and shook his head: "When we Vietnamese get married, it isn't for any reasons of the spirit, is it? Most boys and girls just look at parents or ancestors or property when they marry. Actually it isn't two people getting married at all, it's just wealth and honor being joined."

"So you intend to let that fellow Chi come here to visit Nga?"

"I'm very much in favor of it, but I don't entirely have the authority. . . ."

"Why don't you explain all this to older brother and sister so they'll understand that Chi's visits are necessary! . . . Then just wait until she's been cured and let them decide if they want to get married."

"But they have to get married, because they do love each other. The doctor was not ambiguous in his diagnosis."

"What do you mean by that?"

"The doctor said we should let Chi come to visit Nga freely, let them talk to each other as they wish. No one should pay any attention to them. Anything they want to do, let them do it; just so she recovers from this illness."

Mrs. Head Clerk giggled and slapped her husband on the back, blushing: "You monkey! Who ever heard of such a thing?"

But Mr. Head Clerk remained serious. "No, I mean it," he replied. "Precisely that is our only chance."

"Well, then, are you going to tell Chi all this quite openly?"

"Oh, yes. I'll tell him she is his wife, and that he has the right to tell her anything or instruct her as he will."

"Isn't that a heck of a thing to do?"

"Let the medicine fit the illness," Mr. Head Clerk frowned. "If we keep on being bothered by this and afraid of that, she just might die on us. Who knows?"

"We'll be ridiculed by everyone."

"Being afraid of people's laughter is no better than sitting back and waiting to cry over her death. This is a human life; is that some game? There! You see? That's the burden of a high and mighty family. A good family is forced to follow morality. And as I told older brother, morality is not any law of nature. It's just something that was made up by other people a long time ago. That's why a certain morality may not always be appropriate for a particular time or a particular place, and sometimes morality can hurt people. To get right down to the natural law, when necessary, people must do whatever they have to do to prevail; they must go against even natural law, let alone morality."

Mrs. Head Clerk urged her husband to try to explain everything to his older brother. "I'm just a woman, and when you spoke to me just now even I understood."

"But a Confucian scholar can split hairs worse than . . . a thousand women," Mr. Head Clerk replied. After further discussion, Mrs. Head Clerk sighed, "I'm beginning to see the problems of a prominent family."

Mr. Head Clerk smiled. "It was because Nga saw this, and knew that she couldn't break out of this circle of big family teachings, that she became a victim. But if we want her to recover, we have to smash those teachings."

With his duty clearly before his eyes, Mr. Head Clerk braced himself to confront his older brother. Mr. Prefecture was predictably outraged by his brother's behavior, and even more so by his arguments:

"What sort of brother is such a miserable creature as this? Just because you've learned to mumble a few words of French you think you can openly criticize the beautiful traditions of our forebears. Now you're a man of substance. You have a nice house, ample possessions, a beautiful wife and lovely children—and who do you have to thank for these things? How can you be so ungrateful? Morality must be respected above everything else. And good families like ours must be especially respectful of morality. Even when morality seems constraining, you just have to close your eyes and follow it, or you're going to go wrong! You listen to that doctor telling us to have that so-and-so come up here to cure little Nga. Do you want to bring some elephants around to tear down our ancestral tombs?"

But Mr. Head Clerk was determined to save his niece. He misled Mr. and Mrs. Prefecture and secretly allowed Chi to visit Nga many times. He told Chi:

"She thirsts after nothing but your love. You use love to cure her."

Chi was embarrassed, so he blurted out: "Yes, sir, I'll follow your every word to the best of my ability. Because I know that there were many times when Nga just wanted to be nice to me, and it was only because I treated her so coldly that she became disappointed. Then she began thinking about class, and she became heartbroken, and ended up like this. And that may be half my fault."

Mr. Head Clerk sighed: "In a family of noble descent like

mine, if you want to cast away class barriers, it's a very
difficult thing to do. One group wants to close their eyes and
preserve old traditions. The other group wants to put new
ideas into action. So the people on both sides come to view
each other only in terms of these primal notions, and they
come into conflict."

Chi said sadly, "Only we are not bound by these things."

"That's right. And nothing is so wonderful as the freedom
to follow your own ideas."

Gradually, Nga's condition improved. Chi worked diligently at
devising ways to talk with Nga and bring her closer to reality. He
proceeded entirely out of concern for Nga's welfare.

But love could not have been avoided. It came stealthily. It
came drawing two tender young hearts close together. It
came causing Chi to grow reckless and bold. So there came
a time, while Chi was sitting beside Nga and rubbing her
back, when he said softly: "Nga, darling, if I hadn't been so
hard-hearted toward you, you wouldn't have become so
unhappy."

Nga was moved by this, and she raised her innocent eyes
to look at him. Chi felt his face grow warm until it seemed to
be ablaze. He put a trembling hand on Nga's neck. He wove
the five fingers of his other hand through Nga's fingers and
held her hand to his mouth. While those two rib-cages
expanded, four eyes gently met, shining through a halo of
tears, as though to demonstrate that the tunes in those two
hearts were harmonized to but a single beat.

Nga recovered completely. Everyone rejoiced, until one day
Mrs. Head Clerk whispered to her husband: "Nga might be pregnant." Poor Mr. Head Clerk was totally dumbfounded. He had to
muster the courage to persuade his older brother to let Nga and
Chi get married at once. Mr. Head Clerk dared not postpone this
dreaded task, but when the meeting took place he had difficulty
speaking the heavy words. After broaching the advisability of an
early marriage for Nga, he was finally prodded into revealing that
he was suggesting that she marry Chi. Finally, Mr. Head Clerk was
forced to tell his older brother that Nga was pregnant. Mr. Prefecture went rigid and then slumped in his chair, as if struck by a
thunderbolt. A heartrending scene ensued.

For several days Mr. Prefecture refused to appear in public.
He felt so shamed, he didn't want to see anyone. Even

though not a single person had been told that Nga was
pregnant, he still felt as if everyone knew about it. Every
day was the same, from morning to night the doors and
windows of their residence were shut tight. . . .

Mr. Prefecture kept Nga restricted to the house, but forbade her to
show her face in his presence. Each suffered in private, writhing in
humiliation, wanting to die. Nga agonizingly reviewed in her mind
all that had happened.

So Nga felt very sorry for her parents. But no matter how
sorry she felt for them, she felt even more sorry for Chi. She
felt not the least bit repentent. She just resented the
prominence of her family and the rigid and subservient
attitude that descendants of such families had toward their
forebears. This was what forced her father to be a slave to a
meaningless code of ethics. This was what made her father
contemptuous of everyone in the poorer class of people. This
was what—alack and alas—had disrupted her true love and
thwarted her life.

And the basic cause of all this was simply that she had
looked upon Chi as a person, merely as a person, just like
herself. . . . So the notion of social class had been unable to
triumph over Nga's feelings of respect for human dignity.
When she thought of her father, she saw him as an opposing
force, pulling her back, placing her in the old framework
again. Yet, when she stood confronted by love, Nga no
longer felt that any other force could possibly restrain her
heart. So she had boldly overturned the concept of class
distinction.

And now it had come to this. She had failed to fulfill her
duty as a daughter. Her love had been broken up. The old
was gone. The new had not materialized. It was as if she had
been bumped out of the four circles: out of love, out of piety,
out of the old, out of the new. Truly she was a little bamboo
sampan in distress. . . .

Meanwhile, Madam Prefecture had mysteriously disappeared.
When she returned, she went to Nga's room.

"Your father and I are angry with you, but we still love you
very much, my child. You're still young and inexperienced. . . . Your father and I are certainly never going to give
our permission for you to marry that fellow. Don't hang on to

any vain hope of that. . . . How, then, are you ever going to be able to marry a decent person? After this, who would take you as a real wife? . . . Things haven't quite yet come to the point where you have to be a concubine. Your father and I just have to figure out some way for you to be as good as anyone else. Then we'll find some Mr. District or Mr. Prefecture who's lost his wife and talk things up so he'll ask for you to take her place. Then you can become Madam this or Mrs. that and have an honorable status, my child. . . . And so, your father and I have decided to cover up this entire story. In a little while I'm going to bring in some medicine and I want you to drink it, okay?"

"Mother, ma'am, what kind of medicine?"

Madam Prefecture leaned forward to speak softly into Nga's ear. "Something to get rid of the fetus, my child."

Nga refused to cooperate. "It's just a bowl of medicine to wash away dishonor," her mother cried, storming out of the room. Eventually the task of administering the medicine was turned over to Mr. Prefecture himself. When Nga resolutely defied him, he had Chi arrested and beaten. When Nga still defied his instructions, Mr. Prefecture put a gun to Chi's head. At last, to save Chi's life, Nga gulped down the medicine. The potent mixture was too strong for her system, and the book ends with her death.

The Ngas of this world were doomed to be victims of forces more powerful than themselves. In print and over bowls of soup at sidewalk cafes along the side streets of Hanoi and Saigon, young men and a few women grumbled about their families' old-fashioned ideas or lamented the narrow and self-serving conservatism of the colonial bureaucracy, but few of them put their ideas into action. At the office they were polite, respectful, and tried to please the boss. Most continued to live with their parents and to fulfill the demands of *hieu*. Virtually no one challenged his or her status superiors. To indulge in such self-assertive behavior during interaction with others of higher status was so un-Vietnamese a thing to do as to be an act of social suicide. It involved so many psychological and linguistic contradictions that it was almost a rejection of one's Vietnamese identity. Vietnamese did not do things like that, and they most heartily disapproved of people who did.

Girls like Nga were rare, and for a very good reason. To stand up to parental authority and social convention in Vietnamese society was to invite disaster. Novelists of every persuasion, feeling constrained to place believable toads in their imaginary gardens, acknowledged this social reality in all of their works. Even in novels, love matches never ended with everyone living happily ever after. In literature as in life, the new young people either contented themselves with mouthing pretty phrases in carefully compartmentalized aspects of their lives, or they were doomed.

MILITANT INDIVIDUALISM: *BREAKING THE TIES* To Nguyen Tuong Tam this was an intolerable state of affairs. He longed to provide a more powerful advocacy of the new over the old, of the individual over social constraints. He wanted to give the readers and writers of Vietnam a more potent role model. Determined to see a more militant espousal of individualism in Vietnamese fiction, Tam composed his own *roman à thèse*, appropriately entitled *Breaking the Ties*, to be published in *Mores* in 1935.

The protagonist of *Breaking the Ties* had to be a woman. In drawing the portrait of his heroine, Loan, Tam was simultaneously offering an exegesis of To Tam, of the character of Nga, and even of Mai. Through the character of Loan, Tam expressed his own attitudes and values in an all-out assault upon the citadels of conservatism of every kind, to effect a change in the setting of the social thermostat.

The novel opens in a familiar pattern. Like Kieu and To Tam, Loan falls in love with one man but is forced to marry another by the dictates of *hieu*. Like To Tam, and Khai Hung's character Loc, Loan places *hieu* above *tinh* and marries a man she scarcely knows to secure her parents' happiness. It was her own decision, but it was made under tremendous pressure, and from the outset she resents it. Loan begins married life with deep regrets and a chip on her shoulder.

On her wedding night, Loan retired early to await her husband, who was still chatting with the last of the guests. She viewed the lavishly prepared room with distaste.

> Tears began streaming freely down her face. . . . She smiled painfully, comparing her fate to that of a prostitute. If a prostitute had to offer herself to anyone and everyone in order to live, so too did she have to close her eyes and offer herself up to Than, whom she did not love, in order to see her parents happy.
>
> Loan suddenly remembered the very moment she had first arrived at her husband's home. Instead of stepping over the

charcoal brazier that had been left in the doorway, she had paused to look down carefully; and then she had knocked it over with her foot, pretending it was an accident. . . . Then, at the ceremony of the rosy threads, she had been placed to sit behind Than. Just as the prostrations were about to begin, she had calmly stood up and seated herself directly beside him.

In retrospect, she chided herself for being rude. She had promised herself beforehand that she would try to be submissive, to look upon her husband's parents as her own natural parents, and then she had immediately found a way to be provoking. If she couldn't love her husband's mother sincerely, she would try to respect her and be considerate of her, if only to shield herself from misery. She shook her head and grumbled: "Hypocrisy! We force ourselves to be hypocrites." . . . In the big family system, if there are no natural ties of love to bind one person to another people have to take false ones and bind each other with them.

In due course Loan gave birth to a baby boy. The infant was soon taken ill, and Loan's mother-in-law, Mrs. Clerk, took her grandson to a traditional healer.

Loan didn't intervene because she knew she had no power to prevent it. Submissively, twice a day she had gone with her mother-in-law to visit her child. After watching the boy grow paler day by day, Loan had grown suspicious. She inquired among her friends and was told that the amulet fellow's healing technique consisted of giving a drink of incense ash in water and that sometimes he even used a mulberry switch to drive away the evil spirits. In other words, he beat sick people. . . . She had never imagined there could be so savage a means of treatment. When she finally carried her child out and took him to be treated with Western medicine, it was too late. She could only wait for death to take him away.

Loan's sister-in-law, Bich, visited the infant at the hospital and brought home a gloomy report:

"That little child looked as green as a leaf, with black rings around his eyes, a glassy stare. . . . How vile! I don't know what those people can have done to bring him to such a plight."

Loan could see that Bich wanted to dump all the blame onto her. Bich repeated mournfully: "I don't know what they did to him."

"They tried to cure him of course; what else would they have done?" Loan replied.

Mrs. Clerk spoke up. "Oh, they cured him all right. . . . And it's only because I listened to you, because I believed in you that . . ."

Mr. Clerk, who was fond of his daughter-in-law, spoke up for her. "When using Western medicine you have to be patient to get good results."

Mrs. Clerk glowered at her husband. "You only have a voice to contradict me. Be patient until the moment of death, until he can't breathe any more, is that it?" Then she turned to ask Loan: "What do you think now?"

"I'm not thinking anything now," Loan answered. "I've already decided to use Western medicine until the end."

"Aha! You have decided!"

Bich raised her hand to wipe away the tears with the flap of her tunic.

Loan knew that Bich was crying partly out of pity for the child, but mostly as a rebuke to her. She asked herself bitterly how these people could be so lacking in human feelings that they would stop at nothing to give her a hard time, that they didn't even know enough to think of the agony of a mother whose child was about to die. She looked at Bich with resentment, and the more she watched her cry the more clearly she saw Bich's hypocrisy.

"I knew it," Bich said. Loan felt the hot flush come on her face. Unable to restrain herself any longer, she told Bich: "And just what is it that you knew? Please leave me in peace to take care of my own affairs." Bich looked up at her mother. "You'd better take it easy there," Mrs. Clerk said. "Your affairs?"

"Mother, my child is sick. It's my duty; I have to worry about it." As soon as she finished speaking, Loan knew that she had said the wrong thing. Mrs. Clerk was scowling. "You've got to learn that he may be your child, but he's my grandson. If you feel like killing him, then, are you to go right ahead and do so? You don't have the right."

Loan tried to mend her words. "Ma'am, I didn't intend to say that, mother." But Mrs. Clerk ignored her. She turned away and called out: "Where is my eldest son?" Seeing that Than was standing right there, she continued: "You intend to let your wife abuse her authority, do you? To be a man like you are and not be able to make up your own mind about anything for yourself! Your son is sick to the verge of death, and you just let your wife go ahead and do as she pleases, is that it? If you want to do something worthwhile, you go bring your son back here, bring him back to me right now."

Than looked at Loan and said: "Mother, ma'am, let it go until tomorrow, because right now . . ." Mrs. Clerk broke in: "I want you to bring your son home today, that's what I want."

Loan looked at her husband and said slowly: "Why bring him home? I'll tell you the truth. The doctor told me nothing can save him anymore. . . . I ask you please to let him die there in peace."

Bich was instantly on her feet. "Don't try to twist things around now, older sister, slandering and hurting other people. You ask yourself, just who in this house has ever mistreated that child so you could dare to say such a thing?" Mrs. Clerk pointed her finger in Loan's face and shook her fist. "Who mistreated him? Who killed him? Huh? You brat!" Loan leaned against the desk. Her hands gripped the edge of its surface tightly. While her husband's mother and his little sister both grumbled away at the same time, she felt her face darken. Without thinking, she blurted out: "Miss Bich! Do you have to know why he's dying? That amulet fellow, he beat my son to death! Have you got that straight yet? Don't you put the guilt for killing my own son onto me, for pity's sake. You think about that! Who killed my child? Who killed him?"

In her rage she had forgotten all about guarding her speech. Mrs. Clerk, sobbing, stood up and shook her finger in Loan's face as she shrieked: "There you go blaming me for killing him. He's your child, but he's my grandchild. . . ."

Loan was furious. Her hands were shaking. . . . She was just opening her mouth to argue when Than rushed over and grabbed her arm, scolding her. "Shut up! Will you be quiet this instant!" Mrs. Clerk said: "Do you mean that girl can speak so insolently to your mother and you aren't even going to give her one good slap? Give her a slap for me and see if she still has so much to say." Loan angrily jerked her arm away from Than and he stunned her with a slap across the face.

Things went steadily from bad to worse. Than had an affair, and when the girl got pregnant Mrs. Clerk told her son to take her as a concubine. Loan had no objections. But she found the ceremony

by which the girl, Tuat, was installed as a junior wife to be a loath-
some experience.

Loan looked down, unable to bear watching the spectacle of
Tuat bowing down on the mat in ritual prostrations to the
ancestors and to Mr. and Mrs. Clerk, because the sight
reminded her of the time several years ago when she first
walked into her husband's home. She felt that she was then
as Tuat was now. Even though her status and that of Tuat
were not the same, nevertheless they were both people who
had been purchased and brought home with great to-do to
prostrate themselves before other people in acceptance of
their role of being baby-making machines, of being little
servant girls without any wages. Loan had been married to
become a proper wife. Those rites had not been as hypocrit-
ical as these were now, when they brought her out here to
conceal, and even more to formalize, an adulterous affair.

Suddenly the voice of Mrs. Clerk was saying: "Where is
eldest daughter-in-law? Sit up here so she can perform the
ceremony." Loan looked around without comprehension.
With a start she asked herself: "Tuat kowtow to me? Tuat
kowtow to Than?" By then Tuat had come up before her,
looking down at the floor, cheeks flushed, looking embarrassed and pained, but very submissive, as if she were waiting only for Loan to give the command before falling to the
ground and prostrating herself before her as if she were
some kind of god who could cause happiness or disaster.
"Why," thought Loan, "should two people with a common
fate kowtow to each other to bring more shame upon
themselves?" . . .

Loan raised her hand in a gesture of refusal and said: "No
more, that's enough. I can't accept this." At once Mrs. Dao's
voice was heard. "That won't do. Sit up there so she can kowtow to you. If you don't want it, that's up to you. But a ritual
has to be a proper ritual. Above has to be above and beneath
has to be beneath. This person is going to live with you for a
long time. If you don't accept this, she may feel that you
disapprove of her, and that can only lead to trouble."

Now Loan understood why Mrs. Dao had come. She was
the representative of the senior wife's clan. Her task here was
to demand satisfaction. Loan was about to stand up and leave
when Tuat sat down on the mat and bent her head to begin
the ceremony. Loan was forced to sit back and accept what
was already taking place. She didn't want to exhibit displea-

sure for fear that people would think she was unwilling to
have a concubine taken for her husband. She felt her face
flush, and she was embarrassed for Tuat. She frowned down
at Tuat, who was bowing deeply at her feet, and thought: "Is
this a person or a thing?"

As time passed, Loan became even more estranged from the
entire household. It seemed to Loan that everyone was picking on
her, and her resentment kept growing. She noticed herself that this
constant conflict had "turned her into a different person, had given
her a sour disposition and stunted her soul."

One night, irritated with her husband, she left the light on and
pretended to read just to annoy him.

"Why don't you turn off the light when I ask you to?"
"Goodness gracious! You go to sleep. I need the light to
read by."
"I can't sleep while you have the light on."
"Just turn over and sleep with your face to the wall."
Loan was somewhat surprised by her gruff response, and
for the first time she had the idea of getting some pleasure
from putting her husband down. This is because when one
wants to resist after being bullied for a long time, it is always
necessary to overdo it in order to demonstrate that one can
tolerate no more. Loan had reached that point. For over a
week now she had had the idea that if it is easy for someone
to bully you, they are going to keep on bullying you. Whereas
if you want someone to be considerate of you, there is no
better way than to oppose them. Loan didn't realize that in
doing this she was actually beginning to reject the authority
of her mother-in-law, beginning to reject the existing big
family system. Loan had reached the point where she didn't
care about anything any more. She simply didn't understand
how she had put up with so much for so long.
She kept asking herself: "What is there forcing me to go on
and on in pain, misery, and shame?" The rationale of sacrificing herself just to please her parents was no longer strong
enough to lead her any further. She recognized that for a long
time now she had cowardly been living according to tradition.
She had not had the courage to destroy the customs that her
education had made her understand deserved to be abandoned, deserved to be destroyed. Loan was determined not
to turn off the light until she was ready to do so. "Please
leave me in peace so I can read. If you want the light off, get
up and turn it off yourself."

Finally Than became so exasperated with Loan's defiance that he slammed his foot into Loan's back, knocking her off the bed onto the floor. As Loan struggled to her feet, Mrs. Clerk's voice was heard from the hall:

"What are you doing in there to make such a racket? If you want to teach your wife a lesson, go ahead, but do it some other time. Keep quiet now so other people can get some sleep."

"Who teaches whom?" asked Loan. "If someone does the smallest thing, you want to teach them a lesson. I don't need anybody to teach me anything." "Oh, yes, and it is just that which makes you so ill-bred." "Being ill-bred is striking a helpless woman, is being one of a pack of cowards."

Mrs. Clerk came roaring into the room in her bare feet and demanded of Loan: "What was that? What did you say, you little brat?" Loan turned away and looked back into the room without replying. Mrs. Clerk continued: "I think I'll try a good slap on you and see if you still want to call anyone a coward."

"No one has the right to berate me. No one has the right to hit me."

"I have the right. You talk back to me, and you'll see."

"I am not in the habit of berating anyone. When we abuse others, we only dirty our own mouths."

That was the first time Mrs. Clerk had ever heard Loan say anything like that. She jumped with rage and her eyes bugged out; then she hurried herself forward to seize Loan and began to slap her furiously. . . . "I'm going to beat her to death." Then, gasping for breath, she told Than: "I don't want to dirty my hands by hitting her any more. Give her a good trouncing for me."

Loan smoothed her hair and looked straight into her mother-in-law's face. "You are a person and I am a person. Neither of us is any better or any worse than the other. If you strike me, I won't . . ." Without finishing her sentence, Loan jerked free and backed away. Mrs. Clerk clasped her chest and fell to the bed, crying: "She beat me."

"Don't slander me," said Loan. Than raced over. Loan told him: "I ask you, please, don't touch me." No sooner were the words spoken than a powerful blow to the chest made Loan knit her brow and rest her head against the wall. Then she was pushed to the floor. She struggled to her feet and retreated to the corner of the bed. At that moment she felt as if her dignity was not equal to that of an animal.

"If you want to keep on living, stand up." Mrs. Clerk was sitting up. She pointed her finger and said: "Beat her to death for me. If she dies, I'll be responsible."

Loan kept backing up. Than looked around in an agitated manner. Then, because it was near at hand, he picked up a copper vase and hurled it in her direction. Loan saw Than coming toward her and in a moment of panic she grabbed up the little knife for cutting book pages, from her nightstand, intending to hold it up to ward him off. Like a wild tiger, Than kicked at the copper vase, sending it flying at Loan. She ducked, but in doing so she stumbled and fell upon the bed with the knife still clasped firmly in her hand. Than had kicked too hard, and he too lost his balance. He fell heavily on top of Loan. She felt the knife press forcefully back against her hand and heard Than let out a yell.

Within minutes, Than was dead. Mrs. Clerk charged that Loan had planned the whole thing in advance, pretending to read before picking a quarrel so as to have at hand the knife to plunge into her husband's heart. Loan soon found herself on trial for her life, accused of premeditated murder. In the courtroom, where the officiating parties were French, the prosecutor calmly built his case step by step, with Mrs. Clerk testifying as a key witness. After summing up the evidence against Loan, he raised his arm to accuse her:

"This woman is a murderess. Her hands are stained with blood. Moreover, it is the blood of her husband, a gentle man, whose only single fault in his entire life was to marry a heartless woman. Miss Loan has gone to school. She has, in fact, completed four years of advanced study in elementary education. In Vietnamese society, such a person must certainly be intelligent. So we have here an intelligent woman. Why, then, in all of her household, in all of her lineage, is there not a single person who does not criticize her, who does not despise her? Is it not just because she was so intelligent that she became arrogant, that she had no regard for anyone else? She was contemptuous of her mother-in-law, contemptuous of her husband, contemptuous of her husband's father. To her, everyone else was uneducated. I'm sure you all clearly understand the danger of reading novels written by that gang of youngsters who know some French, that unseasonal blast of romantic wind which is blowing by and leaving so much destruction behind.

"Because she was arrogant, because she was romantic,

because she compared the wonders she read about in books with the commonplace reality before her eyes, she sought a means of escape. But what if she did wish to escape? She had no lack of opportunity. But Miss Loan did not see things that way. She was ready to kill her husband in a moment of rage. She used a means of escape that was merciless and inhuman. At that moment, more than anything else she was seeking to relieve her own feelings of anger. She did not realize that more than anyone else she herself was the person responsible for this anger. . . .

"I ask the court to punish her severely to set an example for others. This is not the first time that the court has had to try a case like this. These family conflicts are too numerous to count. Who knows how many young girls whose heads have been turned by that blast of romanticism I've just mentioned have forgotten all about their heaven-mandated roles of being devoted daughters-in-law and gentle wives, of being pillars of the family like the virtuous women in old Vietnamese society. In their twisted state of mind they want to destroy the family, which they mistakenly look upon as a place of imprisonment for them. When families are shaky, the society will be shaky, because Vietnamese society has been stable only thanks to the family.

"The French are here to preserve the social foundations of the people within the protectorate. We cannot be lenient, because to be lenient will mean to be weak. If the family is destroyed, the society will be destroyed; and it will be our fault. This is especially true in the case of these girls who resort to the theories we brought over here and taught them to destroy the very things it is our duty to preserve. Of course, they misunderstand. That is precisely the reason why we must demonstrate to them that they are wrong and that the reformation of society is no job for a bunch of youngsters who are still immature, still only half-educated, whose only conceit is that they are uninhibited."

By the time the prosecutor finished his speech, it seemed that Loan was doomed, but she showed no trace of emotion. Her defense lawyer rebutted the physical evidence and the sworn testimony condemning Loan, then in his summation turned to the larger issues raised by the prosecution:

"Unless I am mistaken the prosecutor himself said that the entire household hated Loan. But there is nothing to indicate that this was her fault. People hated her. This does not prove that she was arrogant. Loan is an educated woman, which means she is a woman who has progressed. But 'progressive' is not a synonym for 'romantic.' Loan is a new woman, but nevertheless she was willing to obey her mother, to marry a traditional husband and go to live with a traditional family." . . .

The lawyer proceeded to recount the story of how Mrs. Clerk had taken her grandson to the Taoist practitioner. . . . "It was Loan's mother-in-law herself who killed her own grandchild without even knowing it. And then it was she who blamed Loan for killing her own child. Now it is she who is blaming Loan for killing her own husband, and little does she realize that it is her own fault that her son is dead. Miss Loan's mother-in-law and that old-fashioned morality are the guilty parties.

"But if we move to a higher level and think of this more broadly, without looking at any particular person, we see that nothing that has happened is the fault of any one individual, but rather it must all be blamed on the current fierce conflict between the old and the new. We cannot avoid recognizing that fact. It is the French who have come here carrying Western culture with them. It is the French themselves who have taught people new ways of reasoning, who have given people new concepts about life.

"The prosecutor claims that the French are here to preserve the foundations of the people in their protectorate, and that this foundation is the family. I can agree with that. But we have also wholeheartedly taught them to progress, and so now we must let them progress. It is not only improper to restrain their progress; it is impossible.

"Vietnamese society today is not the Vietnamese society of the nineteenth century. The Vietnamese family cannot be left intact to be exactly like the Vietnamese families of previous centuries. In all the countries of the Far East—Japan, China, Thailand, especially in China, the original ancestor of Asian civilization—the status of the family is not as it was before.

"Preserve the family by all means. But please do not confuse preserving the family with preserving slavery. The system of slavery has long since been abandoned, and whenever we think of it we cannot avoid shuddering with horror. And yet, little does anyone realize that this wretched system still exists in the Vietnamese family. Loan's mother-in-law, without realizing it, out of a habit handed down to her, has resorted to just such powers, like a hundred thousand other mothers-in-law in Vietnamese society.

"These people who have absorbed the new culture have been imbued with ideas of humanity and individual freedom, so quite naturally they seek to escape from that system. This desire is very legitimate. But escape is not so easy as we might imagine. Except for those people who patiently live in submission, like Loan here, how many others are there who rashly sacrifice themselves to escape the burden?"

The lawyer pulled out of his briefcase some old daily newspapers marked with red pencil and read a few lines as examples. "There, do you see, distinguished sirs, that it is we who have the greatest guilt? We have these people learn new ways, and then do not create for them an environment that is appropriate to their new concepts.

"Find Loan guilty of the crime of murder? Loan did not murder anyone! Find Loan guilty of disturbing the family? Loan was the very person who most earnestly wanted to live in peace with the family. The only thing of which Loan is guilty is going to school, with her books tucked under her arm, to try to develop her intellect and become a new person, and then to return to live with old-fashioned people. That is her only crime. And that crime she has already atoned for with untold misery.

"Free Loan and you will perform an act of justice. You will actually be expressing the fact that this inhuman family system has come to the day of its demise and that it must now yield place to a different system appropriate to the new life of today, one appropriate to the concepts of those with a new education. Free Loan and you will free a person who has been unjustly accused. You will free a woman who has had the green spring of her youth wasted, who has sacrificed herself for this stern society of the old and the new."

Before the session closed Loan declared herself resigned to whatever punishment society saw fit to impose upon her:

Loan then turned to Mrs. Clerk. . . . "Now that I am no longer your daughter-in-law, I can speak frankly of the feelings I've had toward you for a long time. You and I are two people who can never understand each other, can never love each other. Yet, this being the case, we have had to live with each other; so there is no way we could have avoided conflict. This is not anyone's fault."

Loan was found "not guilty" by the French court and struck out alone to lead an independent life after breaking the ties that bound her to submission in the traditional model of family life.

Breaking the Ties was probably the most celebrated novel of the decade. Republished many times during the four decades following its initial appearance, it was required reading for high school students in South Vietnam until 1975. It may be the most powerful single document in the concerted early modern attack on the *yang* structures of tradition. Loan's response to her mother-in-law in the dramatic bedroom scene that resulted in Than's death was considered scandalous by many people at the time and has been controversial and widely quoted ever since. "You are a person and I am a person. Neither of us is any better or any worse than the other." With these two short lines, the entire sociocultural system of tradition was declared to be invalid.

Through the character of Loan, Tam attacked numerous elements of traditional culture: healing practices, rituals (weddings, death anniversaries), and values (especially *hieu*, or filial piety). The concept of role-based social hierarchy was denigrated in a variety of emotion-laden contexts. Loan was intended to personify the ideal qualities of the new Vietnamese woman. Yet, to some readers, Loan is too aggressive to merit complete sympathy. Sincerity and self-confidence verge upon arrogance and self-righteousness. To some extent Loan seemed to bring troubles upon herself by being intolerant, conceited, and quarrelsome. She was predisposed to take offense and to dismiss other people as "uneducated" or "old-fashioned." Significantly, these were qualities attributed to Nguyen Tuong Tam himself by some of his contemporaries.

Loan's defense lawyer was a device through which Tam could speak in defense of himself, his colleagues at *Mores*, and his followers. It was not Loan alone who was on trial, but the entire individualistic ideology of which she was a symbol and for which Tam was the leading and most articulate spokesman.

A REBUKE TO INDIVIDUALISM: *MISS MINH, THE SCHOOLTEACHER*

Loan, and Tam, had thousands of passionate supporters. But some other readers were disconcerted or annoyed by the novel. One reader of *Breaking the Ties* was outraged. Nguyen Cong Hoan promptly set about writing a novel that would be a direct criticism of it. This work appeared in 1936 as *Miss Minh, the Schoolteacher*.

Hoan's character of Minh was obviously based on Tam's portrait of Loan. Both girls were of the same age and social background, with almost identical educations. The first half of Hoan's novel was so similar to *Breaking the Ties* that Tam charged Hoan with plagiarism. Miss Minh was, like Loan, pushed by her mother into a marriage against her wishes. She too was disappointed with her husband, quarreled with his family (especially his younger sister), and clashed fiercely with her mother-in-law. Like Loan, Minh felt bullied and oppressed by an old-fashioned family, and her disposition soured.

> She asked herself whether she would be able to spend the rest of her life with Sanh if things continued like this. As for Sanh, Minh bore no hostility toward him. She knew that her husband was just a machine being directed by his mother and his sister. Sanh was a person who did not realize that there was something in this world called freedom and that it was a necessity of life. Once, out of curiosity, she had asked Sanh why he had ever asked her to be his wife. He responded that it was only because of the binding words of his father, spoken long ago.
>
> The honesty of her husband's answer made Minh feel sad. The marriage bonds between her and Sanh had no meaning at all to either one of them. They were no more than some sticky rice to be steamed and some peanuts to be boiled and shelled, so they could be mixed together and used to fill a dish to be placed upon the ancestral altar. And no one even knew whether there was anyone there to appreciate it or not. What these people had done was absurd! . . .
>
> Hurt as she was, she felt even more sorry for Sanh. She pitied Sanh because he was a young man, and as such he had more rights than a girl where marriage was concerned, but he had not known enough to exercise those rights. She really had never hoped to have so stupid a husband. She had never been one of those girls who wanted a meek man just so she could bully him. She had wanted a husband who was intelligent, who was loving, who understood the meaning of life. A husband who was fond of freedom himself and knew how to respect the freedom of others. She loved individualism. She was economically independent. She wanted emotional independence as well. She wanted to follow the new completely.
>
> Because of *hieu* she had been forced to marry Sanh. All she wanted now was to find some peace and tranquillity in which to live out her insipid and empty life devoid of love. But people would not leave her in peace. . . .

And so for Minh, as for Loan, things drifted from bad to worse. Being a schoolteacher and having friends in the Office of Education, Minh secretly arranged to have herself transferred to a teaching post in one of the provinces outside of Hanoi. She eagerly awaited the orders that would give her a pretext for evading the constant pressures of the old-fashioned household in which she was so unhappy.

> Minh received her transfer to Vinh Yen. But throughout the Tet holidays she concealed this piece of good news from her husband's family. She intended to wait until the seventh day of the new year, the final day of her vacation, to mention it to them. Then Madam Province Chief wouldn't have a chance of keeping her in Hanoi, no matter what she wanted to do about it.
>
> In the afternoon of the sixth, all of her girlfriends had a going-away party for her. . . . It was a gay party. They made each other laugh by rehashing old stories from their student days. But when the period of joking ended, they were all worried about Minh's plight. . . .
>
> Minh grew sad and sighed. Thuc slammed her hand down on the table and said: "Who can blame me for putting up with all that talk about not being able to find a husband? In fact, when I see the situation that exists between mothers-in-law and daughters-in-law in this society, I panic at the thought of marriage. It's better to live alone all your life."
>
> Duc held up her hand, saying: "That's why I admire my older sister so much. I doubt if any of you have run into a situation as tricky as hers. She has a life worse than anyone else's. Not only is her mother-in-law as cruel as can be, her husband is a good-for-nothing playboy. Yet she has the guts to put up with all of it."
>
> "That's because those women are shaped in the old mold," said Thuc. "My father's sister is the same. I'd have walked out of there long ago, but she keeps throwing herself back to get more humiliation. . . ."
>
> "My sister's that way too," Duc added. "I just don't understand women like that."
>
> "Well, I think they're weaklings, cowards! They don't have the nerve to resist because they don't have any jobs. They're afraid they couldn't survive away from their in-laws."
>
> Minh, who had been listening in amazement, was very moved. All at once Duc asked: "Sister Minh, you have to figure out some way to avoid getting stuck with the repu-

tation of being one of that crowd with a 'new-fangled' education, don't you? Or are you going to become a proper married lady and submit to your husband, no matter how silly he is, just to conform to that good old ethical system that's been around for a couple of thousand years?"

Xuan answered for Minh by asking Duc: "And what would you do if you were in her situation?" "I wouldn't consider getting married. I'm too much of a pessimist. I could never cooperate with that old-fashioned crowd." "But you must at least have some idea about how to cope with it." "You've got to realize, I've had lots of proposals, and I've turned them all down because the fellow still had parents, especially a mother, still alive. If any man expects to get me, he has to agree to let me set up a separate residence from the very beginning, and that we'll have nothing more to do with his family." "And what if they won't let you?"

Duc stood up and broke off the conversation. "If they don't agree, then that's the end of that! We don't have to get married."

Xuan asked Thuc: "And what would you do if you were in Minh's place?" "I'd have started off by not letting my mother-in-law push me around. I'd have done as I darned well pleased." Minh smiled with a sigh. Thuc continued: "That's right! In my opinion the old and the new can never meet. And if you let them come too close together, both suffer from it. You have to follow the age in which you live. That's the only sensible way. If you cling to outmoded customs, who can put up with that? We've got to let those old-fashioned people know that we really are new, that we're better than they are. After all, we are educated, and we've got to show some self-respect. We are people, and we must have our rights!" . . .

Xuan shook her head sadly. "The problem of marriage still hasn't been solved for us, and we're going to be miserable until it is." "And why should we have to wait for someone else to do something about our problems? What I say is, chuck out all those empty discussions and idle words we read in newspapers. We need some suicide squads, some people willing to sacrifice themselves, to give up their own happiness. That's the only way to get those old ladies to stop being so cruel." "What do you mean? Are you talking about a lot of suicides? Of divorce suits? People just leaving their families?" "That's just what I mean!" "That's terrible! Just listening to you say those things gives me the creeps."

Thuc raised her hand and said with determination: "We've got to overturn the old system, breaking the ties with the old-fashioned family." Minh spoke up with enthusiasm. "I'm very much in agreement with sister Thuc. That old family system has turned me into someone who is always angry at life, always dissatisfied. I used to be such an easygoing person, but now I'm foolhardy and rash. I anticipate dreadful things and then I want them to take place quickly. If they don't happen, I'll precipitate them. Just wait and see."

But Minh's in-laws learned of the impending transfer and prevented her from leaving. The family conflict then worsened. One day Mrs. Province Chief gave Minh a sound thrashing. Minh seized upon this as a chance to escape, a good excuse for breaking the ties with the old-fashioned family that was oppressing her.

Minh had everything figured out in advance. She stopped by Xuan's house to borrow some money and went directly to a doctor's office to get the marks of her beating certified in writing. She was determined to do something big. With the doctor's certificate in hand, she went to her family home to discuss the matter with her aunt, the wife of her father's younger brother. She wanted to get her aunt's permission to take action against her mother-in-law.

When the aunt saw Minh, sobbing, display her black and blue marks, she was moved to pity. Shaking her head, she said: "I never thought the woman would go so far. But, still, you should follow the example of your father's sister and be patient." Minh was still crying. "I can't be patient. This time I've made up my mind to do something about it." But her aunt persisted. "Try patience first, and see what happens. Patience is the only way, without it people cannot live together."

"But auntie, I can't live with that woman any longer. Especially now, since the whole clan rejects me." Her aunt smiled. "Then how come other people manage to live with their mothers-in-law?" "That's because they don't understand maintaining personal dignity, they don't know how to respect themselves. Mrs. Province Chief looks upon me as an enemy. Why in the world should I have to regard her as a mother? Ever since I got married my life has been nothing but misery and humiliation. Everyone wants to be happy, don't they? Without happiness, who would feel like going on living?"

"You shouldn't get so discouraged."

"I know I've been wretched since the day I got married. I've

got an education. I know how to think for myself I understand how to follow the new completely. Yet I still have to
accept being put down under the system of an old-fashioned
family. People will laugh at me as a new person who doesn't
know anything!"

Solemnly, her aunt replied. "That's right, this new of yours
is better than the old. You can't tolerate being repressed by
the old family system. But there was nothing new about your
mother. There's nothing new about me. There's nothing new
about our whole family. How were you able to put up with
us? The way you distinguish between the old and the new, I
think you're just imitating words you've heard used by other
people. You're trying to justify yourself, trying to separate
yourself from other people because they don't share your
ideas. Must the old and the new really be as far apart as you
imagine them to be?"

Minh was silent. Her aunt continued. "There is only right
and wrong in this world. It seems to me as if you want to live
only for yourself. What do families become then? Who cares
about anybody else any more? What if everyone seeks their
own happiness, if your mother had lived her own life, if I
lived my own life, if Mrs. Province Chief lived her own life, if
all of us went our own way, thinking of nothing but selfishness? If everyone's household became that way, what would
life be like? I think that even though we all live with certain
natural rights, because our lives touch upon each other, we
should each sacrifice a bit of our rights for everyone else. And
nothing is lost that way, because we get back whatever we
give many times over in sacrifices that other people make for
us. Happiness comes from our way of thinking, the way we
see things. But it seems as if nowadays people believe that
the external trappings of happiness are most important."

Minh was still determined to make her escape. With Xuan's help
she arranged for an old admirer of hers to pick her up late one
night to take her on an emergency trip. No one, not even the
young man who was to drive away with her, realized what she
was doing. It was a foolproof scheme. She had planned with great
patience. At last the night arrived when she would be breaking the
ties with the old family system.

Minh latched the door and went down to her room, listening
to the ticking of the clock. She was anxious. . . . She was
going to go far away. This journey was going to take her to

some happy place and never again would she return to this house in which she had been so long confined.

She glanced around the room. . . . Suddenly she noticed a picture of her mother on the wall. In her haste she had almost forgotten and left it behind.

She took the picture down and held it in her hand, looking at it intently. . . . In her mind she reviewed the days of her childhood. She saw them as a carefree and happy time. She imagined Mrs. Province Chief's stern face, and Oanh's impertinent conversation. She thought of her mother's sister and grew uneasy. Then she thought of her father's sister, and she had to sigh and smile. She shook her head. "Patience!"

When that word "patience" came to mind, she closed her eyes and tilted her head back against the chair. She found ringing in her ears all those words spoken by familiar relatives praising her father's sister for being such a good daughter-in-law. She compared her aunt's situation with her own. She thought of the harmonious family setting in which her aunt lived, how everyone in the entire lineage cherished and admired her aunt. She was moved and felt perplexed.

"Should I really follow European ideas to smash an Asian family?" Her mind wandered in confusion, but then she thought decisively: "I must let the new triumph over the old!" Triumph over the old! If Minh was determined to follow the new, she had to triumph over the old. She thought of Mrs. Province Chief. Mrs. Province Chief hated her. If she ran away now and abandoned the woman's son, she'd be alienated forever. Never again would she accept a new-type girl as a daughter-in-law. She would hate the new with unswerving bitterness. Her resentment of the new would be incredibly deep. All at once, Minh felt a surge of elation. She was pleased at the thought of making Mrs. Province Chief afraid of the new. "Afraid of the new." Minh was jolted by those four words. Her head reeled. She rested her chin on her hand. "People fear the new because they—" Minh hesitated, then pressed her hand against her chest. "Because they hate it, they resent the new. People think the new is something altogether bad." She bounded to her feet. "But the new isn't bad. It's very good, better than the old. If we want to avoid having a bad reputation for being new, what we have to do is get the old to respect the new."

She sighed and kneaded her forehead with her hand. "We have to demonstrate that the new is superior to the old. The best thing to do is to get the old to admire the new. That's the duty of the new people. So what should we do?"

Minh screwed up her face and glanced around, as if looking for an answer. The churchbell chimed, bing bong bing bong, four times, then leisurely sounded eleven gongs. She was in a panic. Every stroke of the bell shook her to her very soul. . . . She folded her arms and shuddered. "What should I do?"

In a frenzy she dashed up to the garret, threw open the shutter and peered out. She saw Nha slowly button up his jacket and glance at his watch, then look toward the house. She looked at the car and noticed how old it was. The old and the new, she thought, Nha and that old jalopy. Then she thought of her father's sister and her family.

The engine began to turn over. Minh raced down the stairs on tiptoe. She grabbed up her suitcase, then put it down. Picked it up again. Put it down. . . . The sound of the engine drew near. Boldly she peeked out the door. "I've got to decide. One way or the other!" On that thought she crumpled to the floor, sobbing.

Out on the street the sound of the automobile was very loud. It was directly in front of the house. Minh was at her wit's end. But the engine did not falter. It roared, diminished, and gently faded away into the silence of the night.

Minh abruptly came to her senses, opened wide her eyes and clasped her breast. Looking bewildered, she strained to hear the sound of the car that was no longer there. "In the heat of the moment I almost debased the new. Breaking the ties with the old family is a selfish thing to do. It leads people to ridicule the new, to be repulsed by it, to resent it. Whether one follows the old or the new, the goodness of the person is what is important."

So Minh stayed with her husband's family. She tried very hard to be cooperative, helpful, and polite. She learned to see things from her in-laws' point of view. She used her intelligence and education to help the family, never to oppose it or escape from it. Gradually mutual respect and even fondness for each other emerged on both sides. The old and the new could live together. It was not easy; but, with patience, it was possible. "Breaking the ties" was a foolish and selfish thing to do.

Nguyen Cong Hoan had pronounced Loan—and by implication

Nguyen Tuong Tam—to be guilty as charged. They were guilty of glorifying selfishness and inciting conflict. Tam and Loan were brash, impatient, and immature. Tam's brand of individualism, Hoan implied, was shortsighted; it was wrong. With his portrayal of Miss Minh, Nguyen Cong Hoan signified a resounding rejection of Tam's proposed setting of the thermostat. Hoan believed Tam was advocating a course that could lead only to disaster. He should, like Miss Minh, come to his senses and open his eyes.

The Paradigmatic Battle Continues

The Vietnamese reading public understood all this by-play quite well. *Miss Minh, the Schoolteacher* was widely read and discussed. Nguyen Tuong Tam was furious, and Hoan's work came under scorching attack on the pages of *Mores*.[30] Meanwhile, Tam had been at work on a new novel of his own, called *Loneliness* (*Lanh Lung*), an attack upon the Neo-Confucian interdiction of widow remarriage.

The protagonist of the novel is Nhung, an attractive twenty-three-year-old widow with a young son. She continues to live with her mother-in-law after her husband's death, as part of the extended family. Nhung, too, falls in love and makes a bid to break the ties and live her own life. But she is a weaker character than Loan; and she fails, condemning herself to a lifetime of "loneliness."

Khai Hung too maintained the attack upon tradition by writing a series of novels championing the freedom of the individual against oppressive and corrupt social institutions. *Family* (*Gia Dinh*, 1935) was a scorching indictment of the "family mentality" that had been so prized in traditional times, and still was by most people. One of the major themes in this complex novel involves the corruption and emasculation of a basically decent and intelligent young man named An. Painstakingly, Khai Hung depicts the tacit conspiracy between traditional families thirsting for prestige and status and a corrupt colonial bureaucracy in need of pliable minions.

> An was a progressive thinker. He wanted to live an appropriate life amidst the ricefields, but both his paternal and maternal lineages wanted him to become an official. This strong family pressure reached a point where, although he was stubborn and persistent, in the end he had to give up his ideal of personal happiness and continue his studies to become an official. He had to do this to satisfy the ambitions of his wife,

of his mother's brother, of his father's younger brother, to eat above and sit before the others in the inner *dinh*, in order to satisfy his family's mentality of status competition.[31]

An did what he had to do under extreme family pressure, but with great reluctance. While his family took great pride in his official status, he was embarrassed and disgusted by it:

> These days the very word "officialdom" has taken on a strangely terrifying meaning. Even I tremble when I hear the stories about what we do, about the cruel schemes of some unscrupulous district and prefecture chiefs who only wanted to become officials so they could exploit the ignorant peasants. I knew all this, but I got mixed up in it anyway. Aghh! And it's all because of my wife, because of father's brother, because of mother's brother—it's entirely because of my family.[32]

In *Inheritance* (*Thua Tu*, 1936) Khai Hung portrays the petty quarrels and intrigues within an upper-middle-class family squabbling over who shall control the family estate. *Escape* (*Thoat Ly*, 1936) is the heartbreaking tale of a girl who tries to escape from her constricting family life several times, only to be thwarted by fate and a cunning stepmother who resents her taste for independence. Only through her untimely and pathetic death does she finally escape from the prison of family life.

From 1932 until 1936 the pages of *Mores* contained a steady barrage of such attacks on the traditional *yang* elements of society, focusing especially on the traditional family system that was the bulwark of the oppressive social structure they had to overthrow if their ideals were to be realized. Authentic participation in traditional society was restricted to people who were firmly embedded in the hierarchical pyramid of *yang* subsystems: family, village, national bureaucracy. But the Self-Strength Literary Movement in particular, and the new Vietnamese literature in general, launched status-leveling attacks on those who were attached to such roles and glorified or defended those outside the traditional system, the "nonpersons" of traditional Vietnamese society.

The credo underlying many articles, short stories, and novels of the day is that these "nonpersons" are the most genuine of people. They make mistakes. They suffer. They sin. They fail themselves and others. But they are authentic, alive, aware. They may not have the right answers, but they are right to question and to challenge the sterile conventions of a decadent, unjust, and irrational society. In the view of the world shared by Tam and his colleagues and followers, the lowliest among them was "more of a person" than the high and mighty hypocrites who rose to the upper levels of society by blindly following convention and unthinkingly doing whatever others expected of them.

Vietnamese society was beginning to polarize around a profound and elemental disagreement over the definition of "personhood," two contradictory and irreconcilable bases for one's sense of selfhood. This was at the very heart of the conflict, not just between the old and the new, but between diverging visions of what the new should be as well. Other writers painted the nonpersons of society in less flattering terms, but went even further in excusing their deviancy. With a more deterministic view of the world and less faith in the power of individual free will, these writers asserted that all people were what society had made them.

This evolving debate over the nature of modern Vietnamese culture and society entered a new phase and broadened considerably in May 1936 when a Popular Front government assumed power in France. Leftists were able to participate much more openly in public debate in Vietnam. Between 1936 and 1939 the Marxist worldview, especially but not exclusively as interpreted by the Indochinese Communist party (ICP), was propagated with great intellectual vigor in several new publishing ventures. Party intellectuals articulated their views on everything from rural poverty to literary criticism: educating sympathizers, savaging opponents, and offering the confused and uncommitted youth of Vietnam an all-encompassing worldview and a set of principles for action.

Three young men who were drawn together in this spate of activity began their move from obscurity onto the pages of history. Pham Van Dong and Truong Chinh (Dang Xuan Khu) had both become involved in anti-French activity in their teens, both had traveled to Canton, met Ho Chi Minh, joined the Revolutionary Youth League, and been converted to communism. Both had then returned to Vietnam to become organizers/proselytizers for the party. Both had been imprisoned in the 1930–31 crackdown by colonial authorities. With their resolve hardened by five or six years of harsh imprisonment, alongside like-minded individuals, they both returned to Hanoi early in the Popular Front period to advance the interests of the Indochinese Communist party.[33]

Vo Nguyen Giap was five or six years younger than these two

party stalwarts.[34] He had attended the prestigious Quoc Hoc School in Hue—following in the footsteps of Ho Chi Minh and Pham Van Dong, and Ngo Dinh Diem and his brothers. While Giap was a schoolboy in Hue, Phan Boi Chau, the hardy old "soldier of *nghia*," was living there under house arrest, and sometimes young Giap went to visit the old man and listen to his stories, imbibing his patriotic rancor. He also read, and admired, some underground literature by Ho Chi Minh. By the time he was fifteen, Giap was expelled from school for involvement in protests. At age sixteen he was a revolutionary; at eighteen he was in prison.

But soon the young Giap was out of prison and studying at a lycée in Hanoi. By 1933, at age twenty-one, he did so well in the fiercely competitive examination system that he gained admittance to the University of Hanoi, the capstone of the French educational system in Indochina, where a few hundred carefully selected "native" students were permitted to receive a university education. There he met Pham Van Dong and Truong Chinh, who converted him to their cause.

In 1937, when he was about twenty-five years old, Vo Nguyen Giap achieved a law degree from the University of Hanoi, got married, and joined the Indochinese Communist party. With prodigious energy Giap undertook a multitude of tasks, excelling at each. He continued his university studies, specializing in political economy. He taught history, at the same school where Nguyen Tuong Tam and Khai Hung had met a few years earlier. He was active as a journalist, editor, and author for several journals and a publishing house—all controlled, directly or indirectly, by the ICP. And he was active in a variety of organizations. When the Indochinese Democratic Front was formed, its leaders were Pham Van Dong and Vo Nguyen Giap.

Meanwhile, Nguyen Tuong Tam and his colleagues in the Self-Strength Literary Movement had overextended themselves financially, artistically, and politically. In autumn 1934 they began to publish *This Day* (*Ngay Nay*), a Vietnamese version of *Paris Match* or *Life* magazine, built around timely feature stories and investigative reports illustrated with high quality photographs. The managing director of *This Day* was Nguyen Tuong Cam, Tam's older brother; the editor-in-chief was Tam's younger brother, Thach Lam (Nguyen Tuong Lan). But Tam and his brothers lacked the money, the time, and the staff to maintain quality on two publications, and *This Day* was ruinously expensive to produce. Faced with a loss of prestige (and circulation), Tam halted publication of *This Day* after only thirteen issues. Then, in 1935, *Mores* was suspended for three months by the colonial authorities for its sharp criticism, and finally had its license permanently suspended in early 1936 for its savage satire and biting criticism of the colonial establishment. A hard-hitting critique of French colonialism by Hoang Dao (Nguyen Tuong Long) apparently triggered the official closure.[35]

This Day reappeared. Over the next three years it published some fine essays, fiction, and poetry, but the élan of the early years of *Mores* was gone. Neither Tam nor his many competitors could recapture the enthusiasm of those days. In 1937 Tam, Hoang Dao, and Khai Hung turned to direct social action, organizing a group called Beam of Light that energetically initiated a low-cost housing project on the outskirts of Hanoi, complete with a reading room and a public athletic field. Vo Nguyen Giap, among his many activities, joined with others (including the conservative scholar/educator Tran Trong Kim) to launch a massive literacy program. Writing about problems was no longer enough to satisfy any of these men. Even under the Popular Front, French actions were niggardly, despite rhetoric that was more liberal. But these articulate intellectuals never stopped writing and talking, about the French, Vietnamese society, and each other.[36]

To the Communists, the work of the Self-Strength Literary Movement was whining and effeminate. Why write about the psychological traumas of middle-class housewives, they asked, while thousands languished in French prisons and millions of other people were going hungry? Class consciousness became a more important theme. Now the poor people were decent and the well-to-do were evil. Criminals were merely responding rationally to an unjust and uncaring society. Among those who wrote in this vein was Nguyen Cong Hoan. In *Abandonment* (1937) Nguyen Cong Hoan presents the story of a young orphan boy who is driven by the cruelty and wickedness in society to abandon his innocence and turn to a life of crime. When asked about it, the young man explains his way of life in stark and simple terms:

> "You talk like a fellow with some education, like someone
> who knows how to use his head. If you wanted to lead a
> decent and proper life, there are all sorts of things you could
> do. Why do you choose to steal?"
> "Sir, I know this is a perilous occupation, and I am familiar

with many a way to earn an honest bit of money. But the world wouldn't let me live in peace, so that's why I naturally turned to crime."

"What a strange way to talk!"

"That is so, sir, but it's true. I went to live with people, but they didn't take care of me. I learned to do things, and people gave me no chance to do them. Every family I met treated me badly. People weren't nice to me, so I became an enemy of the people. Now I force people to give me what I need in my life."

Hoan repeats the same theme in *Dead End* (or *Impasse*, 1938): "Why do you steal, you rascal? Why don't you look for some honest work?" "Because, sir, I am hungry. Any work that will permit me to feed myself is honest enough for me."

The Psychic Costs of Colonialism and Failed Individualism: A Desperate Generation

The poet The Lu also wrote fiction. In one of his least successful endeavors, he created a Vietnamese "private detective." Detective stories are one of the quintessential myths of Western individualism, and perhaps only a cowboy could have been more out of place in the streets of Hanoi than The Lu's independent and detached Vietnamese sleuth. Even with The Lu's immense popularity to recommend them, these Vietnamese "mysteries," with their Holmesian flights of deduction and cold-blooded rationality, were received with massive indifference.[37] The emotional basis for such individualism was underdeveloped in the personalities of most Vietnamese.

Despite his varied and strenuous efforts to imitate Western models and assimilate Western cultural elements into Vietnamese vernacular literature, there was a strong "Vietnamizing," boundary-maintaining element in The Lu's work. One of the best-known and most powerful statements of Vietnamese nationalism and ethnic identity ever written is The Lu's superb poem "Remembering the Jungle," subtitled "The Words of the Tiger in the Zoo":

Gnawing upon our resentment, we stretch out in an iron cage,
Watching the slow passage of days and months.
How we despise the insolent crowd outside,
Standing there foolishly, with tiny eyes bulging,
As they mock the stately spirit of the deep jungle.

Here by misfortune, shamefully caged,
We are no more than a novel sight to amuse them, some
    plaything,
Forced to endure exhibition, just like the oafish bears,
Put next to a penned pair of panthers, carefree in their captivity.

We sustain ourselves with fond memories of days long past,
A time of freedom and assertiveness. . . .

When in dark caves we crinkled our god-like eyes,
All creatures fell silent,
And we knew we were lord of all living things,
In a garden nameless and eternal.

Where are those golden nights beside the bank of a stream,
When, intoxicated with the hunt, we stood to drink the melting
    moonbeams?
Where now are those rainy days that transformed the
    surrounding scene,
As we silently admired the renewal of our homeland?
Where now are the dawns with green trees bathing in sunshine,
Our radiant naps to the lullaby of singing birds?
Where now are the afternoons overflowing with blood beyond
    the jungle?
We awaited the death of the irksome sun to seize possession of
    our privacy.
Alas! Where now are those glorious times?

We now embrace the rancour of a thousand autumns,
Hating these never-changing scenes,
Scenes that are altered, commonplace, and false.
Flowers tended, grass trimmed, trees planted in tidy rows,
Trickles of black water with pretensions of being brooks,
Barely flowing down the crevices of these puny elevations.
A few leafy areas, meek, without mystery,
Seeking to imitate the wild visage
Of a realm steeped in a thousand years of nobility and darkness.

O stately soul, heroic land,
Vast domain where yesteryear we freely roamed,
We see you no more.
But do you know that during our days of frustration
We follow a great dream, letting our souls race to be near you,
O formidable jungle of ours![38]

This allegorical treatment of Vietnamese frustration under
French colonial rule articulated clearly yet with prized indirection

the common Vietnamese perception that their true worth was being denied, that they were being judged unfairly and out of their true context in an artificial situation that denied them genuine dignity. But the poets just a little younger than The Lu who came into prominence during the mid 1930s tended to be preoccupied with their own internal worlds. Their favorite topic was their own internal occurrences and private sensibilities.

A poet ten years younger than The Lu began publishing poetry in *Mores* in 1935 and soon became even more popular than The Lu himself. Ngo Xuan Dieu wrote what may have been the most individualistic, the most personal, and the most emotional poems of the time. For these and other stylistic reasons, Xuan Dieu's poetry also seemed the most Western. To the older, classically trained Vietnamese intellectuals, he epitomized the decadence of the younger generation. To one unfamiliar with Western literature, his poetry often seemed to be incomprehensible gibberish. To Xuan Dieu:

> To be a poet is to be lulled by the wind,
> To follow the moon in dreams, and drift with the clouds.
> To let the soul be bound by a thousand strands,
> Or splinter because of a hundred precious loves.
>
> .   .   .   .
>
> A thousand hearts are carried in one heart
> In order to understand the voice of the stream, the speech of
>   birds,
> The sound of sobbing in the rain, the cry of words struck by
>   beams of moonlight.
>
> Without wings, yet always eager to soar in flight;
> Mindful of celestial matters while entering a barnyard;
> Halting time in one teetering moment,
> Admiring the scenery between two sides of a leaf or a blade of
>   grass.
>
> I am but a tiny needle,
> And nature is ten thousand magnets.
> If the evening dew awakes intoxicated with the full moon,
> How can a poet be criticized for being too sensual?[39]

Far removed from the eternal cycles of family and village life where ancestors and posterity, life and death, harvest and planting formed a seamless whole as natural and reassuring as the recurring seasons, the modern urban intellectuals found themselves standing alone and frightened on a precarious perch from which both human relationships and natural processes appeared as threats to a fragile existence. Love meant not only fulfillment but vulnerability. The passage of time meant not only maturity but death. A morbid sense of alienation and vulnerability is apparent in much of this introspective poetry. To Xuan Dieu "Love" seemed risky and ephemeral:

> Love is just a little bit of death in the heart,
> For how often can one love in certainty that love will be
>   returned?
> Giving so much love, and receiving so little of it;
> Because people are fickle, or indifferent? Who knows?
>
> .   .   .   .
>
> They wander lost in the somber darkness of sorrow,
> Those fools who follow the footprints of love.
> Because life is an endless desert,
> And love is an entangling web.
> Love is just a little bit of death in the heart.[40]

Melancholy often lapsed into despair, as in "Nothingness":

> But alas, I'm going to die!
> I'm a chap who uses his teeth to pinch the sun,
> One whose heart contains the bloody tides of the earth,
> Who clings to life with the fingernails of both hands.
>
> One who drinks of love till it overflows his lips,
> But alas, I'm going to die.
> Some day my glowing eyes will no longer be black,
> Youth will wither, my face will grow ugly.
>
> Some day when old age is binding my hands,
> And I struggle to perceive the rays of day,
> While disease gnaws into my bones like a piercing serpent,
> I'll sit and grope for the memory of today.
>
> .   .   .   .
>
> The other night I sat alone in agony,
> Listening to the hours pass, wracked with sorrow.
> I had only a small light for a friend beside me,
> But the flame, while it lasted, resisted the long night.
>
> I tremble like a leaf, grow pale as winter,
> Sweat flows down my brow, eyes well up with tears.
> Pushed by years and stuffed with months,
> I have arrived to face the cold border of nihility.[41]

This was an extraordinarily morbid frame of mind for a young man in his mid-twenties. But Xuan Dieu was probably the most popular poet in all of Vietnam during the late 1930s and early 1940s, especially among younger Vietnamese, particularly high school students. For many young psyches, these were desperate times.

Another bright star on the literary scene in the late 1930s was a young man from central Vietnam who wrote under the pen name Che Lan Vien. His reputation was based primarily on one slender volume of poems, entitled *In Ruins*, published in 1937 when he was only seventeen years old. Although he was Vietnamese, his poems are mostly about Champa and written from a Cham rather than a Vietnamese point of view. It seems, however, that behind his preoccupation with the long-crumpled glories of Champa, deemed worthy of countless centuries of lamentation and regret, lay a view of Vietnam in the 1930s as a decadent and dying society whose true glory was "in ruins."

These early poems of Che Lan Vien are sad, musical, pensive, and metaphysical, containing an element of controlled madness. They often border on the grotesque. Death, decay, mutation, and grief were his favorite and most successful themes. Che Lan Vien's early poetry had a strained intensity, expressing a desperate quest for sensation, for meaning, for reassurance. Yet whatever he sought lurked beyond his grasp. His frenzied search for respite from a disconcerting sense of lonely individuality was hampered by the morbidity he projected onto everything he saw. This vicious cycle is revealed in a poem called "The Graves":

Bury deep that smile upon bright lips.
Kill those words of song that spring from far down in the
    throat.
Seek no more fresh flowers, vibrant colors,
Myriad birds, nor sounds of jade, my friend.

For each moment of joy but prompts the more
That madness buried at the base of dreamy souls,
That sadness in the dark citadel of the heart,
And in sorrowful eyes, images of innocence from the past.

All the Past is but an endless string of days,
All the Future is but a series of graves not yet fulfilled,
And the Present—do you know, my friend—
Is also the silent burial of the green days of youth.

In the summer sun, fresh leaves begin to change in hue,
Weaving the autumn whose arrival is imminent—as in our
    lives
The green days follow in fading succession,
Weaving the shroud that covers our souls.[42]

All experience was reflected back into the self in an orgy of intro-
spection, as in "The Funeral Procession":

Pale, cold torchlight.
Slender shadows from a row of tall bamboo
Flicker dimly on the coffin of a child
Carried through the chilling dew.
A sobbing old woman lays bare her heart.
I stare at the countless stars in silence, asking myself:
Since when has my soul been destroyed?
And might that dark coffin of a child
Not contain my corpse as well?
Vaguely, from the immensity of space,
I heard a star cast a soft reply.[43]

The poem "Creation" describes the frame of mind in which Che
Lan Vien wrote:

O Heaven! Today I am sick and tired
Of the colors and forms of this world!
The flesh is defeated; my eyesight exhausted;
The pleasures of madness and hope remain difficult to ward off!

I close my eyes to disregard the present,
Gradually shifting into the past upon my eyelids.
Changed, changed, and ever changing,
The world still has moments of transformation which await!

I close my eyes to let the dark shadows arise boundlessly,
Immense as in the deep of night,
To let my soul grow dark with the artificial,
In the world of the dead so long awaited.

Let the shades of ghosts and demons one by one appear.
Let their cries, their shouts of epilogue, reverberate in my ear.
Let me roll about, my soul intoxicated with illusion,
To put out of mind for a few minutes the scenes of this world!

Let my soul soar rapidly over great distances
In the dark night shadows of my eyelids,
And proudly assert: Here is a world
Created in a moment of grief.[44]

Cu Huy Can was born in 1919 and became acquainted with Xuan Dieu while they were both in high school in central Vietnam. In 1938, at the age of nineteen, he published his first and perhaps most famous collection of poems, *Sacred Fire (Lua Thieng)*. His poetry follows in the footsteps of The Lu and Xuan Dieu, and the influence and encouragement of Xuan Dieu has been publicly acknowledged. But a shift in tone can be detected in the poetry of Huy Can. The romantic exuberance that marked the early years of the "new" poetry had begun to decline. The emotions in *Sacred Fire* are muted. A sense of weariness and foreboding was beginning to outweigh the extravagant hopes and fears of the initial outpouring of romantic verse. Yet the alienation, loneliness, and sorrow that was so strong in the works of Xuan Dieu and Che Lan Vien bursts forth in the poetry of Huy Can as well. The pervasive melancholy of the times is captured in "The Sadness of a Rainy Night":

This rainy night makes me long for space.
The shivering of my heart intensifies the chill of the immense
    coldness. . . .
My ears take refuge in drops of rain upon the roof;
The sky seems heavy: I seem to be sad.

I listen to the confusion in my soul
Of distant feet on a long and lonely road. . . .
Drip, drop . . . softly, softly, drip, drop—
A hundred million gentle drops connecting unclear words.

Lovesick and lost, confused in direction,
I return to my propped-up pillow of dreams and listen with
    indifference.
The wind returns, my heart trembles unprotected.
The breath of clouds blows lightly on all four sides of my
    thoughts.[45]

The agony of many Vietnamese who espoused individualism has seldom been described with such intensity as in the poem "Reporting," also from *Sacred Fire*:

I shall come before your face, oh God,
To complain, when I have parted from this life,
When leaves fall, and my soul has sunk
To the other side of the world of humankind.

Before merciful God, I shall place
My heart, which shriveled and ached while on this earth.

I shall say: "Here are my tears,
Jade of sorrow, still intact, unmelted."

. . . .

Icy step by icy step, I have walked on alone,
In the naive belief that one soul could understand another,
Little suspecting that flesh and bones are rivers and mountains,
Separating people into distinct and lonely regions.

All of my soul I carried to the integrated whole.
From a poor family unaccustomed to commerce,
Even to those who but feigned a promising affinity,
To the integrated whole I gave all of my soul.

With knees buckling, I stand exhausted, waiting.
I'm looking with two eyes as black as night.
I've sobbed through many nights of deathly sadness.
Earthly existence—O God, pity me!

While very young, my fondness for friends knew no reserve.
In the greenness of spring, I tired myself in the pursuit of love.
But loneliness secretly engraved itself upon my brow,
And my heart has been adrift since the day of my birth.

Here is my heart, an entire life spent mourning the lack of love.
Here is my soul, abandoned by the world to desolation.
Look here, my feet are marked by thousands of scars,
Punctured by the thorns of life. Here are my hands, reaching
   for love.

O God, I return with head bowed.
My soul has wandered lost through one existence.
My sorrow has ripened. Please, no more! Pick me now!
Accept me, whether it be in hell or paradise.

And then I sob, and my head drops,
My eyes blur, and my hands fall to my side.
I don't know anymore—heaven or hell—
Forget, forget, forget I bear a human heart.[46]

Equally poignant is "The Human Body":

O God!
Just look, Lord. You gave us these bodies,
Vessels of flesh and bone, to contain our souls.

You gave us a pair of hands, like blooming flowers;
Sturdy legs, tapering like bamboo sprouts.

. . . .

Our necks are upright, like firm tree trunks.
Our shoulders are broad, like the surface of a brook.
O Lord! You have labored so mightily!
—But termites have burrowed into the castle.

Weakness follows weakness, thousands upon thousands of
  them.
Tomorrow's steps will accumulate upon the prints of today.
Oh, these bodies are vessels of sin!
The earth from which You made us has turned to muck.

Don't blood and bones ever tire out!
Doesn't the mouth ever spit out the bitter breast!
The body, inhaling death, doesn't tire of that pain in the
  grieving chest.
One hand still clasps the body, while the other embraces the
  grave.

Take pity, Lord, on these withered shoots, these cracked eggs.
These shriveled forms beg for Your mercy!
These bodies are too heavy, so our souls have sunk very low.
Don't be angry at us who have lost Paradise!

If You only knew, Lord, how many hearts have panicked
And shattered their wings like bats in the darkness of grief.
If You only knew how many streams of bitter tears
Have flowed like rivers and still not washed out life's sorrow.
If You only knew how many souls have been decimated
Because they picked up the flaming vessel and held it to their
  lips;
Then even You, O Lord, might blush with regret
That You had brought human life into existence.[47]

Meanwhile Luu Trong Lu was achieving new fame and respect
as a poet with his publication of collected poems entitled *The Sound
of Autumn* (*Tieng Thu*) in 1939. The title poem in particular became
well known and widely quoted:

Don't you hear the autumn,
Throbbing beneath the dim moon?
Don't you hear the anguish,
See the vision of a distant warrior,
Entombed in the lonely woman's heart?
Don't you hear the woods in fall,
The rustling call of autumn leaves,
As the apprehensive tawny deer
Walks upon dry sheaths of gold?[48]

The ennui and emptiness of the late 1930s showed through his poetry as well. The naive enthusiasm evident in his 1934 speech was gone. Lu's desolation and alienation is seen clearly in a poem called "Rain . . . Endless Rain," also from *The Sound of Autumn*:

> Endless rain, always raining,
> Who is there to love?
> The cold wind has gone to the mountains, not to return again
>
> . . . .
>
> Why this rain, this endless rain?
> My heart is always longing!
> For whom do I bear this pain?
>
> Why this rain, this endless rain?
> Half the spring of life has gone in sadness!
> Golden dreams were not picked in time!
>
> Endless rain, always raining!
> And who is there to blame?
> Youth has been squandered in vain.
>
> Always raining, endless rain!
> Who is there to be seeking?
> This is like being banished to a border outpost.[49]

The new poetry shifted rapidly from romantic and exuberant idealism to introspective melancholy. The promise of individualism remained unfulfilled for most people, and the quest for personal happiness ended all too often at a dead end of despair. For many disillusioned youths, life was indeed like being banished to a border outpost, but theirs was a self-imposed banishment within the heart of lively urban centers. It is clear from their poetry that for Luu Trong Lu, Xuan Dieu, Che Lan Vien, and Huy Can, individualism was not working very well. The response of the reading public to this poetry suggests that many other Vietnamese of the time—especially those who were young, urban, and middle class—recognized something of their own feelings in these emotional lines.

Luu Trong Lu seems to have been almost a caricature of disoriented youth, lost and alone in the familiar and bustling beauty of Hanoi. He was a well-known, widely published, and respected poet, writer of fiction, and literary critic. Yet the composite picture that can be obtained of him during this period of his life is insubstantial, inconsistent, almost unreal.[50] He seems more like a stereotype taken from the pages of a third-rate novel than a flesh-and-blood human being. His acquaintances perceived him that way at the time. He seems to have had no intimate friends of either sex nor any close relatives around him. Painfully thin, with a sickly pallor, unruly hair that was never combed, Luu Trong Lu walked into the Hanoi literary world in 1932 at the age of twenty with a "careless step, a haggard stare, a distant smile, and a slender volume of just-published stories in his hand."[51] He had a wife, but he did not live with her. He shared a wretched garret room with two other young men, earning a meager living by writing for newspapers. He was a lazy writer and produced just enough to obtain food, shelter, clothing—and opium.

Poetry and opium were Luu Trong Lu's only pleasures, or perhaps his only sources of solace. Yet he wrote poetry only when the mood to do so struck him. Over the seven-year period during which he made his lasting reputation (1932–1939) he wrote little more than fifty poems, most of them quite short ones. And though he was fond of discussing philosophy and love, in point of fact most of those who knew and liked him agree that his philosophy was badly muddled and his loves were mostly imaginary. His discussions, even of himself, were mainly flights of imagination. Nguyen Vy, a sympathetic observer, felt that Luu Trong Lu himself was a product of his own imagination, like his loves and his stories. Vy likened Lu to a paper kite fluttering in the wind high among the clouds, attached to earth by only a slender thread.

The Darkening of the 1930s

Many members of the "village of literature" in Vietnam at this time used opium. But few were as heavily addicted as Luu Trong Lu. It was rumored that he sometimes smoked as many as one hundred pipes in a single night, occasionally overdosing himself until he fell into a coma.

The poetry of the 1930s was overwhelmingly inward-looking. In their morbidity, their alienation, and their drug addiction, these poets were perhaps extreme cases, but their lamentations struck a responsive chord among many urban middle-class readers who recognized some genuine link between their own feelings and perceptions and this new poetry. Throughout the 1930s a darker trend had been looming up to overshadow the naive optimism and forced gaiety of the new urban middle class. There seemed to be a steady increase in suicide, prostitution, emotional disorder, opium addiction, and alcoholism. Articulate urban intellectuals were beginning to identify and define these and other phenomena as "social problems" and were seeking publicly to assign culpability in terms of their own ideological predilections.[52]

Within this bleak context, throughout the second half of the decade Vietnamese intellectuals fiercely debated the relationship between art and society. With growing vigor, some argued that to be socially responsible literature had to be politically engaged. Proponents of political correctness in art called their position "art for the sake of life," as opposed to what was dubbed "art for art's sake," echoing turn-of-the-century debates in Europe. This vacuous false dichotomy was capable of arousing intense passions in the wounded psyches of this generation of Vietnamese.

Among those who dared answer the taunts of those who demanded a politically correct literature was a young critic from central Vietnam named Hoai Thanh (1909–1989). Although he himself had been expelled from high school in Hanoi for revolutionary activity, he was unwilling to see artistic standards degraded in the name of politics. In 1935 he lashed out in exasperation: "You can have any kind of literature you like, but first it must be literature."[53] He berated those who insisted on politicizing literature for their failure to recognize that people can transcend their social class, in literature and in life. "A thief who is brought into a work of art is no longer a thief. He is a person, and his miseries have become the miseries of Person (Person with a capital letter) and have an eternal quality."[54]

Luu Trong Lu was prominent among those who upheld the capacity of literature to transcend time and space and social class, insisting on the intrinsic value of good literature. In April 1939 he wrote:

> Poetry is common to all people, with youth it speaks of love, with parents it speaks of families, with older people it speaks of the past. People may do as they please. Whether or not a revolution comes to overturn rotten societies, or change that merely alters them a little bit, whatever political changes may or may not take place, there will still be youngsters, there will still be mothers, there will still be old men; in short, there will still be people who know love, who know happiness, who know pain. Poetry is for them. . . . The human heart is . . . always the human heart.
>
> It is not that we are unaware of the urgent duties of the

times, that we are unaware of the pressing demands of a new life. It is not that we do not realize that the responsibility of a writer today is heavy, is perilous, and to be [met] properly must serve the majority, serve the masses. But we also know that beyond the literature of struggle, the literature of a period, there is also a literature that is eternal.

We cannot for any reason neglect the following point. The literature that is eternal takes the human heart as its base. . . . In truth it has no East, no West, no modernity, no antiquity. It has a perpetual essence, like time, because it comes from the human heart, a human heart that remains unchanged through the ages.[55]

Conflict has often been present in Vietnamese society. There were structural reasons for conflict in the traditional sociocultural system, and the conflict itself was an integral part of the system. That conflict served basically as a centripetal force, either pushing people into one or another of society's allotted role sets, or sometimes recruiting them into supplementary roles within the *yin* subsystem (as monks, shamans, hermit scholars, minstrels, etc.). Despite conflict and suffering, people knew who they were and where they stood in regard to one another.

But the conflict that emerged in the early modern period was increasingly a centrifugal force, pulling people out of the system altogether into frameworks and relationships that were in no significant way integrated into or functionally related to the existing family or village systems. Society became less integrated. Multiple functional discontinuities arose within and between the ends and means of social action.

The individual in such a society—especially to the extent that one was young, middle-class, urban, Western-educated, and male—was inevitably subjected to feelings of ambivalence, guilt, and frustration, and in some cases to a painful sense of impotence and inferiority. The personalities of such people, too, I would argue, became less well integrated.

Both intra- and interpersonal conflict intensified in early modern Vietnamese society. On the one hand, the tightly knit core of traditional culture perpetuated itself within the family; on the other, the intrusive nucleus of Western civilization was a burgeoning influence, instilled through a widespread, French-controlled public school system and magnified by a rapidly expanding vernacular press and popularistic literary productions. The core of traditional

culture exhibited a remarkable persistence, sustained by a powerful sense of family instilled in almost all Vietnamese from early
childhood.

Vietnamese children still imbibed the folk wisdom that insisted
that boys and girls who did not follow the dictates of *nghia* would
come to a bad end, and would injure their families in the process.
They still learned, even as they were learning to speak, that the
primary social world consisted of a rigid status hierarchy that implied various dichotomies of mutual expectations based on role sets
with linguistic and other behavioral definitions. But when the child
went to school, as hundreds of thousands were doing in the 1930s,
precepts and examplars from Western civilization provided spontaneous, inner-directed, autonomous individuals as role models.
Men and women in the schoolbooks made their own decisions and
were answerable only to their own consciences, were willing to be
judged by that "tribunal in one's heart," and by that alone. It was a
critical, skeptical, independent spirit that was admired; not blind
obedience, not filial piety, not fidelity to convention.

Contradictory demands and expectations exacted a heavy toll
from many Vietnamese, especially young educated males from
"good" families in urban areas. Socialization within the family had
systematically stunted the psychological independence required for
efficacious performance within the individualistic culture of the
West. At the same time immersion in Western culture at school
and office and in books had eroded the psychological capacity for
dependence and nurturance required for efficacious performance
in family life—which was "autocratic" and "hierarchical," but
hugely satisfying to those who submitted to its discipline. Thus
were the best and the brightest of a generation of Vietnamese to
some degree rendered ineffectual both at home and in the office.
They never felt quite comfortable, never fit in completely. The feelings of alienation and anxiety they experienced were exacerbated
by the humiliation and rage they experienced as second-class
citizens in their own land. For many of them had come to see
themselves as the French saw them: members of a poor, backward,
and subjugated race. Such a state of mind was clearly intolerable.

Nguyen Tuong Tam had defined the dilemma clearly immediately after assuming control of *Mores*, asserting that only one
course of action was possible: complete and radical change:

> Those deeply concerned about these times, when speaking
> about the destiny of our nation, usually rub their bellies and

heave long sighs, feeling sorry over the fact that morality has come to the end of the road, so that many ancient ideals, having entered a period of transition, seem to be getting pushed into nothingness. They regret the demise of that for which they felt affection, and this leads to a desire to reach out and rescue a bit of the essence, the unadulterated remnants— now becoming concerned with the restoration of Confucian studies, now giving speeches about the national spirit, the national soul—and it remains to be seen if the work of these conservatives will avoid the fate reserved for the labors of a sand-crab.

At the advent of a new age, those who remain friends of the ancient literature, who cling to the old morality, are not very many. So in the very heart of this group of conservatives we find Pham Quynh advancing the theory of the "golden mean." Retain the best of that which is Eastern, acquire for ourselves the best of that which is Western, synthesize the two cultures, and create for ourselves a distinctive civilization. That is where Pham Quynh's vision rests.

Upon first hearing this theory everyone must agree that it is a fine one, one that should be followed. But when it is brought into practice there are endless difficulties. Even Pham Quynh will agree with that. Myself, I go one step further: it is impossible to implement this theory successfully.

Eastern culture venerates the family. The individual can be no more than an element of the family. The ideas or actions of the individual must be subjugated to the family hierarchy. And a nation is just a larger family, also with a hierarchy just like the one in a small family.

The West attaches importance to the individual. Within the family, or in society, anyone can develop his or her own ideas. No one is forcibly restricted to following the teachings of Aristotle or any other sage. . . .

In the West anyone can follow his natural reason and start a discussion. In the East everyone must follow the teachings of the ancients. So many matters concerning society, the family, relations between the sexes—all must be resolved in different ways because they are based on different premises. In regard to these differences, merely examining European society with an objective eye is sufficient for us to determine which is superior and which is inferior. But because of the differing sets of premises, we cannot synthesize all the good features of the two cultures of East and West. . . .

Our nation, for better or worse, is a place where Eastern and Western cultures have met, and we have been unable to

follow the rule of the golden mean. We must choose one of
two paths: one is to retain our old mores, to follow the old
men of antiquity; the second is to follow the new civilization,
taking science as our base, having our roots in reason.

Following either path has advantages and disadvantages,
and it is not yet certain where truth lies. But when the old
civilization is put into practice with the results before our very
eyes, we are dissatisfied with those results. We can only place
our hope in Western civilization, although we do not yet
know where that civilization will lead us. Our destiny is to go
into the unknown, to keep changing and to progress.[56]

Pascal observed some three hundred years ago that as one
crossed the Pyrenees what had been truth on one side became
error on the other. In Vietnam, however, for the past sixty or
seventy years widely divergent views of reality, patterns of value,
and subjective meaning have not been separated by any mountain
range but have coexisted in uneasy intimacy around a common
breakfast table, side by side on ferry boat and trolley car, on news-
stands, within offices and classrooms, and in village meeting halls.
One man's truth might well have been error or perversion to his
neighbor, employer, father, brother, sister, wife, son, or daughter.
Even—perhaps especially—those who achieved a modicum of
material prosperity or tangible means of asserting a claim to higher
status found these to be uncomfortable times in which to live.

In such a world the "social construction of reality" became a
problematic and even painful exercise.[57] The intersubjective commonplace world unraveled for many Vietnamese as incompatible
ideas regarding what was "true," what was "good," and what was
"proper" competed to become the commonplaces of tomorrow.
Virtually all literary figures, as well as all political activists, were
working to create a new and different world. With one voice they
were prepared to condemn both the traditional sociocultural system of Vietnam and the French colonial administration that overlay
it. Where they were divided, and with increasing bitterness as time
went on, was in deciding how change could best be accomplished,
and in defining the nature of the new society that would replace
the existing one.

The tragedy of twentieth-century Vietnam emerged as men and
women banded together to impose upon society some setting of
the thermostat with which they could live comfortably and in
doing so came into conflict with other groups who were equally

committed to competing and incompatible standards by which to judge and ultimately to enforce the ends and means of social action. Few of the participants in this drama realized how traumatic their journey into the unknown would be. In September 1939 World War II erupted in Europe. In June 1940 a badly battered France surrendered to Germany. Fighting was spreading around the world and the outcome of this global conflict was uncertain. Vietnam was drenched in a sense of foreboding, with both hopes and fears for the future heightened by the prospect of the inevitable changes war would bring. And Vietnamese of all persuasions braced themselves to career onto a collision course with history.

4 The End of Colonialism and the Emergence of Two Competing Models for Building a Modern Nation, 1940–1954

From Polemics to Politics, 1939–1945

As the specter of war loomed over Europe some Vietnamese came slowly to realize that out of the darkest of scenarios might yet come an exceptional opportunity to escape their colonial status. And as the decade wore on it became obvious that France might be in serious trouble. Adolph Hitler had renounced the Treaty of Versailles and was building a powerful German army. In 1936 Ethiopia fell into Italian hands; German troops marched into the Rhineland; Germany and Italy formed the Rome-Berlin Axis and jointly intervened in the Spanish Civil War on the side of Franco. Then in March 1939 German troops captured Czechoslovakia.

On March 25, 1939, Nguyen Tuong Tam stopped writing to devote all his energy to political activity. At about this time he organized a minor political party called Restoration of Vietnam. This soon became incorporated in a somewhat larger (but still small) organization called the Greater Vietnam People's Rule party, of which Tam was secretary-general.[1]

Meanwhile, as many Vietnamese had anticipated with hope and trepidation, France was in desperate trouble. On September 1, 1939, Germany invaded Poland, and two days later France and Great Britain declared war against Germany. German tanks rumbled across Europe toppling one nation after another.

Nguyen Tuong Tam, Hoang Dao, and Khai Hung were now working frantically to build a political base within Vietnam. But they were not the only Vietnamese preparing to exploit French weakness to generate a revolution. Others had begun long before them. By 1940 the Indochinese Communist party (ICP) network extended throughout all of Vietnam and much of southern China. And early in 1940, Ho Chi Minh returned to resume active command.[2]

After uniting feuding Communist factions to form the Indochinese Communist party in 1930, Ho Chi Minh—by then a senior official in the Far Eastern Bureau of the Comintern—had been captured by British intelligence agents in Hong Kong in 1931. Through a notorious legal battle that went all the way to the Privy Council in London, Ho was classified as a political refugee and released in 1932. There was no evidence that he had broken any laws in Hong Kong itself, and as a political refugee he was not subject to extradition. After wandering from Hong Kong to Amoy to Shanghai pursued by French security agents, Ho finally made contact with the Chinese Communist party, which helped him get back to Russia safely. There he received further schooling at several Communist party centers, capped by his attendance at the famous Lenin School, which provided the Communist elite with their highest level of training. A few years later he was back in China with the Communist 8th Route Army. It was on a mission from that legendary unit that he traveled toward the southern border in early 1940.[3]

In May 1940 Pham Van Dong and Vo Nguyen Giap slipped out of Hanoi to make their way to Kunming. Giap would never again see his wife; she would die in prison a few years later. But within a month Giap, Pham Van Dong, Truong Chinh, and other key party cadre were reunited with Ho Chi Minh in Kunming, where party members in exile had been organizing since 1930.[4] As they began to expand their activity there, the Germans smashed their way into Paris and France surrendered.

In September Japan joined the Axis powers, emboldened by the shaky world situation to expand its own empire in Asia. Already in control of Korea, Manchuria, Inner Mongolia, and northeastern China, Japan now set out to conquer all of East Asia. The Japanese quickly took over French Indochina, triggering several local uprisings, all short-lived and unsuccessful episodes that served to swell the ranks of émigrés in southern China. Chinghsi, a small town some sixty-five miles across the border in Kwangsi, soon held over seven hundred Vietnamese exiles. The Communists, the Vietnamese Nationalist party (VNQDD), and various other political factions competed for the allegiance and support of this activist overseas community.

In 1940 Khai Hung and Hoang Dao traveled to China for the

Greater Vietnam People's Rule party. With little political experience or organizational skills, they found themselves pitted against a tough and well-organized Communist apparatus. At the same time, the VNQDD also had its headquarters in Kunming. Both the Communists and the VNQDD were publishing newspapers there, and both had party cells strung across many towns in southern China, particularly along the crucial railway that linked Chinese forces fighting the Japanese with vital supplies coming from Haiphong.[5]

Hoang Dao and Khai Hung returned to Vietnam having made only minor gains against their better organized and more experienced competitors. Not long after their return they were arrested by the French, along with some other prominent members of the Greater Vietnam People's Rule party, and they spent the next two years in prison. To allay the suspicions of French security agents, Tam began earning his living by playing the clarinet in a Hanoi nightclub band, and he refrained from making any public statements. But following the Japanese attack on Pearl Harbor on December 7, 1941, he could restrain himself no longer. In 1942 he went to China and hurled himself into the frenetic political maneuvering taking place there.[6]

The outcome of the worldwide war was far from clear in Vietnam at this time. And as the dream of revolution against French rule spread, it was equally unclear who would lead it or what form it would take. In the early 1940s the Indochinese Communist party was in serious trouble and had many credible competitors. In the words of David Marr:

> Members of the Indochinese Party, the Nationalist Party, the Dai Viet, the Cao Dai, and Hoa Hao each sensed that their moment in history had arrived. . . .
> In 1941 the Indochinese Communist Party was in complete disarray, its members dead, incarcerated, demoralized, or surviving precariously in forests and swamps. Organizationally it appeared to possess less potential than any of the groups mentioned above.[7]

How did the Communists manage to revitalize themselves and seize control of the revolution?

Late in 1940 or early in 1941 Ho Chi Minh had slipped across the border and set foot once again on Vietnamese soil after an absence of thirty years. He took refuge in the remote grottos of Pac Bo near the Chinese border. There in early May 1941 the Central Committee of the Indochinese Communist party held its eighth meeting, creating the most famous of a long series of Communist front organizations. Its name was Viet Nam Doc Lap Dong Minh Hoi, literally the Association of Allies for the Independence of Vietnam, or the Vietnam Independence League, as it was sometimes called. But it was generally known simply as the Vietminh.[8]

For their own purposes, the Chinese authorities wanted to consolidate the Vietnamese revolutionaries in China. During 1942 many of these Vietnamese had gathered in Liuchow, a sizable town some six hundred miles northeast of the Vietminh's secret headquarters near the border. There were soon over six hundred Vietnamese in Liuchow, including over twenty leaders of various competing and contentious groups and parties. In June 1942 ten other Nationalist (VNQDD) leaders were invited to Liuchow from their headquarters in Kunming. After much bickering and delay, a new organization finally came into being in October 1942. A number of Vietnamese agreed to form the Vietnam Revolutionary League (Viet Nam Cach Mang Dong Minh Hoi), commonly known as the Dong Minh Hoi, with the support of the Chinese.

The Dong Minh Hoi brought together diverse elements in the exiled Vietnamese revolutionary community, but it did not create real unity. The Indochinese Communist party and the Communist-dominated Vietminh were specifically excluded, and other groups were considered by the Chinese to be too closely linked to the Japanese (who covertly aided some of them in anti-French activity) to be trustworthy. Both Ho Chi Minh and Nguyen Tuong Tam, for example, had been imprisoned in 1942 as undesirable influences on the political scene. In fact the Dong Minh Hoi consisted of only four or five out of well over a dozen Vietnamese factions vying for power both within Vietnam and in southern China. The VNQDD dominated the league but could not exercise effective leadership. After a year of operations largely subsidized by Chinese authorities, its accomplishments were negligible; so General Chang Fa K'uei, the dynamic commander of the Fourth War Area, initiated a major reorganization to give the league a broader base of support and more effective leadership.[9]

In October 1943 a Reunification Conference was scheduled to be held in Liuchow. Both Ho Chi Minh and Nguyen Tuong Tam were released from prison to become members of the league. The ICP as an organization was still not permitted to participate, but the Vietminh was, which amounted to the same thing. After much squabbling the VNQDD managed to retain its dominant role in the organization, but the numerous revolutionary factions continued to compete with each other, spy on each other, and engage in a bewildering series of complicated intrigues and clandestine negotiations. Each group was in contact with many others as well as with the various civilian and military agencies and organizations contained in the Chinese, Japanese, French, British, and American missions in southern China and Vietnam, as well as with locally powerful religious sects like the Cao Dai and the Hoa Hao. Each group was striving for a free and independent Vietnam, but one to be controlled by itself and structured in its own ideological image; and to this end each tried to play off its opponents and rivals, one against the other, in a constantly shifting configuration of alliances and truces, temporary cooperation, and betrayals.[10]

The Greater Vietnam People's Rule party was by this time part of a loose coalition of several parties, referred to simply as the Dai Viets (or Greater Vietnam parties), that were for the most part cooperating with the Japanese in hopes of enlisting their help in removing the French from Indochina. Hoang Dao and Khai Hung were avowedly part of this group, and they were secretly negotiating with the Japanese Kempeitai for a role in the new Vietnamese government, which the Kempeitai had some interest in forming. At the same time Nguyen Tuong Tam was in China seeking support from China and the Allies; he actively collaborated with the VNQDD and other forces friendly to and dependent on the Chinese and with a strongly anti-Japanese posture.

As a result of this amateurish maneuvering neither the Japanese nor the Chinese (nor many other Dai Viet or VNQDD leaders) trusted Tam or his friends very much. And since they were notorious for their extreme anti-French and anticommunist positions, this meant that Tam, Hoang Dao, and Khai Hung were effectively isolated. They had a small band of devoted followers and some popularity with the urban middle class, especially in Hanoi; but they had neither an effective mass organization beneath them nor any powerful sponsors among the international power brokers. Ho Chi Minh, meanwhile, was in the process of acquiring both.[11]

In view of the continuing ineffectiveness of the Dong Minh Hoi, General Chang organized a second Reunification Congress in Liuchow. At this Congress of Overseas Revolutionary Groups in March 1944, fifteen delegates were entrusted with the task of hammering out the new form of the Dong Minh Hoi in four days of vigorous and often bitter debate. Ho Chi Minh and Pham Van Dong were two of at least three Communists in the group. Tam was the lone Dai Viet, and he is sometimes referred to as a Dai Viet and sometimes as a VNQDD leader at this time. The end result of this conference was a shift in power that gave the Communists the leverage they needed to assume a powerful role in the very organization that encompassed most of their significant competition. Nguyen Tuong Tam was one of four out of the fifteen delegates who was left without any official seat in the new organizational structure.[12]

Tam felt cheated out of his rightful place in the revolutionary leadership, but he was at his worst in negotiations of this kind: blunt, uncompromising, antagonistic to any tactical maneuvering. Ho Chi Minh, older and much more experienced, was soft-spoken, moderate, flexible, pragmatic. He made a great impression on General Chang. The general was not himself a Communist, but many on his staff were; they urged him to entrust to Ho Chi Minh the task of preparing conditions within Vietnam for the planned entry of the Chinese to disarm the Japanese at the end of the war. On May 7, 1945, Germany surrendered, and Japanese forces faced almost certain defeat in the Pacific.[13]

By August 1944 the Vietminh and Ho Chi Minh had gained ascendancy in the Dong Minh Hoi. The VNQDD elements had been weakened and discredited. On August 9 Ho left Liuchow with sixteen young Vietnamese who had been receiving special training from General Chang for three years. Pham Van Dong, Vo Nguyen Giap, and other top Communist leaders had been working along the China-Vietnam border for several years to prepare for this moment. They had recruited and trained men (and some women), established lines of communication, worked out transportation problems, and scouted out safe base camps in mountain and jungle. Now Pham Van Dong and Giap went north into China to meet Ho as he came south to join them. Ho vetoed their proposals to launch an armed insurgency in Cao Bang province and stressed the priority of political over military considerations. On December 22, 1944, a small armed propaganda unit went into operation led by Vo Nguyen Giap. The People's Army of Vietnam (PAVN), to all practical purposes, came into being on that day.[14]

While Giap's guerrillas carried on a modest but successful campaign of ambush, political agitation, and propaganda in the Vietnamese highlands, Ho Chi Minh remained in China and sought support for their efforts. The United States Office of Strategic Services (OSS), the forerunner of the Central Intelligence Agency, had a headquarters in Kunming, and in early 1945 Ho Chi Minh visited them several times, receiving modest assistance and agreeing to gather intelligence from Vietnam for the Americans. He also obtained, simply by asking for it, an autographed picture from General Chennault, the legendary commander of the Flying Tigers. At the same time Ho maintained close contact and cordial relations with General Chang and his staff, consolidating his grip on the Dong Minh Hoi and keeping himself well informed as to Chinese plans for moving into Vietnam.[15]

In May 1944 Ho Chi Minh was back in Vietnam, this time to stay. He established himself in a mountain hamlet, Tan Trao, some sixty-five miles north of Hanoi and began his final phase of preparations for exploiting the opportunity that he—more clearly than anyone else—saw coming.[16]

Returning to the Roots: Literature and Society, 1940–1944

World War II and the Japanese occupation had a profound impact on Vietnam, but the effects were largely indirect. No major fighting took place on Vietnamese soil; and bombing—first by the Japanese and later by Allied forces—was not severe compared with the suffering and destruction experienced by most other countries in both Europe and Asia. Japan exerted its authority with indirection and restraint, especially during the early years of the occupation. The French colonial apparatus continued to administer the country. In many ways these colonial administrators had more autonomy than ever before to set their own policies and make their own decisions. But they remained formally under the authority of the Vichy government, and both protocol and the realities of power constrained them to accede to Japanese "instruction."

France had, after all, suffered its second humiliating defeat at German hands in little more than twenty years. In occupied France under the Vichy government, the official policy for simultaneously binding the wounds of defeat and maintaining order under difficult circumstances was a reactionary "national revolution" that looked to the past for solace while stressing in the present a disciplined devotion to "work, family, and fatherland." The same policy was applied to Vietnam. Parades were held; youth groups were formed; extensive sports programs were organized. School curricula at all levels were reorganized to include religious education and ethical instruction. There was a marked emphasis on increased study of Latin and Greek. In Vietnam this also took the form of a return to a greater emphasis on Chinese and the ancient classics. Frivolity, romanticism, and individualism were anathema—spurned as the seeds of weakness and defeat.[17]

Because France itself had been so badly weakened by the war, French authorities were forced to adopt a more cooperative and conciliatory attitude toward those Vietnamese who were willing to collaborate with them. New opportunities for political participation were granted, albeit at a superficial level, and Vietnamese membership was increased on the various binational consultative committees. The number of Vietnamese in the civil service soared, and Vietnamese were permitted to hold higher positions and wield more authority than ever before.

The humiliating salary differential between Frenchmen and Vietnamese was abolished, and at long last Vietnamese could receive equal pay for equal work. Since the colony was so effectively cut off from France, local manufacturing also flourished. Vietnamese businessmen began to reap profits formerly reserved for French syndicates. Educational opportunities too increased dramatically at all levels. The number of students grew from 450,000 in 1939 to 700,000 in 1944. All in all, the urban middle class multiplied and prospered as never before. On the surface tranquillity reigned. For many Vietnamese in numerous ways things had never been so good.[18]

The intellectual and artistic activity of the years 1939 to 1945 exhibited a distinctive tone of sober restraint. Historical and philosophical writing flourished after a decade of relative neglect, as did literary scholarship and criticism. Even the fiction and poetry of this period reflected a spirit of critical detachment. The romantic, individualistic element in literature drastically declined in 1939, and the use of the first person singular point of view was abruptly reduced. This was a literature "returning to its roots." Historical and heroic themes were popular, but "rural realism" was the dominant orientation. Writers and poets conjured up rustic scenes of daily life vibrant with authentic details of speech, custom, and landscape. Sometimes with an ironic undertone, alternately delightful or poignant, they recited the commonplace dramas of frustrated young lovers, overweening notables, farmers struggling to make ends meet, the tragic excitement induced by sickness in a prized water buffalo.

Meanwhile, newspapers ran essays on historical figures like the Trung sisters, Tran Hung Dao, Le Loi, and other popular heroes who had successfully led Vietnamese troops into battle against Chinese invaders. Histories and dictionaries of various kinds appeared. Textual research and critical essays provided fresh insights into many classics of Vietnamese literature.[19] As part of this process, Hoai Thanh, the champion of "art for art's sake," produced a scholarly anthology of the "new poetry."

Hoai Thanh had become involved in revolutionary politics at an early age. As a result he had been expelled from high school in Hanoi and had gone to work as a journalist. But the colonial authorities kept close watch over him. Suspecting him to be a potential troublemaker, they decided to expel him from Tonkin altogether, sending him back to his native village in central Vietnam. In 1931, still only twenty-two years old, Hoai Thanh went to Hue to make his way in the world. He worked at a print shop, then found work teaching at a private school, all the time continuing to write articles for newspapers, many of them literary criticism.[20]

In 1941 Hoai Thanh was living in a very modest house next door to a blacksmith in Hue. He was supporting a sizable household with his earnings as a teacher: his father, several younger brothers, his wife, and four children. Then the colonial authorities, nervous about increasing political activity, withdrew his teaching certificate. For six months Hoai Thanh was unemployed. Helped by his younger brother, Hoai Chan (who had already spent time in jail for his own political activities), Hoai Thanh began work on an annotated, critical anthology of the "new poetry."

Working in the heart of Hue in that crowded household, sick with worry about how he would support his household, assaulted by the constant thump and clatter of the blacksmith's work next door, he produced what was to become a classic work in Vietnamese literary history. *Vietnamese Poets, 1932–1941* was published early in 1942 and became an instant success. So popular did it become that it was reissued before the year was out, an astonishing event in Vietnam at that time. This anthology contained 169 poems by 46 poets. The five poets discussed in some detail in the preceding chapter accounted for 52 of the poems, 31 percent of the total (Xuan Dieu, 15; Luu Trong Lu, 11; Huy Can, 11; Che Lan Vien, 8; and The Lu, 7). Hoai Thanh also included highly subjective introductory essays for each of the poets and a thirty-nine-page introductory essay that provided a brief history of the "new poetry" movement and the social world from which it arose. From the vantage point of 1941, he observed:

> In general, the entire spirit of ancient times—or the old poetry—and the present time—or the new poetry—may be summed up in two words: "I" and "we." . . . When the word "I" (speaking of it in its fullest sense) appeared in the realm of Vietnamese poetry, many people viewed it with disfavor. Even though it always followed words like "older brother," "uncle," and "grandfather," it seemed improper. Let alone now, when it shows up all by itself.
>
> But, day by day, gradually it has ceased to be so startling. People have gotten used to it. They have even found it to be worthy of affection and compassion. And it is indeed a piteous thing! . . .
>
> The word "we" is too big for [our poets] now. Their souls have shrunk until they just fit the framework of "I." . . .
>
> Our lives now lie within the sphere of "I." Having lost breadth, we seek depth. But the deeper we go, the colder it gets. . . . Never before has Vietnamese poetry been so sad, nor so much in an uproar, as it is now. Along with our sense of superiority, we have lost even the peace of mind of previous times.[21]

It was a time for sober stocktaking, for dispassionate cultural reassessment. This reflective mood was in part a result of the policies and influences of the French and the Japanese. But in colonial Vietnam the net result of such historicism and localism was not at all what had been intended by Marshal Pétain. Both the French and the Japanese tried to build a "restoration movement" and, at least in Vietnam, in the process created something that was much more of a "renaissance." Beneath the innocuous surface of scholarship and story telling, the smoldering fires of nationalism were being fanned to a fresh glow.[22]

The revolutionary feelings of the intellectuals and students of Vietnam were being inflamed in the early 1940s, but their passion was in general amorphous, unfocused, and uncommitted to any particular party or program. They simply wanted to gain independence, to regain their dignity. The remnants of all the existing political parties, as was noted above, were intensifying their efforts to recover from the brutal French repression that had decimated them in 1939–1940, and new parties and groups were forming. But these were all relatively small, secret organizations, and altogether they involved only a tiny percentage of the intelligentsia and a miniscule proportion of the population. Bui Diem, who entered the University of Hanoi at the time, remembers:

> Like my high school classmates, I heard all about them. Although no one knew anything concrete about these parties, what their policies were, or even the names of their leaders, we were caught in a rush of excitement. We felt our country was on the verge of striking out for its freedom, and there wasn't a soul who didn't want to be part of that.[23]

When Bui Diem went to live at the University of Hanoi in 1943, he remembers:

> The change meant far more than just a different place to sleep. . . . When I was in high school I knew of the secret political parties mainly through rumor and secondhand sources. Somebody's cousin had joined one; someone else's father's friend had been arrested for membership in another. But now . . . the movement had gained strength and credibility. The Cité was alive with students who were Vietminh, Dai Viet, or VNQDD. Political discussions and party recruitment went on all the time against a background of more diffuse but equally fervent nationalism of the university's Student Association, of which I immediately became an active member.
>
> Aware that French agents and provocateurs were everywhere, the Student Association acted prudently. We avoided confrontation by arranging meetings and outings that were ostensibly innocent but in fact were intended to stimulate patriotic feelings. Our weekend bicycle tours always had historical and political connotations. We visited . . . temples and sites associated with great heroes of Vietnam's past who had routed and destroyed earlier foreign invaders. The parallels between their times and ours were not exactly subtle, but the French authorities could hardly object to such orderly excursions. Sitting around campfires, we would discuss how the Trung sisters had overthrown the Chinese occupiers of the first century or how Tran Hung Dao had smashed the Mongols twelve hundred years later. Afterward we would sing, so loudly the woods seemed to reverberate:

Brothers, students, stand up!
Answer the call from rivers and mountains.
Go forward, always forward.
Have no regrets ever
About sacrificing your lives.

These meetings touched something deep inside each of us. With the Temple of the Ancestors just out of sight in the dark, we could feel that we ourselves were part of the continuous, heroic flow of Vietnamese history. The Trung sisters, Tran Hung Dao, Le Loi—they all led up to this very moment, a moment that was about to witness the rebirth of the nation's struggle for freedom. Magically, this was taking place in our generation. It was our time.[24]

Few of these students had ever heard of Ho Chi Minh. Few of them could distinguish the differences between one party or another. Even as late as 1943 or 1944, the majority of these students could have ended up in any of half a dozen political camps. But by August 1945 the Vietminh had clearly triumphed. How and why this happened is a story yet to be fully told.

We know that the Vietminh effectively served as a "screen" behind which the ICP could operate effectively, adapting to changing circumstances with neither revealing nor rejecting its long-term goals. For years the ICP had stressed social revolution, class conflict, and international solidarity with the forces of the proletariat (i.e., the revolutionary transformation of the world to communism). But the Vietminh downplayed these goals. National liberation was assigned overriding priority. This was an important step, but it was only part of the story.

Up to this point, the ICP had failed to attract any significant following among students, intellectuals, and other urban elements during the 1930s. The party, and especially the hard-core leadership, was composed of students and intellectuals recruited during the 1920s, when the motive force for joining the movement had been patriotism and the simple desire to overthrow French colonial domination. But during the 1930s and into the early 1940s the party had lost much of its appeal for urban intellectuals. In February 1943, the party launched a "cultural front" to rectify this situation.[25]

The key figure behind the cultural activism of the ICP during the 1940s was Truong Chinh, who held the powerful post of secretary-general of the Communist party from 1941 until 1956. His fervent belief that Marxist-Leninist ideology provided the single correct path to national independence, social justice, and prosperity drove Truong Chinh to demand a fundamental transformation of Vietnamese culture—eradicating all that impeded the march toward socialism and nurturing everything that facilitated it. Vietnamese literature was perceived to be an important battleground in this campaign. As the "cultural czar" of Vietnamese communism throughout the 1940s, Truong Chinh had a profound effect on Vietnamese literature as well as on Vietnamese history. He worked both directly through the party apparatus and indirectly, through an intricate network of front organizations and overt agents who penetrated most groups active in cultural affairs.

Truong Chinh himself effectively employed the pen as a weapon in his campaign. Using the pen name Red Wave (Song Hong), Truong Chinh published his own poetry in underground newspapers, condensing and symbolizing the doctrines set forth in his theoretical writings and party directives. In 1944, writing in the clandestine newspaper *Flag of Liberation* (*Co Giai Phong*), which was an important tool for proselytizing new members, Truong Chinh skillfully played upon the feeling of guilt, impotence, humiliation, and inferiority that beset the poets of the 1930s, in his poem entitled "To Be a Poet":

. . . .
If to be a poet is, transported with passion,
To sing of white breasts
That tremble for love, the next moment to find
Life is but dreams and illusion all told,
Smothered in flowers and doting on bodies of jade;
If to be a poet is to spread an elegant brocade
To cover the sores of tyranny in decay,
Straining to sing sweeter and louder
To cover the groans of the people's distress
The cry of the laboring people's long pain.
Then, oh my friends, such a poet
Is a curse to the whole human race!
He is tormenting his own heart, destroying the springtime of
    youth.
To extoll brutality and praise injustice
To bend the knee before power in the poor servile hope
Of catching a whiff of the droppings of the rich.

. . . .

To be a poet is to be true, pure, brave,
Firm-willed, to have purpose and fire;

. . . .

He must free all the ardour and power of his heart
To bring again to his people's dark winter the courage of Spring.

. . . .

Seize the pen to cast down the world's tyrants
Make rhymes into bombs and from verse make grenades.

. . . .

Light up with the clear beam of verse
The gangrene that devours our land.
Your verse together with our workers' hands
Shall plow the furrows of a splendid future.
                                (Translation from Nguyen Khac Vien
                                    and Huu Ngoc, n.d., 568–70)

Among the many intellectuals and students who were attracted to support the Vietminh in the final year and a half before the August Revolution of 1945, Huy Can was an early and important convert. As a covert agent of the Vietminh, he played a vital role in harnessing the patriotic aspirations of young intellectuals and students to the purposes of the Vietminh. In June 1944, when the Vietminh sponsored the creation of a new political party, innocuously called the Vietnamese Democratic party, Huy Can was an influential member. Among those Huy Can managed to draw into the Vietminh network was the poet Xuan Dieu, a good friend since high school days. Most other key figures from the poetry of the 1930s, however, were still trapped in their individualism and alienation.

Also in 1944, the ICP formed yet another front organization, the National Salvation Cultural Association. Several well-known writers and artists discussed the party's cultural programs and policies. They attracted others. The popular short story writer To Hoai joined the Association, and brought his friend Nam Cao into it. A convert would gain other converts. Often a first step would be to show a copy of *Flag of Liberation* or some similar clandestine paper to a friend and ask his opinion of it. Clandestine papers were distributed in easily concealed formats, a few at a time, sometimes hidden inside the handles of a bicycle.[26]

By the end of 1944 these interlocking networks of front organizations and covert agents had successfully introduced large numbers of urban intellectuals and students into the Vietminh network, bringing them under the influence of the ICP. In the cities of Vietnam, the tide was turning toward the Vietminh. Curiously enough, little has been written about this, one of the more important and successful of all party programs. The Communist party itself has been strangely reticent about the National Salvation Cultural Association.[27]

These successes stood the Vietminh in good stead when diverse forces began to converge in the spring of 1945 to accelerate the tempo of change. There was first of all a great rice shortage in the northern half of the country. For many people inconvenience was becoming genuine hunger. The collapsing Vichy-Japanese administration was exposed as impotent, or ruthless, or both. Starving people did not care why those in authority did not transport rice.

The Japanese realized that their days of empire were ending. And since France itself had been liberated, French authorities in Indochina were no longer under orders from Vichy. So in a swift and precise military operation on March 9, 1945, Japanese forces in Indochina turned upon their French "allies." Within twenty-four hours the French were disarmed and their colonial administration was dismantled. All adult French males were soon either in prison camps or fleeing into the mountains.[28]

On March 11 Emperor Bao Dai was declared chief of state of a new government, nominally independent but firmly under Japanese control. Tran Trong Kim, by now a renowned scholar, educator, and writer who had kept aloof from politics, was asked to form a new cabinet. On April 17 Tran Trong Kim became prime minister of Vietnam; he appointed a cabinet of talent and integrity, men he personally could trust and respect, men who shared his attitudes and values. This was a government of technicians and specialists, however, totally lacking in political skill and influence. Neither the French nor the VNQDD wished them well. The Vietminh urged strikes, demonstrations, sabotage, and raids. The Japanese, preoccupied with their own problems, gave them less authority and less help than had been expected. The entire enterprise degenerated into a tragic farce.

As Prime Minister Kim and his ministers sank into a political, administrative, and technological nightmare, conditions in the country grew more desperate. Nothing worked; despite Kim's relief efforts, people were dying of starvation and disease. Millions of people suffered unspeakable deprivation. Everyone was indignant at someone over something, and massive demonstrations took place. The turmoil only made things worse and contributed to the paralysis. The fledgling government—composed of honest and capable men of good will—soon became frustrated, bitter, and apathetic.[29]

On May 5 Hoang Dao and Khai Hung once again began publishing *This Day*. But it was now a maverick political organ of the VNQDD, published at Tam's behest. Its shrill and angry tone bore little resemblance to its days of glory in the 1930s. There was little literature of note, little objective news, and virtually no humor in these issues. The French and the Vietminh came under especially ferocious attack, but vituperation was flung in all directions. Only the Japanese escaped the more biting attacks of this politicized rear-guard action of the Self-Strength Literary Movement.[30]

Excitement kept building as Germany surrendered on May 7, and each week brought news of more Japanese defeats. In the Mekong delta, the Cao Dai—with units armed and trained by the Japanese—had their own semiautonomous enclaves, as did the Hoa Hao. The Vietminh forces, growing steadily under Giap's command, established guerrilla bases and revolutionary governments in six provinces ringing the Red River delta. In July a Dong Minh Hoi "action brigade" also began operating in the border areas. It was divided into three separate units: one led by a VNQDD man, one by a Communist, and one by a noncommunist Nationalist from yet a different group. Two other small units also independently crossed into Vietnam, one led by a Communist and one by a non-Communist. The relationship between the various forces was ambiguous at best. There were attacks, ambushes, and obstacles erected by group against group, especially between the Vietminh and the noncommunist Nationalists.[31]

A Fateful Summer, 1945

Administratively, politically, and militarily Vietnam was a chaotic nightmare in the summer of 1945. At least a million people starved to death. Many times that number were sick, weak, desperately frightened. People gnawed on roots and tree bark to lessen the pain of their hunger. Transportation and communication facilities ceased operating. Businesses foundered. Shortages, malfunctions, rumors, and hysteria spread across the land. Then, in August 1945, events plummeted toward a breathtaking conclusion.[32]

An embittered Nguyen Tuong Tam had been in Kunming

through all of this turmoil, urging his views on all who would listen. None of the key Americans in southern China, apparently, ever met with Tam or gave him any support. Tam's colleagues, and the Dai Viets in general, were perceived to be "pro-Japanese," so the Americans were unsympathetic to Tam from the outset. Also, the Americans were collaborating with the French and, by the spring of 1945, working closely with the Vietminh. Ho Chi Minh helped downed American airmen, provided useful intelligence, and offered to cooperate in joint operations against the Japanese. Since Nguyen Tuong Tam was correctly perceived to be working against both the French and the Vietminh, the OSS regarded him with suspicion and watched him. But apparently they never met with him and considered him to be more a problem than a potential ally.

On August 4 Tam dined by appointment in a small restaurant in Kunming with a French army officer. Major Jean Sainteny was a hero of the Free French Resistance during the German occupation and had recently been appointed by General De Gaulle himself to command France's crucial Mission 5, an elite intelligence group stationed in Kunming. The able and energetic Sainteny listened to and learned from a wide variety of sources. He kept in close touch with the Americans (whom he found hostile and naive) and with the Chinese (whose aims he mistrusted). The OSS officer in charge of Indochinese affairs found Sainteny to be devious and more concerned with salving French pride than with fighting the Japanese. When he heard that Tam and Sainteny had met, he could scarcely believe it. But the two men seemed to take a liking to each other.[33]

Sainteny was favorably impressed by Nguyen Tuong Tam as "the perfect model of a Vietnamese intellectual, but with something additional, a virility and directness which is rather rare." Tam, for his part, was delighted to find a highly placed Frenchman in the Far East who was so perceptive and open-minded as Sainteny appeared to be. The two men had an amicable discussion. Two days later Tam handed Sainteny a letter to give to Hoang Dao when he reached Hanoi, after the war ended. In it Tam urged his younger brother to speak frankly with Sainteny. Neither man thought the war would end soon and assumed that the letter would not be delivered for quite a while. But on August 6, the very day Tam handed Sainteny his introduction to Hoang Dao, the United States destroyed the entire city of Hiroshima with an atomic blast.[34]

On August 7 Tran Trong Kim resigned. Many members of his disheartened cabinet had already abandoned office. When a second atomic bomb was dropped on Nagasaki on August 8, Japan surrendered. In Vietnam a total vacuum of political leadership existed. Of all the candidates for power, none was nearly so well prepared as Ho Chi Minh. Not the least of Ho's many advantages was the appearance that the power of the United States was behind him.[35]

No sooner had Ho established his mountain headquarters in Vietnam than an American unit hiked in from China to join him, escorted by fifty Vietminh. They quickly established radio communications with Kunming, and soon other Americans were parachuting into the Vietminh headquarters. Working together with cordiality, the American military and intelligence units and the Vietminh built a small airstrip and pored over maps, news bulletins, and intelligence reports. Busy as he was, and sick part of the time, Ho made an effort to spend part of each day with the Americans. And Ho's autographed picture of General Chennault was prominently displayed.

As Ho strove to win support among the disparate and contentious group of influential Vietnamese revolutionaries, the appearance that he knew the Americans and had their backing while his opponents did not was very helpful. And this appearance, although skillfully exaggerated by Ho, had a solid basis. The OSS people knew Ho Chi Minh and Vo Nguyen Giap, Pham Van Dong and Truong Chinh, and other top Communists. They provided them with arms, ammunition, radios, and eventually even training.[36]

The Democratic Republic of Vietnam, August–October 1945

One of Ho's most urgent concerns during June and July was the extremely difficult task of arranging for two groups of people to be brought together in the wilderness north of Hanoi. On August 13 and 14, the Central Standing Committee of the Indochinese Communist party held the ninth meeting in its fifteen years of existence. An insurrection committee was formed (including Vo Nguyen Giap and Truong Chinh), and the order went out to all party members to prepare at once for an all-out general uprising. A message was transmitted to Bao Dai, who was by then abandoned by his own officials, urging him to yield his authority to the forces of revolution.

Then, on August 16, a People's National Congress was convened under Vietminh auspices. Over sixty delegates representing various ethnic minorities and political groupings were briefed on the favorable internal and international situations. By the end of the day a National Liberation Committee of Vietnam had been formed. Ho Chi Minh (whom most of the delegates had just met for the first time) was president. This committee, which included Pham Van Dong, became the Provisional Government of the Democratic Republic of Vietnam.

On August 17 Ho Chi Minh and the rest of the Liberation Committee were sworn into office, as Communist cadres led mobs pouring into the streets of Hanoi and Vo Nguyen Giap mounted a successful assault on the city of Thai Nguyen. On August 18 news of this first major victory of the People's Army of the Democratic Republic of Vietnam (PAVN) flashed across the nation. Emperor Bao Dai sent a letter to General De Gaulle urging him to recognize Vietnam's independence to safeguard French interests in Indochina. All semblance of public order was breaking down in Hanoi. Ho Chi Minh sent messages (through the Americans) to the Allied powers requesting their support for Vietnamese independence. On August 19, amid mass demonstrations, the Vietminh took over the city of Hanoi without firing a single shot. In Kunming, Major Jean Sainteny was fuming. He had been trying to get transportation into Hanoi for ten days, but unfriendly American personnel obstructed his every effort. When a French aircraft summoned in desperation finally arrived, the American General Wedemeyer, who was theater commander, issued a curt order forbidding the departure from Kunming of any airplane for Hanoi.[37]

Not until the afternoon of August 22 did the Americans finally allow Major Sainteny to accompany an OSS team flying into Hanoi. By then Sainteny was acting as special French representative for northern Vietnam, a last-minute commission dumped on him by flustered superiors. The attitude of most Americans in the area was expressed by the OSS team leader who accompanied him to Hanoi. Sainteny was told to his face by Major Archimedes Patti that the French had no right "to intervene in affairs which were no longer of any concern to them." When Major Sainteny finally met with Vo Nguyen Giap, representing Ho Chi Minh, on August 27, 1945, Major Patti arranged the meeting and was present when it took place.[38]

A few days later Bao Dai formally abdicated his throne. A three-man delegation from the Vietminh attended the ceremony, headed by the prominent Communist leader Tran Huy Lieu. But one of the other two men was none other than the poet Huy Can, still only twenty-six years old in 1945. Though nominally a member of the Democratic party, he had become a trusted Communist cadre. No longer "lovesick and lost, confused in direction," with a heart that no longer "shriveled and ached," Huy Can was of immeasurable value to the Vietminh as a symbol of their appeal to the youth of the nation, all the more so because he was not known to be a Communist.[39]

On August 28, in accord with Allied agreements made in Potsdam, Chinese armies moved into Vietnam to disarm the Japanese and serve as a temporary occupying force to preserve order. The British were playing a similar role in the southern half of the country. Accompanying the Chinese armies were the great majority of VNQDD and Dong Minh Hoi leaders, who hoped they would be left in control of Vietnam when the Chinese left as promised. Apparently at Ho Chi Minh's urging, Vo Nguyen Giap, who did not know where Nguyen Tuong Tam was nor how to get in touch with him, asked Major Patti to get a message to him, personally inviting him to come to Hanoi and hold discussions.

Typically, Tam had set off for Hanoi on his own. Soon after his arrival he was feverishly at work with Khai Hung, Hoang Dao, and other colleagues mounting a press campaign to gain popular support in the anticipated struggle for power. But the careful planning and preparation of Ho Chi Minh permitted him to act decisively while everyone else was still getting ready. Firmly in control of Hanoi and much of the surrounding countryside, Ho Chi Minh and the Liberation Committee he headed proclaimed themselves to be the sole government for all of Vietnam. *This Day* was promptly closed down, and Nguyen Tuong Tam was isolated once again.[40]

Half a million people jammed into Hanoi's Ba Dinh Square to watch the Provisional Government of the Democratic Republic of Vietnam formally assume office on September 3. A hush fell over the excited crowd as Ho Chi Minh stepped forward to read to them the Vietnamese Declaration of Independence. This frail-looking man with a warm and kindly manner was still somewhat of a mystery to the crowd, for he had appeared in Hanoi for the first time less than two weeks earlier. American military officers from the OSS were present, conspicuously hearty and well dressed; and they must have been smiling in pleasurable anticipation, because

Ho had consulted them well in advance about the wording of this historic document. "All men are created equal," the new president began. "They are endowed by their creator with certain inalienable rights; among these are life, liberty, and the pursuit of happiness." When Ho had finished reading, General Giap strode forward to deliver a speech in which he said pointedly: "The United States of America . . . has paid the greatest contributions to the Vietnamese fight against fascist Japan, our enemy, and so the great American Republic is a good friend of ours."[41]

The Americans had indeed been good friends of the Vietminh in their bid to grasp power in Vietnam. Americans in the field had consistently snubbed the French forces and refused, sometimes cruelly, to help them, while they had openly demonstrated their sympathy for the Vietnamese revolutionaries in southern China, and especially for Ho. The Americans who had met Ho Chi Minh liked him and wanted to help him in his struggle against both the Japanese and the French.[42]

Ho Chi Minh not only was president of the new Republic, but also served as his own minister of foreign affairs. Vo Nguyen Giap was minister of the interior (and thus controlled the police) as well as commander-in-chief of the army. Pham Van Dong controlled the purse strings as minister of finance, and Tran Huy Lieu was minister of propaganda. Huy Can was appointed deputy minister for youth. Nguyen Tuong Tam and the other Nationalist leaders, the entire right and center of the political spectrum as well as the Trotskyists, had been completely outmaneuvered. They were all dumbfounded to realize that Ho Chi Minh and his followers were now the government, the only government in Vietnam. And anticommunists were already beginning to disappear. Pham Quynh had already been executed near Hue; and Ngo Dinh Diem's older brother was said to have been buried alive.[43]

American goodwill for the new government remained abundant. In October a Vietnamese-American Friendship Association was organized in Hanoi. Its first meeting was attended by high-ranking Vietminh officials and the small American community in Hanoi. General Gallagher, the recently arrived head of the American military mission in Hanoi, even sang over the Communist-controlled radio station and expressed his best wishes to the new regime. There was an unfeigned sense of camaraderie.[44]

Although the Americans' behavior aroused in Sainteny and his fellow Frenchmen in Hanoi a furious resentment that never quite disappeared, American goodwill was of little use to the Vietminh once they were firmly in power. Their inexperienced administration was confronted with many serious problems, of which the most pressing was the continuing shortage of food. The second poor harvest in a row came in the fall of 1945. An existing rice shortage was further complicated by the presence of 150,000 or so Chinese soldiers who had entered Vietnam with no provisions of their own, some 50,000 of whom remained there for over six months. Not only were there more mouths to be fed from an already inadequate supply of rice, some of the Chinese troops indulged in unconscionable looting while their leaders were preoccupied with scandalous currency manipulations amounting to legal extortion. In addition to, and exacerbating, the food shortage, the Red River delta and central plains were stricken by inflation, currency disputes, strikes, demonstrations, and sporadic acts of violence. The Vietminh revolutionaries were ill prepared to cope with the enormous administrative and technical problems confronting them.[45]

Things Fall Apart in Saigon, 1945

Meanwhile, in the south a quite different set of problems was unfolding over which neither the Vietminh nor their major Nationalist opponents could exert much influence. The south had adequate food and was spared the depredations of undisciplined and underpaid Chinese troops, but the political situation there was equally chaotic and even less amenable to the movement for independence.

The French had found the British, both in India and in Vietnam, to be more sympathetic than either the Chinese or the Americans. The Tran Trong Kim government had never ruled the southern third of the country, known to the West as Cochinchina. There the Japanese held on to direct rule until they were finally replaced on August 16 by the United National Front. This fractious coalition of Cao Dai, Hoa Hao, Dai Viet, Trotskyite, and various other factions held power for only one week. Because the Vietminh had closest ties to the victorious Allies, many southerners thought it would be best if they were in power to receive the victorious occupying forces. A Provisional Executive Committee for the south took up the reins of government in Saigon, led by Tran Van Giau, head of the southern branch of both the Vietminh and the ICP.[46]

When the British commander, General Gracey, arrived in mid-

September, Tran Van Giau and his colleagues called on him, eager to make a good impression and establish some sort of working relationship. But in the general's view, there was nothing to discuss. "They came to see me and said 'welcome' and all that sort of thing. It was an unpleasant situation and I promptly kicked them out." While still mounting his troops in India, General Gracey had decided that "the question of the government of Indochina is exclusively French. . . . Civil and military control of Indochina by the French is only a question of weeks."

In Saigon, violence had begun before General Gracey's arrival. When huge crowds turned out on September 2 to celebrate the declaration of independence taking place in Hanoi, sniper fire from an unknown source turned the demonstration into a riot and several Frenchmen were killed. Against this background, General Gracey yielded to the clamoring of a frightened French community and released and armed French troops who had been confined to their barracks. These soldiers, who had endured some hardship and much humiliation since being arrested by the Japanese six months earlier, took to the streets in a provocative and arrogant manner. Vietnamese extremists responded with provocations of their own. Many ugly incidents took place amidst sullen and frightened crowds.[47]

Then in the predawn darkness of September 24, French troops seized all public buildings in Saigon, expelling the Vietnamese Executive Committee from its symbolic headquarters in the city hall. At daybreak an exultant crowd of Frenchmen exploded in brutish expression of pent-up anger, resentment, and fear. Vietnamese were chased up and down the streets, assaulted, abused, and humiliated. The following day even larger crowds of equally hysterical Vietnamese unleashed their own passions, brutalizing any Frenchmen they could lay their hands on and setting fire to the market.

General Gracey angrily disarmed the French troops once again and attempted to crack down on all groups equally, but tempers were inflamed beyond control. On September 25 a crazed mob of Vietnamese stormed into a French housing settlement and killed hundreds of men, women, and children with bloody abandon. The Vietminh leader, Tran Van Giau, then tried to exploit the violence he could not prevent. Calling for a general strike and a complete state of insurgency, he told the Vietnamese to evacuate Saigon and leave nothing but burning rubble behind them.[48]

A temporary truce was negotiated, to last only a week. On October 11 violence flared up again. But French troops were arriving in Saigon, and by October 25 General LeClerc was ready to reassert French rule over Indochina by force of arms. It would take, he estimated, about a month. Saigon became a beleaguered French city; the Mekong delta, a battlefield. The French encountered few pitched battles in their pacification campaign, but a sullen and hostile population rendered them vulnerable to guerrilla attacks and terrorist raids against which there was no adequate defense.[49]

From Politics to War, November 1945–December 1946

Ho Chi Minh, Sainteny, the various Vietnamese Nationalists, and the Chinese occupation forces continued to maneuver against each other in the north. Throughout the fall of 1945 there were sporadic outbreaks of fighting between Communist, VNQDD, and Dong Minh Hoi armed units, especially in the upper reaches of the Red River valley. The Chinese, for a variety of motives, were eager to bring pressure to bear against the French, so they strongly urged the competing Vietnamese factions to present a united front against the French imperialists.

Ho Chi Minh then seized the initiative once again. Aware of his need to placate the Chinese if he were to maintain his position against both the French and the Nationalist opposition, he made two crucial decisions. First, on November 11, 1945, the Indochinese Communist party was voluntarily and officially dissolved "in order to destroy all misunderstanding, domestic and foreign, which can hinder the liberation of our country. . . ." Beyond this, Ho offered noncommunist leaders posts in his government, suggesting that Nguyen Tuong Tam become minister of foreign affairs. On November 19, under pressure from the Chinese, the Vietnamese factions contending for power in the north agreed not to resort to armed force to settle their disputes. From mid-November until mid-December the Vietminh, the VNQDD, and the Dong Minh Hoi negotiated fruitlessly in an attempt to come to some agreement.[50]

But on December 3, 1945, Ho Chi Minh once again stole the march on his opponents by abruptly announcing that general elections would be held in three weeks' time. Taken completely by surprise, the Nationalists realized they could not compete successfully on such short notice. Nguyen Tuong Tam denounced Ho's "treachery," labeling the elections a deceitful Communist trick.

Some VNQDD elements were so agitated that they kidnapped Vo Nguyen Giap and Tran Huy Lieu (whom they especially disliked and distrusted) in an effort to force the Vietminh to cancel or postpone the elections.

Orders went out to all VNQDD provincial units to prevent the elections from taking place. Then a counterorder went out. An agreement of unity was reached at the last minute. Ho Chi Minh promised that if the elections were permitted to go ahead without disruption he would grant fifty seats in the National Assembly to the VNQDD and twenty to the Dong Minh Hoi. Fearful of French military advances in the south and under strong pressure from the Chinese, VNQDD and Dong Minh Hoi leaders reluctantly agreed to a platform of unity.[51]

General elections were held on January 6, 1946, with relatively few incidents, and a Provisional Coalition Government was formed. But bickering continued, and before either the new cabinet or the National Assembly had met, Nationalist aspirations received another severe blow. The Chinese wrested numerous economic and political concessions from the French and repaid them by agreeing that between March 1 and March 15 the Chinese occupation force in northern Vietnam would be replaced by French troops. On March 1 French ships left Saigon bound for Haiphong. British forces, too, were to begin withdrawing on March 4, leaving the French with a free hand to impose their will on the Vietnamese once again.

To Nguyen Tuong Tam and the other Nationalist leaders, who were desolate and bitter, this was an unconscionable betrayal. The treaty was also a blow to the Vietminh, but one that had been anticipated. Ho Chi Minh had already begun to negotiate seriously with the French. He, Sainteny, and General LeClerc were on the verge of achieving a compromise that would postpone if not avert open warfare.[52]

In this setting the National Assembly convened for the first time on March 2 and voted the new coalition government into office. On March 6 the French fleet arrived in the harbor at Haiphong; on that very day, Ho Chi Minh concluded an agreement that permitted the stationing of French troops in northern Vietnam in exchange for French recognition of Vietnam as a "free state," which was, however, "part of the Indochinese Federation and the French Union."

Nguyen Tuong Tam, installed only four days earlier as minister of foreign affairs, was outraged at the agreement, immediately denouncing this "surrender" in his typical outspoken and uncompromising manner. When his vociferous protest was blandly ignored by Ho Chi Minh, Tam stomped off in a huff and remained away from his new office for six crucial days to demonstrate his disapproval and to dissociate himself from this spirit of compromise. Meanwhile the Chinese commander in Haiphong (who was himself apparently unhappy over the turn of events), claiming he had not been officially notified of such agreements, opened fire on the French and ordered them to leave. Withering fire from French naval guns and a sharp rebuke from his superiors quickly combined to convince him that he had "misunderstood," but the tone of the disembarkation had been established by the gunsmoke hovering over the waterfront.[53]

On March 12 Nguyen Tuong Tam returned to his post, still angry and sharply critical of nearly everyone. In addition to the Vietminh, the French, and the Chinese, he attached special blame to the United States for failing to exercise its moral responsibility. But Tam's voice went unheeded, and both the Vietnamese pact of unity and the Franco-Vietnamese truce were shaky and frequently ignored.[54]

Throughout the winter months sporadic fighting continued between the Vietminh and the VNQDD in the northern provinces, between the Vietminh, the Cao Dai, and the Hoa Hao in the south, and between all these groups and the French. This uneasy, many-sided truce inspired little confidence or genuine goodwill on any side. Even within the new coalition government there was in fact little opportunity for genuine debate. The Vietminh-controlled National Assembly met only briefly on March 2, rubber-stamped a number of proposals laid before it, then adjourned. A Permanent Committee established to act for the Assembly when it was not in session was composed entirely of Vietminh members. Few important issues were debated; none were resolved by compromise.[55]

The controversial March 6 Franco-Vietnamese agreement was a masterpiece of ambiguity. If this treaty were to prevent the continuing guerrilla war in the south and the periodic clashes in the north from erupting into the full-blown war that wiser parties on all sides dreaded, it remained necessary somehow to perform the almost impossible task of translating vague rhetoric into a mass of concrete details to which all parties could agree. To this urgent purpose, a preliminary conference was convened in the tranquil mountain town of Dalat on April 18, 1946.

The ten-man Vietnamese delegation was led by Nguyen Tuong Tam, under the watchful eye of Vo Nguyen Giap. A third member of the team, there as an "agricultural expert" and still considered to be a noncommunist delegate, was Cu Huy Can. On the French side Pierre Gourou was present as an expert adviser. Discussions were heated and fruitless, marred by accusations of treachery and deceit, charges and countercharges. There were so many fundamental differences between the Vietnamese and French conceptions of what it meant to be a free state within the Indochinese Federation and the French Union that it was often difficult even to find a basis for discussion. The two sides hammered away at each other for over three weeks. Vo Nguyen Giap was the most impressive participant to Western observers.

Tam, as usual at his worst in negotiations, was stiff and sullen. At the end he was trembling with rage, and Vo Nguyen Giap was in tears. Neither man had expected much to come of the conference, but it had been worse than they had anticipated. Tam summed up the sole accomplishment of the long hours of negotiations as being "a general agreement on the fact that the Conference had failed to reach agreement on any item on the agenda."[56]

Ho Chi Minh, however, tried to put the best possible face on the fiasco and began preparing for a major, definitive conference on the Franco-Vietnamese relationship to be held in France a month later. But Tam would make no more concessions to either the French or the Communists. He felt his presence at such negotiations was being used to discredit the noncommunist Nationalist position. By the end of the month he was back in China trying to organize a coalition that was both anti-French and anticommunist while Ho Chi Minh and Pham Van Dong were leading a new Vietnamese delegation to France in one final attempt to negotiate an acceptable relationship with France.

The Fontainebleau Conference formally opened on July 6 and continued throughout the entire summer with no discernible progress. It had, in fact, been thoroughly sabotaged before it even began by the wily Admiral d'Argenlieu, French high commissioner to Indochina, who had unilaterally and without proper authority recognized the "Republic of Cochinchina" as a "free state" on the very day when Ho Chi Minh and his party were traveling to France.

Since the status of Cochinchina was to have been one of the major topics of discussion at Fontainebleau, the Vietnamese rightly took this act to signal an arrogant and intransigent attitude on the part of the French. On September 13 the Vietnamese mission left for home, empty-handed and disappointed.[57]

Ho Chi Minh remained personally aloof from the conference proceedings, letting Pham Van Dong serve as official leader of the delegation. When the others left for home in disgust, Ho remained in France, unwilling to return to Hanoi with no agreement at all. "Don't leave me this way," he pleaded to Sainteny and Marius Moutet, the socialist minister of overseas France. All he could obtain from them was a modus vivendi that avoided the crucial areas of conflict. This he signed on behalf of his government. It was not much, but he thought it was better than nothing. It did stipulate that all acts of hostility and violence between the French and the Vietnamese would cease and that another conference would be held no later than January 1947 to negotiate a final treaty.[58]

During Ho's absence Vo Nguyen Giap ran the government. With the departure of Nguyen Tuong Tam and other prominent Nationalist leaders and with Ho Chi Minh absent (and thus able to dissociate himself from any actions that went wrong), Giap brutally cracked down on the opposition. When the last Chinese troops left in early June, the purge began. The French aided Giap in this repression, believing Ho Chi Minh and his Vietminh to be not only the strongest but also the most moderate of the contending Vietnamese factions in the north.

After driving the Dong Minh Hoi troops out of their areas of control in the region north of Hanoi, Giap's forces were ready to attack the VNQDD-controlled zones in the Red River valley. The major crackdown in Hanoi came in mid-July. While French vehicles blocked off the surrounding streets, Vietminh troops launched an assault on the VNQDD headquarters in Hanoi, arresting over a hundred cadre, burning files, smashing printing presses. By November the Vietminh troops had fought their way almost to the Yunnan border, expelling the VNQDD forces from all populated areas in the country.[59]

When Ho Chi Minh returned to Vietnam in October 1946, several important changes had taken place, mostly in his favor. The Chinese troops were gone, organized opposition had been effectively suppressed, a separate Vietnamese state had been established in the southern third of the country, and well-armed French troops were installed in all parts of Vietnam, including Haiphong and Hanoi. Incidents between French and Vietnamese units were taking place with increasing frequency. On both sides tempers were frayed and there was a growing danger that a minor mis-understanding might spark full-scale warfare.

Meanwhile, just a few days before Ho left for France and Nguyen Tuong Tam slipped off to China, another front organiza-tion had been superimposed on the Vietminh, just as the Vietminh itself had been imposed on the ICP four years earlier. This new group was known as the Lien Viet front, or more formally as the Vietnamese National Union League. Dominated by the Vietminh but broadly based, the Lien Viet front was a loosely organized coalition under a leadership committee containing twenty-seven leaders of disparate ideologies and backgrounds. It included hard-line Communists, pro-Vietminh members of different religious and political groups, friendly neutralists, and a few members of the opposition. Hoang Dao, Nguyen Tuong Tam's younger brother, was a surprise member, representing the VNQDD. The secretary-general of this new organization was also a surprise, none other than Cu Huy Can, still nominally a member of the Democratic party and better known as a poet, intellectual, and agronomist than as a politician. The Lien Viet front provided an effective facade and some very real substance of national unity against the French.[60]

As soon as Ho Chi Minh got back to Hanoi, the time was ripe for consolidating these gains on the home front. On October 28, 1946, the National Assembly was convened for its second session. The session opened with 291 members present. Of the 70 Dong Minh Hoi and VNQDD seats, 33 were empty. The 37 opposition members who did appear felt intimidated by the conspicuous pres-ence of heavily armed policemen, and some claimed that their houses had been searched. One of the more courageous (or more naive) of these men was bold enough to inquire as to the fate of the missing representatives. Who answered for the government? Cu Huy Can spoke up at once, authoritatively announcing that "they had been arrested with the approval of the Standing Committee for common-law crimes." Before the session was over the man who asked that question had himself disappeared, and no one cared to ask out loud about that.

Ho's proposals, including a new constitution and a sweeping

reorganization of the government, were passed without criticism or revision. The final vote taken at the close of the session on November 8 was 240 to 2. The Vietminh controlled the National Assembly, the cabinet, and the military on a constitutional basis. Through the Lien Viet front, they had the support of a large segment of the population; but at the same time they faced the unremitting enmity of a very large minority group.[61]

Tension between the Vietnamese and the French forces reached a new high a few days later when a misunderstanding at Haiphong flared out of control and excited Vietminh militiamen slaughtered twenty-three French soldiers, some of whom were unarmed and shot down while doing nothing more provocative than purchasing fruit in the market. Two days later, six more French soldiers were killed north of Hanoi. The French military commanders then determined to teach the "treacherous Viets" a lesson. But what began as a show of force in Haiphong on November 23 quickly got out of hand through a series of misjudgments made in panic. Before the day was out, over six thousand Vietnamese civilians had been slaughtered in a grotesquely disproportionate response. By this time the rank and file of the military on both sides were increasingly ready to shoot first and ask questions afterward.[62]

A French proposal that the "trigger-happy" Vietminh militia be disarmed was received with indignation. On the morning of December 19, 1946, Ho Chi Minh sent a friendly letter to Sainteny (who had been rushed back to Hanoi in a last-minute attempt to avoid open warfare) expressing hopes that some way could yet be found to reduce tensions and achieve a peaceful resolution of differences. At the same time, Vo Nguyen Giap suggested to the French military that permitting some of the French troops who were standing by on alert to go on leave might induce a more relaxed atmosphere in Hanoi. At noon many French soldiers received their first passes in days. At eight in the evening the power station in Hanoi exploded and in the ensuing darkness the Vietminh militia executed a well-planned attack on all French installations. Within hours fighting spread from one end of Vietnam to the other. The Resistance War had begun in earnest.[63]

The Resistance and the Intellectuals, 1946–1947

By February 1947 Ho Chi Minh and his entire government had withdrawn to the mountainous Viet Bac region. Giap had long since pulled his meager regular-force units into that zone for further training and to fortify and stockpile a secluded wartime headquarters there. The French controlled only the major towns. Ho Chi Minh attempted to organize the entire population to participate in the Resistance War by forming multiple overlapping groups for "national salvation." Not the least important of these groups was the Literary Association for National Salvation, headed by a relatively unknown young man named To Huu.

To Huu's unique qualification for this job—beyond his extraordinary energy and intelligence—was the fact that he was perhaps the only person in the land who was artistically successful as a Communist poet. While The Lu, Xuan Dieu, Luu Trong Lu, Che Lan Vien, and Huy Can were enjoying their enormous popularity among high school and college students in the late 1930s, To Huu had been a high school student himself. And he had gone almost directly from school to prison, for while still a student he had been converted to communism and embarked upon a revolutionary career. He has been, he tells us, a different man "Since Then":

> Since then summer light has burned in me
> The sun of truth has pierced my heart
> And my soul has become a splendid garden
> All scent and chirping birds.
>
> I link my mind with other minds,
> My love flows a hundred ways
> My soul mingles with multitudes:
> Side by side, we're creating life.
>
> I have been son to numberless families,
> Brother to thousands of lost destinies,
> Elder to millions of children
> Who wander, naked and hungry, over the earth.
> (Translation from Nguyen Ngoc Bich 1975, 180)

Many writers and poets made their way into the mountains to join the resistance. One of the first to rally to the Vietminh cause was Luu Trong Lu. During 1943 and 1944 Lu lived alone in a wretched hut on the outskirts of Hue, ill, penniless, and depressed. At first a few acquaintances had brought him food, medicine, and encouragement. But he seemed only to get dirtier, lazier, and more withdrawn. By the end of 1944 Lu was abandoned out of disgust and helplessness by all who knew him, left utterly alone with his sickness, his poverty, the opium addiction he could no longer afford to indulge, and his ever-deeper anguish and despair.[64] For years he had written nothing, but in 1945 Lu wrote a simple ditty about a young woman named O who carried supplies for the Vietminh:

> Learning of life's deep intent
> Off to carry supplies O went.
> At her twenty years of age,
> What knew she of life's darker page?
> Looking forward, to and fro,
> O passed by camps of the foe.
> O moved on without delay,
> Asking sisters on her way.
> Moving with a stealthy step,
> Down deserted roads she crept.
> O sang a tune, she hummed a lay.
> The enemy camps were far away.
> O laughed, and then she chattered.
> All over the road her echo scattered.
> Sometime she could rest again.
> It didn't matter where or when.
> O went on, and on and on.
> Light of day would soon be gone.
> A ravine forced her to go wading
> And her pants got soaking wet.
> Suddenly she stopped to rest,
> Looked at the water and saw her face.
> O noticed, all at once,
> The bloom of spring was fading.
> Her white complexion was turning brown.
> O feared her husband's frown,
> But she walked on at a steady pace.
> She was working for her nation.
> If he didn't like it, let him frown.[65]

Luu Trong Lu explicitly renounced his earlier metaphor of the "apprehensive tawny deer," and with it his old life and his earlier literary theories and creations. After the August Revolution, a new root metaphor dominated his soul, reinvigorating him, as he made clear in a new version of "The Sound of Autumn (II)." The wind of revolution had now blown away the autumn leaves. Since the revolution, he asserted:

> The apprehension is gone
> The deer has found its way.
>
> . . . .

> Shattered destinies are reborn,
> In the rebirth of my soul.
>
> . . . .
>
> With Heaven and Earth in turmoil,
> The deer plucks up its ears,
> And quivers on the trail of warhorses.
> (Translation from Nguyen Khac Vien
> and Huu Ngoc, n.d., 604)

The revolutionary movement lead by the ICP was a weapon with which Luu Trong Lu and thousands like him could combat the feelings of inferiority, impotence, alienation, and despair that had blighted their lives. It gave them hope, a newly discovered sense of efficacy and self-worth. For some, in general those with the greatest need, it provided a new and more satisfying sense of self. These newly reconstituted identities were associated with personal rejuvenation as well as with patriotism, and with a new worldview that reconciled previously unresolvable conflicts and contradictions between the old and the new, between East and West, between the individual and the group. These men now espoused "art for the sake of life" and rejected "art for art's sake."

Perhaps the most enthusiastic of all the writers and poets to join the Resistance was Xuan Dieu. No longer was he clinging to life with the fingernails of both hands, facing the cold border of nihility. Under the influence of his good friend Huy Can, Xuan Dieu became a dedicated, proselytizing Communist, joining the party in 1947. His popularity and skill as a poet made him a valuable addition to the Vietminh organization. To compensate for his bourgeois background and his notoriety as the most romantic, Westernized, and individualistic poet in Vietnam, Xuan Dieu became the most extreme of the new Communist literary talents. He was second to none in praising "Uncle Ho" and "the Party":

> Whenever the struggle grows fierce,
> Uncle Ho always comes to visit.
> As we children listen to his teachings,
> We want to follow in his path.
> We children swear a solemn oath:
> To be resolute in our devotion,
> To shed our skins from this day forth.[66]

By the phrase "to shed our skins from this day forth" Xuan Dieu meant nothing more nor less than to be reborn into a new identity.

This was a summons to be "born again" in communism, an evangelical call that far transcended any purely political intent. This was an appeal for a conversion in identity that amounted to a religious experience, a total transformation of self. Both Luu Trong Lu and Xuan Dieu had found new meaning and purpose in life, changing their very personalities.

Huy Can was already a high-ranking Vietminh official. Phan Khoi, sixty years old when the fighting began, hobbled over mountains and through jungle with the aid of a cane, doing whatever he could to support the Resistance. The Lu was on the editorial board of the magazine being published in Viet Bac by the Literary Association for National Salvation. Che Lan Vien and Nguyen Cong Hoan had not only gone into the mountains with the Resistance forces, they too had joined the Communist party in 1947.[67] Hoai Thanh also quickly placed his pen in the service of the Vietminh and joined the party in 1947.

Hoai Thanh shared in this radical reorganization of sense of self, and the concomitant reappraisal of the understanding, evaluation, and creation of literature. During the 1930s and early 1940s, he later wrote, "I was very infatuated with the new poetry, from the time it first appeared. It was as if the 'new poetry' was my one and only pleasure in life at that time."[68]

He reported that, after joining the Vietminh-led Resistance following the August Revolution, he experienced a "miraculous resurrection." Speaking for himself and other "victims of the century of individualism," Hoai Thanh later proclaimed that in "the new atmosphere" following the August Revolution, "we now realize how little our individual life means in the immense life of the community." This syndrome of psychic and social "rebirth" experienced as a "miraculous resurrection," especially insofar as it characterized many of the more articulate and influential members of the intelligentsia, is an important element in explaining the resurgence of the ICP in the years immediately preceding (1944–1945) and especially immediately following (1945–1947) the August Revolution.

Despite a surge of support in the year and a half preceding the "revolution" of August 1945, when the "revolution" took place there were only about five thousand party members, and many of them were in jail. After Ho Chi Minh announced the "dissolution" of the party in the name of national unity in November of 1945, during its state of official nonexistence membership grew to about twenty thousand by 1946. Between 1947 and 1949, the party inducted hundreds of thousands of new members.[69] When the Vietnamese Communist party reappeared under the new name Vietnam Workers' party, it constituted a vast, tightly disciplined force that exerted near total control over the Resistance movement. This created for the many patriotic noncommunist Vietnamese, especially intellectuals, a difficult and frustrating situation.

The Anticommunist Factions, 1947–1950

At this time Nguyen Tuong Tam was still trying to build an anti-French and anticommunist organization in southern China, cursing both sides in the war with equal passion. Few of his former colleagues were still with him. Khai Hung had been kidnapped and assassinated early in 1947, presumably by the Vietminh. The Lu had joined the Vietminh. Xuan Dieu and Huy Can, who had launched their careers in the pages of *Mores* and *This Day*, with Tam's support, were Communists. Hoang Dao had gotten nowhere with his activity in the Lien Viet front organization. So in March 1947 Tam flew to Hong Kong to confer with the former emperor Bao Dai.

After voluntarily yielding his authority to the Vietminh, Bao Dai moved to Hanoi, where he was "supreme adviser" to the Ho Chi Minh government. In March 1946 he had traveled to Chungking as part of an official delegation to the Chiang Kai-shek government; but instead of returning with the other members, he took up residence in Hong Kong, where he began to earn his reputation for profligacy and carousal. Yet he continued to follow political developments with a shrewd eye, realizing that he might still play a role of some significance in his nation's history.[70]

After an inconclusive but not discouraging discussion with Bao Dai, Nguyen Tuong Tam returned to China and announced the formation of a National Union front, anti-French and anticommunist, dedicated to the creation of a new government to be headed by Bao Dai and with which both the French and the Vietminh would be forced to negotiate and make concessions. At the heart of this movement in its earliest phase were the Dong Minh Hoi, VNQDD, and Dai Viet leaders; but the participation of a widely disparate group of prominent Vietnamese quickly followed. The founder and leader of the Hoa Hao sect, Huynh Phu So, had been slain by the Vietminh in April, and his followers became fanatically anticommunist. The Cao Dai, too, were abandoning their tenuous truce with the Vietminh. Hoa Hao, Cao Dai, Buddhist, and Catholic groups and leaders were drawn to the coalition, as were a number of older conservatives, including Tran Trong Kim.[71]

In March the French appointed a new high commissioner for Indochina whose mission was directed primarily toward negotiating an end to the fighting there. One of the first moves this new high commissioner made was to appoint to his staff as his political adviser Paul Mus. During the month of May, Mus was dispatched on two critical missions, one to Ho Chi Minh and the other to Bao Dai. Neither was successful. Bao Dai was not encouraging. He would, he informed Mus, demand from France at least as much as Ho Chi Minh, and possibly more, should he participate in any negotiations. Ho Chi Minh, too, rejected out of hand the offer Mus had been authorized to deliver. "If you were in my place, professor," he asked, "would you accept these terms?" Mus confessed that he would not. "There is no place in the French Union for cowards," said the Vietminh leader, "and if I accepted these terms, it would be the act of a coward."[72]

The National Union front made spectacular progress in the south, where even officials of the French-sponsored "free state" known as the Republic of Cochinchina were cooperating with it. By late August there were even demonstrations in Hanoi, with crowds shouting their support for Bao Dai. On September 9 and 10 National Union front leaders met with Bao Dai in Hong Kong on an optimistic note. The popularity and influence of Nguyen Tuong Tam was high at this time, and his brother Hoang Dao had joined him. But to Tam's dismay other Bao Dai supporters representing much more moderate points of view were increasingly in evidence, including some who had traveled to Hong Kong at the suggestion of the French. As the movement in support of Bao Dai grew, Nguyen Tuong Tam and his closest associates found their influence withering. On October 29, 1947, Tam resigned in anger and withdrew into lonely exile in southern China.[73]

Throughout late 1947 and 1948, the Vietminh mounted a vigorous propaganda campaign against Bao Dai and Nguyen Tuong Tam. In the markets and schools, the villages and towns under Vietminh control, numerous meetings and rallies were staged at which crude straw effigies of Bao Dai were ridiculed, insulted, spat upon, punched, kicked, stabbed, and finally burned. The treason of Nguyen Tuong Tam was denounced in songs. At a more sophisticated level, study sessions were held in which Vietminh cultural cadres patiently explained Tam's flaws as a man, as a writer, and as a thinker. He was characterized as a product of the flaccid and confused reaction of prerevolutionary intellectuals to their colonial plight. It became fashionable to compare the works of Nguyen Tuong Tam with those of Nguyen Cong Hoan, demonstrating Hoan's more advanced social consciousness. The contrast between Tam's *Breaking The Ties* and Hoan's *Miss Minh* was a common theme. Tam, they said, advocated selfishness; Hoan, social responsibility.[74]

Under Truong Chinh's policy of party cultural hegemony, literature served as a powerful weapon for the party. Huy Can, Luu Trong Lu, Xuan Dieu, Che Lan Vien, The Lu, Nguyen Cong Hoan, Hoai Thanh, and quite a few other poets, writers, and critics in the Vietnamese literary community accepted—and many of them reveled in—the cultural matrix laid down for them by the party, a doctrinaire, naively pedagogical approach that aspired to wed artistic skill and talent to propagandistic intent. In a July 1948 report delivered to the Second National Cultural Congress, Truong Chinh reminded the converts to the cause what was expected of them, echoing the martial rhetoric of his 1944 poem, "To be a Poet": "Just as we have manufactured bazookas, mortars, guns to fire at the enemy, we must likewise create cultural bazookas, mortars and guns to destroy him."[75]

The prescribed mode for all art, for all cultural cadres, was "socialist realism." In the early years of the revolution, not many Vietnamese had a very clear idea of what was meant by "socialist realism." In his July 1948 speech, Truong Chinh explained:

> As we understand it, socialist realism is a method of artistic creation which portrays the truth in a society evolving towards socialism according to objective laws. Out of objective reality we must spotlight "the typical features in situations" [a quote from Engels] and reveal the inexorable motive force driving society forward and the objective tendency of the process of evolution.[76]

The National Union front foundered. Its dynamic leader in the south, Nguyen Van Sam, was assassinated in October, within twenty-four hours of the killing of an important leader in the north; it was during this same month that Tam resigned. Also, a key policy speech by the French high commissioner in late September had been a bitter disappointment, totally devoid of any imaginative concepts or substantive proposals that might have provided a rallying point for the divided Nationalist community and led to serious negotiations.[77]

Eventually Bao Dai did manage to wrest from the French nominal concessions of both "independence" and "unification" for Vietnam. He returned to Vietnam late in April as chief of state for a unified Vietnam. He had achieved through patient diplomacy more than Ho Chi Minh would gladly have settled for in 1945, or in 1946, or perhaps even in 1947. There was no single dramatic breakthrough, however, and Bao Dai's new government came into being with no crowds, marching bands, or parades. It came instead through a gradual and tedious procession of paperwork, committee meetings, and bureaucratic obfuscations. It came, in fact, too late to achieve its purpose. While arousing the total enmity of Ho Chi Minh and the competing government of the Democratic Republic of Vietnam, it continued throughout its existence to feud with the French over hundreds of technical details, and still it failed to win the support of many noncommunist Nationalists.[78]

Ngo Dinh Diem for over two years played an active role in bringing about the return of Bao Dai. But he refused to head Bao Dai's government. The limited independence that Vietnam had obtained was not enough for Diem. Diem had talked with the French, the Japanese, the Vietminh, the National United Front, and now he talked with Bao Dai, from whose cabinet he had once resigned in 1933. But he never actually negotiated. He was still waiting to meet his time. In August 1950 he left Vietnam for a four-year sojourn in Japan, the United States, Rome, Belgium, and Paris.[79]

The "Supervillages" of Vietnam

Vietnam in the meantime was becoming an ever-more fragmented and confused society in which people were taking refuge in smaller and more tightly bounded social groupings. Families and villages strove to maintain their precarious equilibrium by closing their boundaries more tightly. The same strategy was revealed in the regional sectarian autonomy that flourished; states within states closed and maintained their boundaries by a potent combination of inflated ideological rhetoric, armed militias, and a resurgence of in-group solidarity. The sense of personal rejuvenation experienced by To Huu, Xuan Dieu, Luu Trong Lu, Hoai Thanh, and other converts to the Communist revolutionary movement was not restricted to the Vietminh. At this critical juncture of history all competing Vietnamese groups were engaged in a rite of passage, suspended in and out of time in a transitional moment between colonialism and independence. The revolution was an extended transition from one cultural state to another for many groups and individuals in Vietnam.

As the writings of Victor Turner (1969, 1974) have led us to expect of such liminal (threshold) phenomena, the revolutionary movement minimalized previous distinctions based on wealth, age, gender, kinship, occupation, or social status. Individual egos were immersed in a mystical bond between individuals who shared dreams, hardships, danger, and uncertainty. This state of spontaneously generated relationship (similar to the "I" and "Thou" of Martin Buber), marked by such "intense, effervescent camaraderie," has been called "communitas" by Victor Turner, to distinguish it from the more mundane and formally structured sense of community. Communitas flows through the interstices of structure; it is inherently transient, pleasurable, and typically rejuvenating.[80]

Along the fertile coastal plains of the South China Sea in the lower portion of the northern delta, in the bishoprics of Phat Diem and Bui Chu, the militiamen of militant Catholic groups kept both the French and the Vietminh at bay. The white and yellow flag of the Vatican flew over the villages scattered across this rich riceland; and local-born Catholic priests dispensed justice, organized economic activity, and directed the emplacement of watchtowers and machine guns. There were enthusiastic village and intervillage "resistance committees," and they resisted all outside forces and influences with breathtaking zeal.[81]

Far to the south the Cao Dai too ruled over a small world of their own, one focused on the Holy See in Tay Ninh with its garish eclectic architecture, its pantheon of saints and spirit advisers ranging from Lao Tse to Victor Hugo to Sun Yat-sen, and its single, staring, all-seeing eye painted on the innermost wall of the sacred temple. The Cao Dai also had their own militia (well trained by the Japanese), their own schools and courts, and their own social welfare programs including everything from agricultural cooperatives to a well-run orphanage. They fought with a zeal comparable to that of the northern Catholics, spurred on by grandiose schemes for the future. They envisioned transforming a modest cluster of villages on the outskirts of Tay Ninh into a major metropolis with broad boulevards and spacious parks. On their professionally executed maps for planned development they even allocated space for the railroad station, although no existing tracks ran anywhere near them.[82]

Farther down in the Mekong delta, centering upon the province of Long Xuyen, where Huynh Phu So was born, the Hoa Hao had carved out another semiautonomous zone, the boundaries of which were maintained by fiercely wielded machetes and rifles. With their own purple and yellow flag, their own administrative hierarchies, the Hoa Hao were more provincial and less grandiose in their designs than the other sects, but their followers were no less zealous or devout.[83]

There were at roughly the same time other less important and less pure examples of these states within a state. For a time a diehard band of VNQDD partisans held out against the French and the Vietminh in a remote mountain stronghold near the Chinese border, proclaiming themselves to be a national government. Most bizarre of all, in and around Saigon an overgrown gang of river pirates (the Binh Xuyen) ran both the police department and a monopolistic vice empire of vast proportions. They also levied a "tax" on the transport of goods and extorted money from various business enterprises. They too had their own armed forces and slyly assumed the facade of a "sect"; but any ideological pretensions they had were strictly an operation in public relations.[84]

Each of these semiautonomous enclaves was to a greater or lesser extent characterized by an élan, some palpable disciplined enthusiasm that was conspicuously absent from Vietnamese society as a whole. Each was in its own peculiar way an extension of traditional Vietnamese village organization. Each might best be understood as an improvised "supervillage" that emerged to protect its members from the vicissitudes of a modern world in which no other truly modern and national identity had evolved to provide an adequate sense of structure and stability to their lives.

Like each traditional village, each of these social enclaves had its own politico-religious center, its own charter, its own hierarchical structure of roles, and its own rather clearly defined sets of mutual obligations and expectations. As these "supervillages" took shape and grew, developing through interaction with each other and the larger society, their boundaries closed and became more vigorously maintained. As ideological consensus, mutual assistance, and cooperation emerged internally, accompanied by an invigorating sense of communitas, the distinction between members and nonmembers grew sharper and the "price of belonging" (in terms of orthodoxy and commitment) grew higher.

The Bao Dai government nominally presided over all of these groups, and ultimately it gained their cooperation in the war against the Vietminh. But the Bao Dai government never partook of their enthusiasm, and it was singularly unsuccessful in generating any sense of communitas at a higher level. The central government was endured as a necessary element of defense against the Vietminh and against further French colonial designs, but it obtained active support precisely because (and only when) it respected the various groups' autonomy and did not intrude in any significant way in their freedom to conduct local affairs as they saw fit. In a society so heterogeneous and so polarized, perhaps nothing more was possible.

From the national point of view, these groups (Catholic, Cao Dai, Hoa Hao) were purely *yin* structures, alternative or even counter ideologies; but at the local level they thrived because they provided a new *yang* structure that engendered personalities and social groupings more highly structured and integrated than any that had existed in Vietnam for the past fifty years. They increased entropy at the national level, but drastically reduced it within the localities they dominated.

In contrast to all of this, the complex organizational structure under the leadership of Ho Chi Minh was unique. As the Vietminh, it was a "supervillage" in much the same sense as the Catholics, Cao Dai, and Hoa Hao. As the Democratic Republic of Vietnam, it was also a fully developed and constitutionally based national government. The French conducted studies that provided a penetrating analysis of what was happening but failed utterly to assess its proper significance. A report prepared by the French military accurately described Ho Chi Minh's organizational apparatus, including:

> youth groups, groups for mothers, farmers, workers, "resistant" Catholics, war veterans, etc. It could just as well have included associations of flute players or bicycle racers; the important point was that no one escaped regimentation and that the [normal] territorial hierarchy was thus complemented by another, which watched the former and was in turn watched by it—both of them being watched in turn from the outside

and the inside by the security services and the party. The individual caught in the fine mesh of such a net has no chance whatever of preserving his independence.[85]

Preserving one's personal independence, however, was not a high priority for many Vietnamese. Many peasants and intellectuals sought instead some well-defined, encompassing, and bounded framework within which to pursue their socially oriented goals and ambitions. This stress upon ideological orthodoxy and conformity to socially imposed constraints on individual behavior on the part of the Vietminh was a return to rather than a departure from traditional Vietnamese culture. The traditional village (or court or mandarinate), the Cao Dai, the Hoa Hao, and the Phat Diem/Bui Chu Catholics shared this emphasis on social constraint of individual behavior—as they all did with the Vietnamese family, which socialized the population from which these groups all recruited their members. This was the source of their dynamism and strength, not a weakness. Within the relatively closed system that these villages and "supervillages" constituted, it generated commitment rather than resentment. The true test of survival for these groups was their ability to bring enough people into the system to make it viable against external pressures and then to develop techniques of communication and control adequate to the task of maintaining the larger system. In this the Vietminh were unexcelled.

Both Neo-Confucianism and communism were primarily ethical systems, prescribing a way of life. The revolutionary ethics of the Communist party skillfully assimilated the essence of the traditional system and transformed it to serve their purposes, tapping the deepest levels of the Vietnamese personality to motivate and discipline their members. A handbook used by party militants defined the core values of tradition in contemporary terms. *Nhan* and *nghia* were still core elements of the ethical system. *Nhan*, the work explained, "consists of loving deeply and wholeheartedly assisting one's comrades and compatriots. That is why the cadre who displays this virtue wages a resolute struggle against all those who would harm the party and the people. That is why he will not hesitate to be the first to endure hardship and the last to enjoy happiness." *Nghia*, the summative value of duty and social obligation, was elaborated to mean "not having ulterior motives, doing nothing unjust and having nothing to hide from the party. It also means not being preoccupied by personal interests in conflict with those of the party. Any task assigned by the party, large or small, should be done conscientiously."[86]

This handbook for cadres might be summarized in a single sentence: behave toward the party as if it were your family. All of these supervillages constrained individuality and insisted upon conformity. But to most Vietnamese this was familiar territory. They had not been raised to be independent, as American children are.

At the individual level, conformity was a strategy for obtaining respect, status, cooperation, and assistance from one's fellow group members. At the group level it was a strategy for establishing equilibrium and maintaining stability. The price to be paid was one of reduced autonomy of thought and action for the individual, and a decrease in flexibility and possible loss of some development potential for the group. The relative desirability of these trade-offs was a question that could only be answered in terms of values.

For a person who had internalized the value of individualism this high degree of conformity to group pressures involved such a loss of personal dignity and feelings of self-worth that it was intolerable. For one who possessed a collective orientation derived from the root paradigm of the traditional Vietnamese family, one's own ambition and needs generated a positive desire to meet the expectations and to conform to the social pressures of other group members. This was the heart of the debate between Nguyen Tuong Tam and Nguyen Cong Hoan fifteen years earlier; it was the essential difference between Loan (in *Breaking The Ties*) and *Miss Minh, the Schoolteacher.*

While these competing, closed, "supervillage" communities were developing into the major forces in Vietnam and reaching their zenith as models of social conformity, Nguyen Tuong Tam was at the nadir of his career. While many writers and poets were undergoing varying degrees of personal rejuvenation within the Vietminh organization, Nguyen Tuong Tam languished alone in China. Added to the death of Thach Lam, his younger brother, in 1943 and the assassination of his close friend Khai Hung in 1947, in 1948 Tam suffered another severe personal loss. His brother and closest remaining comrade in arms, Hoang Dao (Nguyen Tuong Long), suffered a fatal heart attack. These events, coupled with his political frustrations, the loss of his treasured publishing empire, the unhappy dispersal of the Self-Strength Literary Movement, and the avalanche of criticism and abuse being hurled at him from all sides of the political and literary spectrum, combined to push Nguyen Tuong Tam to the verge of a nervous breakdown.

Tam had been notable in Hanoi in the early 1930s, when he took over *Mores*, as an abstemious man. He was faithful to his wife. He did not smoke, drink, gamble, hang out in nightclubs, or use opium. In the heyday of *Mores* it had not been unusual for him to work on the paper until eleven or twelve o'clock at night and then arise and be at his desk again by three or four in the morning to write another ten or twenty pages of fiction before anyone else arrived at the office. As the decade wore on he began to turn to opium to relax and escape from the frustration and rage that was consuming him. When opium seemed to be getting too strong a grip on him, he began to drink as a means of abstaining from opium use. But until 1939 he had continued to be a productive writer, and he was always a hard worker. When he found himself alone and frustrated in China, alcohol helped him combat rage and depression. But now he wrote nothing, did nothing. It is said that he would sit alone in a darkened room for days on end, speaking to no one, gulping down cheap whiskey by the tumblerful, and smoking one after another of the strongest and cheapest cigarettes available.[87]

The Cao Dai, Hoa Hao, Vietminh, and similar groups in Vietnamese society during the 1940s all developed their strong sense of identity and tightened their boundaries and internal cohesion in reaction to one another—as well as to the French, the Chinese, and other political, military, religious and ethnic groups and ideologies both domestic and foreign. Each group came progressively to define, articulate, and insist upon the primacy of its own worldview, a unique configuration of beliefs, attitudes, and values that represented to them the only truth and the sole basis of social or political legitimacy. As they aspired to and attained greater autonomy, closed their boundaries and grew more dogmatic, the relationships between them became increasingly fierce. According to Bernard Fall, opponents were commonly tied together in bundles like logs and thrown into the Mekong River to drown and float to sea.[88]

The Vietminh and its most effective opponents tended to be both authoritarian and totalitarian regimes. They demanded, and by and large received, a very high degree of conformity from their members in virtually all aspects of social life. As in the traditional families and villages of northern and central Vietnam, this extreme conformity to group pressure did not normally involve any genuine constraint on personal will or ambition. People chose to act this way and to be part of such a framework, because it was an efficacious way of attaining their goals and fulfilling their needs. They were willing to give up a great deal of personal autonomy to confirm their membership in a group in which other people too would conform to an equal degree. In such groups, each individual knew what to expect of another person and also what was expected of him or her by the other person. For an individualist like Nguyen Tuong Tam, these were all repressive feudal structures of precisely the sort against which he had declared war almost twenty years earlier. But to many other Vietnamese, such groups were exactly what they had long been looking for.

The Bao Dai Government and the French, 1948–1954

In sharp contrast to the Democratic Republic of Vietnam (based as it was on the Vietminh) and the competing "supervillages"— the Cao Dai, the Hoa Hao, and the Phat Diem/Bui Chu Catholics— the Bao Dai government, although authoritarian in the extreme, was not at all totalitarian. It was instead relatively open, poorly defined, and ideologically bland if not impoverished. It had laws, edicts, regulations, and administrative guidelines by the thousands. It generated mountains of memoranda. This was a bureaucratic coalition government based on compromise, ambiguity, caution, and intrigue. To the blunt and outspoken Tam and people like him, this was a world as alien as that of the Communists and the sects.

Far too many French administrators, military officers, and businessmen clung with shortsighted tenacity to their accustomed colonial prerogatives in Vietnam, vitiating both the substance and the symbolic value of Bao Dai's painstakingly negotiated progress toward genuine unity and independence. Yet Bao Dai's government steadily if slowly replaced the French. There had been over 27,000 French civil servants in 1939; there were only 2,574 by early 1952 and a mere 1,700 by 1954. The Vietnamese also obtained their own military academy in 1949. A separate all-Vietnamese army had grown to 80,000 by 1952, and by 1954 it was over 200,000 strong and operating at the level of regimental combat teams. This army controlled a large area of the Mekong delta and parts of central and northern Vietnam; it had its own paratroop units, naval commandos, and even a fledgling air force. Progress was real, but far too slow. French officials in Saigon insisted on occupying the most prestigious residence in town, and when Bao Dai settled for lesser quarters many Vietnamese drew their own conclusions about the reality of "independence" for the new Republic of Vietnam, which he led as chief of state. This symbolized the mean-mindedness of the process by which the French grudgingly transferred to Bao Dai the concrete reality of the independence that had been promised him and his people.[89]

The New Yang *of the Resistance*

In late 1949 and during the year 1950 the Vietminh underwent a significant transformation. It was now confronted not merely with the massive and well-armed French expeditionary force, but with the competition of another formally established Vietnamese government, which had a plausible claim to legitimacy and which had at least in part achieved the twin goals of independence and unity sought by all Vietnamese national sentiment. At the same time, the Cao Dai, Hoa Hao, and Phat Diem/Bui Chu Catholic movements toward autonomous self-rule and revitalization were at their peak, and the Dai Viet were beginning to stage a comeback in the Red River delta (and taking on "supervillage" characteristics).[90] Meanwhile, and of crucial importance, Chinese Communist troops arrived at the border in December 1949 (only two years earlier their victory had seemed problematic and distant). Shortly thereafter the United States was increasing its aid to France and beginning to praise the "new unified state of Vietnam" under Bao Dai.

The Communist infrastructure of the Vietminh was also tightening its control over noncommunist elements, and both the rhetoric and the techniques of the Democratic Republic of Vietnam rapidly became more overtly Marxist in nature. While retaining its popular front strategy, the Vietminh became a leaner, tougher force, with the orthodoxy of its Marxist ideology more actively propagated and more strictly enforced.[91]

The stunning Communist victory in China coincided with the outbreak of Communist insurgencies in Burma, Malaysia, and Indonesia, not to mention the recent chain of events in Eastern Europe. So when the Soviet Union recognized the Democratic Republic of Vietnam in early 1950, Dean Acheson, President Truman's secretary of state, promptly announced that this had removed "any illusions as to the 'nationalist' nature of Ho Chi

Minh's aims and reveals Ho in his true colors as the mortal enemy of native independence in Indochina." One week later the United States and Great Britain recognized the Bao Dai regime as the sole legitimate government in Vietnam. Earlier American assistance and promises to the Vietminh were seen from the vantage point of policy makers in Washington as "only the braggadocio of a handful of isolated officers."[92] Thus Vietnam was not only being polarized internally by conflict between Vietnamese leaders, it was also becoming enmeshed in a global process of polarization.

Under the influence of all these developments, at the Eleventh Congress of the Indochinese Communist party, after five years of pretending to have disbanded, the decision was made to bring forth an overt and specifically Vietnamese Communist party. On March 3, 1951, the Vietnam Workers party officially came into existence. As the party resurfaced its dominance of the Resistance movement was overt and virtually absolute.

In these times life was extremely difficult in the Vietminh-controlled regions, and mobilizing several million ragged and ill-fed peasants to increase production and bear a heavy burden of taxes was as important and as difficult a task as keeping up the fighting spirit of the troops and maintaining organizational discipline.[93]

With a long tradition of underground newspapers and having from the earliest days stressed literacy campaigns, the Vietminh now claimed a daily distribution figure of over 200,000 for newspapers in their zones of control. These were a valuable resource, as were more specialized journals, such as the one published by the Association for National Salvation. There were also many meetings and rallies, speeches, posters, banners, and party and governmental directives. But the Vietminh effectively supplemented these formal communication channels with a variety of less formal but no less important and carefully planned means of indoctrination. The use of songs as an instrument of communication and control was remarkably effective. Many of these songs were widely known and long remembered, providing a highly redundant source for transmitting to a mass audience the core values on which the ideology of the new regime was based.[94]

These songs repeated the recurring themes of collective mastery, a future-time orientation stressing deferred gratification, and the historical inevitability of victory. One striking song was simply called "Operation":[95]

Our group goes to carry out new duties with resolute will and
firm hearts;
Carrying heavy loads over long roads for the party, for the
people;
Over mountains, across rivers, through jungle, through
streams.
Still we are joyful. These are hard times, achievement comes
tomorrow!
Upon meeting adversity, we gaily sing; the road of struggle is a
road of adversity;
The more confidence by revolutionaries of one red heart of
steel, the firmer our strength.
To pass through perils is to triumph over the enemy troops.

Everyone was encouraged to "Follow in the Steps of the Party
Vanguard":

People, rise up and exterminate the enemy!
With hearts enthusiastic and passionate to carry out the
revolution,
Struggle for a prosperous life.
Although there are perils, we still maintain our position.
This is the revolution of the peasants, of the citizenry.

The battle would not be won or lost on the battlefield alone. The
revolutionary struggle extended to labor "In the Green Fields":

In the green fields
My hands quickly scoop the water
While you dig ponds and build dikes to let the water outside
the fields
Irrigate all our rural region.

Hamlets and villages increase production;
You and I pay the agricultural tax
And quickly carry the rice to a good store.
This is a heart with love of country.
Brethren! Our strength is like the tidal flow of a great river!

. . . .

Remember the words of Uncle Ho
Whenever we sing and echo back: increase production!

Everyone was urged to vie with all others in sacrificing for the
revolutionary cause. People were told "This is the time to
Compete":

This is the time to compete.
With ardent hearts the entire patriotic population of Vietnam
    is competing.
Here the old, the young, boys, girls are of one determined
    heart:
How to live up to the encouraging words of the old father [Ho
    Chi Minh]?
Compete, compete in what? Compete, compete in what?

Officials, farmers, laborers, tradesmen, soldiers!
Compete against hunger, compete in destruction, compete in
    resisting the foreign invaders.
Work quickly, work well, work hard! Lead our race to success!
Attention all! Unite! Tomorrow is arriving!
Independence, happiness, and freedom at last!

Throughout 1950 the Democratic Republic of Vietnam constantly announced by word and action that it was firmly a part of the international Communist community. A crash campaign was launched to study the Chinese revolutionary experience. Within three years forty-seven key Chinese Communist writings were translated into Vietnamese and distributed in nearly 200,000 copies. Some of the work of Mao Tse-tung was translated by Ho Chi Minh himself. The national government, broad popular front, and "supervillage" aspects of Ho Chi Minh's vast and complex organizational structure were reconciled and meshed as a "democratic dictatorship." Led by the Workers party, the regime was "democratic toward the people, dictatorial toward the imperialist aggressors and the reactionaries."[96]

In 1952–1953 a "rectification" campaign was carried out to purify the party and the government. Nearly 16,000 cadres underwent "thought reform" sessions in a single year. Communist party membership dropped from a peak of about 500,000 in 1950 to about 400,000 by 1954. Preparations began in 1952 for a land reform program, which would go through numerous "waves" but had two clearly delineated phases: a moderate beginning phase in 1953–1954 emphasizing rent reductions, and the radical reforms of 1954–1956. In all of this the Chinese Communist model was closely followed.[97]

The writers and poets of the Vietminh played an active role in this activity. In 1953 a National Literary Congress was held in which a specially designed rectification program was carried out for writers and poets to ensure their wholehearted support in these revolutionary Communist programs. Nguyen Cong Hoan wrote some melodramatic short stories about evil landlords and their downfall before the just struggle of noble peasants, providing vivid role models for cadre and villagers to act out across the countryside. Most members of the Literary Association for National Salvation spent time trudging around the territory under Vietminh control, speaking in support of land reform, stirring up landlord denunciation sessions, and helping to reform the thoughts of local soldiers and cadremen.[98]

Once again Xuan Dieu distinguished himself, tramping from village to village giving speeches, urging the cadre teams to greater efforts, and still finding time to incite a wider audience through his poetry:

> Brothers, band together in determination,
> Struggle to wipe out all remnants of our enemies:
> Until landlords, notables, and opposition figures are turned to ashes,
> Until the bones of laggards and reactionaries are ground to dust.
> Light the torches to brighten every lane.
> Light the torches to brighten the village *dinh* tonight.
> Drag that whole gang out by their necks,
> Force them down on their knees, and threaten them with death.[99]

The year 1950 had been a turning point both politically and militarily. In a complicated series of military operations and stratagems between late 1949 and October 1950, the Vietminh had seized the initiative and driven the French entirely out of the northern half of northern Vietnam, inflicting heavy casualties. The overconfidence with which the French had entered into this decisive series of encounters gradually disappeared as time after time the Vietminh troops performed feats of which the French had not imagined them to be capable. In the military as in the political sphere, the French were slow to accept reality.[100]

Dien Bien Phu, 1954

By the time Vietnamization of the anticommunist forces began in earnest and American aid began pouring in, to all intents and purposes the war had already been lost. It took another dramatic shock, however, for this brutal fact to be accepted: the epic battle for Dien Bien Phu. Once again, the Vietminh succeeded because they performed a task the French thought impossible.

The international ramifications of the conflict in Indochina were deeply influenced by the Korean War between 1950 and 1953, especially when Chinese Communist and American troops met head-on in bloody fighting that aroused both nationalistic and ideological emotions on both sides. When a cease-fire was reached in Korea in July 1953, the French in Indochina perceived it as another "stab in the back" by the Americans. But both the People's Republic of China and the United States were thereby enabled to divert considerably more resources in support of their respective "sides" in the Indochina fighting, and this was to influence the way both parties conducted themselves in the final years of the war.[101]

Dien Bien Phu was a remote and sparsely settled valley of little political or economic value. For complex reasons, all seeming quite logical, the French had contrived to make it militarily important; calculatingly, hopefully, they schemed to make this obscure piece of wilderness the scene of a set-piece battle that might decisively tip the balance of a stalemated war that neither side had any realistic hope of ending successfully after seven years of combat.

On November 20, 1953, three battalions of French paratroops captured Dien Bien Phu. Within four months the garrison held twelve battalions of men, superbly armed and trained, with abundant concentrations of artillery and heavy mortars, tanks, and even an airstrip with fighter planes. The valley bristled with painstakingly constructed "strongpoints" designed to be mutually supporting. The French looked forward to the battle of Dien Bien Phu, confident that their position was impregnable. They anticipated limitless resupply by air, and even dreamed of the possibility of massive air support provided with added muscle from U.S. aircraft carriers offshore.[102]

At first the only worry was that General Vo Nguyen Giap would not send a large enough force against them. French experts had calculated that in that remote and rugged wilderness any major Vietminh force mounting an attack upon Dien Bien Phu would run out of supplies in four days. It was certain that such an attack could be withstood. Then, as the massed Vietminh forces were compelled to retreat, the well-supplied and air-supported French troops would counterattack and annihilate them. At first the French marveled at the lightness of contact. Then on March 13, 1954, Giap struck: suddenly, massively, fiercely. Wave after wave of assault troops poured out of the mountains under a concerted blaze of heavy artillery fire. Contrary to expert opinion, the Vietminh were able to close the airstrip and keep it closed. And this attack was sustained for fifty-five days! It was the exhausted, half-starved, and shell-shocked defenders who eventually ran out of ammunition.[103]

Not only did the Vietminh still have ample supplies at the end of the fighting, their original sixteen antiaircraft guns had been supplemented by another sixty. Pulling on ropes, pushing improvised carts made of old bicycles, Vietnamese peasants had hauled in all the cannons, antiaircraft guns, shells, and bullets required to keep the valley under constant fire for eight weeks! And as they toiled they sang:

How do we sing, two three how.
How do we sing, pulling our artillery through mountain
    passes.
How do we sing, two three how, pulling our artillery across
    streams.
How do we sing, two three how, pulling our artillery across
    mountains.

The mountains are steep, but the determination in our hearts
    is higher than mountains.
The chasms are deep and dark, but what chasm is as deep as
    our hatred?
How do we sing, two three how, the fowl are about to crow
    on the mountain tops.
Pulling our artillery across mountain passes, before the early
    dawn.[104]

The Vietminh massed forty thousand troops on those rugged hills overlooking the French fortress. They sang as they marched in, and marching out in victory they sang even more loudly:

Flowers bloom out of season.
The northwest region is radiantly happy as in olden times.
Terraced ricefields are newly planted.
Yonder a group of youngsters in the middle of a field.
Flowers in their hands,

Along the road of victory upon which we advanced
Happily greet us as we return.

. . . .

Oh, what happiness from the day we went northwest!
Our compatriots are excited, and happily greet our return.
Hills and rivers are ablaze; our nation is radiant.
Above the fields of Dien Bien, red banners of victory brighten
  the sky.

The Vietminh had timed their victory almost to the hour for
maximum psychological impact. While the battle raged at Dien
Bien Phu, an international conference had convened at Geneva,
hoping to bring about an end to the fighting in Indochina. The conference opened on April 26. Dien Bien Phu fell on May 7, the day
before the Indochina situation came up on the conference agenda.
The French were ready to compromise. Great Britain, represented
by Sir Anthony Eden, urged compromise. Both Russia and the
People's Republic of China, represented by Foreign Minister Molo-
tov and Chou En-lai, respectively, urged compromise. Only three
parties at the conference took an uncompromising attitude. These
were the Democratic Republic of Vietnam, flushed with military
victory; the Republic of Vietnam, fighting for its very existence;
and the United States, unwilling to make any more concessions to
the international expansion of communism. The weakest delegation of all, the Republic of Vietnam, ultimately adopted the most
uncompromising stance.[105]

The Nationalist Dilemma

In its precarious five years of existence, the Republic of Vietnam
had made a credible showing. It was recognized by many more nations than was the Democratic Republic of Vietnam and was an active member of many international agencies. It had in fact wrung
considerable concessions from the French and created a moderately
effective administrative structure and a competent military force.
Yet it lacked, always, the ability to generate genuine commitment
from any significant number of people. It was the very antithesis of
a "supervillage"; it was a bureaucracy that embodied principles
that related in no fundamental way to the family and village paradigms of Vietnamese culture.

In 1950 and the years immediately following, the radical Communist nature of the Vietminh resistance force caused some defec-

tions from their ranks, but many who left the Vietminh still withheld their full support from the Bao Dai government. Bao Dai had from first to last great difficulty in attracting men of prominence and competence to serve in his government. Many feared that their reputations would be tainted by association with policies in which national fervor was seriously diluted by a spirit of caution, Byzantine negotiation, endless compromise, and the lack of firm ideology and purpose. Others felt that their personal identity and integrity were threatened by an impersonal bureaucratic machinery in which one's individual efforts made little difference. Among those who did serve there was widespread corruption and malfeasance in office.[106]

Bao Dai's prime minister from June 1952 until December 1953 had been the energetic but corrupt Nguyen Van Tam, whose passionate hatred of the Vietminh was combined with such a mild and conciliatory attitude toward the French as to arouse loathing in large sectors of the noncommunist Nationalist community. Nguyen Van Tam was a self-made man from the lower middle class, a shopkeeper's son. While not brilliant, he was disciplined and hardworking. After attaining a law degree, he worked as a district administrator, eventually became a provincial governor (the first Vietnamese in decades to hold such a post), and then headed a special political police in the early days of the Bao Dai government.

Nguyen Van Tam had been tortured by the Japanese; he had sons killed by the Vietminh; and both intellectuals and upper-class Vietnamese snubbed him as a social-climbing mediocrity. His terms as province chief and top police administrator provided him with ample outlets for relieving his many frustrations, but won him few admirers and even fewer friends. He enjoyed going out with a carbine and "bagging" a few Communists to relieve the tedium of his administrative duties. He had actually earned his nickname as the Tiger of Tan An for his enthusiasm and prowess in fighting the Vietminh. Usually stern and overbearing toward Vietnamese, with Frenchmen he was relaxed and friendly. When he became prime minister under Bao Dai, he actually chose to employ a Frenchman as his private secretary, in effect placing a Frenchman between himself and his Vietnamese cabinet ministers.[107]

Nguyen Van Tam was a competent administrator who tried to implement many sensible reforms, some of which might be considered to have been nationalistic in nature. Among them was a modest but apparently well-thought-out land reform program. Yet whatever he proposed or attempted was strenuously opposed and fiercely criticized on all sides. As a leader of the noncommunist Nationalists he was worse than a cipher, he was a severe liability. Not only the man, but the government he led, lost the ability to mobilize and control large segments of the population because of a general feeling that he was unworthy to be head of state.

Although he was an able and hardworking bureaucrat and possessed physical courage, Prime Minister Tam was stigmatized by a social insensitivity and moral coarseness that precluded his eligibility for leadership in the tribunal of public opinion. Disapproval was translated into mechanisms for social influence and control much like those of the traditional village. A body of folklore circulated widely in Vietnamese society reflecting, transmitting, and reinforcing negative evaluations of the man's character, learning, and intelligence. In particular, Prime Minister Tam was the butt of many jokes, which reduced his prestige and hampered his effectiveness as a leader.

Ridicule had always been a potent resource of the weak against the strong in Vietnam. The subtle use of word-play as a form of humor was highly developed; and this had often been converted into a devastating weapon for personal or political ends. Several wonderful examples of this technique concerned jokes played on Prime Minister Tam, who was an inviting target for satire. These stories may be apocryphal, but they were no less effective on that account. A group of notables from Cochinchina presented the prime minister with a beautifully inscribed gold lamé scroll to celebrate Tet. The four characters could be understood to mean "All the world experiences nostalgia." But an alert and well-read observer would have recognized an allusion to a statement attributed to an ancient Vietnamese Zen master. In its original context, the saying might be translated as "All the crimes in the world can be traced back to our own hearts." But the word for "heart" was homophonous with the prime minister's name, Tam. So, to those in on the joke, the scroll could be read as "All the crimes in the world can be traced back to Mr. Tam."[108]

On another occasion Prime Minister Tam was greeted in a tour of north Vietnam by a huge banner that read "Outstanding among all officials." But if one translated the Sino-Vietnamese reading of the first two characters literally into vernacular Vietnamese and then inverted the letters in a common Vietnamese version of what we call "pig Latin," the meaning became "the dog Tam." Performing the same operation on the second two characters, the result could be read as "houseboy of the West." Thus, while watching this self-important man glow with pompous satisfaction, these northern wits thrilled to the sight of the prime minister sitting beneath a banner they read as "Tam is a dog who serves the French." In both cases, the joke was made all the more edifying by the fact that Prime Minister Tam expressed his gratitude for the sentiments without being aware of the ironic double meaning, thus adding to his own subsequent discomfiture.

For Prime Minister Tam such experiences were mortifying. But more important, the public knowledge that he had been subjected to such humiliation so successfully dealt a crippling blow to his capacity for leadership. Trivial as they may seem, these anecdotes about Prime Minister Nguyen Van Tam reveal more about the dilemma of the Republic of Vietnam than much of the purely political analysis written about the period. The basic problem was a moral, almost a spiritual shortcoming rather than any administrative, military, or economic defects. It was a political problem, but it must be understood as political in the context of Vietnamese culture.

Many people were wary of the Vietminh; and certainly the great majority shuddered to think of coming under the control of the Cao Dai or the Hoa Hao. The Binh Xuyen were held in contempt by all but the most naive or the most corrupt members of society. Even many Catholics were made uneasy by the militancy of their coreligionists in Phat Diem and Bui Chu. The Republic of Vietnam offered the only existing alternative to these competing "supervillage" groups with their disconcertingly doctrinaire approach to government, yet most people continued to withhold their support and adopted a stance of disengagement. As they said of themselves, they stayed "under the blanket."

Most Vietnamese, it must be remembered, did not belong to any of the powerful politico-military groups. And as "outsiders" or "nonmembers," they were distrustful of all "supervillage" organizations. Villages, after all, took care of their own; little was given to or expected from those outside the boundary. These people resented the intransigence and arrogance of the French. For them, the security and prosperity of their families was their religion, their politics, and their ethical touchstone. Beyond this they had no genuine commitment or allegiance. This disengaged, cynical public was the only group Bao Dai and his government could be said to represent. Yet Bao Dai himself knew that the best he could hope for was tepid endorsement as the least threatening of an unpleasant assortment of choices. By mid-1954 he needed much more than that.

The Polarization into Two Vietnamese States, 1954

And so it was that in the middle of the Geneva Conference, after the fall of Dien Bien Phu, Ngo Dinh Diem returned to public life after over twenty years of aloof disdain. On June 4, 1954, after years of shilly-shallying, France finally ratified a treaty granting the Republic of Vietnam full independence; with this condition fulfilled, on June 19 Ngo Dinh Diem accepted the task of forming a new government. On July 26 the Geneva Agreement was signed by France, the Democratic Republic of Vietnam, Great Britain, the USSR, and the People's Republic of China. The United States, viewing the agreements as one more in a series of surrenders to armed Communist aggression, "took note of" the agreements, but refused to sign them. Diem's new minister for foreign affairs, angry and frustrated by his feeling that he had been excluded from the inner circles of negotiation, repudiated the results of the conference as "immoral" and cabled Saigon that his mission had been a "total failure." It had been, he said, "absolutely impossible to surmount the hostility of our enemies and the perfidy of false friends."[109]

On this note of recrimination and distrust Vietnam was partitioned at the 17th parallel. The northern half of the country (containing somewhat more than half of the population) was the territory of the Democratic Republic of Vietnam (DRV). The southern half was controlled by the Republic of Vietnam (which did not recognize the DRV as a legitimate government). A 300-day moratorium was granted for the regrouping of partisans into the zone of their choice.

Within ten months, from 850,000 to 900,000 people poured from the north to the south. Most of them were Catholics; the fighting bishoprics of Phat Diem and Bui Chu were virtually deserted, and other militant Catholic villages packed up and left en masse. Others who chose to move were soldiers in the national army or in the French Union forces and their dependents, Dai Viets, VNQDD, and a sprinkling of intellectuals, writers, poets, journalists, and teachers. Perhaps only one-tenth of that number moved from south to north, in large part because the Vietminh had never been nearly as strong in the southern third of the country as in the northern and central regions.[110]

The partition of the country and the regroupment of partisans in 1954 and 1955 produced an even sharper polarization of Vietnamese society. From all over the land, and even from exile in foreign countries, the ideologues of Vietnam assembled in clusters of mutual hostility. Vietnamese Communists gathered in Hanoi while their many enemies were brought together (physically if not spiritually) in Saigon. Under the leadership of Ho Chi Minh, the "superfamily/supervillage" Vietminh/DRV organization now had virtually uncontested control of the closed corporate village communities of the northern half of Vietnam whose families (still for the most part strongly traditional) constituted almost 60 percent of the population. Ngo Dinh Diem, the devoutly Catholic son of Grand Councillor Kha, presided uneasily over multiple, competing supervillages thrust together cheek by jowl in the more sparsely settled, culturally heterodox, ethnically diverse, open, and much less traditional rural landscape of the south. Within and between the two regions, diverse forces still roiled a society in search of a new equilibrium. Many battles remained to be fought over the setting of the social thermostat.

5 *Yin* and *Yang* in Modern Guise, 1955–1970

The Return of Ngo Dinh Diem

When Ngo Dinh Diem emerged from an airplane in Saigon in June 1954 as premier of the Republic of Vietnam, he entered an alien world. He was unsmiling and barely acknowledged the small band of supporters who welcomed him. Curious crowds lining the sidewalks along his route from the airport received no nods or waves. Diem was courageous, incorruptible, pious, ascetic, hardworking, and a dedicated nationalist. He was also stubborn, self-righteous, and a complete stranger to compromise.

Diem assumed office with an unshakable certainty in his own moral and intellectual superiority. If people disagreed with him, he ignored them. If they interfered with him, he crushed them. If he could not prevail, he would withdraw. The thought of genuine compromise or reconciliation with opponents never crossed his mind. He often said, "I know what is best for my people." And he sincerely believed it.[1]

In his rigid insistence on conformity to the orthodoxy of his own *yang* model of society, Diem was sustained by a mystical belief in the inevitable workings of a determinative moral order in the world. He expected to be obeyed, not because he was popular or because he was strong, but because he was morally superior. He expected to triumph over all opposition simply because he was right and they were wrong. He was devoid of externalized guilt that attached to objects or events in political life. His guilt was strong, but entirely internalized, focused on personal inadequacy in fulfilling his duty to his god, his country, and—lurking beyond

234

all else—his stern and domineering father. He felt neither a psychological nor a political need to be liked, but respect and obedience were essential. This was Neo-Confucianism with a vengeance!

This devout son of Grand Councillor Ngo Dinh Kha possessed to an exceptional degree that common Vietnamese quality of "absolutism." Even those early modern Vietnamese who acquired Western educations and internalized certain modern Western values retained an implicit assumption of some underlying, determinative moral order in the world. For Diem this moral order manifested itself as a mixture of the Neo-Confucian concept of *ly* and a militant, conservative Catholicism that was closer to the Spanish than the Gallic tradition. For Ho Chi Minh and the hard core of the Vietminh *ly* was overlaid with the evolutionary determinism of dialectical materialism as programmatically formulated in Marxist-Leninist thought.

All such men were characterized by a rigid insistence on conformity to the orthodoxy of their own *yang* model of society. To them the acceptance of heterodoxy was worse than laxity or weakness; it was a form of moral turpitude that would blight one's destiny. Like the ancient kings, villages, and families of Vietnam, they strove to replicate uniformity as a means of hitching their wagon to a star.[2]

The similarities and differences between Ho Chi Minh and Ngo Dinh Diem are revealing. Both were bachelors and (as Bernard Fall has noted) "personally lonely men." Both spent large portions of their adult life in obscure, self-imposed exile. Each tried, in his own way, to be the father of his country. Both were strong authoritarian leaders and stern disciplinarians; neither was very nurturant or forgiving. But Ho Chi Minh avoided both the aloofness and the direct responsibility inherent in the father role by calling himself "uncle." In public interaction the people were not his children, they were his nieces and nephews. He was not always disciplining and directing the "family" as fathers were supposed to do. Others were assigned those tasks. Uncle Ho was *bac*, father's older brother. He intervened when problems arose and exercised discipline for the sake of the collectivity. This was an incredibly effective device.[3]

After the abortive Nghe An Soviet uprising in 1930, most Communist leaders went to prison and incurred severe criticism from inside and outside the party. Ho Chi Minh was in Hong Kong, untainted by the failure, and a few months later he emerged as head

of a united Indochinese Communist party. When radical land reform got out of hand in 1956–57, millions of North Vietnamese
were furious. Uncle Ho immediately disavowed the "excesses" of
the program, removed Truong Chinh as secretary-general of the
party, and fired the minister of agriculture. He was being a proper
"father's older brother" through all of this, and his personal popularity suffered little damage.[4]

While Ho Chi Minh brilliantly exploited the metaphor of family
through rhetorical kinship, Ngo Dinh Diem took family loyalty all
too seriously. Ho Chi Minh had an older brother–younger brother
sort of relationship with his top aides, whereas Diem's blood
brothers actually played an important role in running the southern
half of the country. Diem was "president." Like a father, he took
direct responsibility for the nation/government/family as a corporate unit.

Ngo Dinh Diem never understood either the peasants or the
bourgeoisie of the south. He was temperamentally incapable of
appreciating the unique character of Saigon. Saigon had always
been an extraordinarily *yin* city. It was considerably younger, bigger, richer, more diverse, and lustier than Hanoi or Hue. Buddhism, Taoism, and Catholicism joined with rampant secularism to
dilute the rigid *yang* orthodoxy of its Neo-Confucian heritage. Morals and manners in Saigon were always more eclectic, pragmatic,
and flexible than anywhere else in Vietnam. One could scarcely
have found a more unlikely site for the conservative and ascetic
Ngo Dinh Diem to have based his attempts to build the foundations of a new "supervillage." This devout Catholic who once
wanted to be a priest was grotesquely miscast in presiding over the
"Pearl of the Orient."

Yet Diem proceeded with vigor and dispatch. He closed the
more conspicuous vice operations, discouraged private enterprise,
attempted to rein in the Buddhists, and outlawed spiritualism
(turning influential shamans into criminals). The use of contracep-
tives was banned; and a legislative attempt to prohibit women
from wearing "falsies" failed only because questions raised about
enforcement procedures proved to be embarrassing. Divorces,
passport applications, promotions and reassignments of military
commanders and civil servants, and property transfers involving
foreigners all required Diem's personal approval; and he would sit
up half the night studying each case before making his own irrevocable decision. He forced the Chinese and other ethnic groups to

become Vietnamese or leave Vietnam. In 1962 first dancing and then sentimental songs were banned. The cumulative affront to Saigon's *yin* sensibilities was incalculable.[5]

Programs in the countryside also suffered from Diem's myopic vision of Vietnamese rural life. Southern villages were never as distinctly nucleated, as tightly organized, nor as thoroughly closed socially as those to the north. Patrilineal organization was notably weaker. The entire *yang* structure of tradition was modified in the south. Diem's early "agroville" program and later the strategic-hamlet program essentially consisted of making rural communities more closed, more nucleated, more like what Diem took to be the "real" or "authentic" model of tradition, that is, like the northern and central coast villages. Diem never appreciated the distance between reality on the ground in the south and his own mental model derived from folklore and literary works and confirmed by his firsthand experience in central and northern Vietnam. With no significant corporate ownership of property and a much less active communal ritual life in the Mekong delta, such closure as Diem envisioned had little functional or psychological relevance to the southern peasantry.

The insouciant manner in which Diem attempted to uplift the moral tone of his constituency lays bare the quintessential *yang* nature of his regime. Why did Diem insist on pressing for 98 percent of the vote in elections he was bound to win in any event? The 60 percent margin that American officials urged him to settle for would have been more than adequate in a social milieu that accepted diversity and sought to organize it. But Diem was preoccupied with replicating uniformity. Such a man, like many of his opponents, could not conceive of a "loyal opposition." He saw only two kinds of people: wholehearted supporters, and heretics to be suppressed.

At another place or time Diem might have made a truly great Vietnamese leader. What he did achieve against all odds was little short of miraculous. But in the Saigon of the 1960s it was like trying to swim up a waterfall to impose his ascetic *yang* view of the world upon the *yin* appetites of this lively, heterodox metropolis.

The mere fact that Diem survived his first few years in office was remarkable. Within three years he managed to get rid of Bao Dai, to gain control over an army that resented him, and to subdue the Hoa Hao, the Cao Dai, and the Binh Xuyen through a deft mixture of trickery, bribery, bluff, and combat operations from the Plain of

Reeds to the streets of Saigon. The one tactic to which Diem did not resort was compromise. Through this fateful period the daring new president of the Republic of Vietnam was skillfully aided by a small group of energetic Americans, led by the legendary Colonel Lansdale, whose similar exploits in the Philippines were portrayed in *The Ugly American* and whose activity in Vietnam during this period was caricatured by Graham Greene in *The Quiet American*.[6] Diem's instinctive reaction to the chaos around him was to transform the Republic of Vietnam into yet another variant of the "supervillage" model, infusing it with a rigid *yang* structure of his own making. In so doing he acquired some devoted followers, and many other people were reasonably content. But millions of people within the constituency of his state were starkly outside the boundaries of his "village." The most dangerous of these were men who had just been displaced from supervillages of their own.

The organized insurgency that flared up in South Vietnam in 1958 and 1959 was fostered by Diem's failure to hold elections, by the inadequate execution of land reform programs, by censorship of the press and the arrest of political opponents. Many issues contributed to unrest. But the effective nucleus of armed opposition was from the beginning a residue of the competing supervillages Diem had suppressed. The insurgency was at core Vietminh, and Communist dominated and led.[7] But former Hoa Hao, Cao Dai, and Binh Xuyen played an important role in providing armed troops and experienced middle-level leadership. The insurgent movement attracted both land-hungry peasants and disaffected intellectuals to its ranks; but it was the eclectic supervillage component that provided the skills, the muscle, and the armament to make it a viable force in its formative years.[8] For most peasants and intellectuals who belonged to no competing supervillage, life in South Vietnam was simply not bleak enough in the late 1950s and early 1960s to drive one to desperation.[9]

But apart from the growing armed insurgency in the countryside and the mutterings of religious and intellectual leaders, Diem was faced with other political efforts either to displace him or to force him to alter his narrow ideological stance. In the early years, while Diem was preoccupied with other matters, there was spirited discussion in the National Assembly. But after the 1959 elections there was only one legislator who openly stood up to the powerful president. Dr. Phan Quang Dan had been elected with the greatest plurality of any candidate in the election despite heavy government opposition and interference. Dr. Dan was said to have worked for the OSS during World War II, and he possessed a degree from Harvard. He was a leader of the Greater Vietnam People's Rule party, the very party organized by Nguyen Tuong Tam and his colleagues some twenty years earlier. Dr. Dan and Tam had been in close contact in the hectic days of 1945–1946. And with Nguyen Tuong Tam himself now living in Saigon, Diem was naturally suspicious.[10]

Tam had gone to live in Hong Kong in 1949, and he stayed there until 1951, existing on money sent by his family and writing an occasional short story "only to help pass the time." In 1951 he had returned to Hanoi because he missed his family. But he firmly announced, publicly and privately, that he would have nothing more to do with politics, rejecting offers to join a resurging Dai Viet movement in the Red River delta. He soon moved to Saigon, and then settled in Dalat.[11]

In the haunting beauty of this pine-covered highland resort, Tam lived in a simple wooden house built with his own hands. Much of his time was spent raising orchids. Sometimes friends from Saigon would join him for hikes through the forest in search of new orchid varieties. Tam would take along a loaf of bread, a few bottles of beer, and his clarinet, alternately delighting and exasperating his companions by unexpected and sometimes hilariously inappropriate bursts of music from his horn.[12] Like countless other Vietnamese before him (including Diem), Tam had withdrawn from participation in a world lacking reason and righteousness, with patient good humor, indulging in the *yin* virtues of leisure and contemplation as he awaited vindication by history.

Although he had no diagnosed physical defects or disease, and the writing he sporadically produced attested to the soundness of his mind, Tam's behavior in Dalat was eccentric. While friends and family worried about him, others whispered that he had a fatal disease, had gone insane, or was putting on an act to conceal some monstrous conspiracy. He still did smoke and drink heavily, yet he was up at five every morning sipping tea. And he steadfastly refused to discuss his health or his politics. He loved to read detective stories from the United States and Western Europe, and he once estimated that he had read at least five hundred of them.[13]

In 1958 Tam moved back to Saigon to go into the publishing business once again. The journal he published was scrupulously nonpolitical, and the only organization in which he was known to be active was the recently established Vietnam PEN Club. Yet he was reported to have dined with various generals and politicians whose loyalty to Diem was suspect, and all sorts of people were said to have visited him at his home.

Tam was one of many disaffected intellectuals in Saigon. Some wanted a more open and flexible governmental process. Others smarted over a variety of slights, injustices, and disagreements. Several dozen men of diverse backgrounds, beliefs, and aspirations—united chiefly by a shared resentment toward Diem and his family—formed the habit of getting together occasionally for drinks or dinner. Since the bar at the Caravelle Hotel was a favorite meeting place, this informal network of disgruntled middle-aged men became known as "the Caravellists."

Political conversations were always common occurrences at certain bars and restaurants in Saigon. At these lively but predictable events recent actions by those in power in both Saigon and Hanoi would be denounced. Then, with lowered voices, the group would indulge in speculation about hidden motives. Byzantine conspiracies were imagined and their potential intricacies explored over another round of drinks. Then, with voices again raised, dire pronouncements would be made regarding various calamitous circumstances soon to eventuate if "something were not done about this mess." Every evening in downtown Saigon several such groups might be found.

In November 1960 a paratroop commander executed a hastily conceived coup that put him in control of Saigon for several days. The more optimistic of the Caravellists stepped forward to support and advise the young colonel. When Diem regained control a few days later, these men went to prison. Tam was suspected of involvement in the coup, but evidence was lacking, so he escaped the fate of his drinking companions.[14]

The National Liberation Front of South Vietnam (NLF) was formed in December, and a growing insurgency in the countryside diverted the attention of Diem and his anticommunist opponents. There was no real unity, but for a few years opposition voices were muted and some measure of political stability appeared to have been achieved in Saigon as the situation continued to deteriorate in rural areas. But Diem had refused continuing pleas from the noncommunist opposition and the United States to broaden the base of his government.[15] Discontent simmered beneath the surface, and the unspoken truce proved to be fragile.

A Coalescence of Yin *Forces*

In May 1963, on the birthday of Buddha, celebrants in Hue were prevented from flying their flags in celebration. Protests followed, and inept efforts at crowd control by poorly trained troops led to violence in which some demonstrators were killed. Although the escalation of protest and repression was initially restricted to the Hue area, other Buddhist groups conducted sympathy marches and demonstrations throughout the country, but especially in Saigon. This well-organized, nonviolent wave of protest evoked little government response and failed to engage the emotions of the larger population. Then, on June 11, in a precisely timed operation, the venerable Thich Quang Duc, with the permission and complicity of Buddhist leaders, assumed the lotus position at a busy intersection in downtown Saigon and struck a match as his saffron-robed companions poured gasoline over him. For ten minutes he remained in this position with his hands folded while the flames consumed his body.[16]

Malcolm Browne, Associated Press correspondent, was on hand with a camera, having been alerted that something important might happen. Within just a few days Brown's graphic close-up photographs of the immolation were on tens of thousands of postcards, circulating all over Vietnam and around the world. Huge enlargements of some shots were held overhead in scores of demonstrations around the country during the next few weeks. Disenchantment with the regime spread, and Diem was urged by his brother Nhu to take a harder line with dissenters of all stripes.

To demonstrate firmness, the government decided to prosecute some opposition leaders suspected of fomenting unrest. On Saturday, July 6, 1963, Nguyen Tuong Tam was summoned to a military police post and informed that on Monday morning, July 8, he was to be tried for complicity in the abortive coup attempt that had taken place three years earlier. With a smile Tam proclaimed his innocence, dismissing the charge as a crude effort at intimidation. Yet he was painfully aware that his entire life, even his dreams, would be on trial in that courtroom. The past forty years of his life would be forever labeled as he was judged by criteria he could not accept by men he did not respect.

On the afternoon of Sunday, July 7, he sat down for a leisurely chat with his family at home. He had treated himself to a bottle of Johnny Walker scotch, but otherwise this was a normal and relaxed family get-together. No one knew that he was mixing veronal with his whiskey in a carefully calculated lethal dosage. It was the seventh day of the seventh month, traditionally an auspicious day, and the day on which Ngo Dinh Diem had formed his government nine years earlier.[17]

That final afternoon Tam scribbled the last and most stirring words of his long and controversial career:

> Let history be my judge, I refuse to accept any other judgment. The arrest and detention of nationalist opposition elements is a serious crime, and it will cause the country to be lost into the hands of the Communists. I oppose these acts, and sentence myself to death . . . as a warning to those who would trample upon freedom of every kind.

His children rushed the handwritten original of their father's last words to the United Press International (UPI) office in Saigon and had photocopies made, which they distributed among their father's many friends and among the American press community, including American newsmagazines such as *Time* and *Newsweek*. Within forty-eight hours tens of thousands of people in Saigon had read a copy of this document, although not a single newspaper dared to print it. I had a copy pressed into my hand by a friend who was a student at the Faculty of Law at the University of Saigon. For many a damp-eyed reader, these lines irrevocably removed Diem as leader of the nationalist cause.[18]

Thousands of people turned out for Tam's funeral, despite the inconvenient hour, despite the conspicuous riot police and the threatening surveillance of Diem's security agents, despite the gray skies. This was no ordinary crowd. It was well-dressed, dignified, articulate. There were many women, distinguished old men, and groups of students. Hundreds of cars crammed to capacity with riders inched through a sea of bicycles and motor scooters. A group of well-groomed teenage girls marched in ranks behind a banner proclaiming them to be students of Trung Vuong High School, a girls' school named for the famous Trung sisters who had themselves led a march against oppression nearly two millennia earlier. With slender bodies clad in immaculate white tunics, and glistening long black hair framing pale and delicate faces, these young women were incongruous as a warrior band, but that is what they were. Among the tough old politicians and grizzled veterans of combat in the Resistance War who came forward to pay their respects to Nguyen Tuong Tam on the day of his burial, these wasp-waisted girls marched with unsurpassed authority. They were neither Tam's comrades in arms nor his foes; they were his readers, young Loans, who by their very presence pronounced him "not guilty." This was a symbolic declaration of war upon those who had driven the author of *Breaking the Ties* to make this ultimate affirmation of his belief in individual freedom.[19]

Never before had Diem encountered such dangerous opponents. These girls were the pride and joy of upper-middle-class Saigon. It was their adoring fathers, uncles, cousins, and older brothers who staffed Diem's ministries and commanded his troops. What soldier or policeman would dare to lay a hand on such a girl, not knowing who her father might be? Diem's agents would soon arrest these youngsters, thus signing Diem's death warrant.

Appropriately, Tam's funeral procession turned down Madam Thanh Quan District Street and paused at the politically active Xa Loi pagoda, center of the Buddhist protest movement. After a brief prayer service there, the procession turned back to The Two Trung Sisters Street to proceed to a suburban cemetary. A billboard-sized portrait of Nguyen Tuong Tam stared out at the crowd, overlooking an altar laden with flowers, incense, and candles. The service was conducted in an air of excitement and overpowering emotion.[20]

Representing a group of "independent writers" who had come to pay their respects, individuals "with no political coloration, members of no political party," one of Saigon's finest and most respected writers stepped forward: Nhat Tien. "Your death," he promised, "will always be a bright torch to light the dark path we must tread, a great encouragement for us in the hardships we shall encounter, a brilliant mirror in which we who take up pens after you must look at ourselves and reflect."[21]

By expressing the idea that Tam's death served "as a mirror," Nhat Tien was emphasizing that Tam's death symbolized not despair but conviction; not defeat but an affirmation of threatened group values. This act, echoing a tradition as old as the myths of the Hung kings, was an extreme act of "abstention" as a means of protest. This large and heterogeneous crowd had gathered precisely to affirm this interpretation of Tam's suicide.

The Vietnam PEN Club was also present in full force: writers, poets, scholars, and literary critics, many of whom had been warned that it would be wise to stay at home. The chairman stepped forward nervously. He was Thanh Lang: Catholic priest, college professor, literary historian, and a northerner. In a voice trembling with emotion he began to speak. A skilled orator, he gained rhythm and resonance as he warmed to his topic:

> The handfuls of earth which I and all your friends here pile upon you are not to bury you. If literature . . . is viewed as an existence . . . then from this moment on, as you lie here, you will truly begin to live, you enter into the authentic life of literature. So these clods of earth we heap upon you in this painful moment are not really clumps of dirt, they are rose petals which we strew upon you, with which we swathe you, to escort you into the glory of history. . . . You and your friends pronounced the birth of an entire generation of new literature, in which you were the chief, the president of our Republic of Literature from 1932 until 1945. You gave young men and women a whole new path of thought and feeling and writing. . . . In this moment, while tears stream down our faces, while sobs surge up in our throats, while our trembling hands fling upon you this soil that I call rose petals, this is the very moment you go into resplendent history. We come here today to bow down before the throne history has prepared for you. My brothers and I, the PEN club of Vietnam, have escorted you here to place you upon that throne.

Then Father Thanh Lang cast the soil he had been holding in his hand upon Tam's coffin. Mrs. Nguyen Tuong Tam fainted, and the crowd burst into tears.[22] Tam's death was his most successful artistic creation and his most effective political act. Four months later Ngo Dinh Diem was dead and buried in an unmarked grave.

A few days after Tam's funeral monks and nuns at the Xa Loi pagoda staged a hunger strike. The temple was ringed with barbed wire and several hundred sympathizers were beaten back with rifle butts and clubs as they stormed the lines to join those fasting inside. Then, during the first three weeks of August three more monks and a nun burned themselves to death, unleashing wave after wave of protests and hunger strikes. Hue and Nha Trang were placed under martial law. As Buddhist militancy grew, councillor Nhu's "special forces" raided major pagodas. Over a thousand were imprisoned, and dozens were killed in the ensuing clashes.

On August 20 Special Forces troops swooped down on the Xa Loi pagoda in a swift and unnecessarily brutal raid. Many were arrested, but two monks skipped over a back fence of the pagoda and took refuge in the mission of the U.S. Agency for International Development (AID) around the corner, where they were given shelter.[23] American officials rejected demands that they be turned over for arrest. The next day the entire block was cordoned off by Vietnamese troops in combat gear. Their commander entered the mission and formally demanded that the "fugitives" be surrendered to his custody. He left without them and returned later, again to be denied.

Unaware of what was happening, I arrived soon afterward to enter the mission and was firmly stopped by a group of soldiers. After I produced identification proving I was an American (but not a journalist), the soldiers executed an informal but snappy salute, and the officer in charge came up and shook my hand. "I'm sorry, sir. I'm just following orders," he mumbled in embarrassment. I went in and out of the area several times while the siege was on, and to a man the Vietnamese military were friendly, courteous, and apologetic.

When I returned to the province in which I was working I stopped by the house of an officer of the Army of the Republic of Vietnam to tell him of my experience and what had happened at the pagoda and the AID mission. He stared blankly for a moment, then slammed his fist on the table with great violence. "It's that goddamned Nhu," he shouted as our drinks spilled across the table. This man was in charge of Nhu's strategic-hamlet program in the province.

A few days later the senior U.S. military adviser in the province was ill, and three other key Vietnamese army officers stopped by one evening to wish him a speedy recovery. Casually, they asked me to join them as they visited the colonel in his room. When the five of us were alone they launched into a bitter denunciation of Ngo Dinh Nhu. If Nhu didn't go, they warned, both the military and the civil government would soon crumble. The strength of their anger and the openness with which they expressed their views were a shock to us. They risked not only their careers but their lives with such talk. And, collectively, they commanded most of the province's military forces and security apparatus.

Soon after that incident a very senior civilian official invited me to drop by one evening to share a bottle of wine. It was the first and only time I was in his home; and it was not an exceptionally good bottle of wine, but rather one that obviously had been hastily purchased as a stage prop for the occasion. In the room where we sat was a shiny new Buddhist altar. During a lull in the conversation the man pointed to it saying, "I'm a Buddhist now." After a pregnant pause, we chatted for a few more minutes and I said good night.

As diverse groups and personalities converged into a powerful *yin* force opposing the increased rigidity and intolerance of the government, American pressure on Diem to get rid of Nhu was growing, firmly expressed by Henry Cabot Lodge, the new American ambassador. Suddenly, many kinds of information I routinely collected from Vietnamese offices as part of my job in coordinating relief and development assistance programs were no longer available to me. Within days a number of Vietnamese civil servants privately offered to provide me with whatever information I needed. I would write out my questions and hand them to people in a parking lot or a canteen, and a few days later they would slip me an envelope containing all the data I had requested. This spontaneous gesture came from secretaries, clerks, and higher officials. Most of us wanted to get on with the work at hand, and we loathed Nhu's egotistical antics.

Diem's refusal to get rid of his younger brother was distorting and steadily destroying his relations with the Americans and with his own civil service and armed forces, as well as with Buddhists, students, and the more liberal members of all other groups. The United States finally indicated that it would support a replacement government, and within weeks Diem and Nhu died together after refusing American offers of safe conduct out of the country during a military coup.[24] For the next several years coup followed coup and a shaky government structure muddled through as best it could. But Americans were increasingly taking over the conduct of the war and dominating many civil matters.

In late 1964 and early 1965 entire North Vietnamese regiments, accompanied by sizable quantities of weapons and supplies, began pouring into the south and overrunning district towns, and even the provincial capital of Song Be in early May.[25] In May 1965, United States military units began arriving in the country to counter this assault. The war quickly became bigger and more ferocious.

Anxious Souls in the Republic of Vietnam

Meanwhile the *yin* metaphor had been capturing Saigon even more completely. The literary movement characterized by individual sensibility, spontaneity, and unfettered emotionalism that had burst forth primarily in Hanoi during the 1930s reached its apogee in the Saigon of the 1960s. Shortly after the partition of Vietnam in 1954, Saigon journals like *Creativity* began publishing a torrent of experimental verse: unconventional in content and form, disturbing, intensely personal, often agonizing, and frequently confusing.

These works were produced by individuals who demanded a life and a poetry that was more sincere, more creative. To them all established ideologies were contemptibly committed to old mistakes. Man's only hope lay in himself; but to find himself truly, the more extreme of these young poets argued, he first had to destroy himself in his current conceptual existence and be born again through his own creative efforts. By this they intended no social upheaval, but individual acts of self-transformation. To make this possible these young artists demanded "absolute freedom," even demanded of themselves freedom from the self-imposed influence of habit and custom.

Foremost among this new generation of poets was a young man from the north, writing under the name Thanh Tam Tuyen, who cried out:

> i have a need to weep that is like a need to vomit
> on the street
> in the crystalline sunshine
>
> .   .   .   .
>
> i need a secret place to kneel
> for my tiny little soul
> which fears the vicious dog
> the colorless hungry dog.[26]

The emotionally charged discussions of his poems attest to their significance. Although Thanh Tam Tuyen's poetry derived much of its power from tension generated by a jarring choice of words, the primary impact of his poems comes from a sequence of disturbing images, as in this excerpt from "Night":

> Low sound in the night
> A deep lonely feeling
> Green bar of music with a black do re
> Eyebrows borne down with old winter
> Vaporizing death
> Formless ragged sound of a bugle
> Girl in a black tunic with high flowing hair
> Two long arms writhing like boa constrictors.

The air is infected
Smash it
The past insults upon a drumhead
Throw a broken bottle up at the blind sun
Whisper Whisper
Cold drizzle
Slow eradication of time
Sound like burning gas beneath a living swamp
Excited pounding of a hammer
The future screaming in pain
Will-o-the-wisp abruptly extinguished
Fierce laughter
Girl in the black tunic vomits blood
Dizzy vaporizing death
Throwing up on feet enraging the gravel
Smash Smash Smash Smash
The deep lonely feeling
In the low sound of the inhaling night.[27]

Another young poet who came into prominence in Saigon during the late 1950s and early 1960s was To Thuy Yen:

So that's life
Keeping the eyes exposed
Not wearing dark glasses
Keeping a normal level
Not becoming acid
· · · · · · · · · · · ·
With a type of soul forbidden by the nation
I am imprisoned for life
Between four walls of air
· · · · · · · · · · · ·
I run headlong upon the thread of terror
Stretched across the cold pit of emptiness.[28]

As the insurgent war intensified and partisan controversy continued, To Thuy Yen wrote "On the Battlefield," expressing the bitter disillusionment and alienation he and many of his friends were experiencing:

My secret is that I have lived
On an earth covered with a scum of sombre shadows
Where the rays of the sun were a sentence of arrows, knives
    and axes.

They said the night was ebony light
Only a black sun was a true sun
We had to puncture the blindness of good vision.

. . . .

Saying the dead corpses would fertilize for peace
They slew the people in the house down the lane
They slay people as if clearing a wilderness.

Reject with one word both capitalism and communism
No one stands out here in this war of vengeance
That mashes my body on the edge of a scimitar formed by the
     two factions.

I fall to the ground with clean hands.[29]

Perhaps the most popular poet in Saigon in the early 1960s, at least
among urban youth, was Nguyen Sa, who wrote in a variety of
free forms. The poem "Stating My Intentions" conveys his preoccupation with fleeting youth and the meaning of life:

I detain you on a crowded sidewalk
Don't be reluctant, I just want to tell you that I love you.
I say it with no shyness, no hesitation, and no examination.
Because, my dear, I'm no merchant asking the price of goods
     in the tumult of an afternoon market.
Nor am I an old clerk sitting in excitement with a few
     paperclips as I plot to become manager.

. . . .

One moment of procrastination, and upon the boundless
     fields of life
I shall in an instant be transformed into a disabled veteran
     who sits and bitterly weeps,
The trickling tears falling upon rusted medals and tarnished
     gold.
Yes, I will cry and the tears will dissolve into little bits of
     blood.

. . . .

Let me speak at once. If not, I will have to go seek myself like
     a maddened horse galloping down the road at twilight,
     chasing the sun as it disappears beyond the mountains

. . . .

Let me speak at once.

When tomorrow comes the breath will still be moist and have
   the stench of sin
. . . I will look at life through the eyes of a cadaver.
And, dear, all of me, all of life, the path ahead and the long
   fragrant hair—all shall become an illusion.[30]

Nguyen Thi Hoang became an extremely popular poet and novelist
by depicting the innermost conflicts of young people in Saigon during the 1960s. Her poem "Confession" was written in 1963:

Let me now bid farewell to the convent.
Oh, Christ, my misery knows no bounds.
Night after night I strain to listen to the vespers
While agonizing over a hundred lonely griefs.
How many times did the rain fall and the wind gust,
Bringing dishonor and sin upon this body?

. . . .

Each love broke off but half fulfilled
So I sought to escape from life
And bury the green days of youth behind the bolted convent
   doors.
My soul is drifting away from the faith.
I cannot forget the images of yesteryear.
When was it that faith shattered . . . ?

. . . .

Let me bid farewell to Paradise
And from now on seek the violent passion of Hell.
Year after year, month after month, day after day.
Out of shame I clutch my grief and conceal it in my arms.
My soul is a lonely island.
. . . .

Where have they gone, those green days of golden youth?
I have already known the burden of too many loves,
Already my heart is marked with a thousand scars.
Let me now bid farewell to Paradise;
Let me now go seek once more the sorrow of loving in the
   midst of life.
But the road back has no span for returning again.
Oh, Christ, I am afraid—of being alone tomorrow.[31]

Young poets joined in to express the oppressive weight of a lifetime of war and conflict upon their psyches. With a sensibility
honed to razor sharpness by conflicting cultural influences and
ideological strife, Vien Linh, who had come from the north as a

boy, wrote several striking poems about himself and the meaning of "Life":

> I see myself upon my way
> As churchbells sound the knell of death.
> Carrying life's principle in my hand,
> From this point on I am expended.
>
> He who is not here today,
> Once was present and alive,
> Though the traces day by day
> Fade with the grave marker.
>
> Lest someone should look down at me
> And think that my body's at peace,
> Know that even in hell we are people,
> And I'm still afraid after death.
>
> . . . .
> .
>
> I just tell of a portion of life,
> Of a person as he has died.
> But how is he different from me?
> How changed in appearance from you?[32]

Another young poet who came to Saigon from North Vietnam in 1954 wrote in a similar vein of doubt and anguish. Do Quy Toan grasped attention and compelled thought with poems like "Shooting the Sun":

> Take a gun and shoot the sun.
> Right in the breast, the blood flows.
> It rolls over, struggling.
> It rolls over, dead.
> Yet it still stands,
> Twists its mouth in a smile,
> Gives pursuit, grasping for your shirt,
> Pleading piteously:
> "I beg of your kindness, sir,
> Please don't shoot me.
> Please don't shoot me."[33]

In the 1960s Saigon almost always had a curfew. It was eerie and unnerving to watch the city, pulsing with activity, suddenly fall silent as people scurried into their homes and locked the doors. Do Quy Toan wrote about "Curfew":

"Doors are closed at nine o'clock."
As when death abruptly claims a body:
All breathing stops,
Breathing stops and eyes are closed.

Closed at nine o'clock.
Dark night descends upon the city,
Dark night in which we cannot see each other.
But we live upon a changing earth
And upon a sea that alternately writhes and settles.
So our souls are eternally anxious.

How can our souls sleep peacefully?
Our eyes open and stare into the silent night.
While our ears
Keep listening for the sound of footsteps,
For the rumble of vehicles on patrol,
For the sound of doors slammed and of shouting.
While all the innocent pairs of eyes
Quietly open in all the bedrooms,
The entire city
Is petrified with fear.

While a pealing of strange bells rings out,
And resounds, becoming a deep echo,
And that deep echo besets our souls
With eternal nights of wakefulness.[34]

Tran Duc Uyen also expressed anxiety, anguish, and disillusionment with existing ideologies, as in "A New Testament Poem":

.   .   .   .

The abundant sources of great happiness
Alas, are only in the future
But the future is blind and deaf, so there is nothing to be said

The offering was presented, but the cow was old and dry
So the calf grows angry, goes away, disappears
I stand there laughing, blinking my eyes in scorn

Though I do not wish to prolong the days of misery
I no longer believe in the power of miracles,
In the efficacy of old cows and their calves
Upon green pastures fouled by the stench of urine.[35]

Ninh Chu, another young poet who had come from the north, wrote of "fleeing life down a long and lonely road." He reveals his outlook in "A Black Poem":

People grow up
A sob upon their lips

People grow up
A far-away look in their eyes

The misery of war
A future of death

People grow up
A coffin for burial

People grow up.[36]

The war grew more fierce with each passing year and burned deeper and deeper into poetry in the south, as in "Some Gifts to Express my Love" by Tran Da Tu:

I give you a roll of barbed wire
Some kind of creeping vine of this new age
Which has stealthily crept around my soul today
That is my love, accept it without question

I give you a truck with plastique
It explodes in the midst of a crowded street
Explodes and hurls about chunks of flesh
That is my life, do you understand it

. . . .

I give you the relentlessness of twenty years
Twenty years seven thousand nights of artillery
Seven thousand nights of cannon fire for a lullaby
Are you asleep yet or still awake

. . . .

I would like to give you many more things
But that's enough
I'll just give you a tear gas grenade
To force out tears neither happy nor sad
Like those streaming down my waiting face.[37]

Du Tu Le expressed an equally tortured consciousness. With scathing irony he told his troubled readers that "It's Nothing":

I told you to go to sleep, little girl
The gunfire is steady, but it's still far away
And even though tomorrow the shooting may draw near
So what? There's nothing strange about that.
That's not strange
Of course not!

Ever since we opened our eyes
Bombs have fallen gladly, bullets have whistled happily
Days have been full of misery, nights full of remorse
Blood still flows and corpses still topple over
—I told you to go to sleep, little girl

. . . .

Barbed wire watches over us rascals ready to abandon our
    duty
The brass bugle urges us to madness
Flares light the road to guide us night after night
Patch by patch of gently sleeping earth, destiny by destiny,
Eye by terrified eye, foot by unsteady foot,
Finger by eager finger, clutching the trigger on the rifle
    Hey! I told you to go to sleep, little girl.
It's nothing, the nights have long been like this.
It's nothing, the nights have long been like this.[38]

The young men and women who wrote this kind of poetry, and the tens of thousands of others who read and appreciated it, moved into the *yang* roles of society. They became army officers, schoolteachers, business executives, administrators, journalists. It was, increasingly, people like this who led troops in combat, who implemented government policies in every sphere of life, who reported on the fighting as journalists and newscasters. Growing numbers of such people molded younger minds as classroom teachers, wrote and reviewed books, turned out training and indoctrination materials for the armed forces, and as the decade wore on created television dramas and motion pictures.

With this traumatized sensibility, they buried their fathers, uncles, brothers, cousins, classmates, neighbors, and friends, more every year than the year before. Many nights they could see flares and hear gunfire from the surrounding countryside as they undressed and climbed into bed. Why, they asked, must life be so absurd?

The Supervillage of Insurgency

But beyond the city lights, deep in jungle and swamp, a force had arisen to challenge the complacency of the world in which these people merely wanted to be left in peace to study, to work, to love, to play, to build a better life for themselves and their families. And in stark contrast to the *yin* world of Saigon, against the growing individualism, diversity, alienation, and cynicism of the urban middle class and their imitators in the countryside, zealous young men in guerrilla camps sang out with the clear and unambiguous voice of *yang*, expressing unity, conformity, the power and satisfaction of collective action, the communitas of shared affliction:

Our unity is strength
Our unity is steel, iron,
But neither steel nor iron is as durable as we.
We swear to rout the enemy troops, colonialism, the wild
     beasts of imperialism, as well as reactionary elements.

We shall utterly destroy them!
Advance rapidly!
The bugle of freedom is sounding in the purple rays of battle.
Build a new life in a new democracy![39]

With this song the insurgents opened their meetings, rallies, and frequent songfests. And as they grew, they sang about past and present victories. Continuity with the previous successful Resistance War was stressed. They sang the work song to which cannon were hauled into Dien Bien Phu and many other songs from the Resistance War against the French. One was called "Grasp Weapons Firmly":

Weapons in hand, rounds in the chamber;
Two duties: resist imperialism, advance the movement.
On operation, strive to kill!

Return to help increase local activity.
We are the side of victory, the armed force.
We and the people struggle to certain victory.

We are peasants in soldiers' clothing
Waging the struggle of a class oppressed for thousands of
     years.
Our suffering is the suffering of the people.

One well-known and very revealing song did originate out of this struggle in the south—"The Experiences of Several Autumns of Resistance":

We are people from the four directions, all emancipated from
     our families, gone out,
Meeting each other in the greater family, guerrilla troops, the
     troops of liberation.
When near each other, we live happily in a feeling of love,
With an ever-stronger spirit of comradeship, tender and
     inexhaustible.

.   .   .   .

We live together side by side, sharing all during fits of hunger,
Each bowl of rice, each dry morsel.

.   .   .   .

There are moments in the cold winter wind when we share
     the warmth of tobacco ashes,
The howling arises, wafting fragrant odors, wrapped in a veil
     of frost;
The night grows colder, and the blanket is spread to cover all.
When near each other, we live happily in a feeling of love,
With ever-stronger spirit of comradeship, tender and
     inexhaustible.

.   .   .   .

There are moments lying near each other when a feeling arises
     of not concealing anything from each other.
The more we understand each other, the more we love one
     another.
We love one another more, together in one spirit,
The spirit of struggle to preserve our country.

The spirit of belongingness in this song contrasts sharply with
the songs and poems prevailing in Saigon at the same time. It is a
hymn of insurgency that glorifies the communitas of shared affliction; and it was effective because it was based on a real and important phenomenon. In spartan camps stretching from lush, jungled
highlands to the dank bowels of mangrove swamp in the U Minh
forest, the wretched guerrillas who sang this song recognized
the basic truth it contained. They did make virtues of their hardships, and they did get psychological rewards for their physical
deprivation.

The metaphor of family is explicit in this song. These insurgents
were "liberated" from their families, freed from the pettiness and
strain of family life. But they were not "liberated" in the sense intended by Khai Hung or Nguyen Tuong Tam or the many other
writers and poets who had been championing individual freedom
since the mid-1930s. Individualism had no place in the value system of this insurgency, and the insurgents were not free as individuals. They were, in a very meaningful sense, freed from their
families to become, and truly free only because they had become,
totally immersed in a larger, stronger, and more enlightened social
group: the "supervillage" of insurgency, which was so organized
as to become a surrogate family, a replacement for the family, a
"superfamily." Individualism had no more legitimacy in the insur-

gent "supervillage" of the 1950s and 1960s than it had in the villages of the nineteenth century, and the individual had no more freedom of action in his new "superfamily" than individuals had ever had in the Vietnamese families of traditional times.

Setting the Thermostat in the North, 1955–1958

The family/village metaphor representing the disciplined and tightly knit social group to which the insurgents belonged was homologous with the Vietminh/Democratic Republic of Vietnam ideological model, and the linkage and similarity between the two became increasingly explicit with the passage of time. From 1946 through 1954 the Vietminh had emphasized the single overwhelming ideal of independence from French colonial rule, drawing upon a tradition of resistance to foreign aggression that went back to the Hung kings, the Trung sisters, and General Tran Hung Dao. But the leadership of the revolution had been exclusively Marxist, with no room for competing ideologies.

Phan Khoi described the situation with the intellectuals in the Literary Association for National Salvation:

> When the Association was in Viet-Bac its line of conduct seemed very simple. In order to serve the country, the people, and above all the pressing war of resistance, one had to follow Marxism. It cannot be presumed that writers and artists in those days correctly and properly fulfilled their duties, but it was certain that they did their best to follow the above line of conduct. Did they have any dissatisfaction with their leaders? Scarcely any. Or if there was any, they did not pay much attention to it, since their souls were immersed in the greatness and the glorious misery of the Resistance War. They had no leisure to think of other matters.[40]

When the fighting came to an end, the poets and writers returned to Hanoi bursting with pride and enthusiasm, eager to participate in the construction of an independent Vietnam. But to many of them, the rigid discipline that held them together through the long years of resistance, and which they had readily accepted under those circumstances, seemed no longer necessary. Some young poets demanded freedom of artistic expression, feeling they had earned this right by their sacrifices for the revolution.

From late 1956 until early 1958 the role of the artist in the new society was vigorously debated. As early as February 1955, a young writer, Tran Dan (born 1924), a party member, had tried to work through official channels to convince the party to adopt a more liberal policy toward literature and the arts. He allegedly had the temerity to argue publicly that "truth transcends all directives, all theories." Criticizing party-controlled literature as rife with "artifice" and even "hypocrisy," he plainly called the new revolutionary literature "hackneyed" and "simplistic."[41] Phan Khoi, seventy-year-old patriarch of modern poetry, was as usual among the first to take a firm position.

> Each of us possesses his own art and reflects his own
> personality in it. Only this kind of art and personality can
> create the spectacle of a hundred flowers rivaling each
> other in charm. On the contrary, if one compels all writers
> to write in the same style, there may come a day when all
> the flowers will be changed into chrysanthemums.[42]

As editor of *Literary Selections*, a new quarterly journal, he boldly published the more extreme examples of the growing protest literature. A significant number of writers and poets, many of whom had developed their talent writing for National Salvation publications, were increasingly critical of the dogmatism and regimentation imposed upon them by party leaders. Tran Dan came under especially heavy attack when he wrote:

> I walked and saw no streets and no houses,
> Only rain falling upon the red banners.[43]

When warned that with such an attitude it would be better not to write at all, he responded:

> I can ignore a thousand vulgar insults,
> All save one: "To live without creating."[44]

Phung Quan, another protestor, replied to the party cadres who criticized his writing:

> I want to be a true writer;
> When I love somebody, I say it outright,
> When I hate somebody, I say so.
>
> . . . .
>
> Even if someone threatened to kill me with a knife,
> I would not say "I love" if I meant to say "I hate."

Having been threatened that such writing might have consequences he would regret, he proclaimed:

The honey-strewn road of riches and honors cannot sweeten
  my tongue,
A thunderbolt striking upon my head cannot knock me down.
Who then can snatch away my pen or my paper?[45]

Le Dat, perhaps the most controversial of all the protestors,
decried

Placing police stations and machinery in the center of the
  human heart,
Forcing feelings to be expressed according to a set of rules
  promulgated by the government.

And, sharpest of all these critical thrusts, Le Dat composed the following quatrain aimed at the top party leadership, including Ho
Chi Minh himself:

Human lives, which can attain a hundred years,
Are like pots of lime.
The longer the life, the more mediocrity.
The longer the life, the smaller one becomes.[46]

Phan Khoi added a polemical essay, rich in indirection and irony,
entitled simply "Mr. Lime Pot":

The chewing of betel is a custom practiced all over Vietnam,
so lime pots may be found everywhere. As far as I know,
there are two kinds of lime pots used in our rural areas. Both
are made of baked clay. One looks like a small jar, but has a
high neck with a funnel-shaped mouth. This kind was used
by ordinary families. The other is like a round vase. It has a
flat bottom, a handle, and its mouth is one-sided. . . . This
kind was used by rich people. Both were used as lime
containers. Each time the lime was poured in, people also
deposited some lime on the mouth of the pot, gradually
building it up.

In our family, when my paternal grandmother was still living,
we had that luxurious kind of lime pot. Each time that lime was
brought home from the market, my grandmother would sit
down and meticulously spread a coat of lime on the mouth of
the pot with a small spatula, saying she was "feeding Mr. Pot."
From time to time the mouth would receive another coat, causing it to puff out more and more as time passed.

When I say "my family had a lime pot," that is not accurate. For from the time I was a small boy until I reached the

age of twenty-five, when my grandmother died, my family had three lime pots, one after the other. This was because after long use, the inside of the pot would fill up with hard, dry lime and the neck would become clogged as more and more lime accumulated in deposits around the mouth. Finally a pot would become unusable and we would have to buy a new one.

At that time my family had an altar to three deities. The god of good fortune was in the middle with the earth god on one side and the kitchen god on the other. Whenever a lime pot was to be discarded, my grandmother would tell me to place it on the altar to be worshipped along with the others.

Worshipping pots of lime in this manner was not at all peculiar to my family. When discarding a lime pot an entire village might carry it to be placed on a wall of a village shrine or a pagoda. People considered this to be venerating that particular "Mr. Pot."

Why was a pot of lime called "Mister"? Having read this far, you must understand why already. Because in our rural district, and perhaps throughout all of Vietnam, anything that might be able to harm one is called "Mister." Anything that is huge or that has lived for a long time is also called "Mister." The tiger that can eat you is called "Mister." The monkey that can destroy your crops is called "Mister Monkey." . . . The cooking tripod, used for five or ten years before being replaced, is called "Mister Tripod." . . . Whatever they may become in the future, the Vietnamese in the past have always given the title of "Mister" to anything capable of being harmful, big or small, and to anything large or long-lived. This was to indicate their reverence and respect.

I committed a misdeed when I was eighteen years old. Let me now engage in self-criticism and make my confession. At the age of eighteen I no longer believed in all this. One summer night . . . I took a walk along the village road with some friends of my own age. As we passed the village shrine and the pagoda we took down every one of those "Mr. Lime Pots" from its place of veneration and tossed them on the ground. Why did we do that? We just did it, and we didn't need any reason. But, a few days later, when we went back to look, they had been neatly replaced by some unknown person.

That was, however, not a crime of which I alone was guilty. In those days any young person of that age might have done exactly the same thing. If at the present time I must engage in self-criticism, then that entire generation of young people, now gray-haired, should criticize themselves as I am doing.

In summation, people show their reverence and respect to a lime pot by calling it "Mister" because it has lived a long time, filled up hard and dry inside, its mouth covered over, sitting in melancholy on an altar or up on a wall, like an earthen or wooden statue, speechless, motionless. I wrote this short study to explicate a few lines of poetry by Le Dat:

> Human lives, which can attain a hundred years,
> Are like pots of lime.
> The longer the life, the more mediocrity.
> The longer the life, the smaller one becomes.[47]

Ho Chi Minh had been the leading Vietnamese Communist since the late 1920s when he organized the Youth League among young political exiles in Canton. Pham Van Dong, Vo Nguyen Giap, Truong Chinh, and almost all the other important leaders had played an important role in the party for decades. The implication was that these men might have grown too rigid, too closed, that like lime pots they had lost their usefulness after long use. Perhaps it was time to put Ho Chi Minh and his gray-haired cronies on the shelf; to venerate them, to give them titles showing reverence and respect, but to get new leaders to conduct the affairs of government.

Phan Khoi also highlighted the irony of this intolerance toward youthful protestors on the part of the government. You and I, he reminded the party leaders, were just like them when we were young. Tran Dan, Phung Quan, Le Dat, and the other youthful critics are simply doing what the young always do, what we did when we were young: they are challenging the shibboleths and encrusted assumptions of their elders.

Phan Khoi was immediately attacked as a reactionary, a revisionist, a Trotskyite, a senile old man unable to overcome his ingrained capitalist mentality, and a habitual troublemaker who enjoyed controversy for its own sake. In the merciless stream of criticism, hints grew stronger that he was a dangerous enemy of the state. Yet he continued to aid and encourage the most controversial of the young writers and poets. The third issue of *Literary Selections* (October 1956) contained a short poem he had written earlier during the Resistance:

What sort of rose is a rose without thorns?
Just let it not be a rose without blossoms.
If it is to be a rose, it must have blossoms.
Who would tend a rose with only thorns and no blossoms?
O rose, I love you very much.
You have thorns, but a fragrant scent as well.[48]

Only four issues of the controversial *Literary Selections* appeared: in March, August, October, and December 1956. The other major source of publication for the protest writers had been the journal *Humanities*, also edited by Phan Khoi, of which only five issues appeared, between September and November 1956. The sixth issue, scheduled for publication in December, contained one line so shocking that the head of the printers' union ordered his men to refuse to man their presses: "The people have a right to demonstrate." The publishers of the journal were arrested, and Phan Khoi was out of work and in very serious trouble.[49]

Despite suppression, the flow of works from outraged artists and intellectuals continued through 1957. When the protest literature could no longer be published, it was typed or handwritten and distributed covertly. A violent peasant rebellion in Nghe An province in November 1956 had increased government sensitivity to any and all forms of opposition and criticism, and the radical and brutally executed land reform program (supervised by Truong Chinh) had aroused fierce resentment among some segments of the rural population. In late 1956 and early 1957 Ho Chi Minh himself admitted that "errors had been committed" and urged more moderation and tolerance. A "rectification of errors" campaign was launched, and thousands of political prisoners were released as a gesture of government goodwill. In the north as in the south, *yin* and *yang* elements of the sociocultural system were in a relationship of conflict rather than complementarity.[50]

Early in 1960 Phan Khoi died in Hanoi just a few days before he was to go on trial for "deviationism."[51] The grandson of the legendary Hoang Dieu (who hanged himself as French forces overran the citadel in Hanoi), the father of modern poetry, the veteran revolutionary who had spent nine years of his life imprisoned on Poulo Condore and another eight years in the mountains with the Resistance forces—Phan Khoi died in disgrace, labeled an enemy of the state in the north, as Nguyen Tuong Tam was to die in the south three years later.

Both Ngo Dinh Diem in the south and Ho Chi Minh in the north were ardent Vietnamese patriots, dedicated men who led austere personal lives. Both knew French and English and were intimately familiar with Western political traditions. Yet neither could understand, or sympathize with, the individualism of men like Phan Khoi or Nguyen Tuong Tam. Neither was any more concerned with individual human rights than were the benighted French colonists against whom they had leveled so much bitter criticism. Many of their countrymen thought none the less of them for that; others were troubled.

Hoang Cam, commenting on the transition from colonialism to communism, wrote:

> Stop, write no more letters,
> Lest each line be one more crime.
> My parents have passed away.
> Now I have new parents.
>
> . . . .
> When can I be an orphan?[52]

The desire for greater artistic and intellectual freedom was fairly widespread, and the protesters had many admirers. But many other people—and there were a large number of poets, writers, artists, and intellectuals among them—were angered by this kind of criticism. There was a massive backlash against these champions of individual freedom.

Che Lan Vien disassociated himself from the protesters and proclaimed his willingness to place his talents wholly at the service of the state. This, he felt, was the best way to serve his people and his nation. He had no sympathy for the young writers and poets who were being arrested, or sent to reeducation centers, and forced to work at state farms in remote rural areas. They should, he asserted, learn "The Practical Truth":

> All his life he has eaten the rice of the people.
> Today he is transplanting rice for the people.
> What good is all that futile verse that flows like water,
> And does not serve the people so much as a single bowl of
>   rice?[53]

On January 6, 1958, the political section of the Party Central Committee formally demanded a rectification of the mission of arts and letters in the Democratic Republic of Vietnam. The question of what was right and what was wrong, what was acceptable and what was not, in poetry and in all other art forms was now a public and unequivocal one. There was no possibility of remaining neutral and ambivalent. Either one was for the protesters and against the Communist party or one was for the party and against the protesters. The decision had to be clear-cut, immediate, public; and it was irrevocable.

The entire cultural, educational, and information resources of the regime were brought to bear against the malcontents. During the first four months of 1958 every author of protest literature was subjected to a barrage of public attacks. Their characters were slandered, their philosophy ridiculed, and their written works dissected and refuted almost word by word. The February 1958 issue of *Arts and Letters* set forth the general thrust of the counterattack in an article entitled "Serious Erroneous Tendencies in the Journal *Humanities*." The March issue then contained several articles that continued the attack, including "Struggle with Determination Against Revisionism in Literature," and "Reviewing Some Mistakes in Journals and in the Mission of Arts and Letters," capped by a major article by Xuan Dieu entitled "Some Issues of Struggle Concerning Thought in Poetry."

Xuan Dieu vigorously attacked all the critics of the government and of the party. Declaring that he, too, disliked dogmatism, Xuan Dieu responded to Phan Khoi: "We too are awaiting, are encouraging, and are striving for a hundred types of socialist poems to blossom like flowers, to show off their freshness." But there was, he contended, no need of diverse tendencies or viewpoints:

> Yes, we have no need to imitate America, or England, or France, where conflicting literary tendencies are inevitably molded. Here in our Democratic Republic of Vietnam, although conflicting classes still exist, under the leadership of the party we are advancing toward socialism. We want to have hundreds, thousands of approaches to writing, tens and tens of thousands of creations, but our literature has only one tendency, and this is progress toward socialism.

After a brief analysis of poetry by Le Dat and others that stressed the theme of human dignity, Xuan Dieu concluded:

> But their conception of a human is based on their own model, and not on ours. In his poem "The New," Le Dat sees us, we who have striven, who have labored, who have respected the

daily anonymous tasks, as "a formula for a wire through the
nose. There are some people who live a long time—And are
just like lime pots—The longer their lives, the fouler they
get—The longer their lives, the narrower they become."
Being educated by the party, the older people among us do
indeed become narrower day by day, as we struggle to restrict the individualism within us, the smaller the better, in
order that the new human, the collective human can grow
and develop: And this is a source of happiness for us.

Having noted the conflicting criteria for self-esteem, the conflicting models of human beings and their derivative conceptions of
"human dignity," Xuan Dieu justified his demand for ideological
redundancy as a necessary means of resocialization. This argument
demonstrates why and how ideological controversy in Vietnam
was a zero-sum game. The thermostat could have one and only
one setting; one and only one set of values had to achieve dominance. Each group's values threatened the other's self-esteem. Between and within the north and the south, vehement accusations
were hurled back and forth, careers were destroyed, and people
were being imprisoned and killed—because of the incompatibility
of the constellations of attitudes and values on which precarious
feelings of self-worth were based.

Those who write for Humanities and Literary Selections do
not understand that: The struggle of thoughts is a decisive
one, and there can be no concessions. Thought that esteems
labor, that loves collectivism, and respects the good and
proper discipline of the proletariat is certain to stamp out the
thoughts of anarchy, of unbridled freedom, of supermen and
heroes, and not permit them to keep spreading, not permit
them to arise, not permit them to breathe, not permit them to
live. It is certain that capitalist thought must surrender to us.
With thinking that has gone astray, we will help it, nurture it,
and reform it; but with thoughts that oppose the party,
oppose our regime, no agreements can be reached, and they
must be forced to surrender to us.
. . . Formerly, under the old repressive and exploitive
regimes, if you got drunk, if you smoked opium, then the
repressive and exploitive regime was responsible. If you were
anarchistic under those regimes, at least that had some partial
value of resistance to those regimes. But now, under our
regime, if you get drunk, if you are infatuated with the

capitalist classes, if you indulge in individualism, if you are unorganized, the regime will not accept responsibility for you, and those things are your own fault.

After dealing with the protesters and their works, Xuan Dieu articulated the standards to which all writers and poets in the new regime were expected to strive.

A literature that adheres to Marxism-Leninism is the most humane literature, because that is the first literature in the history of mankind which proposes to be in the service of the masses, of the majority, of the workers, farmers, and soldiers. We study the teachings of Lenin, the heritage of those things which are the essence and the progressive result of that which man has created under the various regimes. At the same time we understand that in previous regimes, basically, the masses had no writers or poets who were of their own class, serving their class directly. Under our regime, the masses are creating history more strongly and more radiantly than ever before, but with a few exceptions, the masses of today still do not have writers or poets who have emerged from their own bosom. Socialism needs technicians who are red, completely red, and not just ones with a pinkish tinge. We also need writers and poets who are red, completely red, and not just ones with a pinkish tinge. While we are reforming ourselves so as to become truly writers and poets of the masses, we must thoroughly comprehend this, that we are far, still very far indeed, short of the necessary level. That level is to be Communist writers and poets, writers and poets who are Communists with all our hearts and all our minds, not just ones who carry a card indicating membership in the party.

In the same issue of *Arts and Letters* (March 1958) as the article by Xuan Dieu, a poem appeared by Che Lan Vien that reinforced the thrust of the article but took a different approach, more persuasive than argumentative. This poem was called "When You Have Purpose":

When you have purpose, a common stick can slay the enemy.
Our brothers of old used their teeth to rend the flesh of
    opposing troops.
One leaflet can activate an entire district.
Dirty hands and muddy feet can overturn even the throne of a
    king.

When you have purpose, on those mornings and afternoons
    without savor,
Which are molded by fortifications meant to protect the "self,"
In the vale of agony weapons can be found
To shatter the loneliness and mix it with "people."

Nothing at all is lost
When life has clear purpose.
The tiniest moss-covered crevice will glisten with light,
When the sunshine of thought plumbs the deep caves.

. . . .

When there is purpose, fear not that the flame of life will end,
For when the wind blows, life will arise naturally.[54]

This sense of purpose, of the psychological rewards of participation in meaningful group action, provided the Communist poets with the inspiration for their finest poetry.

While Xuan Dieu, Che Lan Vien, and other "born again" Communists were attacking Phan Khoi, Le Dat, and the other protestors, Huy Can, now deputy minister for culture, was traveling around the world to gather support for the new regime and to collect materials and seek inspiration for his socialist writing. A good example of his seminal work at this time is his poem "Wide Oceans, Long Rivers," or "Flying Across Siberia," which he wrote while in Moscow in December of 1956:

The plane crosses Siberia,
White snow and more white snow.

. . . .

It is like flying into the past of mankind,
Snow envelops snow, life follows life, eternally.
The plane passes through clouds into a golden dazzle of
    sunshine,
Like glad tidings announcing the morning of days and days.
Above the long whiteness of the snow, beneath the smooth
    whiteness of the clouds,
The plane soars back to the present.

My friend smiles at me affectionately,
Pointing out the rising factory smoke;
My Soviet comrade also shows me
The sea brimming with water, a river whose course has
    shifted.
No newly formed cell here,

Staggering exhausted upon an ancient beach,
But already transformed through a hundred forms over
    millions of years.
And here the snow still falls, the snow still envelops.
But man has made himself king of the universe,
Has reformed society already, and is now reforming nature.
Rivers flow uphill, exceeding even ancient myths.
With two white hands, man has made himself Nature.
Obedient trees bear more fruits and flowers,
Desert becomes garden, spring blooms in arctic regions.
In decorating the garden of the universe, more moons are
    added [Sputniks]
Adorning the earth like a pair of earrings;
Like a telephone without limits upon which we listen to the
    secrets
Of myriad deep skies, of myriad stars,
Undulating in the blue atmosphere like a pair of buoys,
Spreading tidings of life throughout the Milky Way,
In eight ways, in ten directions, to all of the stars, hot and
    cold.
The immortal communications satellite of man,
Who, with earth in hand, now masters even the sky,
And transmits the beat of the human heart into the universe.

Here is Moscow now; at the airport,
Many close friends warmly greet me.
Meeting my brothers and sisters, people of
Myriad glorious ages of the Soviet homeland.
Face looks at face, hand clasps hand, and I know
There is today, and there will also be tomorrow,
Because there are the hearts—like wide oceans and long
    rivers—
Of these brothers and sisters, firmly attached
To millions and millions of laboring people,
To hundreds and hundreds of sorrowful peoples,
Who hear the call to rise up and set upon their way.[55]

Huy Can, Xuan Dieu, Luu Trong Lu, and Che Lan Vien were
among the most alienated and disturbed young poets of the 1930s.
Their poetry at that time revealed extreme individualism and
preoccupation with their own inner feelings. What they seem to
have felt, however, was mainly loneliness and despair. They had
not celebrated the joys of individualism; they had expressed its
anguish. Then, as revealed by their poetry and confirmed by what

we know of their lives, they had been rejuvenated by their participation in the Resistance War and their conversion to communism during the mid-1940s. Party discipline combined with membership in a tightly knit, highly organized social group had enabled them to slough off the oppressive weight of individualism and provided them with new and satisfying identities.

To them individualism was dead and not to be mourned, while the rediscovered virtues of collectivism had taken on almost religious significance. Revolutionary Marxism-Leninism not only provided them with a touchstone for attaining mastery over society and even nature, it offered a metaphysical basis for confronting the previously frightening prospects of life and death. These men were now thriving. Both their personalities and their lives were more highly structured and better integrated. They had become integral parts of an efficacious collectivity that transcended their own lives both sociologically and temporally, like the families and villages of tradition, like the wide seas and long rivers that served as apt metaphors in their poetry.

With unmatched zeal To Huu, Huy Can, Xuan Dieu, Che Lan Vien, Luu Trong Lu, Hoai Thanh, and other "born-again" Communist writers, poets, and critics defended the party, propagated its teachings, and maintained its ideology against all criticism. In so doing they were protecting their own new-found feelings of self-worth. Their new identities required that the integrity of the new superfamily/supervillage structure be assiduously maintained as the primary source of meaning in their lives. But the spontaneous outpouring of poetry, short stories, and articles eulogizing the regime by devout party members was not countering the growing influence of the protestors to the satisfaction of the party leaders. After several months of study and conferences, it was decided that vigorous action was required to resolve once and for all the question of the proper role of the artist in society.

Rectification was demanded in January 1958, and the March 1958 issue of *Arts and Letters* contained Xuan Dieu's major position paper and the poem "When You Have Purpose" by Che Lan Vien. Then, in March, the subcommittee for arts and letters of the Central Committee of the Labor party organized a "study session" for 304 writers, poets, and cultural cadre. Care was taken to ensure that the most outspoken critics of the regime were present: men like Tran Dan, Le Dat, Hoang Cam, and Phung Quan. At this session, confronted with the brilliance of proletarian thought, with the clear truth, and by the determined struggle and patient assistance of their fellow literary artists, elements participating in the *Humanities–Literary Selections* affair took a first step toward recognizing the errors and crimes of their clique toward each and every one of their brothers and sisters who are literary artists.[56]

The entire April edition of *Arts and Letters* was devoted to articles criticizing the writers and poets who had been involved with *Humanities* or *Literary Selections*. Then, in the May issue, confessions and retractions by the offending poets and writers appeared. The controversy over the role of the literary artist, which had begun only twenty-one months earlier, was over. Literature was totally dedicated to the service of the party. Now collectivism ruled supreme. Individualism was anathema. The wheel had turned full cycle. Once again Vietnamese poets in Hanoi would be creating within an official framework, with Marxism-Leninism taking the place of Neo-Confucianism, and poetry would be produced to meet the current requirements of the state, with the party taking the place formerly occupied by the king and his royal court. Poetry was again public rather than personal, didactic rather than expressive, *yang* rather than *yin*.

Throughout all this, The Lu had remained silent, not joining in the acrimonious debates nor writing any poetry. Phan Khoi asked him why he no longer produced poetry as he had before, and received the reply: "I'll write poetry again when my soul is purged and my life adapted to that of the working masses."[57] But in the early months of 1958, along with most other men of letters, The Lu too denounced those who had challenged party dogma and lost. In a brief article entitled "The Counterrevolutionary Clique Has Revealed Its Genuine Form," he wrote of Phan Khoi and the young protest writers:

They have resorted to heresy and sophistry to deceive the people and seduce the rotten elements to follow them, to sell their hearts and minds to them cheaply. And in the ranks that followed them before all else came those literary artists who had gone with the revolution but carried along with them a heavy burden of personal feelings from the old life, and regretted the passing of a way of life characterized by unfettered selfishness, thinking and working in an easy manner, according to their own individualistic preferences, crawling

into a hole of literature that was smoke-filled and debased
and taking that as the universe for their souls to create in.[58]

No longer could even The Lu ask: "What need have I?" when
chided for lack of ideology. As a culmination of the six months of
study sessions and policy meetings that followed the January 1958
resolution of the Central Party Committee demanding rectification
of the mission of arts and letters in society, on the evening of July
13, 1958, there was a festival held to celebrate the departure of
fifty-eight (of ninety-two) members of the Arts and Letters Association "into reality." These writers, poets, and cultural cadre were
going out to work in teams for six months in agricultural cooperatives, mines, lumber camps, road gangs, frontier outposts, and tex-
tile factories. Hoai Thanh, association chairman, hearing rumors
that some individuals were grumbling about the honor bestowed
upon them, reiterated the necessity, desirability, and importance of
this assignment:

> It may be said that you are going into the most strategic
> places, into the first ranks on the frontiers of production, into
> the centers of contemporary life. The primary purpose of this
> phase of travel is not really to create. The primary purpose
> remains the reform of thought. But through this phase of
> thought reform, we believe that the enthusiastic spirit of
> revolution . . . will spread into our literature and our art,
> will give rise to creations that will make an appropriate con-
> tribution to the common task. For this has become a matter
> of regulation.[59]

The Ideological Foundations in the North,
1958–1968

With the disruptive but brutally effective land reform program
completed in the countryside, and the protesting intellectuals si-
lenced if not yet fully reformed in their thinking, the party apparatus was solidly in control of the northern half of the country.
Ngo Dinh Diem, meanwhile, had been unexpectedly successful in
strengthening his control over the south. Within the party there
was considerable debate over what line to take. Some wished to
concentrate on building socialism in the north. Others advocated
giving a higher priority to promoting revolution in the south. During this policy debate, some poets in the Democratic Republic of
Vietnam began to agitate public opinion against the opposing Republic of Vietnam. One early work mobilizing opinion to support

the struggle for reunification of the nation was a poem by Luu Trong Lu dated September 7, 1958. This long poem was written at the point where the river dividing the two antagonistic regimes flows into the sea. It is called "Pounding Waves at the Bay of Tung":

> I am a poet of my nation.
> Arriving here one afternoon,
> I sit upon a boulder. . . .
>
> .   .   .   .
>
> I look at the vast sea,
> Up at the towering sky.
>
> .   .   .   .
>
> All of this is part of my nation,
> Beneath my pointing hand.
>
> .   .   .   .
>
> Yearned for by night, dreamed of by day,
> And still just one handspan away.
> I want to have a million-gallon heart,
> And drink in every bit of my nation.
> I want a pair of arms that are wide and long,
> That can embrace all of the southern region.
> Ah, kind friends throughout the world!
> Why is it on this afternoon,
> Standing on this peak of land,
> My feet cannot advance to reach,
> My feet cannot advance to reach it?
> Why is that so, my friends?
>
> .   .   .   .
>
> Vietnamese soil that cannot be reached by Vietnamese
>
> .   .   .   .
>
> Oh, wave deities with silver heads!
> From a hundred thousand spans of water
> Swell up,
> Roar,
> Shout out
> All the resentment in my heart this afternoon!
>
> .   .   .   .
>
> My poetry gushes forth into the majestic Bay of Tung;
> My feet take one long stride after another.
> The offshore wind will keep howling beneath my feet.

While on the other side of the river sits the American-Diem
    clique,
Their owl-like eyes staring at me provocatively.
When the hawk flies,
The owl must bow its head and turn away.
Hearing this poem, they must start with fright;
For this poem voices the aspirations of millions
And millions of reforged people,
Is heavy with the just cause in its heart.
Our poetry shall never bow down,
Poetry firm as steel and enduring as iron, eternal.
Yet this poetry goes in soft shoes of paper,
Slipping from alley to alley, knocking at every door,
No, no, not with a thud of hobnail boots
In the black night,
A sound that causes doors to be bolted and lamps blown out,
That when heard causes ghosts to whimper and demons to
    cry.
No, our poetry is not cruel.
Wherever our poetry goes lamps burn brightly and houses are
    gay.
The doors of agony open a crack,
The bitterness in hearts is shared
Beside a kitchen fire in the deep of night;
Head leans against head,
While in the house, lamps burn brightly,
Like stars, twinkling in the sky.
The dark night of south Vietnam shall be brightened forever,
A ray of faith spreads light to both sides of the river.
In the misery of the past ten years
Souls have been forged into iron and steel.
Like the numberless waves of the sea,
The struggle does not rest and does not cease.
O southern region of a thousand memories and a million
    affections,
Flesh of our flesh, blood of our blood,
The flesh cannot be torn asunder,
And your blood is still mingled with ours.[60]

In south Vietnam both Communists and anticommunists were
increasing the level of violence. Buried weapons were being dug
up; kidnappings and assassinations, arrests and executions spi-
raled in geometric progression. A few well-trained cadre from the
north were already marching down jungle trails to provide lead-

ership and technical expertise to rag-tag bands of guerrillas. Diem had built some "reeducation camps" and filled them with men and women guilty of leftist thinking; and—with increasing American assistance—he was upgrading and enlarging his military and police forces. And in the north the poetry was growing stronger and more explicit. In a poem dated January 25, 1959, Huy Can created a poignant case for the urgency and necessity of the armed struggle that was developing and the sacrifices it would require. "Your Uncle's Child in the South Is Eager to See His Father's Face" was published in *Arts and Letters* in April 1959:

> Each morning when he awakes, my child tugs at my face,
> Sits on my shoulders like a flower blooming upon a branch.
> . . . .
> My face presents a strange terrain
> For my child to explore each day.
> Do flowers ever talk with trees?
> My child questions with a hundred words not yet spoken.
> . . . .
> I experience an immensity that is the feeling of fatherhood
> Each morning as my child tugs at his father's face.
>
> O my child, my child! You have an uncle, a man of the south,
> A good friend of your father, who is often wakeful long into
>   the night,
> As he lies there missing his child. . . .
> As your uncle dreams and wonders how big his child has
>   grown.
> He pulls out old pictures of his child, mischievous, laughing,
> But—and this is painful—the pictures stop at an early age,
> The newer ages of his child are not to be seen in those
>   pictures.
>
> O my child, my child! You remain at home, my child.
> Study hard, and practice talking with grandmother.
> Let father go to work with your uncle from the south.
> Your uncle's child in the south is eager to see his father's
>   face.[61]

Other poets and writers quickly took up the theme. One example of the contributions of younger writers and poets, products of the Resistance, is this poem by Nguyen Anh Dao, which appeared along with the previous poem by Huy Can in the April 1, 1959, issue of *Arts and Letters*:

At the age of ten I followed the revolution,
Exactly thirteen years ago, one morning in the fall,
In a gay mood, with a flag clasped firmly in my hand, I
    asked to enlist
        in the army.
        Father was already dead!
            Mother, why do you look at me without speaking?
Mother choked back her tears and whispered:
        Stay here and avoid it, my only son,
Your mother doesn't want to hinder you,
        But so many members of our family
Have gone into the thick of battle for the Revolution!
I think you have no need to rush,
For you are not yet a man,
You're still so very small, my son,
And I love you very, very much!
. . . .

Mother,
        Was there ever a time
            When I did not love you,
        Was there ever?
        No, no, no! That could never be!
. . . .

        And did you ever find me to be contrary
Or not listen to what you told me?
But today the flag has waved above my head,
With the words of the Fatherland, pulling my heart toward
    them.
The wave of revolution is roaring up into a blowing wind,
Impelling me to set out, and I cannot be stopped, dear mother!
        I've grown up,
            And somehow our house seems confining!

. . . .

You love me. But please don't worry.
On the day of Independence I will return.

Mother,
        Why do I miss my home so fervently today?
What should I write to send home to the South?
I have my heart
        I have my hands
            I have my Party!
With my heart, my life is attached
To the South, to my mother, to my brothers and sisters . . .

Like arteries and veins of red blood are attached
   to the heart!
With my hands I can do anything,
Working along with millions of other rapid, busy pairs of
   hands
I cut logs
   I construct bridges
      I build roadways up and down the land,
Determined to open wide the pathways of the Fatherland!
Oh, road to the South,
      Your name is Route Number One,
Because our nation cannot be divided into two!

. . . .

On the distant bank there is a figure,
   Head sprinkled with gray and shoulders stooped,
Yet still standing erect, . . .
      Awaiting the return of her son,
         Victorious in battle,
            Her beloved son!
And I am determined to return.
      There will be a warm and sunny day when the flag will
         rustle
And that day will come
      Because I have
         My Party.

The new content, style, and tone of the new public and didactic poetry in the north were well established, and the messages it transmitted were highly redundant. Poetry, fiction, and other mass media were skillfully employed to prepare the way psychologically for (and sometimes to influence) party decisions and policies. The above poems with their emotional pleas for unification of the country were written between September 1958 and April 1959. The party's formal decision to "liberate the south and unify the nation" was apparently made in May 1959. But not until September 1959 did the party give even tacit public acceptance of the notion of "liberating the South" and the formation of the National Liberation Front of South Vietnam (NLF) did not come until December, three months later. By then the published literature in the Democratic Republic of Vietnam had been preparing public attitudes for two years.

In both the north and the south the significance of published literature at this time was much greater and of much more immediate effect than in earlier decades. Not only had transportation and communication facilities been vastly improved over the years, the size of the reading public was growing at an unprecedented rate. The number of students in schools for all of Vietnam grew from only 450,000 in 1939 to about 700,000 in 1944. By 1954 this number had grown to about 1,125,000, and by 1961 school attendance in Vietnam had reached 4,000,000. In both halves of Vietnam the literacy rate was spectacularly increased, and the public was subjected to a barrage of printed material.[62]

The major poets of the state in the north continued to explain their new approach to poetry and to life to other writers and poets, to their reading public, and to the world at large. In an introduction to the French book *Anthologie de la Poésie Vietnamienne* we find Che Lan Vien writing for the Western reader on the subject of Vietnamese poetry:

> Our poetry is essentially realistic. It is repelled by getting too much involved in the domain of the abstract, and at leaping the boundaries of the metaphysical. . . . In the new poetry we still have some metaphysical poets, but it seems this may be merely some spirits impatient of finding a solution to the problems of life. For when the waves of the Revolution broke, they let themselves be carried away with the others to rejoin the ranks of the people. There they have come, strong with the optimism of those who fight in the present, convinced that all will in the end be resolved by the hands, the brains, and the heart of man. . . . The more unhappy a mother is, the more she wishes for her child to be gay. Vietnamese poetry at this time is like such a child. It sings of happiness and liberty recently won. It is the joyous cry of a man who, through his work and his struggles, is becoming master of himself. . . . But actually, it was not in an instant that we were able to measure the magnitude of the change. For fifteen years I have saluted To Huu, the poet of the Revolution, in these terms: "You have changed the geography of the national poetry." I meant that before the Revolution poetry sang of unchanging subjects: life, death, mankind, but that with the Revolution it approached new regions: struggle and politics. But now I hold the position that it is not simply a question of changing geography, but is also a question of changing history. Without doubt poetry has brought itself to other lands: the Revolution, politics; but it did not limit itself to that. It renewed itself and gave new content and significance to life, to death, to the face of a loved one or a rose.

Obviously the first days showed signs of infantilism. But to the degree that the country, the nation, was reaching maturity, poetry too was maturing. Those who searched have found. The stammerings of the debut have become clear calls of assurance. . . . Nevertheless, tears are still with us. Our country is still divided in two. The body and soul of those who are coming from the past and bequeathing us the justice of this war are not able to take on new flesh and blood in an instant. But if we speak of our suffering and sorrows in our poems, it is in order to abolish them. These poems resemble a corps of engineers preparing the route for the army of joy.

In former times, imprisoned in chains, we loved the man plunged into the valleys and abysses of sadness. Now, in freedom, we love the man at the summit, in his work and in his glorious struggles. . . . Our verse speaks of man in his moments of light: revolutionaries . . . , resistance fighters . . . , peasants trusting all to their hands and with their human force transforming rocks and gravel into rice . . . , and also those who are in the process of proceeding from the particular to the general of whom Xuan Dieu writes, those who leave the horizon of "one alone" to attain "the horizon of all," a horizon more vast, which makes them more vast themselves. . . .

The Lu, Luu Trong Lu, Xuan Dieu, Huy Can, . . . coming from the valley of tears to the plain of laughter, these are the poets who having had to suffer the wounds they inflicted upon themselves are now able to fight those of the others and to construct the springtime.

These poets of suffering have understood that the revolution is theirs. They march side by side with the younger poets . . . , all emerging from the crucible of the revolution and the resistance. . . .

Our country is now our soul. And our soul today is nothing other than a part of the Democratic Republic of Vietnam. A new rapport has been established between poets and their readers. . . . No more is there a "no man's land" between the soul of a poet and those of his readers.

Is it necessary to recall the fact that this is due to the existence of the Labor party of Vietnam? . . .

For us, the party of the Vietnamese proletariat has resolved and is in the process of solving the problems posed to our people during the centuries. It has abolished feudalism and capitalism. It subdues nature, effacing misery. It brings happiness. This happiness is not content to bring men to life, to nourish them; it also teaches them to sing.[63]

In the May 1961 issue of *Arts and Letters* Huy Can presented an article entitled "Thinking About Poetry" that succinctly sets forth the rationale behind the new public poetry and its role in the new society:

> To think about poetry is actually to think about art and life, or, even more accurately, to think about the relationship between artistic creativity and a way of life. Formerly, when I first began to write poetry, I faced this issue, but from a metaphysical point of view. Since then the Revolution has shown me the proper way of looking at it; and I now see clearly that: Before all else, poetry is a question of "What is the proper way for one to live?" and at the same time how should one live so life will be beautiful and profound. Once one has untied that central knot, the source of creativity has been opened for poetry. The ultimate thing in poetry is that it must bring to fruition something that will raise the level of life. Sometimes we say this in an abbreviated way: mobilize to struggle, mobilize to good works. It is very accurate to speak in this way. But we must probe more deeply; mobilize here means to evoke the creative force of humanity, to elevate life to be more beautiful, more proper, to develop all aspects of mankind in accordance with the works and programs of Karl Marx.[64]

Luu Trong Lu contributed to the same issue an article entitled "A Few Reflections on Poetry." After emphasizing that "the pre-Revolution poets, under the admirable reformation of the party, have undergone a great transformation and are making a notable contribution to the revolutionary poetry," he gave his colleagues an eloquent reminder that there could be no acceptable excuse for not producing poetry of high quality that would contribute to the common cause:

> The political meaning, the didactic meaning of a poem should not be too cheap and conspicuous, but should arise from the sinews and fibers of the poem! Say what you think, say what you feel. If the wings of your heart have not yet spread, then go knock on the door of life. When life has come, the heart will flap its wings, and poetry will soar. When a bird is under a blue sky, it is difficult for it to repress its song. A bud just soaked with morning dew, when struck by morning sunshine, can scarcely restrain itself from blossoming. And just so as poets of the regime, intoxicated by the regime, we must speak of the beauty of the regime, of the great sentiments of

the times, of the resplendent and unsurpassed humanity of communism. Our Poetry must give voice to our policy positions. But is not every policy of the Party loving and meaningful? Do they not all arise from a heart of love for the people? If there is not a profound agreement of sentiments with the Party, one cannot speak.[65]

These comments by Che Lan Vien, Huy Can, and Luu Trong Lu accurately set the tone for the poetry published in the Democratic Republic of Vietnam during the 1960s and 1970s. They themselves adhered to this philosophy and served as powerful exemplars to the younger generations. Che Lan Vien, who thirty-one years earlier had been "sick and tired of the colors of this world," who wanted to "close [his] eyes to disregard the present," whose poetry had been "a world created in a moment of grief," wrote in 1968:

Each day I meet someone, and he is one fragment of the genius of mankind.
The blood and sweat of people forge so many images, so much language,
The shirttails of a million poets could not encompass all the gold and silver that life spews forth.
Each person, stranger or friend, aids by adding one word to my poetry.
Glean the words of life and write them down on paper.[66]

This exuberant spirit of relatedness was shared by many members of the party, the government, and the armed forces of the Democratic Republic of Vietnam. Che Lan Vien, Luu Trong Lu, Xuan Dieu, Huy Can, and To Huu are more prominent and more articulate than most of their comrades, but the transformation in outlook they so forcefully express was characteristic of a significant number of people. They spoke for a much larger group of men and women who grew up in early-twentieth-century Vietnam to become unhappy, disoriented, and frustrated young adults. For many of these people, the revolution was a turning point in their lives, usually corresponding with a conversion to communism. The revolution and its ideology symbolized their personal revitalization, their rebirth into a new identity rooted in what was for them a more congenial and succoring environment. This new environment, based on an absolute, binary view of the world, was so intimately related to their feelings of belongingness and self-worth that from their perspective it had not merely to survive, it had to flourish, to prevail. Anything else was unthinkable.

The new ideology stressed the joy and power of collective action, mastery over both Nature and human nature, a future-time orientation, and the historical inevitability of the triumph of Marxism-Leninism in a worldwide clash of ideologies, of which Vietnam was an integral part. This not only provided these "reborn" intellectuals with a new and valued role in Vietnamese society; it also gave them a well-defined identity that was both modern and international, one that was embedded in a comprehensible, all-explaining historical process. The intellectuals took added strength from their conviction that they were, with the ideology they now embraced, men whose time had come. They had "met their time" in the deepest sense of the traditional Vietnamese concept. There was a natural moral order at work in the world, and they were attuned to it and assured of ultimate success and victory by its operation.

This entire process is exemplified in the person of Huy Can (no longer "lovesick and lost, confused in direction," no longer with a heart that "shriveled and ached") as he appeared at the Worldwide Cultural Conference held in Havana on January 15, 1968, and presented the following poem, written in French, to a receptive international audience. Standing only a few hundred miles off the Florida coast, he could incorporate even major themes from American culture into his personal but widely shared binary map of reality. Now he could stand erect before the world and proudly proclaim "A Greeting to All Peoples":

Walt Whitman, if you should come back to life,
What greeting would you make to the world, to all peoples?
You have hailed the nations with your green voice,
With a voice of perfumed and quivering leaves of grass,
You have saluted them with a young voice gushing from a
hairy chest,
Gushing from a flourishing beard, from an immense prairie,
You have greeted them with a voice of democracy.
But, Walt Whitman,
It is now that the free peoples love you,
It is now that you should greet them with a new voice.

The people are stronger and truer than ever before, Walt
Whitman.
The people have sprung up again on this earth, more firmly
rooted than ever before.

· ·

Walt Whitman, you have seen the mountains and the plains,
You have heard the great voice of rivers and seas,
And your voice has thundered like the ocean swells,
Like the cosmic wind of the stratosphere.
Today you shall see the people surging more powerfully than
    all the waters of the world put together.
You shall hear this great wind that bursts out from the people,
The great wind that blows from the heights of man,
This great wind that is the natural breath of revived nations.
In this new climate of the planet your broad chest will expand
    to new dimensions.
The longitudes and latitudes are drawing closer together,
The people are drawing closer together to make the world
    more grand,
A younger earth in a universe that men have rejuvenated.
. . . .
Salute to the people, masters of their destiny.
Walt Whitman, it is time to enrich our language.
We often say: The sun is shining; it's a fine day.
We should also say: It's peopling; it peoples at all latitudes
    and longitudes.
Our century is not nearly finished, Walt Whitman;
A good third of it remains in which to make up for lost time.
Its final portion will be the most beautiful part of the journey
    through the ages.
O century of ours, so unhappy and so exultant, you will be
    the century of people, as your predecessors have been the
    centuries of kings or feudal lords.
Salute to the people, to their problems and to their hopes, to
    their struggles and to their victories.
Salute to our heroes, living and dead, unchanging as
    diamonds, pure as jade.
. . . .
Let us sing, comrades, the ancient and the new songs of the
    people.
Let us sing the ancient and the new rights of the people.
And you, Poetry, the honey of men and of peoples, a salute to
    you also!
The great hive of humanity is breaking open with a great
    beating of wings and filling itself with new pollen and new
    nectar.[67]

The writers and poets of the party were amply provided with a
sense of mission, of purpose, of self-esteem, of efficacy. There was

nothing remarkable about Huy Can's appearance in Havana. For years he had been visiting Moscow, Peking, Prague, Ulan Bator, and numerous other cities in the Communist world, leading delegations and troops of performers, exchanging pleasantries and ideas with his fellow socialist artists and cultural cadre. Not long after his trip to Havana, Huy Can was instructed to prepare urgently to travel to Paris to organize cultural and propaganda activities in support of the DRV delegation attending peace talks there. He took Che Lan Vien with him. For those who were politically reliable, travel was not unusual. Nguyen Cong Hoan had traveled to Poland, Czechoslovakia, the People's Republic of China, and the Soviet Union for interaction with his fellow socialist writers.[68]

These cultural exchanges were a small but integral part of a well-coordinated communication system, one that reinforced in these men (and through them others) a feeling of power and purpose, of membership in a collective body whose concerted effort was destined to conquer and transform the world, to remake the earth in its own image. Literary works in the Democratic Republic of Vietnam were carefully orchestrated with newspapers, radio programming, and school curricula to illustrate, propagate, and provide continuous reinforcement to a single, coherent cluster of attitudes, values, and beliefs. Tendencies toward deviation were reduced through public criticism and periodic sessions of self-criticism. Extreme uniformity was desired, even demanded, because it was essential to the operation of the system. The key value was collectivism, with all the conformity and suppression of individualism that implied.

All things were possible when everyone worked together toward a common goal. If people yielded to individualistic tendencies, the strength of the collectivity was thereby diminished. The "secret" power of traditional Vietnamese families and villages was made explicit and placed at the very heart of the new ideology on which the "superfamily," "supervillage" organization of the Democratic Republic of Vietnam was to be based. The power of collective action had been demonstrated many times, and the theme of efficacy through collective action was repeated over and over again, as in this Vietminh song:

The sun shines, shines and dries up the ricefields.
The people are fighting as one against the drought.

We draw each other into digging dams and raising dikes.
We must make trenches, handle the scoops so that the ears
    will be full.
We must not rely on the sky,
We must rely on the prodigious efforts of man.

Only yesterday, rice plants were parched and dry.
Tomorrow water will flow abundantly and they will become
    green again.
Thus, the million enterprises depend on man.
When man is determined, even the sky is defeated.[69]

By 1964 the meta-message of this immense communication system was that everyone had to band together against a new enemy more terrifying than France or Japan, more dangerous than drought or flood. This new foe was the United States of America. With remarkable dedication the people of North Vietnam worked and fought and sacrificed to liberate the south, reunify the country, and drive out the Americans and those Vietnamese to the south who they believed had "sold their country" and become "puppets."

The North and the South: Inverted Images, 1959–1968

Meanwhile communication channels in the southern half of the country carried much more diverse and complex messages. Individualism was rampant in the literature published in Saigon. The works of Albert Camus and Françoise Sagan were best-sellers in the late 1950s and throughout the 1960s. The pre-1945 works of The Lu, Xuan Dieu, Huy Can, Che Lan Vien, and Luu Trong Lu were published in many reprintings, and Pham Duy and others set many of their poems to music. Many of these poems became popular songs, appearing as sheet music on street stands, played on the radio, taped to be listened to again and again over the home stereo systems that were becoming so popular among the urban middle class. *Breaking the Ties* and *In the Midst of Spring* were part of the public school curricula. All the major works of the Self-Strength Literary Movement were reprinted, many of them in several editions, and they were prominently displayed in every bookshop.

Buddhism, too, enjoyed a powerful resurgence during the 1960s, while Taoist drums continued to throb in villages and in the side streets and alleys of Saigon. A dedicated few struggled to generate a Confucian revival, even putting out their own journal of

Confucian studies. The supervillages in the south never ceased to raise their competing voices. Communism was denounced as the common enemy from radio stations, church pulpits, newspapers, and loudspeaker systems in public markets. The communication channels in the south were jammed with competing messages. There were the shrill-voiced advocates of various *yang* orthodoxies, and there was in contrast the simultaneous surge of individualism and heterodoxy. But there was in the *yin* aspects of Saigon a dimension that went beyond all this, a soft voice responding to the angry controversy. Saigon and the south were never without an insistent advocacy of *nhan* and *dieu*, of compassion and reasonableness, that provided constant counterpoint to the drumbeats of war and dissension.

In early 1970 I spent an evening with the poet Ninh Chu. We wandered around the city sampling the specialties of various kiosks and sidewalk cafes, drinking beer, and talking about literature and politics. Just before curfew he took me to his home and pressed a book into my hand. It was *Try the Fire*, by Thao Truong. "This," Ninh Chu told me, "is real Vietnamese literature. Here is the deepest and best spirit of our people." He especially drew my attention to a selection I translate as "Color and Hue," written about 1959:

> It's just a river. Just a bridge. Old. Very ordinary. But this place has meaning, a clear significance. I often ask myself why this place is a boundary. I don't yet dare use the word border, perhaps because there remains within me a hidden confidence. This is that no matter what, this division is merely a phase. There will come a day when people will no longer have to halt at this or that end of the bridge. . . .
>
> I stand looking intently at the other side. It is very quiet here now. It is as if by listening carefully I can hear the rhythm of the heartbeats of the people on the two banks. It is as if my blood vessels are linked to the blood vessels of those people on the other side. I think that whether desired or not, whatever the obstacles, whatever the distance, the people in the two regions are tied to each other in many ways.
>
> I reject the images of the protest demonstrations, the resolutions, the conferences, the banners, the slogans, the political attitudes of this side and that side. . . .
>
> Fold up all the maps. Everything that bears any trace of the concept of division, I want to cast it all away.
>
> Let me hear from the bowels of the earth, from the flow of

the water, from the bushes and clumps of grass, the breathing, the smiles on pairs of lips and in the corners of the eyes of the people in the two regions some whisper, some echo, something absolutely divine, absolutely gentle, absolutely harmonious.

I want to stretch out, spreading my arms and legs across this bridge. Closing my eyes, not smelling, not hearing, not seeing, not thinking of anything around me, of any of the painful things that are happening. I want to forget reality.

But a commotion on the bridge makes me realize that I am standing on this side of the bridge. I look up to see two cadre from the two regions strolling on the bridge. Their equipment is different. They have a different air about them. They are walking in different directions. One walks toward this side of the bridge; one, toward the other. Both slowly. Both cast their shadows on the river. They don't smile at each other. They don't even look at each other. As indifferent as two towers of the bridge facing each other, like chairs in a set of table and chairs. They keep their heads bent and keep walking slowly. My God! I cannot stand this attitude. Why can't they smile at each other? Is the person beside you no longer a person to you? Is the person facing you no longer of any significance to you? Can you no longer be moved, no longer feel anything for other people?

The person from the other side has crossed to a place near where I am standing. He's beginning to take notice of me. Of course he is! He must know that I am standing here on this side. He must see me! What! Don't look at me like that. Don't give me that questioning look. I'm not a thing to be looked at as if I were a gun or a mine. I'm a person. I like other people to smile at me, to be relaxed with me and in harmony with me. You stand bent over, your elbows resting on the bridge railing, looking down at the water and then over toward me. I know that you are deciding about me.

I don't want anyone to grasp me entirely. I want to be alone, not to have anything to do with you. I'm going to sit down on the bank of this river. So I can just think of the sacredness of our country, listen intently to the ringing of the water, listen intently to the welling up of our souls.

I have just read an article by a man of letters from over there . . . printed in . . . Hanoi. . . . He too went along the bank of the river, on the other side, and he looked from that side to this side. Whereas I have just looked only from this side to that side. What a shortcoming! We look at each other from only one direction like that. I want myself to be you, and you to be me. We must be able to look at the other person from the outside, and must also look at him from inside himself, just as we must also look at ourselves from the inside and from the outside as well. I don't speak of the attitudes, of the unnatural looking of the cadres. I want to tell my literary friend on the other side that we should try looking at each other in literary ways. Naturally, everyone has a point of view and looks at things from his point of view. I don't tell him to look through my glasses, but suppose we all looked through all the glasses and looked on all sides.

Hey, friend cadreman over there. You've categorized me already, haven't you? To which part of society do I belong and what attitude have you decided to take toward me that you rub your hands and smile like that?

I've lived near this boundary for five years now. Tomorrow I will return to the capital. I came out here today to seek the sensation of one who has lost his homeland, to sit at the edge of this bridge in order to see clearly that our country is not now unified. For years now I have retained the vague feeling that this division was temporary, that in a day or two it would be no more. But now I must accept the fact that healing such a division is no easy task. Especially healing the separation of our souls. In the conference rooms of those with authority, those with red pencils in their hands, drawing a line along the river is such a simple thing to do, but how can they know they have . . . drawn deep into our souls a terrible separation.

The river is narrow, and is spanned by a bridge. Simple and modest. That gate blocking the road on the other side will not be able to hold anyone back. People can pass it. People can erase a line on the land, but it's difficult for them to cross the division separating the souls of the people in the two regions.

When will the two cadres guarding the bridge cease to treat each other as two objects? When will they ever learn to regard each other with sincere affection? When will they ever be stirred to remember that they are brothers? Only because of two differing doctrines has enmity arisen. Even though the two doctrines are directed at people in order to save them.

Here I do not speak of the error or honesty of any doctrine in particular. I put that matter aside. I simply raise the question that both sides are for the people, so why do they become enemies? Today, before returning to the capital, I come out here to the entrance to this bridge to think about that. Friend on the other side, let us not think about taking over each other. Keep thinking about how people can earn a living and enjoy themselves, and still be free and at ease.

How long have people been using man in order to seek a way of destroying him? For how many thousand years; so many theories, so many doctrines; why is man still hungry and miserable? Man has been deceived many times. Keep thinking of him and let him be free.

The cadre from the other side of the bridge again rubs his hands and smiles, and takes a few more steps until he reaches this end of the bridge. You're laughing at me over politics. You ask how I am. Then suddenly you say to me:

"You see which side is strong, don't you? The Soviets have just launched a four and a half ton satellite around the earth, for all to see."

Having spoken, you look up at the sky, as if seeking proof of your words in the clouds.

I look down at the water. The reflection of the clouds is there, as is the bridge, and even your shadow.

I don't answer you. I'm looking at a boy tending buffalo in a patch of grass near the river. He's wearing a ragged pair of black shorts and a filthy shirt, lying asleep upon the body of a skinny beast.

I think the tasks we must perform are not what you were just asking me about, but are rather the things concerning people who are poor. Children who do not go to school.

I get up and go home to pack my suitcase. Tomorrow I will no longer be here. From the day I arrived until the day I leave, the river has been a road of division, an interruption. The people of the two regions still reject each other, still shun each other's souls, and regard each other as enemies.

But actually this matter is not in the river, nor in the bridge, nor in flagpoles. It is in the hearts of the people in the two regions, in our hearts. Our separation is caused not only by a boundary, by a line, but by a shapeless wall that forms a partition between our souls. We face each other, but do not look at each other. We are very near each other, yet seem to be lost. O friend on the other side, is love for each other not yet enough that we must have hatred and resentment as well? The pain comes not only in being far from home, but it is in the crack from which the heart's blood oozes. I want each person to examine the ties that bind us together.

O people of the two regions . . .

Tomorrow I will no longer be here. But the river will still be here. The task of bringing the two regions together, of erasing the border on the land and the border in our souls is primarily our task.

Don't rely on any satellite or spaceship. If tomorrow we are no more and this problem is not yet resolved, if we still look upon each other as enemies, then it will be the turn of the generations that follow us. The children who are now sitting at desks in school or sleeping on the backs of buffalo will have a day when they learn to love each other, and on that day this river will no longer be a border.

So please don't teach them to hate.

Pham Duy, meanwhile, was probably the most popular folk-singer and composer in the south. He had joined the Resistance, but he was one of those who became disillusioned by the party's increasingly narrow and dogmatic ideological regimentation beginning in 1950. He finally abandoned the Resistance forces. He did not wish to live in the Communist supervillage, nor in any other. He sang:

The water runs quickly
The gibbon carries her child
Climbing the mountain to pick fruit.
I pity you,
I pity you,
Orphan girl.
Oh, little girl, oh!
I pity you,
Orphan girl.

The rain falls interminably.
The spider is in a cave,
Webs spread in confusion.
I pity you,
Lost on your way.
Brother, oh, brother,
I pity you,
Lost on your way.

The wind echoes loudly
The raven complains
All day, all night.
I pity people
Borne down with hatred.

People, oh, people,
I pity you,
Borne down with hatred.

The sun shines brightly.
Cricket without charm,
No sound of singing.
I pity people,
Green youth fading.
People, oh, people,
I open wide my arms.
Hurry back![70]

One of Pham Duy's best-known and best-loved songs, written in 1965, was "The Rain on the Leaves." Steve Addiss has provided English lyrics that nicely capture the tone of the original:

The rain on the leaves is the tears of joy
Of the girl whose boy returns from the war.
The rain on the leaves is the bitter tears
When the mother hears that her son is no more.

The rain on the leaves is the cry that is torn
From a baby just born as life is begun.
The rain on the leaves is an old couple's love,
Much greater now than when they were young.

The rain on the leaves is a passionate voice
In a final choice when last love is near.
The rain on the leaves is a voice surprised
As it realized its first love is here.

The rain on the leaves is a heart's distress
And a loneliness as life passes by.
The rain on the leaves is a last caress
And a tenderness before love can die.[71]

In the north, all messages to which the public was exposed through any form of mass media were filtered through a screening process firmly controlled by the government and ultimately by the Communist party; in the south, despite the existence of censorship, widely diverse views of social, economic, military, and even political questions were always expressed with incomparably greater freedom. In the *yang* atmosphere of the north, all public channels of communication were characterized by high redundancy, low entropy, and a preponderance of positive feedback to amplify confidence in and support of government programs and policies. News, songs, paintings, poetry, fiction, editorials, posters, films, radio programs, and lectures all reinforced the attitude/ value/belief system that constituted the powerful ideological keel of the ship of state. There were many more channels of communication in the *yin* atmosphere of the south, and many more messages were transmitted there; but this ensemble of messages was characterized by low redundancy, high entropy, and a large proportion of negative feedback.

There were few newspapers in the Democratic Republic of Vietnam, and one paper, *The People* (*Nhan Dan*), dominated all others. This party organ was widely available throughout the DRV. No single paper in the Republic of Vietnam had a readership that amounted to more than a small fraction of that of *The People*. In 1967 about twenty-seven different Vietnamese-language newspapers were published in Saigon. Several other papers appeared in English and French and over half a dozen in Chinese. There were nearly 700,000 copies of Vietnamese-language newspapers printed daily in Saigon, with slightly more than one-third of them sold in Saigon and its suburbs and the rest distributed throughout the country. Between 10 and 20 percent of the rural adult population of the Mekong delta read a newspaper at least once a week, and about half the rural adult population had some direct exposure to newspapers.[72]

There were in addition about ten weekly magazines and another ten to twenty biweekly or monthly magazines and journals of various types. These diverse magazines and journals contained everything from gossip about film stars to esoteric philosophical debates, from sentimental love stories to political polemics. They also contained some excellent literature and some fine journalistic reports, as well as some sensationalistic trash. In this precarious, highly competitive field, newspapers, magazines, and journals were constantly going out of business or being closed down by either their creditors or the government, but new ones kept springing up to take their place.

As with newspapers, magazines, and journals, far more books were published in Saigon than in Hanoi, but there were far more copies of each book in Hanoi than in Saigon. The works of Ho Chi Minh reached half a million readers in a single year. A book of poems by To Huu had a first printing of 10,000 copies. The average edition of a book in Hanoi ran between 5,000 and 8,000 copies. In

Saigon most books appeared in about 3,000 copies, and only a best-selling novelist would be published in an edition reaching 5,000 copies.[73]

In both halves of the country there was a tremendous surge in all print media associated with a dramatic growth in education and literacy. But in the south especially there was an information explosion that far exceeded the reach of the printed word. The full extent and impact of this communication revolution was unplanned, unanticipated, and never adequately appreciated. Both the magnitude and the nature of this abrupt change in the flow of information was associated with increased American involvement in South Vietnam.

The War, the Americans, and Vietnamese Society

In 1960 some 5,000 or 6,000 guerrillas were pitted against a moderately effective Army of the Republic of Vietnam (ARVN) numbering about 250,000 men. At that time there were about 4,000 American military personnel and a few hundred American civilians in Vietnam. At the end of the year the National Liberation Front (NLF) was formed, and the war escalated at a more rapid rate. As 1965 drew to a close ARVN had expanded to 500,000 men, there were about 221,000 antigovernment forces (now including entire units sent from the north), and the American presence had continued to grow, from about 900 in 1961 to 11,326 by the end of 1962, to 16,000 in 1963, to almost 200,000 by the end of 1965. In September 1966 the number of Americans reached 300,000, and by the end of the year it was more than 385,000. By this time ARVN had grown to a force of 650,000, and it was opposed by over 280,000 troops, including the cream of the People's Army of Vietnam (PAVN), battle-hardened in the War of Resistance. About 58,000 men marched to the South in 1966. Militarily, both sides continued to grow stronger despite heavy losses. But among the South Vietnamese population, the sociocultural fabric began to exhibit signs of severe strain.[74]

As the war escalated, the U.S. civilian presence grew with equal speed. The United States poured funds, commodities, and technicians into Vietnam to provide assistance that would "win the hearts and minds of the people." We built classrooms and trained teachers and printed textbooks on a scale that permitted the number of students attending school in the Republic of Vietnam to double between 1955 and 1960 and then double again by 1969. Saigon was linked to major towns like Bien Hoa and My Tho by broad and well-paved roads, the likes of which had seldom been seen in Southeast Asia, greatly reducing the travel time standing between millions of villagers and the wonders of big-city life. Parents who had never ridden in an automobile watched their children climb aboard modern airplanes. The number of radio sets soared from an estimated 125,000 sets in 1960 to 2,200,000 by 1970. Television was introduced to South Vietnam in 1966. By early 1969 programming averaged about four hours per evening. An estimated two million viewers were reached through nearly 300,000 privately owned sets and approximately 3,000 community sets. By 1970 there was one television set for every forty persons in the Republic of Vietnam. To accommodate the half million Americans in the country, there was a U.S. Armed Forces channel broadcasting American programs. Every evening countless thousands of Vietnamese sat down to their evening meal while watching "Batman," "Gunsmoke," "Mission Impossible," or—incredible as it may seem—"Combat" (a great favorite of both Vietnamese and American viewers).[75]

Rapid urbanization was also taking place. At the outset of the War of Resistance in 1945 the population of Saigon was about half a million. By 1954 it was about two million. It dropped for a few years then climbed again by leaps and bounds, approaching three million by 1965. Nearly 20 percent of the ethnic Vietnamese population south of the 17th parallel lived in the Saigon metropolitan area. For every fifteen Vietnamese in Saigon there was one American. The salary of the lowest-ranking American was enormous by Vietnamese standards. And Americans (even civilians) were paid in military script, "funny money" we quickly converted into huge amounts of local currency. Like so many other things in Vietnam, money was unreal to most of us.

Competing with Vietnamese housewives and students from the middle sector for a taxicab in downtown Saigon, an American (usually in a hurry even during leisure hours) might gladly pay three or four times the normal fare. And he would be joined and replaced on the corner by dozens of his comrades, all of whom would successfully summon cabs and be carried off while the Vietnamese seeking taxis waved to one driver after another, all of whom would avoid looking at them as they raced to pick up another group of Americans.

As the American buildup continued it became increasingly profitable for the lovely shops and restaurants along the nicer avenues of downtown Saigon to be converted to bars and other business establishments designed to American taste and priced for American patronage. For most people the American consumer economy represented a source of income too great to be spurned. It enabled many people to survive and some to prosper. Those who owned businesses, shops, bars, hotels, or fleets of taxis grew rich beyond their wildest dreams. Inflation was no problem for those who could tap the wealth of the Americans; and tens of thousands of Vietnamese served us as companions, bartenders, hostesses, waiters, busboys, and doormen. Other Vietnamese made our beds and shined our shoes; washed, pressed and mended our clothes; gave us haircuts, manicures, and massages; sold us chewing gum, peanuts, candy bars, cigarettes, dirty post cards, gaudy paintings on velvet, custom-made suits and shirts and shoes, wallets, and briefcases; washed and drove and repaired our vehicles. On the whole, we paid well for the goods and services we received, and our spending generated many jobs.

Many of the urban middle class, however, experienced the massive American presence as a social and economic disaster. Doctors, nurses, schoolteachers, accountants, civil servants, journalists, scholars, army officers, writers, poets, lawyers, dentists, scientists, laboratory technicians, pharmacists—all those who served their own people but not the Americans—these people tended to suffer a severe loss in relative economic well-being and hence in social status and influence. As their favorite shops and parks and restaurants changed drastically, these people came to feel like strangers in the streets they had strolled for years. Meanwhile bar girls outbid middle-class housewives for the better materials in the dress shops, and the family next door whose daughter was a secretary for an American agency outbid them for the better cuts of meat in the market. A nineteen-year-old boy working as an interpreter for an American engineer made more money than his father and his uncles, who were college graduates and had held the same jobs for years.

For the socially sensitive, status conscious, hierarchically oriented Vietnamese, the world was turned upside down. No longer was there any relationship between the ends and the means of social action. The old determinants of social status no longer had any relationship to reality. Education, position, wealth, and social influence no longer went together. There were, of course, analogues to this phenomenon in the French colonial period, and even earlier. But the size, the wealth, the profligacy, the transience, and the exuberant energy of the American forces (there only for one-year tours) made their impact distinctively more disruptive.

As the years went by the influx of American spending combined with the normal inflation of war to disrupt things even further. An egg cost 2.1 piasters in 1960, 6.4 piasters in 1966, 8.8 piasters in 1967, and 13.4 piasters by 1968. In 1970 it cost 21.9 piasters. A kilogram of rice cost 5 piasters in 1960, 13.4 piasters in 1966, 28.2 piasters in 1968, and 53.2 piasters by 1970. From a 1963 base of 100, by 1970 the consumer price index for working-class families had risen to over 600. For the middle class the jump was at least as drastic. Meanwhile, wages and salaries lagged far behind, especially for government employees and members of the armed forces.[76]

Civil servants and military men of various ranks sat outside Saigon bars hoping to make a little extra money by chauffeuring American GIs back to their barracks. Army majors and high-ranking civil servants drove taxicabs during their off-duty hours. University professors took on heavier teaching loads, sometimes teaching full-time at two or three colleges simultaneously. Once I asked a provincial service chief why he was the only official in the province who did not solicit bribes. "Didn't you know?" he responded with surprise. "My mother is a very successful business-woman in Saigon and she sends me money every month."

Unless one could find some way to be plugged into the inflationary economy of the American spending, it was impossible to keep up. Government workers in urban areas were hit especially hard. In 1967 most of the city sanitation workers and street department employees in Saigon quit their jobs to go to work for American construction firms. Mountains of garbage rapidly accumulated in a city of nearly three million people while sturdy and freshly painted buildings sprang up in immaculate, fenced-off U.S. bases in the suburbs.

As the indirect effects of war and the American presence continued to accelerate, the direct effects of war reached horrendous levels. During the six years of war from 1960 through 1965, the armed forces of the Republic of Vietnam suffered about 11,000 dead and 23,000 seriously wounded. In the two-year period of 1966 and 1967, over 24,000 died and more than 50,000 were seriously wounded. Then, in 1968 alone, almost 30,000 were killed and another 70,000 were wounded. By the end of 1968 combat losses of the government's forces exceeded 63,000 dead and 144,000 wounded. In nine years about one of every five soldiers, perhaps one of every twenty adult males, was killed or seriously wounded while fighting for the government. And losses on the insurgent side, while known with even less precision, were certainly much higher. By 1969 they might have reached nearly half a million. Since virtually every soldier who was killed or wounded had a wife, parents, children, brothers, sisters, and friends who were affected, there were few people in the society whose lives were not blighted by deep personal loss.[77]

Civilian casualties, although very difficult to estimate, also increased in approximate terms from about 100,000 in 1965 to about 175,000 in 1967 and then leaped to 300,000 for the deadly year of 1968. By the end of 1968 total civilian war casualties were approaching the level of one million people, including perhaps 300,000 deaths. By late 1969, some 80,000 civilian amputees and paraplegics and about 25,000 blind and deaf civilians were officially registered with the government for disability caused by the war. There were an estimated 50,000 widows and several hundreds of thousands of orphans (no one knows how many, but by late 1971 official U.S. estimates ran as high as 700,000). And by the end of 1968, the number of in-country refugees had grown to well over three million, representing about 20 percent of the population. By 1971 this number would reach five million, and it was estimated that from 25 to 30 percent of the population of the Republic of Vietnam had at one time or another been forced to flee their homes because of the war.[78]

Continuity and Change in Values in the South

Americans who derived their image of Vietnam from the visible turmoil of the 1960s, however, often failed to realize how deeply the core values of traditional Vietnam remained embedded in the hearts of almost all Vietnamese. Even in the south, among dislocated peasants and superficially Westernized urban elites, to the left and the right of the political spectrum, the dictates of *nghia* exerted a powerful influence. Vietnamese families retained their capacity to instill a sense of *on, hieu,* and *de* into a new generation.

In her survey "Family Attitudes and Self-Concept in Vietnamese and American Children," Mary Leichty (1963) demonstrated the persistent emotional importance of family in Vietnam and the strong sense of familial obligation being inculcated in Vietnamese children. In her sample from a village in the upper Mekong delta, where traditional familism was weakest, the internalized values of *on*, *hieu*, and *de* leap out of her data, even though she did not employ them as analytical concepts.

Responding to a sentence-completion item that began "The people I like best are . . ." the U.S. children usually mentioned friends, while Vietnamese mentioned family members. To the stem "I like my mother, but . . ." the U.S. children tended to add some negative action by the mother ("sometimes she gets angry with me"). A fourth of the Americans even mentioned negative feelings toward the mother. Only 7 percent of the Vietnamese mentioned any negative action by the mother, and none expressed any negative feelings toward her. Over half of the Vietnamese mentioned an obligation to do something for the mother. This sense of *on* among nine-, ten-, and eleven-year-old children in the Mekong delta was revealed by lines like this: "I love my mother very much, but I am still young and I cannot pay my debt to her."

In the items intended to elicit fears, U.S. children expressed "an externalized fear, emphasizing animals and the dark." But Vietnamese children "seemed to be emphasizing more internalized sorts of fears. They emphasized fear of personal inadequacy, failure in parental-familial relationships or some violation of sociocultural mores." And whereas U.S. children indicated that their fears led them to "do something bad or undesirable," "most Vietnamese children indicated that their fear led them to perform some duty."

While the U.S. children expressed a guilt that was externalized and attached to some object or event, "the emphasis by the Vietnamese was on internalized guilt, some expression of personal or interpersonal inadequacy." In hopes for the future, nearly half the Vietnamese children expressed a hope for something good for someone else, usually something for their families. Not one U.S. child made a response of that kind. American children wanted things for themselves: a swimming pool, a new wagon, a trip. In response to the item "When I am older . . ." over half the Vietnamese responses involved family obligations: repaying parents, helping younger siblings, and so on. Typical U.S. responses were "have a car," "be a nurse," or "go to California."

The psychological primacy of family obligations in these children would continue to underlie the trappings of ideology and technological sophistication they would acquire as they grew up during the war. In the late 1960s one young man argued for over a year with his father, who did not agree with his choice of occupation. Finally, all other means of blandishment and coercion exhausted, the old man threatened to deny his son the privilege of mourning his death and participating in his funeral. Shocked and extremely upset, the young man immediately resigned from his well-paying and (as he and most other people thought) respectable job. A college graduate with a wife and children, he returned to school to prepare himself for the career his father wanted him to pursue.

The *yang* domain of the family remained the most powerful element in Vietnamese life, and was still balanced by its corresponding *yin* elements. Virtually every home still had an ancestral altar, and it was still important. Death anniversaries and Tet celebrations still brought many families together, and these gatherings were still prized as a primary source of identity by many Vietnamese. Nothing was more important than participation in the rituals of family life.

In a remote provincial capital in South Vietnam in 1964 a group of Vietnamese had a labor dispute with their American employers. The Americans had offered what seemed to them a generous package of wage increases, paid holidays, sick leave, and other benefits of the kind desired by American workers. But they allowed only one day off at Tet, and many workers had to travel long distances to reach their family homes. Many were prepared to quit what they agreed was a relatively easy and well-paying job because it interfered with their participation in the celebration of Tet with parents, siblings, nieces, nephews, and visiting ancestors.

"We'd trade all those other benefits, including a dozen other holidays, for the chance to spend three days with our families at Tet," they said. One man offered to work every other day in the year if he could have one week off to go home for Tet. The Americans perceived such statements as bargaining ploys to get even more benefits. They simply could not comprehend the true significance of Tet to the Vietnamese. It was inconceivable to them that Tet could mean more than Christmas, Easter, Thanksgiving, New Year's Eve, and the Fourth of July all rolled into one celebration. But for almost all Vietnamese, Tet remained a singular occasion involving a unique privilege and an obligation to validate one's place in the overriding primary reference group in one's life.

Although of diminished observance generally, a sixtieth birthday party was still an important affair for some men, one that called for a lavish celebration and a report to the ancestors. I shall never forget one such party I attended in My Tho in 1967. About forty men gathered around tables overflowing with vast quantities of the very best food and drink money could buy. Hearty talk and laughter never ceased as plates and glasses were refilled again and again. During the revelry the host slipped unobtrusively from the room to don a tunic and a turban. He returned to kowtow before the altar and speak to his ancestors. His face glowing with pleasure and pride, he ignored the boisterous crowd around him as he shared the happiness of the gathering, and the social and economic success it signified, with his deceased family members.

When the guests departed, hardly a dent had been made in the mounds of delicacies. Many bottles of imported scotch and cognac and cases of beer and soft drinks remained untouched. This was a relatively well-to-do family, but the cost of that party would have exceeded many months of their normal household expenditures. They appeared, however, to regret not a penny of it.

But this had been a truly special occasion, justified by family tradition and family resources. Sometimes the extent of public generosity could become a source of tension in families. Vietnamese women still controlled the finances in most families, and many men still felt compelled to engage in a high level of public generosity that families could ill afford. Some Vietnamese women complained that they had to keep their husband on a tight allowance. "Anyone could ask him for a loan and he'd dig into his pocket and hand them 500 or 1,000 piasters, whether we could afford it or not. And that was usually the last we'd see of that money. He wouldn't press to get it back." "I don't mind his having a few drinks with his friends, but he'd spend a small fortune buying drinks for people he barely knows. He doesn't even drink that much himself, so he doesn't need to take that much money with him when he goes out."

In 1972 I witnessed an extreme case of competitive generosity in a village of refugees from the north. I was passing through the village with a district official and an American colleague. We chanced to meet a former village chief who pressed us to join him for a drink at the local kiosk. After discovering our business in the area, he began to regale us with numerous anecdotes and much alleged "inside" information. We were soon joined by some of his followers. A few minutes later the current village chief appeared, accompanied by some of his friends and supporters who had obviously rushed to summon him. The current and former village chiefs then proceeded to vie with each other in buying drinks and dishes of food for the entire crowd and in purveying expert knowledge and information on a variety of topics. Each was determined to appear more generous and more knowledgeable than the other.

More beer than we could possibly have drunk was joined by a bottle of cognac. Untouched plates of food piled up on the table. Neither man would let the other have the last word on any subject, buy the last round of drinks, or order the choicest dish. At last we fled in dismay, never learning how the episode ended. The relationship between status competition, prestige, face, and public generosity was quite clear, and a lot of income certainly got redistributed. For both men that was obviously an intense emotional experience. They cared, painfully, what people thought.

The value of public generosity persisted, but it was surrounded increasingly by ambiguity. The same was true of "virtue." Most people still conceived of a "virtuous" or "decent" person as one who observed the time-honored conventions of traditional society, especially the five cardinal virtues (*nhan, nghia, le, tri, tin*) and two of the three bonds—those between parent and child and between husband and wife. The bond between subject and sovereign was so complex and so emotionally charged, and the context had changed so greatly, that it was excluded from moral judgments of the kinds people continued to make in other areas.

Loyalty was a prized attribute, but with such a rapid turnover of governments and leaders and so many competing claims to legitimacy in recent history, it was not always clear to whom or to what one should be loyal. It had been easy to feel and express loyalty to a king, but there were no more kings. And to many Vietnamese, loyalty still meant loyalty to a man. Under such conditions, many people came to feel that too firm a commitment to any particular cause or leader was sheer stupidity, and some were not embarrassed to say so. All agreed that one should show respect for superiors and elders and show courtesy toward all. Politeness and a sense of hierarchy are important to Vietnamese. Yet even in this, change took place.

One example comes from a hamlet of northern Catholic refugees. This was a relatively isolated, progovernment hamlet that bordered on a Communist stronghold. One day the NLF forces flew their flag on the other side of the canal that ran beside the hamlet, and the parish priest dispatched someone to pull the flag down and take it away. In retaliation the NLF instituted a boycott of the local market, which had a noticeable effect on the hamlet economy. A number of people rudely criticized the priest for his bravado. The people of the hamlet themselves said that in the past the priest's decision would not have been questioned in public, and disrespect to the priest would not have been tolerated. By traditional standards, this direct and public criticism of the priest constituted a violation of both *nghia* and *le*. It was a violation of hierarchical obligation and of good manners. In 1967, however, few people condemned the protestors, even though this was a staunchly anticommunist and Catholic community. Those who had been hurt by the priest's rashness were now felt to have a right to complain about it.

Only among some older villagers was trustworthiness insisted upon. Most of the middle-aged and younger adults said that you must expect people to do what they have to do to survive in a difficult and rapidly changing world. Many people said one simply had to assume that promises were often not going to be kept, and that nowadays one often had to say things one did not really mean.

Most significant, even within the context of family the behavioral norms were perceptibly shifting as traditional values were not abandoned but redefined. Many young war widows were remarrying, for example, and a number of people said that while they once would have disapproved of such behavior, now they did not blame these young women for remarrying if they could, especially if there were no children. Another important change that seems to have taken place is that now in most cases the mother could take the children with her if she remarried or moved away after her husband's death, and public opinion supported this as a right and proper thing to do. No longer were children viewed as solely the property of their father's family.

Filial piety, the cardinal virtue of Vietnamese life, was also undergoing operational redefinition. Parents in the 1960s and 1970s neither expected nor demanded the total obedience and responsiveness that previous generations had exacted from their children. Conflict over the choice of marriage partners remained a popular theme in novels, television dramas, and movies; and it was still a source of tension in families as well. But on both sides care was usually taken to prevent serious damage to family solidarity. Parents in the 1960s and 1970s consulted their children more (on this and other major decisions) and gave greater weight to their opinions than their own parents had done when they were children.

And those young men and women who wished to select their own mate still wanted very much to have their parents' approval. Marriages were still often "arranged," but they were much less frequently imposed upon a child who expressed objections. Many parents agreed with their children that times had changed; and a child's unwillingness to submit blindly to parental authority was not necessarily a violation of filial piety. Even among urban middle-class Westernized elites, arranged marriages still took place, and those young people who did challenge their parents' decisions insisted that this did not mean they had forgotten filial piety.

The behavioral expectations associated with filial piety were changing among all social classes in both urban and rural areas. An unmarried young man with a decent income who did not contribute generously to the support of his parents would everywhere be severely criticized for lacking filial piety. But if he were married, and especially if he had children, he would no longer be criticized for refusing to be generous to his parents at the expense of his nuclear family.

Throughout society in the Republic of Vietnam there was a conscious shift toward a more flexible and less exacting behavioral definition of traditional values. In a more complex and rapidly changing world, most people made an effort to compromise, to allow for extenuating circumstances; and this was more true within the family than in any other sphere of life. Both peasants and city dwellers, the elderly and illiterate and young intellectuals alike, all Vietnamese in these times had to live with a high degree of uncertainty, were bombarded with conflicting messages, experienced feelings of anxiety and confusion.

The *yin* values of *nhan* and *dieu* permeated many family and village institutions, inculcating a more charitable, tolerant, and flexible attitude toward deviation from strict adherence to cultural rules under severe situational pressures. This did not mean that any and all behavior was acceptable; it meant merely that definitional boundaries were relaxed and extenuating circumstances were weighted more heavily.

In Saigon in 1970 the black market was at its peak. Government efforts to restrict even its most visible manifestations were achieving little success. Then, after repeated warnings and admonishments, police and soldiers moved into a notorious area of illicit street stalls, smashing counters and destroying merchandise. One woman I knew, who was herself engaged in a variety of black market activities, surprised me by expressing approval of these harsh measures. She explained that the victims had invited their suffering by being "too greedy." Having been warned, they should have curtailed their activity, or at least made some conciliatory gesture. But they had ignored warnings and criticism. They had not known *dieu*.

Villagers in a Mekong delta village in 1967 explained that *nhan* was an attitude that should permeate daily life. One example that typifies the way they talked about *nhan* involved a man who had caught a bad chill from sitting in a draft just a week or so earlier. Word spread through the village that "his arms and legs were trembling like a chicken caught out in a storm." A few neighbors went to his assistance, rubbing him with peppermint oil to ward off the chill. This behavior was cited as an example of *nhan*. But in an adjacent house some other men had remained indifferent to his affliction, loudly singing songs in a carefree manner while he lay suffering next door. This behavior aroused much gossip in the village. Public opinion labeled them as men who "lacked virtue," and they were specifically cited as an example of people who did not know *nhan*.

Patterns in Chaos

In South Vietnam by the late 1960s the distribution of values in society exhibited a complex pattern. Education, in the broadest sense of the term, was generating patterned change in the distribution of values in society. And education cut across geographical and social boundaries within the Republic of Vietnam. The rich had better educational opportunities than the poor, and people who lived in towns found it much easier to continue their educations beyond a certain point than those who lived in remote villages. So too did boys receive more encouragement than girls to continue their education. But all of these factors are relative, and formal school attendance was not the only source of value-laden training and indoctrination.

Wherever a family lived and whatever their socioeconomic status, young males tended to have the most education and older women the least. At the same time, young males were also most likely to receive training and indoctrination in military or governmental institutional settings, and older women were the least likely to undergo such an experience. Other family members were

ranged somewhere between the two extremes. There were no distinctive urban/rural or rich/poor dichotomies in values to rival the
great differences between age-sex cohorts resulting from the great
disparity in their educational/indoctrinational/socialization experiences. The great majority of Vietnamese were ranged along a single continuum representing a gradual shift in emphasis, or rank
ordering, among a common set of basically shared values.

At one end of the continuum were those with modern, Western-
influenced educations, those who had attended school for a certain
number of years or had received extensive training/indoctrination
under the aegis of either the GVN or the NLF. This population was
largely if not exclusively young and male. At the other end of the
continuum were those people who had received little or no formal
education, or had received a traditional education, and had not
actively participated in any effectively socializing modern institution. This population was largely older and female. Thus older
women and young men typically represented the two ends of this
attitude/value continuum.

Compared with the population as a whole, young, educated
males had a more lineal view of time, a stronger future-time
orientation, a greater sense of efficacy associated with a belief that
one could and should attempt to dominate, to change for the better
both nature and society. They were also more individualistic and
less ready to accept uncritically traditional procedures and techniques. Poorly educated older women, on the other hand, had a
more cyclical view of time, were more oriented toward submission
to the world as it was, accepting social hierarchies and environmental constraints as givens to be adapted to, with which one
strove to maintain harmony. They accepted and valued tradition,
and their sense of efficacy was restricted to the exercise of time-
honored techniques of manipulating the familiar world of hearth
and kin and market.[79]

This dichotomy cut across almost every family in Vietnam. And
since the family was still by far the most basic and important social
institution in Vietnam, with various subtle distinctions of degree
and complexity, all individuals and all other institutions in the Republic of Vietnam were affected by it. In the modern as in the traditional model, the family was the primary frame of reference in
which these attitudes and values were translated into action and
found their most profound expression. These modern values did

not replace, but were superimposed upon, the basic values of tradition.

The opposing soldiers and cadre of the GVN and the NLF were more like each other in their value profiles than either was like the majority of their countrymen. Villagers, in turn, tended to be much alike in their value profiles, whether they were under GVN or NLF control, whether they stayed in the country or moved to the city, whether they were Catholic, Cao Dai, or Buddhist, whether they were rich or poor. In many ways an upper-class Saigon matron was more like a peasant woman in a thatched hut than either of them imagined, and both of them were probably much more like their grandmothers than their sons. These similarities were, of course, concealed beneath differences in style and mannerisms reflecting class influences and contrasting social environments.

The Saigon matron and the poor peasant woman would not always behave in the same way nor would they express identical attitudes on many subjects, no more than did the GVN or NLF soldiers and cadre, because they functioned in different environments and were adapting to different sets of situational constraints. The fundamental differences between city and countryside, rich and poor, progovernment and insurgent populations were largely a function of the contexts in which values operated.[80]

Such differences in values cut with increasing sharpness across geographical, religious, political, and socioeconomic differences (which also involved differences in attitudes and values). The dynamic tension between these multiple cleavages in society produced an invisible and largely unperceived network of mutual influence so complex as to confound utterly any lineal model that might be employed to manipulate any single set of variables. Yet such models were employed constantly by all concerned, with uniformly disastrous results.

A growing psychological malaise was constantly exacerbated as various groups and subgroups attributed motives to each other on the basis of inferences drawn from the effects of behavior, not realizing that virtually everyone was similarly frustrated over the vast disparity between the intended and the actual results of social action in a very complex and unpredictible world. As the DRV, the NLF, the GVN, the Americans, and various supervillages within South Vietnamese society each pursued its own illusory goals down pathways dictated by false assumptions and misperceptions, reinforced by communication channels disproportionately weighted in favor of positive feedback, the confused and uncommitted majority adapted as best they could to a tragedy of monumental proportions. The outcome of these adaptations was a huge *yin* society within a society, a world within a world.

Paradoxically, this bloated, unwieldy and unplanned *yin* world was simultaneously independent of the dominant values and structures of all the competing factions and yet parasitically dependent upon them. This, of course, was the way it had always been. *Yin* requires *yang* for its existence. What was unusual if not unique about the *yin* component that emerged in South Vietnam during the 1960s was its vigor, its size, and its complexity. Rather than complementing the *yang* structures of society, it overshadowed them, drained them of their sustenance, and became for large numbers of people an end rather than a means of existence.

6 Continuity and Change in Vietnamese Culture and Society, 1968–1975

A Frustrated Vision

For South Vietnam the only significant, overarching structure in society was the Government of Vietnam (GVN) itself. The armed forces of this government eventually numbered over a million, and its civil service grew to over 300,000. With a population of about 18 million in 1970 (half of which was under age fifteen), this meant that the government directly touched and was touched by a high percentage of the families within its boundaries.[1]

On paper the GVN was, by and large, a modern, rational structure. The military and civil personnel were intelligent, well educated, and well trained; and many if not most were also well intentioned. The technological support systems were outstanding: they included everything from sophisticated computers to jet aircraft and an atomic research center. Yet this system did not work very well. It was not, in fact, nearly as bad in some ways as it has often been depicted by many who were frustrated and outraged by its shortcomings, but it did fall far short of what such a concentration of talent, technology, and money should have been able to achieve.

The *yang* superstructure engaged the attention of most Americans. We watched army units on combat operations. We looked at cabinet ministers, legislators, province chiefs, and district chiefs performing the duties of their office. We saw policemen directing traffic or breaking up demonstrations. Often we found ourselves making invidious comparisons. They seemed to be less efficient, less honest, less logical than we thought they should be (than we thought we would have been in their place). We gave advice, provided new equipment—always expecting that our latest suggestion or gadget or demand would lead to vast improvements in performance, always disappointed. More and more we actively intruded; we took the initiative—quantifying variables, applying the techniques of systems analysis, then sending more American money, soldiers, technicians, and equipment in to bolster what seemed to be the weakest areas.

Yet predictions continued to be proved wrong. Hopes gave way to disappointments. And many of us began to dislike and distrust those people who so stubbornly resisted our efforts to remake them in our own image, who failed to meet our expectations, who produced a reality that mocked the logic of the organizational charts and training manuals we thought we shared with them. Many of us, some in high places, began calling them "gooks." Not always, but often, we had concrete justification for our outrage. Large numbers of Vietnamese civil servants and military officers did solicit bribes and misuse funds. They did pursue personal economic interests at the expense of their official duties. Large numbers of soldiers did desert. They did steal chickens from villagers. And in both the cities and the countryside large numbers of civilians did stand aloof from the struggle, unwilling to make any commitment or bear any burden unrelated to the immediate welfare of their families. What went wrong?

CONTINUITY AND CHANGE: A RAGGED TRANSITION   Let us examine the Republic of Vietnam in terms of the *yin-yang* model. The *yang* dimension of traditional society was predominantly male, Sinitic in origin, legal in basis, orthodox, formal, autocratic, and culturally prescribed. Its organizational expressions tended to be active, complex, highly organized, and prestigious. Component institutions within the *yang* system were highly differentiated and competitive hierarchical systems. They were outward-looking, concerned with face and status, and built upon role-based, part-person relationships. They tended to be relatively rigid and doctrinaire, to be centralizing instead of localizing, and to be characterized by a high proportion of positive (amplifying) as opposed to negative (correcting) feedback. *Yang* systems and subsystems tended to generate asymmetrical reciprocity and to be escalating, self-amplifying systems.

On the whole this description fits the operation of the GVN nearly as well as it did the traditional family/village/national *yang* hierarchy. It is especially apt as applied to the military and the civil service—1,300,000 strong—which provided the only *yang* component at the regional and national level and a major one at the village level. The most significant discrepancy lay in the fact that both the government and the army were now based on a Euro-American rather than on an indigenous-Sinitic model. In fact, by 1970 they had both been rather thoroughly Americanized and existed in a symbiotic relationship with the American mission in Vietnam.

The constitution of the Republic of Vietnam in effect from 1956 until 1963 was drafted with expert American and Filipino assistance, although French influence remained strong. It provided for the governance of the nation by a democratically elected president, vice-president, and bicameral legislature. The chief difference in structure between the GVN and most Western-style democracies was greater centralization and a stronger chief executive. Another constitution was drawn, expressing even more strongly American ideas rather than Vietnamese realities.

For the GVN bureaucracy a National Institute of Administration was established under the leadership of Michigan State University personnel, working under government contract, and thousands of young career civil servants were trained there. Many of the teachers were Americans, and even though the Michigan State contract was terminated in 1962 under less than amicable circumstances, the Institute continued to reflect a strong American influence coming from American teachers and advisers and from Vietnamese who had received advanced academic training in American universities.

American assistance and advice had from the mid-1950s begun to reshape the Army of the Republic of Vietnam (ARVN) into divisions and corps areas, adding firepower and supply services at the expense of mobility and adaptive flexibility. There was soon a hard core of Vietnamese military personnel who had been trained in the United States. Then, beginning in 1962, U.S. military advisers were attached to ARVN units down to battalion level. A crash program was later undertaken to dub Vietnamese narration onto U.S. training films covering every conceivable subject.

Meanwhile, in 1963, 1,014 students from the Republic of Vietnam went abroad to study. By 1970 the number had risen to 2,352. These students went to many countries throughout the noncommunist world, with the United States, West Germany, Belgium, and Japan being the most common destinations.[2] This educational elite returned to staff government agencies, to enter the armed forces, to write books, to teach school, to exert in countless ways the influence of their rational and impersonal bureaucratic/scientific worldview, increasing the pressure of modern Western models on Vietnamese institutions.

Yet at the same time, from top to bottom, the government and the armed forces of the Republic of Vietnam were composed of men (and some women) born and raised in Vietnamese families and socialized to be family members first and foremost. The family was still the most basic, the strongest, the most important institution in Vietnamese society. Vietnamese families continued to produce young men and women whose hopes, fears, guilt, and goals were family-centered. The majority of young adults still bore a heavy burden of moral debt to their families. The family with its complex network of emotional ties remained the primary reference group in one's life and held first claim on one's allegiance.

Within the family the *yang* element was still the male-oriented kinship hierarchy, generating the same basic paradigm arising from *on* (moral debt), *hieu* (filial piety), and *de* (prescribed asymmetrical reciprocity among hierarchically ordered siblings). Young men still grew up bound to their mothers by powerful emotional bonds and an overwhelming and unpayable sense of moral debt and obligation. And the male was still, within the family, often torn between his mother and his wife, both of whom often had a deep-seated emotional need to dominate him psychologically and to satisfy their own ambitions primarily through his achievements.

All this was changing, but very slowly and at an uneven rate throughout society. The family proved to be by far the most conservative element in the traditional system. And the mothers and wives—the women of Vietnam (with the exception of a predominantly young, urban minority)—were least exposed to the modernizing, Westernizing, institutionalizing influences. They had significantly less education and even less participation in the *yang* structures of society. Few women had much exposure to the sources of socialization that inculcated a sense of modern civics, a sense of reciprocal obligations and duties with the larger community in a modernizing nation.

Vietnamese women retained their force of character in the Republic of Vietnam, but their virtues remained for the most part traditional ones. Their undiminished energies and strengths were channeled into support of the *yang* system almost exclusively at the family level. The undoubted influence of the female half of the population was in many cases, however, not functionally integrated, not synchronized to provide support to the discontinuities of *yang* at higher system levels. Primarily concerned with her traditional role as "minister of the interior," the mother or wife of a government official or an ARVN officer generated a set of pressures that cut across the primary thrust of the modern, Western, *yang* ideology that competed with her (and with the family as a whole) for the allegiance of her son or her husband or both.

Many Vietnamese men, especially those in the upper and middle levels of the GVN bureaucracy and armed forces, found themselves caught between multiple competing influences, subjected to a series of partially overlapping but essentially discontinuous socializing agencies. First and with greatest intensity came the family, deeply imprinting the traditional model, substantially unchanged in its fundamentals. Then came school, which in part reinforced this model (especially in the lower grades) but at the same time taught and inculcated contradictory elements (such as notions of individualism, egalitarianism, democracy, the rights and duties of citizenship in a modern-nation state, ideas like those found in *Breaking the Ties*). Adult life then typically brought indoctrination into new *yang* structures, social organizations based primarily on Western models but staffed by Vietnamese who were (like oneself) still traditional in many ways, especially in the modalities of their interpersonal relationships. At the same time the growing mass media assaulted one's consciousness with a large number of often contradictory messages. And the socializing influence of family, of course, continued throughout one's entire life.

MODERN ROLES AND TRADITIONAL CULTURE   For many men it proved impossible to reconcile the conflicting demands imposed by one's family teachings, by one's formal education, by the ideology of one's adult occupational/professional role, and by the societal expectations expressed (both directly and indirectly) through the mass media. It was extremely difficult to maintain a positive and well-integrated self-image under these conditions. Taught from early childhood to be hypersensitive to the barbs of criticism and ridicule, preoccupied with maintaining face, it was difficult to feel the eyes of many different publics upon one, knowing that what was required to satisfy one audience would bring down the wrath or ridicule of another.

A reform-minded Vietnamese educator once confided to me:

> There is no way you can win. People who feel they have
> some claim upon you keep asking for special favors, for a
> bending of one rule or another, for a word in the right place.
> Now if you agree to help them, as you want to do, everybody
> says: "What a hypocrite he is!" But if you refuse, as you
> usually think you should, people will call you "hard-hearted"
> or "ungrateful." Deep down, they don't really admire you
> for it.

No matter what such a man did, he would be criticized. At first he would be hurt and probably feel a little guilty. Finally he would grow angry and resentful, although he would take care not to show it.

Another dimension of this discontinuity in values was revealed to me in a striking manner one day when I went by a military sector headquarters on a weekend. A middle-level sector officer with whom I had only a slight social acquaintance latched on to me as I walked past his office and invited me to "come in and talk." After a minute or two of polite conversation, he told me of some information he had received that called for immediate action, action he was not authorized to take. I slowly came to realize that he was hoping I could help him in some way, but I could not imagine how. Eventually he remarked that both his immediate supervisor and the chief of staff for the sector were away and could not be reached. "Have you informed the province chief?" I asked. "No," was all he said. Finally I told him I thought the province chief would want to know right away. "What do you think I should do, then?" he asked. "I think you should call the province chief at once. Then you'll have done your duty and he can decide what is to be done next." With a woeful smile, he sighed and patiently explained the situation: "Please understand," he said to me. "That telephone was not placed on my desk so I could call the province chief. It was put there so he could call me."

At last the officer and I went together to the provincial headquarters. I found the province chief's secretary and asked if the province chief were busy. Yes, he was busy, but probably could be interrupted. The secretary would find out. A moment later the province chief himself, a genial man, appeared in the doorway and invited me to enter his office. After the requisite preliminary conversation, I suggested that he might want to talk to a certain officer who was seated in his waiting room. The province chief then rang for his secretary, who was dispatched to summon the junior officer. Only when the province chief asked him: "Do you have something to tell me?" could the harried subordinate deliver the urgent information.

Thus were modern systems of communication clogged by traditional values. The formal operational procedures of these modern military and civilian institutions presupposed a rapid, steady, and reliable flow of information. Tons of very expensive equipment were provided to assure that this took place. But the implicit cultural rule was that subordinates do not initiate interaction with their superiors, and computerized switchboards were simply irrelevant to this ingrained sense of hierarchical propriety. Most Vietnamese leaders rewarded loyalty, after all, not initiative.

One maverick GVN official instituted a suggestion program within his department at American urging. Before long, to save face, he was resorting to commanding his subordinates to make a certain number of suggestions per month, instituting a coercive quota system on a program intended to promote a freer flow of ideas. The flow of information and ideas within both the military and civilian bureaucracies was always predominantly from top to bottom, downward rather than upward or horizontal. This resulted in a severely stultified negative-feedback process that prevented decision makers from having an adequate appreciation of the extent to which the actual results of their actions deviated from what they intended and believed them to be. Given the complexity of the total environment, the accelerating speed of change, and the size and power of the organization seeking to shape and control events, such a state of affairs was inevitably disastrous. The formal design of this entire structure assumed and depended on a radically different pattern of communication, one based on radically different values.

Yet, troublesome as this discontinuity in patterns of values may have been, it was not the only one to beset the functioning of the *yang* essence of the Republic of Vietnam, nor was it the most serious. In addition to these specific conflicts between traditional family-inculcated values and modern/Western school and bureaucracy–inculcated values, there was an even more basic conflict involving one's primary loyalties. During the late 1960s and early 1970s it was often impossible to be a dutiful and virtuous family man and a dutiful and virtuous military officer or civil servant. There were incompatibilities between the dictates of proper role behavior in the two spheres.

In a mind-boggling reversal of the traditional order of things, the *yang* element of the Republic of Vietnam was increasingly pressed toward the status of becoming an underprivileged majority in the very social system it was charged with operating and defending. A Vietnamese general or cabinet minister was paid less than the average U.S. enlisted man. Field grade officers and key ministry officials made about a hundred dollars a month. This was less than an enterprising bar girl or taxi driver could make, less than the secretaries, interpreters, elevator operators, and chauffeurs who worked directly for the Americans. Company grade officers—battalion commanders or district chiefs—and the white-collar office workers in Saigon received from forty dollars a month to about half that amount in the lower grades, not enough to cover the bar tabs of most of their American counterparts and advisers. The bulk of the troops in the field typically received somewhat less than twenty dollars per month plus a meager family allowance. The cramped, uncomfortable, frequently unhealthful, and often dangerous living quarters of many military families compared unfavorably with the humblest of village homes. And when Vietnamese military units went on operations no field kitchens accompanied them, no mess tents sprang up; there were no field rations to be issued (until the "Vietnamization" phase of the 1970s).[3] Whatever one's rank or status and regardless of what one had been taught in school or at the National Institute of Administration or an American military base or at the new Military Academy at Dalat, the typical *yang* leader at every level of the Republic of Vietnam was impressed primarily by the fact that his womenfolk kept reminding him that prices were up again in the market and the children needed new shoes and the school his son hoped to attend next year had raised its tuition.

To validate his status and that of his family, to fulfill what he perceived to be his obligations to his family and his family's obligations within the hierarchical social order, no member of the military services or the civil service found his salary and the legal benefits of his office to be anywhere near adequate. His concept of social identity and personal sense of self-worth remained bound up in traditional village conceptions of the status hierarchy; and this was true despite the fact that he might be working within a modern office building in Saigon or leading troops through the briny muck of a mangrove swamp in Camau. In heart and mind he remained essentially a village man, and neither jungle warfare nor modern bureaucracy had any real social significance to him.

TRADITIONAL WOMEN AND MODERN INSTITUTIONS   In the traditional village the market was typically located outside the bamboo-enclosed perimeter, beyond the symbolic gate. It was the women who ventured into the market to buy and sell, to haggle over prices, to supplement the family income through the essential but somewhat demeaning pursuit of petty trade and commerce. And as Saigon was still seen, in a very important sense, in a social sense, as a cluster of overgrown and overcrowded villages, so too it was still the women who dominated the world of commerce, protecting their menfolk from contamination and maintaining the boundary between the world of *yin* and the world of *yang*. The influx of families from northern and central Vietnam, and their disproportionate influence in Saigon society intensified this phenomenon.

The real business day in Saigon began about six o'clock in the morning when the elegant ladies of that city poured their second cup of tea and reached for their telephones. As Madam General called Madam Colonel who called Madam Head Clerk, as Madam Major called Madam Captain who called Madam Technical Service Chief, the daily flow of money and of goods throughout the country was anticipated and careful plans were formulated for diverting some percentage of this bounty into their *yin* domain where it would be transformed into the symbolic *yang* behaviors of family/village interactions according to ancient formulas, only slightly modified to accommodate the modern urban environment. Combining their charm and good manners with a capacity for hard work and hardheadedness, these women exploited their unbeatable resources of information and influence to control and manipulate effectively huge slices of government procurement contracts, real estate investments, new import-export opportunities, and dozens of other entrepreneurial activities.

These women in effect functioned as a *yin* mechanism to extract energy from the *yang* system and convert it to the service of spheres that were meaningful to them, those of the family and the maintenance of its relationship to the village (i.e., Saigon society). In so doing they at once relieved and exacerbated the "double bind" in which the males were trapped. They relieved some of the pressure by themselves taking the initiative to plunge into business ventures that permitted the family to maintain its public face through conspicuous participation in the prestige economy. Yet they also constituted a formidable source of pressure upon the men to violate the mores of the modern *yang* bureaucracies and institutions to which they belonged, to which they had been socialized, and within which they had a certain amount of ego invested as individuals completely apart from their role as family members. According to Le Thi Que, "it was well known in Viet-Nam that if you could not get through the front gate (meaning to the husband), go to the back gate (meaning to the wife or mistress). Anything from a passport to even a position in the State Ministry could be had with the right woman's support."[4]

Many of the allegedly more corrupt politicians and officials were themselves not much different from most of their colleagues. Often they simply had wives (or mistresses) who exploited their positions more energetically. Few of these women experienced any guilt or had serious misgivings about what they were doing. They saw themselves as being good mothers, good wives, good daughters-in-law, good daughters, good older sisters. They were—like their mothers and grandmothers before them—providing the economic support required to make the family socially competitive, to get their menfolk to the head of the table and keep them there.[5]

For the women's husbands and lovers, there was often more ambivalence, greater role conflict; but the men too told themselves that basically they were doing the right thing by making themselves accomplices to the women's economic depredations. These men, from prime minister to file clerk, from general to buck private, were meeting their primary social obligations by the only means available to them in the disjointed society of their time.

DEFINING THE JUST CAUSE   Yet another conflict revolved around what used to be called "the mandate of Heaven," or the issue of legitimacy and its relationship to power. Americans liked to talk about "winning the hearts and minds of the people." To some all that mattered was having God on their side. The most useful and appropriate phrase is probably the old Sino-Vietnamese expression *chinh nghia*, frequently translated as "the just cause."

Both sides in the war claimed to represent the "just national cause." Millions of leaflets were dropped upon insurgent and People's Army of Vietnam (PAVN) troops urging them to "return to the *chinh nghia*," that is, to defect to the GVN side; and many National Liberation Front (NLF) (although very few PAVN) troops actually did. But many of these messages seem to express the anxieties of the originator more effectively than they address the vulnerabilities of the intended recipient. Just who, one wonders, were these propagandists trying to convince?

Few Americans had any conception of the immense ideological, historical, and psychological connotations of the term *chinh nghia*. "Just cause" is a very inadequate translation. The word *nghia* is familiar. Summarizing as it did the burdens of filial piety (*hieu*), moral debt (*on*), generalized mutual obligation within an hierarchical framework (as between older and younger brother: *de*), and loyalty to one's sovereign (*trung*), *nghia* implied social obligation in its fullest possible sense. It was "righteousness," "the path to follow," "the proper way to live." The word *chinh* means "primary," "legitimate," "proper." The term *chinh nghia* conveyed the idea of the transcending, true, proper, legitimate claim of society upon one's devotion and one's behavior. In traditional terms, if one pursued the *chinh nghia* one was in accord with powerful natural and supernatural, social and psychological forces. Victory in battle, the mandate of heaven, and the hearts and minds of the people were a seamless whole that flowed from *chinh nghia* as naturally and inevitably as daybreak follows night. Going with the *chinh nghia* brought moral and ideological power that would transcend and generate all other forms of power: military, political, and administrative.

But *chinh nghia* was not to be determined by individual conviction. Nothing in the traditional system was legitimately so determined. This is the crucial point that Westerners, especially Americans, find so difficult to comprehend fully and that is the source of so much inner turmoil among those Vietnamese who have internalized some elements of Western thought. The *chinh nghia* was expressed as a body of public opinion, primarily literati opinion. This is what Paul Mus had in mind when he spoke of the Diem regime's attempts to capture "an unspoken, intangible . . . the center of which is everywhere, the contour that would permit taking hold of it, nowhere; for . . . it is neither a circle of things nor of people but an elusive and tenacious . . . body of opinion."[6] Phrasing it another way, Mus wrote of Vietnamese village life that "the major premise presents itself neither as a circle of things nor of persons but as the balanced total of the opinions professed on the things that matter by the persons who count in the eyes of the community as a whole."[7]

Chinh nghia was, in other words, primarily a "current of

thought," a socially (not individually) determined judgment as to what was right and proper. At the personal, intellectual level—that is, as individuals—many GVN officials, cadre, and supporters sincerely believed that their anticommunist stance was a legitimate one, that at the level of ideas their more open system—permitting greater individual freedom, more genuine democracy—was superior to that of their rivals in the north and in the south. Their basically Western educations and adult socialization led them to admire and wish to emulate countries like France, the United States, and Japan.

Yet, many of them also believed that (with notable exceptions) their government and army were corrupt and ineffective, their industrial goods and commercial products were shoddy, their arts were imitative. The social system, in short, was not meeting their own standards and expectations. And whatever the facts of the situation, both the foreign press and the local mass media reminded them constantly of their own imperfections. Few men in such a situation could avoid corrosive doubts as to the moral legitimacy of their position. Both their own experience of social life and the expressed opinions of persons who counted in the eyes of the community served to undermine the strength of their personal convictions as to the properly constituted nature of society.

In traditional times both in China and in Vietnam, *chinh nghia* sentiments were broadcast by whatever means were available to the literati.[8] And as the decade of the 1960s brought with each passing year more death and destruction, more inflation, more corruption, more social and economic dislocation, more value conflict and more foreigners, so too did the *yin* voices of society speak with greater authority and in greater numbers, telling these men that they had lost their way, that their actions were not furthering the common welfare. They were being told, in brief, that they (and their American sponsors) were losing their claim to the *chinh nghia*. Right or wrong, the protests in and of themselves, by their very existence, called into question the legitimacy of the enterprise.

The Development of Urban Yin Subsystems

NEW *YIN* VOICES Nguyen Sa, the popular poet of the late 1950s and 1960s, was among those who registered a significant change in tone. Noted for his lighthearted treatment of life and love, in August 1967 he wrote "Forgive Me for Past Mistakes":

Now I carry a Garand rifle on my back
Now I carry a BAR upon my shoulder
Only now do I know how heavy those murderous sticks can be
Only now do I know what a stupid fool I was during my life as
    a teacher
I made so many mistakes over fifteen years or so
For fifteen years or so I failed to tell my students
How heavy those murderous sticks can be
I didn't tell my family or friends or compatriots
My brothers and my homeland
Have carried murderous sticks that heavy
For so very many many years now
Now I lay in ambush by the edge of a ricefield with dew
    soaking my shoulders
Now I stand guard in dark jungle with the cold wind
    penetrating my bones
Only now do I know how cold the dew can be
Only now do I know how cold the wind can be
I want to shout out what a stupid fool I've been
I am a stupid fool
Because every day for the past fifteen years or so
I didn't write down on paper for lovers of poetry to know
My brothers and my homeland have stood like that for so
    many years
Now I move by night move by day move in sunshine move in
    rain
Unable to eat unable to sleep unable to laugh unable to cry
Beloved brothers who have read my poems
Beloved brothers who have sat before me in the classroom
What have I ever done
To enable you to laugh to enable you to cry to enable you to eat
    to enable you to sleep
To enable you to locate coordinates in the jungle darkness
To enable you to find the right spot in a vast expanse of rice
    fields
To keep the bullets from piercing your lungs
To keep the bullets from piercing your heart
Forgive me
Forgive me
My brothers who have died
Brothers who have died on banks died in the dust
Brothers who have died at desolate outposts died in deep
    jungle
Brothers who have died on operation

Brothers who have died from ambush
Brothers with flower-like faces
A thousand times more beautiful than mine
Have died as well
Brothers who have studied so well like prodigies
A thousand times better than I
Have died as well
Brothers just married with the bed still fragrant
Have died as well
Brothers with a will to write poetry in which the words would
    tremble
Have died as well
Brothers with children even younger than my own
Have died as well
Brothers with old mothers even weaker than my own
Have died as well
Brothers a thousand times more worthy of life than I who
Have died
Are dying
Will die
Forgive me.[9]

The great battles of Tet early in 1968 made this *yin* dimension a powerful dynamic force within the Republic of Vietnam. Attitudes changed, especially among the urban middle class, who now for the first time experienced at firsthand the reality of war. Tet was the most sacred and celebrated holiday in Vietnam. It meant the coming of spring and a visit by the ancestors. It was a time reserved for family reunions, for spiritual and material renewal. With purified hearts and freshly painted houses, dressed in holiday finery, friends and relatives exchanged visits of great symbolic significance. This was a time of leisure and rejoicing and hope. Perhaps no other event could have been so shocking to the Vietnamese psyche as the vicious fratricidal slaying that engulfed the cities and towns of Vietnam during the first three weeks of that lunar year.

Nowhere was the shock any greater than in Hue, the most historical and romanticized city in the Republic of Vietnam. In 1968 the coming of spring found the freshly scrubbed houses of Hue in flames, the delicate flower beds trampled, and the shiny new coins so diligently saved for the occasion clutched in the stiff hands of dead and dying children. On both sides, an unusual ferocity was displayed in the battle over Hue. During the twenty-five days in which the attackers partially controlled the city several thousand people were executed in cold blood. Most of the victims were shot; others were beheaded, beaten to death, or in some instances apparently buried alive. Members of the Vietnamese Nationalist party (VNQDD) and Dai Viet party members seem to have been special targets of this terror.[10]

In bloody hand-to-hand fighting in city streets and with a massive use of firepower to drive tenacious PAVN units out of their strongholds, the American and ARVN defenders of the city completed its destruction. About 10,000 people died in this battle for a town of 150,000 inhabitants. Thousands of families were impoverished, many losing all their worldly possessions. The Catholic writer and poet Nha Ca was trapped in Hue during the nightmare of Tet 1968, and she wrote a best-seller novel about it, *Put on the Mourning Cloth for Hue*. At the front of the book she placed "A Brief Preface: Written to Accept Guilt." The powerful sense of impotence and guilt that she shared with many of her colleagues is expressed in a vignette that illustrates their perception of these events:

> A small dog caught in a crossfire ran off, barking, fleeing wildly along the bank of the Ben Ngu River. And it became a humorous target for the ready guns on the opposite bank. They fired until the wretched creature leaped into the river from fear. And then they fired at any spot on the bank where the small dog would attempt to scramble ashore. These shots were fired in jest with no intention of killing that little dog, only of teasing it, keeping it precariously stranded in midstream, in order to have an amusing story to accompany the blood and flames.
>
> How different is the city of Hue, and perhaps even our entire miserable homeland as well, from the plight of that small dog precariously stranded in mid-stream? Our generation, this generation so fond of showing off by using the prettiest of phrases—not only must we tie the cloth of mourning for Hue, for our ravished homeland, but we must accept our guilt for Hue and for our nation as well.[11]

Pham Duy, too, struck a new tone in his music, as in this 1968 song called "A Tale of Two Soldiers":

> There were two soldiers who lived in the same village
> Both loved the fatherland—Vietnam.
> There were two soldiers who lived in the same village
> Both loved the fields and the earth of Vietnam.

There were two soldiers, both of one family,
Both of one race—Vietnam.
There were two soldiers, both of one family,
Both of one blood—Vietnam.

There were two soldiers who were of one heart,
Neither would let Vietnam be lost.
There were two soldiers, both advancing up a road,
Determined to preserve Vietnam.

There were two soldiers who traveled a long road,
Day and night, baked with sun and soaked with dew.
There were two soldiers who traveled a long road,
Day and night they cherished their grudge.

There were two soldiers, both were heroes,
Both sought out and captured the enemy troops.
There were two soldiers, both were heroes,
Both went off to "wipe out the gang of common enemies."

There were two soldiers who lay upon a field,
Both clasping rifles and waiting.
There were two soldiers who one rosy dawn
Killed each other for Vietnam
Killed each other for Vietnam.

Pham Duy later appeared on American television. One of the songs he chose to present was called "On Behalf of." He stated that this song was very popular in Vietnam because it "reflects the feelings of our people." Strumming his guitar violently, he sang:

For my defense I must kill, must kill;
Kill one man, kill one man.
For my place in the sun,
In my defense, I must kill one man.

For my family I must kill, must kill;
Kill ten men, kill ten men.
On behalf of posterity,
Because of my family, I must kill ten men.

For my village I must kill, must kill;
Kill hundreds of men, kill hundreds of men.
On behalf of freedom,
Because of my village, I must kill hundreds of men.

For my nation I must kill, must kill;
Kill thousands of men, kill thousands of men.

On behalf of the fatherland,
Because of my nation, I must kill thousands of men.

For my ideology I must kill, must kill;
Kill millions of men, kill millions of men.
On behalf of the liberation of all mankind,
Because of my ideology, I must kill millions of men.

For the human race I keep killing, keep killing;
Killing everything else, killing everything else.
On behalf of peace, on behalf of peace,
I must kill even myself.

The final line was sung harshly, out of cadence. After a moment of stunned silence the shocked audience began to applaud. But Pham Duy, master showman, cut off the applause as it approached its peak. Loss and destruction, he told them, are only to be regretted, never applauded nor prized. He then began to sing again, providing a new perspective:

For my defense I must save, must save,
Save one man, save one man.
For my place in the sun,
In my defense, I must save one man.

For my family I must save, must save;
Save ten men, save ten men.
On behalf of posterity,
Because of my family, I must save ten men.

For my village I must save, must save;
Save hundreds of men, save hundreds of men.
On behalf of freedom,
Because of my village, I must save hundreds of men.

For my nation I must save, must save;
Save thousands of men, save thousands of men.
On behalf of the fatherland,
Because of my nation, I must save thousands of men.

For my ideology I must save, must save;
Save millions of men, save millions of men.
On behalf of the liberation of all mankind.
Because of my ideology, I must save millions of men.

For the human race I must keep saving, must keep saving;
Saving everything else, saving everything else.

n behalf of peace, on behalf of peace,
must, first of all, save myself.

With this Pham Duy evoked thunderous applause both in Vietnam
and in the United States. Still another song by Pham Duy became
tremendously popular in Vietnam over the next several years. The
words were originally written by Linh Phuong, a young ARVN
combat officer, and then set to music by Pham Duy. A popular re-
cording of this song featured a muted trumpet in the background
and was sung to a slow, majestic beat. It was called "A Souvenir
for You":

> You ask me, you ask me when will I return?
> Let me reply, let me reply, that I will soon return.
> . . . .
> I will return, perhaps as a wreath of flowers.
> I will return to songs of welcome upon a helicopter painted
>   white.
>
> You ask me, you ask me when will I return?
> Let me reply, let me reply, that I will soon return.
> I will return on a radiant afternoon, avoiding the sun,
> Wrapped tightly in a poncho which covers all my life.
> . . . .
> I will return, I will return upon a pair of wooden crutches.
> I will return, I will return as one with a leg blown off.
> And one fine spring afternoon you shall go down the street
> To sip a cold drink beside your crippled lover.
>
> You ask me, you ask me when will I return?
> Let me reply, let me reply that I will soon return.
> I will return and exchange a moving look with you.
> I will return to shatter your life.
> We shall look at each other as strangers.
> Try to forget the days of darkness, my dear.
> You ask me, you ask me when will I return?
> Let me reply, let me reply that I will soon return.

This was still a hit song in South Vietnam in 1971. By then the
words had gained added poignancy because the young man who
wrote the lyrics was said to have been killed in the war. It was a
painfully disturbing experience to watch ARVN troops go into
combat operations listening to songs like this on their transistor
radios.

New *yin* voices were arising with greater militancy. The mood of
many young intellectuals after the grim events of Tet 1968 is

expressed in a 1969 poem by Nguyen Quoc Thai called "Hymns in the Night Upon the Sea":

Let's begin stand up
hold hands and form a circle
in the night shadows on the coast of the eastern sea
from the smallest of you
with heads raised like the sun
tell each other about
shameful indignities
strange new marks of the whip
pouring torrentially over life
tell each other about
loved ones who have died
orchards where leaves have fallen
fields that are black and dry
rivers canals lakes ponds
oil spreading to darken the surface of the water
ragged kindergartens of grass and hemp
scorched streets marked by hatred
from the smallest of you in turn raise your voices
hands footsteps
when the white dove
one morning returns to perch upon our hearts
and tremulously coos in the fragrant pink sunshine

Divide yourselves into small teams
take your hearts your smiles
as baggage as food as fire
go rap on the door of every house
announce the new days and months
light the lamps hanging on porches
let there be light cheering flags waving
raise your solemn voices
with the good news that the long night has been wiped away
· ·
Don't wait for the arrival of spring
the climate has changed
set out in the night
what shadows of darkness can cover our hearts
red fire flaring day and night
what rain and storm can destroy the spring
spring is in our hearts
in our hands upon our feet
· · · · · · · · · · ·

ah young ones source of freedom
pure hearts seeds of humanity

Play speak laugh boisterously
graceful flock of seagulls
warbling upon the waves
radiant limbs of hope
soar up in a tidal mass
let your shadows cover the rivers and mountains with shade
light has returned light has returned
enveloping our bodies layer by layer
maintain your courage
hang yourselves upon the cross
so the world may grow into peace
so breathing may be calm and refreshing
keep shouting out upon the thorns
watch flowers blossom

gold red lavender pink
fill the hearts of mankind
light has returned
in the shade of your shadows
backs raw red sweaty
muddy feet dirty hands oozing blood
wind whistling through garments hair flowing
heads raised high
light summons a new rice season.[12]

A new climate of values had indeed arisen. It was not simply attitudes toward the war that were changing. There was also an important shift in attitudes toward the Americans and their role in Vietnam. Part of this new mood of impotence and guilt was a sense of needing to look the war in the face, and to look the Americans in the face, and speak out.

Flamboyant figures forcefully gave voice to the growing discontent. At this very time the alienated youth of the Republic of Vietnam acquired their own spokesman. Trinh Cong Son, a young folksinger from Hue, soared to the heights of a superstar among high school and college students. At student concerts in university towns he brought his young audiences to their feet, screaming and clapping.

Like Nha Ca, Trinh Cong Son endured the agony of Tet 1968 in Hue, and his memories were equally vivid. "I will never forget a mother running after a truck carrying corpses, which bore the body of her son. And as she ran she clapped her hands and laughed hysterically all the way down the muddy, red-dirt road.

Nor will I ever be able to forget the American troops stretched out by the side of the road who looked at her and laughed arrogantly."[13] In 1969 Trinh Cong Son wrote many songs that quivered with outrage and resentment. All were available at bookstands on the streets of downtown Saigon. One very popular song was called "I Must See the Sun":

> I must see a bright sun upon this homeland filled with
>   Humanity.
> I must see a day,
> A day when our people rise up to obtain peace,
> Calling to each other from all regions:
> Life!
> I must see peace,
> The happy villages of yesteryear have been deserted.
> The people of Vietnam have forgotten each other amidst the
>   bullets and bombs.
> The days of Vietnam have been darkened by hatred.
> I must see peace.
> I must see peace.
> All my beloved brothers,
> Rise up!
> Let's walk in the flickering soul of the nation.
> A million pounding human hearts await a million footsteps.
> Keep moving forward!
> I must see,
> I must see a day with
> Peace glowing brightly all around.

Another favorite written by Trinh Cong Son in 1969 was called "Who's Left Who Is Vietnamese?"

> Open your eyes and look around here.
> Who's left who is Vietnamese?
> A million people have died.
> Open your eyes and turn over the enemy corpses,
> Those are Vietnamese faces upon them.
> Going over the human corpses,
> Whom have we been defeating all these years?
> The homeland has withered.
> Brothers and sisters of North, Center, South:
> Go forth to preserve the mountains and rivers,
> Have hope in your hearts for a tomorrow

Looking at this land,
Joyfully cheering the flag of unification,
With footsteps passing over all three regions.

Open your eyes and look around here.
Who's left who is Vietnamese?
Artificial hatreds,
Open your eyes.
Look at this dark day of Vietnam.
So many years of tattered lives,
Our people bathed in fresh blood.
. . . .

How many loved ones are left?
Turn around and struggle.
Let's go together in the morning.

Reiterating with a slightly different emphasis the theme already
noted in the recent works of Nguyen Sa, Pham Duy, Nha Ca, and
others, Trinh Cong Son wrote "It Is We Who Must Speak":

It is we who must say peace when people's hearts flame with
    desire.
It is we who must have power.
Stand up and demand the unification of the homeland.
I've seen you on your way
. . . .

Hundreds of streets burst into loud rejoicing,
A raging current opening a free life,
Prisons cheering.
It is we who must say peace when this land has turned into
    Hell.
It is we who must take power,
Refusing to slay our brothers.
I've seen you on your way,
Bare hands creating a large storm,
Standing side by side,
Millions of agitated footsteps,
Banners held high.
Let's keep speaking, keep shouting to the sky.
We must go everywhere, we must make our demands.
Fields need hands.
Houses need builders.
Stack your weapons!

Trinh Cong Son was seen by many young Vietnamese—and to
some considerable extent he saw himself—as the Bob Dylan or the

Joan Baez of Vietnam. Although many on both sides decried the fact, the antiwar protesters and the disenchanted critics of the administration in power were influenced by American currents of thought and action no less than the U.S.–trained military officers or the wheeler-dealer businessmen who actively pursued the GI dollars. The intimate but highly complex relationship between American influence and this strong *yin* reaction to the war during the late 1960s in the Republic of Vietnam had many dimensions.

THE VIETNAMIZATION OF ROCK AND ROLL   The first Vietnamese rock bands began to appear in late 1968 and early 1969, and in less than two years they acquired a large and devoted following. During the early 1960s Saigon nightlife had been dominated by a few staid supper clubs where foreigners and upper-middle-class Vietnamese dined on French or Chinese food and enjoyed quiet conversation and sipped beer with their meal, followed perhaps by some French cognac. Sedate background music was provided by bands staffed mainly with Filipino musicians. These orchestras usually had a rich and mellifluous brass sound. After-dinner dancing featured the same perennial favorites: tangos, sambas, cha-cha-cha, and an occasional waltz. The dancing was disciplined and technically well executed. Most of the vocal selections were ballads: romantic, sentimental, and richly orchestrated, sung by Vietnamese women with beautiful, well-trained voices, who wore rather conservative tunics and performed with dignified and highly controlled stage mannerisms.

Jo Marcel had already introduced hard rock music to Vietnamese audiences, but only a small number of enthusiasts were attracted to it. It was during 1968 that rock and roll music in Vietnam was transformed from something exotic to a basic and important part of the Saigon musical environment. This phenomenon was accentuated by the proliferating U.S. military bases, always starved for entertainment, which provided a training ground and a source of income to a new generation of very young Vietnamese musicians who learned much of their material by listening to the U.S. Armed Forces radio station in Saigon. Soon small local clubs were springing up outside the bases as local entrepreneurs sensed the existence of another avenue to the wealth of the free-spending American GIs.

Some very professional Vietnamese rock groups appeared: CBC, the Strawberry Four, the Blackstones. Clubs opened in downtown

Saigon, places where young Vietnamese men and "respectable" Vietnamese girls felt free to go. American patronage helped some clubs get started, but the rock industry in Vietnam continued to thrive, even to grow, as the American presence dwindled. Many young converts to the cult of rock exchanged their dignified tunics and their sharply creased dark-colored pants, long-sleeved white shirts, and carefully groomed hair for more bizarre and much longer hair styles, blue jeans, and brightly colored T-shirts. Some young soldiers even concealed stylishly long-haired wigs in their barracks, and as they went off duty they quickly changed from the drab khaki uniform of structured military life to the multicolored costumes of antistructure, substituting one mask for another, shifting personae in search of a role that might enable them to survive their involvement in an absurd and terrifying situation.

At the same time drug use rose dramatically among young urban Vietnamese. Some began smoking marijuana, and a few began experimenting with cocaine.[14] At night in the heart of Saigon, by the hundreds and the thousands, young Vietnamese, mostly from the middle class and many of them students, flocked to their own *yin* rituals of communitas, antistructure, and surcease from the conflicting social pressures generated by a society subjected to twenty-five years of war and sudden, massive, and unchanneled sociocultural change. With the photic-driving of flashing colored lights, the sonic-driving of highly amplified electronic keyboards and electric guitars, in darkened rooms thick with cigarette smoke laced with marijuana fumes, the alienated and disoriented youth of Saigon tried to boogie their way into hyperventilation to induce an altered state of consciousness. In physiological, psychological, and sociological terms, this phenomenon was strikingly similar to what their structurally oppressed and psychologically disturbed great-aunts and -uncles had done for centuries as they performed their shamanistic rites to the accompaniment of flickering candles, pungent incense, and throbbing Taoist drumrolls. The same physiological transformation was being sought by people who had learned from prestigious foreign exemplars of an altered state of consciousness that could free them, at least temporarily, from the particular pressures that the *yang* structures of their society in their time inflicted upon them.

The Dark Maiden of the Ninth Heaven was superseded by Janis Joplin; high fidelity stereophonic sound systems were purchased instead of traditional altars; and psychedelic posters printed in San

Francisco or Japan replaced parallel scrolls upon the wall. But these substitutions actually made little difference. Distinctions of social class, ethnicity, status, and politics still dissolved in a frenzied search for escape into a free-floating state of communitas. A transcendent, worldwide, alternative subsystem still provided a cultural formula that served to reinforce and legitimate the desire of the individual to flee the perceived oppression of the rigid *yang* structures in which his or her life was uncomfortably enmeshed.

In typical Vietnamese fashion, the cults of rock in Saigon had their own forms of absolutism. The devotees demanded an extraordinarily high degree of conformity and authenticity from those who performed the nightly rituals in the Vietnamese chapters of this international cult. There was little or no creative improvisation, no nuances of satire or parody on the hymns of rock. Vietnamese performers conscientiously and with full awareness of what they were doing imitated even what were clearly unintentional mistakes in the original canons of these rituals. Many Vietnamese singers with a sense of pitch far superior to some of the godlike superstars of the movement steeled themselves to sing off-key at appropriate places. Disciplined ballroom dancers struggled with fierce concentration to "let themselves go" and "do their own thing," as they had seen Western congregations do at major rites presided over by the Rolling Stones or Led Zeppelin. It was so different, so alien, and yet remained so very Vietnamese.

A NEW SUBSISTENCE ECONOMY AND URBAN SUBVILLAGE GROUPS
The emergence of a rock cult in 1968 and 1969 is only one of many examples of the way in which *yin* subsystems emerged and grew in the Republic of Vietnam during the trauma of the 1960s. A surge of Buddhist activism had been an important factor in the downfall of Diem and had persisted. Many other subgroups were appearing in Vietnamese society. They had less articulate ideologies but nevertheless exhibited their own particular structures and cultural rules. These were liminal communities with no past and no future, no legal status and no legitimating charter; yet they possessed clearly marked boundaries, complex institutions, unique constellations of social relationships, well-developed codes of behavior, and even their own distinctive mechanisms for communication and control. They were miniature sociocultural systems that sprang up within the interstices of the larger society. Although decidedly deviant in terms of the dominant culture, these were func-

tionally significant parts of the larger system, adaptive mechanisms that permitted the dispossessed victims of malfunction within the orthodox institutions of society to survive the turmoil of the age.

If the Vietminh, Cao Dai, Hoa Hao, Catholic, Dai Viet, and other such groups can aptly be termed "supervillages," then perhaps these emerging *yin* groupings can best be understood as "subvillages." They were in many ways akin to such unofficial and sublegal traditional village groups as shamanistic cults, mutual-assistance groupings, or the neighborhood or lane organizations.

One fascinating group of this kind comprised the "street children" of Saigon, Danang, and Hue. The old and knowing faces on those slender prepubescent bodies told their own story of a struggle for survival. These children had evolved their own economy based on scavenging, peddling, petty theft, and an aggressive marketing of minor services that bordered on extortion. Each small group had its own particular niche, defined by territory and specialization.

If you parked your car on a Saigon street, some children might offer to "watch it for you" in return for a small sum of money. If you paid, your car was safe. If you refused, a tire might be flat when you returned. If you cuffed them aside or abused them either physically or verbally, serious damage might be inflicted on the vehicle in your absence. Other children roamed the inner-city streets selling bags of peanuts. Approaching potential customers in groups of three to five, they would grasp a hand or hang on an arm as they pleaded for a purchase. Another member of the group would meanwhile slip up behind you and deftly pick your pocket or your purse. There were dozens of such improvised niches occupied by tens of thousands of children.

Prostitutes, too, lived to some extent in a complex hamlet of their own, maintaining internal status distinctions according to the characteristics and number of the girl's customers and the way her services were marketed. There was no overall organizational structure for all these girls, no more than there was for all of the street children; but like the street children, they were linked in interlocking clusters of friends and acquaintances who shared information, provided each other with emotional support, and to widely varying degrees practiced mutual assistance in the form of loans, home remedies for illness, and sometimes shared living quarters and a common commissary.

One of the largest, most visible, and more prosperous of these deviant *yin* groups was that of the bar girls. The streets in do town Saigon, and those near U.S. housing compounds and military bases in Cholon and scattered around the outskirts of the city, were thickly lined with bars. These bars catered almost exclusively to American males, and at any given time each bar would usually have on hand from five to twenty hostesses to make small talk with the customers and push drinks. There were similar clusters of bars in Bien Hoa, Vung Tau, Nha Trang, and Danang, and they sprang up on a smaller scale wherever significant numbers of Americans were to be found. Perhaps several hundred thousand girls worked as hostesses in such establishments during the late 1960s.

Even more than the street children or the prostitutes, these bar girls constituted a distinctive sociocultural unit, a community of sorts, one that was deviant and disapproved of, to be sure, yet one that conformed to dominant mores more than most people imagined. Bar girls maintained their own status distinctions primarily in terms of the characteristics of the patrons of the bar at which a girl worked. Taking into account rank, income, occupation, ethnicity, age, dress style, and manners of the customers, bar girls tended to rank-order the bars in an area and look down on those who worked in places less prestigious than their own.

Few of these girls lived with or near their families of origin, although many of them maintained contact with their parents and siblings and occasionally went home for visits, usually carrying expensive gifts accompanied by plausible stories of employment as a factory worker, secretary, or cashier. Many of these girls had been married, and were widowed, divorced, or separated from their husbands; few had a spouse living with them. Many of these girls had no male Vietnamese friends, and those few Vietnamese men who tried to patronize the bars at which they worked were made to feel very uncomfortable.

Often three or four girls shared an apartment or a small house, sometimes near another group of their friends. In this way these girls provided a surrogate family for one another. Such households seldom had any real head or leader. They were a Communitas of near-equals, with work and expenses divided rather evenly and decisions made on some approximation of consensus. Within these groupings the girls often provided each other with considerable emotional support and financial assistance, confided in each other, and took care of each other when they were sick.

Many of the girls, at one time or another, lived with one of their American patrons with whom a close attachment had been formed. The precise nature of these relationships varied from case to case. Within the group, serial monogamy was completely acceptable, and even admired. Some of the girls hoped to land an American husband someday, but few of them were sanguine regarding their chances. Many tears of genuine sorrow were shed by girls left behind and forgotten when boyfriends or common-law spouses returned to the United States.

Many of these girls were (by their own account) victims of disastrous marriages or love affairs with Vietnamese men early in their lives, and they usually attributed the breakup of these relationships to the man's mother rather than to the man himself. These girls portrayed the man as a passive force over which the girlfriend/wife and mother competed for loyalty and control. "The old lady thought I wasn't good enough for her precious son," many of them complained (in somewhat coarsened and embittered paraphrases of lines from *In the Midst of Spring* and dozens of more recent novels). There was a striking correspondence between many of these self-reported life histories and the fiction of the previous forty years, surely no coincidence.

The darkest element in this vast sub-rosa domain of deviant *yin* subgroups might well have been the young men who roved urban streets on motorcycles in gangs of three to ten. The great majority of Vietnamese merely looked down on the street children, prostitutes, and bar girls with a detached mixture of pity and disdain; but most of them feared and despised these young toughs. Significantly, those who belonged to such groups were called "cowboys." Everyone had heard some story about how a cowboy gang had roared up beside an automobile or taxi, grabbed an arm, and cut off the passenger's finger to acquire a ring. These groups too were part of the emerging context, a small but integral part of the system, one also doubtlessly influenced by and to some extent modeled upon American exemplars such as Hell's Angels.

City streets were also lined with beggars: some hideously deformed, others with ugly running sores, ragged women with malnourished infants in their arms, doddering old men staring blindly into space. Some of these highly visible afflictions were self-induced or intentionally exaggerated as part of the desperate strategy by which these people sought to exploit the only niche open to them in tapping the growing resource of urban wealth, the unintended by-product of the American presence in Vietnam.

A vast subterranean economic system flourished beneath the dessicated and hollow machinery of government programs and policies and the thin veneer of legitimate enterprise. The black market was a vital, efficient, and very important part of the economy. Hundreds of tons of American goods poured into the black market each month along with incalculable sums of American money. Here was a deviant *yin* world where Americans and Vietnamese and Chinese and Koreans and Indians, military and civilians, men and women, young and old, people of all ranks and grades and social classes, of all political philosophies, could work together effectively and profitably.

It all began and ended with money, and with the Americans. Americans who smuggled dollars into Vietnam could sell them at a markup ranging from 25 percent (in military script) to six or eight times that much in piasters. A green dollar was worth over $1.25 in military payment certificates (MPCs) and at least two or three times the official exchange rate in piasters. And a twenty-dollar bill was worth much more than twenty times a one-dollar bill. Dollars were valued so highly for many reasons. Vietnamese liked to have a stack of dollars hidden away as a hedge against the rampant inflation of GVN currency and as an escape fund should they have to flee the country. They also needed them in order to do business with Americans who dared not convert illegally obtained MPCs and piasters into dollars upon returning to the United States. Few Americans in any event changed their money at the legal rates, always set so ridiculously low as to constitute a heavy and discriminatory tax upon the law-abiding minority.

A steady flow of ships steamed up the Saigon River bringing military supplies and American consumer goods to the United States personnel and their allies in Saigon. From dock to warehouse to supply depot to Post Exchange (PX), both Vietnamese and Americans pilfered from incoming goods at every step of the way. Much of what finally did reach a Post Exchange was purchased by card-holding Americans and other "Allied Forces" (all except, of course, the Vietnamese) and resold at a tidy profit. American cigarettes, beer, hair spray, whiskey, and other such commodities often changed hands many, many times before reaching the ultimate Vietnamese consumer, who might pay ten times more than the original authorized purchaser. Lower-middle-class women would pay what was for them huge sums of money to obtain a box of Tide detergent or a bar of Yardley's scented soap.

This illegal traffic in consumer goods and currency generated a vast multinational, cross-cultural network that stretched from plush air-conditioned offices in American facilities to the dingy back rooms of small snack bars, from Noncommissioned Officer (NCO) clubs on military bases to the pseudoposh atmosphere of the International House on Nguyen Hue Street to the slightly threadbare elegance of the Cercle Sportif, from back-alley hovels in wretched slums to opulent suburban villas. Vehicles left U.S. military installations every day containing commercial ovens, cases of whiskey, sides of beef, crates of cigarettes—everything that was not permanently set in concrete—turning down small side streets to transfer their stolen cargoes to the Vietnamese redistribution system.

In an inconspicuous house just off Truong Minh Giang Street one could buy lamb chops, bacon, filet mignon, real creamery butter, fresh or canned fruit of any kind—whatever American-imported delicacy one desired, including many things unavailable through official channels. One could enter a certain market between downtown Saigon and downtown Cholon, near the Saigon River, and buy quite literally anything. If you had enough money and they did not have what you wanted, someone would be dispatched to find it and get it for you, one way or another. The most effective entrepreneurs there, in fact, kept little or no stock in their run-down stalls; but they could send out for anything from a rare book to a hot fudge sundae, from a real Vietcong flag to a Thompson submachine gun. All transactions were cash and carry, with no questions asked and no receipts.

Anonymous enterprising sources, always allegedly located in Cholon, manufactured cheap imitations of American products. There were frauds within frauds, and hijackers got hijacked, but all such disturbing violations of *yin* principles were blamed on foreigners, usually the Chinese. The Indians were involved with much of the currency manipulation, but no one seemed to cheat them or be cheated by them, and they never touched anything but money. Like the rural village economy in traditional times, the *yin* underworld of the 1960s and 1970s in the south was one of great diversity and extreme specialization. Both were finely attuned and highly complex redistributive mechanisms of almost infinite flexibility and capable of being expanded almost indefinitely.

A BRIEF SYSTEM OVERVIEW In a grotesque yet substantive way, these diverse and deviant *yin* subgroupings constituted a transducing (energy-transferring) interface with the smothering, disruptive megasystem generated by the American presence in South Vietnam. The bar girls, prostitutes, street children, cowboys, and black marketeers siphoned immense quantities of money and goods from American personnel and programs in Vietnam and redistributed them throughout the local economy, extending through kin networks to the most remote hamlets in the land. The rock bands, popular singers, poets, newspapers and journals, television sets, transistor radios, tape recorders, and stereo systems likewise siphoned information, ideas, and techniques from American sources, transforming them and retransmitting them through indigenous channels of communication. In sundry ways and from diverse motives, large segments of the swollen *yin* subsystem of Vietnamese society were transmitting some form of energy or information drained from the American sociocultural system and redistributing it throughout the indigenous population. These various *yin* subgroups constituted a powerful ensemble of mechanisms that nourished and in a sense protected Vietnamese society at the very time that they were contributing to its further distortion and disruption.

At an abstract, functional, societal level of analysis, the *yin* subsystem's operation as a complex adaptive mechanism involved a massive redistribution of both goods and people that served to maintain some tenuous balance in a sociocultural system extended to the outer limits of viability through prolonged strain induced by fundamental contradictions and discontinuities between the ends and means of social action. As in traditional Vietnamese society, one discovers a symbiotic relationship between a status-defined, prestige-oriented *yang* subsystem and a functionally defined, subsistence-oriented *yin* subsystem. At a high level of abstraction, this model was as applicable to Saigon in the 1960s as it was to the Red River delta in earlier centuries. The essential difference was the paradigmatic crisis within the *yang* subsystem in more recent decades, which debilitated it to the extent that it could no longer effectively dominate or control the social system it nominally governed. The government and army of the Republic of Vietnam were overwhelmed, neither by the insurgents nor by the Americans, but by their own *yin* support subsystem, which, being more flexible and more subsistence oriented, gorged on the bounty of transient external energy sources.

Through an interlocking set of self-amplifying positive-feedback relationships obtaining within and between the GVN and the Americans, on the one hand, and the NLF, the Democratic Republic of Vietnam (DRV), and the Russians and the Chinese, on the other, the war had rapidly escalated between 1960 and 1968, increasing the speed of many other kinds of change at an exponential rate. Internal readjustment mechanisms within the GVN could not keep pace. The system was no longer even minimally homeostatic. It became in effect heterostatic, increasingly dependent on outside intervention for its very existence, provoking yet another dimension of *yin* reaction.

Estrangement and Farewell

GROWING DISENCHANTMENT WITH THE AMERICANS The proliferation of deviant *yin* elements in the society and culture of South Vietnam was profoundly disturbing to many Vietnamese. The majority of the urban middle sector had initially welcomed American assistance, and as late as 1966 the majority of the people in Saigon expressed no hostility toward the growing American presence despite the increasing number of petty annoyances, the occasional ugly incident, and the already worrisome problem of inflation.[15] But some noncommunist Vietnamese had long been apprehensive of American motives, and an even larger group were concerned about the results of this massive intrusion of alien force into the Vietnamese way of life. As early as 1965 Ton That Thien—social scientist, journalist, and editor—had warned that few Vietnamese of honesty and intelligence would welcome further United States influence in Vietnam or support a closer association between the two countries.[16]

Many noncommunist Vietnamese would "hold back," Thien thought, in part "because they are genuinely unsure about U.S. intentions." Some people felt that Americans in the Republic of Vietnam "shun the nationalists (not necessarily anti-American) who hate the idea of turning their country into a 'little America.'" One year later Thien reported that two important events had recently occurred in Saigon.[17] A group of intellectuals had held a meeting at the city hall "to discuss the problem of cultural and moral 'depravity' and measures to check it." At the same time a meeting of Vietnamese students in Saigon to discuss "current problems" turned into "an indictment of intermarriage between Vietnamese women and American men, and of the government's yielding to American pressure in the economic sphere." Communist agitators played an important role in shaping such events, but their task was facilitated by the very real anxieties felt by many sincere, noncommunist nationalists in these areas.[18]

In Saigon the number of registered marriages between Vietnamese and Westerners climbed steadily: 126 in 1965, 402 in 1968, 557 in 1971. This seems like a fairly small number of intermarriages in a metropolis like Saigon, but its perceived significance was related to the fact that registered marriages between Vietnamese fell from 3,889 in 1965 to 2,871 in 1967, rose somewhat to 3,325 in 1968, and then fell back to 2,868 in 1969, 2,838 in 1970, and 2,851 in 1971. As a percentage of total registered marriages in Saigon, those taking place between two Vietnamese plunged from 96 percent in 1965 to only 81 percent in 1970.[19]

Apparently, in view of the increasing rate at which men were being killed and maimed by the war, in addition to the inadequacy of salaries in the face of rampant inflation, many Vietnamese women were choosing not to marry at all, or were postponing marriage until more stable times. Thus with each passing year during the 1960s more and more Vietnamese males felt threatened, humiliated, and outraged by the sight of Vietnamese women with foreign men, especially with Americans, so conspicuous in their affluence and their numbers. The very real impact of the American presence and the genuine doubts about American intentions combined with traditional attitudes and values to create an unpleasant situation.

Vietnamese have long had an extreme preoccupation with maintenance of the ethnic boundary, first between themselves and the Chinese, later and even more traumatically between themselves and the French. By the late 1960s the crushing weight of the Americans seemed to some to dwarf these earlier influences. The reemergence of a hypersensitivity to maintenance of the ethnic boundary, with strong xenophobic overtones, is illustrated in a revealing paragraph in Toan Anh's useful book on the traditional Vietnamese village published in Saigon in 1968:

> Vietnamese girls don't like to marry a man from outside the village, let alone one from a foreign country. Vietnamese from well-behaved families look upon marrying a foreign husband as a bad thing to do, no matter what rank or status the man may have.
>
> When she marries a foreigner, a Vietnamese woman feels ashamed, no matter what her social class. And women who

marry foreigners are usually ridiculed, especially when that foreigner belongs to a people who have acted in ways that are detrimental to the Vietnamese, either materially or spiritually. . . . This class of women is much scorned by their Vietnamese sisters. The act of taking a Western husband is an act of losing one's origins; the act of going astray by someone who has severed her roots. Most of these [women] are from a degenerate lower-class background, but even they feel deeply ashamed and a piercing hurt, sometimes even more so than other women in the same situation who have better educations and were born and raised in what were called "decent" families. This latter group, poisoned by foreign culture, has lost all concept of peoplehood and nationhood—fortunately there are not many of them![20]

This paragraph is intrusive and jarring as it appears in the original text. It would appear that like many other Vietnamese, by 1968 Toan Anh had been shocked into feelings of frustration, impotence, and guilt, and he felt a need to make this public affirmation of traditional values. In this passionate outburst the traditional Vietnamese preoccupation with system boundaries is disclosed to be standing in naked opposition to the previous thirty-five years of agitation in favor of greater individualism and spontaneity in Vietnamese cultural life.

Thirty-three years after the appearance of *Breaking the Ties* the revolutionary implications of its message were not yet fully appreciated nor accepted by many Vietnamese, even of the urban middle class. One still could find urban intellectuals like Toan Anh (who was born and raised in a village in the Red River delta) railing against those Vietnamese who asserted their right as individuals to exercise their own judgment in selecting a spouse. One still found people viewed, not primarily as autonomous human beings with their own personal worth as individuals, but first and foremost as members of a corporate group. It made little difference whether the corporate group in question was a family, a village, an ethnic group, or a nation. The *yang* essence of Vietnamese culture and society was composed of hierarchical, corporately oriented and rigidly bounded structures that required and demanded a high degree of closure as a prerequisite for survival without undergoing a fundamental change of state. To those Vietnamese in whom an attachment to traditional culture persisted as a vital force in life, the boundary-violating quality of mixed marriages was a threat to their very identity.

Fueled by a dependence on American arms and American dollars that grew apace with an ever-more pervasive and domineering American presence, many citizens of the Republic of Vietnam felt compelled to confront and devaluate the myths of American omnipotence, omniscience, and even of American altruism. Certain issues then took on a symbolic importance that transcended the concrete events from which they arose.

The shift in attitudes toward the American presence in Vietnam went far beyond questions of combat losses, inflation, or interracial marriages. Beginning in 1968 and increasing rapidly over the next few years, some noncommunists began to have second thoughts, not merely about the effects of the American presence in Vietnam, but about the motives behind American actions as well. One example can be taken from the pages of *Chanh Dao* (The Right Path), a semiofficial publication of the Institute for the Propagation of Dharma within the United Buddhist Church of Vietnam. On August 13, 1968, an article appeared that stated:

> Before the war South Vietnam produced not only enough rice for local consumption but also exported millions of tons annually. Since the war broke out, it has to import from the United States six or seven hundred thousand tons of rice each year to feed the people. Naturally, this war has brought a sizable income to farming states in the U.S. such as Arkansas, Louisiana, Mississippi, Missouri, and Texas.[21]

The American use of herbicides in Vietnam seized the imagination of urban intellectuals, who were becoming increasingly disenchanted with American policy and American actions in general. When most of the herbicide was actually being dropped in Vietnam, it was not an important issue in the press even among the opposition newspapers, which tended to be critical of the government and the Americans. Except for a few complaints about the effectiveness of the program to compensate farmers for herbicide-related losses, the reporting of the use of herbicides was highly objective and nonevaluative until 1968; and throughout 1968 and the early months of 1969 the payment of claims for compensation was the only aspect of the program to receive any significant degree of critical attention.

In the spring of 1969, however, the Vietnamese-language press began to publish many more articles about the use of herbicides in Vietnam, and the tone became increasingly critical. A spurt of reports alleged various adverse effects from herbicide use. This shift in reporting in Vietnamese papers was unrelated to actual herbicide usage in Vietnam, which had greatly declined from its peak use in 1967 and 1968, but it did follow directly on the heels of a decision on the part of the *New York Times* to take an editorial stand against the use of herbicides in Vietnam by United States forces. This action by a prestigious American newspaper apparently exerted considerable influence on the reportage of both progovernment and antigovernment newspapers in Saigon.

American scientists, many of whom opposed the role of the United States in Vietnam on moral grounds, were at this time beginning publicly to express valid concerns about possible long-term detrimental consequences to the health and ecology of populations and regions exposed to the massive defoliation program in Vietnam. Certain of these statements were selected for publication in U.S. newspapers, and Vietnamese newspapers began monitoring and selectively reproducing U.S. press reports about the possible effects of herbicides. To an already suspicious and increasingly hostile segment of public opinion in Vietnam, these "published facts" served to confirm their suspicions regarding not just the effects of but also the intentions behind U.S. activities in Vietnam.

On September 1, 1970, for example, an article in *Tin Sang* (Morning News) concluded:

> The U.S. has often proclaimed that U.S. troops are sent to
> Vietnam to help the Vietnamese people, to protect their
> liberty and fight communism. But the U.S. also interferes in
> Vietnamese affairs like a master, and acts cruelly as exem-
> plified by the likes of the My Lai massacre . . . , the indis-
> criminate bombing of B-52's, and the spraying of herbicides.
> These devastate our country.

On November 19, 1971, another article about the U.S. Food for Peace program concluded:

> This program will bring about the devastation and ruin of the
> Vietnamese countryside. The U.S. destroys the rural area of
> Vietnam with bombs and herbicides so that Vietnam is forced
> to import U.S. surplus agricultural products.

And while *Tin Sang* produced the greatest number and the most vicious of these articles (those quoted above are not the most extreme), other opposition papers trumpeted the same themes. The Catholic paper *Hoa Binh* (Peace), associated with former supporters of the Diem regime, sent the same ideas into Catholic communities. *Dien Tin* (Telegram), with a former ARVN colonel as its publisher and editor, was almost equally critical of American actions. On March 8, 1972, *Dien Tin* concluded that "the Americans have been many times more cruel than the French. Besides the destruction of the countryside, spraying herbicides over fields and orchards, they blatantly bombed the cities during the Tet Mau Than (1968) on the pretext of driving out the V.C." *Hoa Binh* was published by a Catholic priest who was well known to be anticommunist. The editor of *Tin Sang* was also a Catholic and a senator. All these papers had very respectable circulations and were read by opinion leaders throughout the country.

The real proof of a shift in attitudes came not from the opposition papers but from *Chinh Luan*, the epitome of respectable conservatism in the south, which came closer than any other newspaper in Saigon to being a paper of record. Its publisher was Dr. Dang Van Sung: doctor of medicine, Dai Viet, staunch anticommunist, and a prominent senator. It had a circulation rate greater than any of the opposition papers and enjoyed widespread popularity throughout the intellectual community. Those who did criticize it called it, if anything, too progovernment and especially too pro-American. Yet in the 1971 elections *Chinh Luan* demanded of President Thieu as a condition of its support that he demonstrate his ability and his willingness to stand up to the Americans and control more strictly American actions in Vietnam. The reasons for taking this position were given in an article published on September 29, 1971:

> The U.S. Armed Forces have a low regard for the lives and property of the people of this country. As a result much indiscriminate bombing has taken place, and careless herbicide spraying has been conducted, a spraying that is beyond the real and reasonable tactical needs. . . . Indiscriminate defoliation activities of the U.S. Armed Forces have inflicted great damage upon trees and crops which are a source of life to the people.

Meanwhile, several intellectual journals of protest had begun to publish trenchant articles that varied greatly in content and style but seem to have been based on a common assumption that the United States was intentionally destroying the Vietnamese economy and sapping the cultural vitality of the Vietnamese people. Two journals representative of this phenomenon are *Doi Dien* (Face to Face) and *Trinh Bay* (Report). *Doi Dien* was published and edited by several Catholic priests and drew many contributors and readers from the Catholic community. The editorial board of *Trinh Bay* included many prominent noncommunist intellectuals. The poets Nguyen Sa and Du Tu Le, whose works were introduced above, were on the board; and so was Thanh Lang, the scholar-priest who in his capacity as head of the PEN club in Vietnam gave such a stirring oration at the grave of Nguyen Tuong Tam eight years earlier. These were prominent men whose integrity, intellectual credentials, and independence from Communist direction were above question.

In January 1972 *Doi Dien* featured an article entitled "A Strategic Goal of the Americans in Their Rural Pacification Policy: To Exterminate the Means of Subsistence, the Sentiments and the Traditional Love of Country of the Vietnamese Peasantry." The author's basic proposition was that the actual purpose of American utilization of herbicides, artillery, air strikes, Rome plows, and even many of their conventional military operations was to disrupt Vietnamese rural life, to dislodge the peasants from their land and their normal productive activities:

> But they still have to live; they still have to eat. And there is only one path available to them: abandon their fields and orchards, change their occupation, take any job at all except farming (this is what the anticommunist strategists want so much). So the farmers "voluntarily" come to the strategic hamlets, the regroupment camps, the refugee camps, the relocation centers in order to "be assisted and more secure." Through the compulsion of their will to stay alive, if they don't use aid commodities and canned goods and after their assistance has been prematurely terminated, the rural people must go to work doing other things, begging, stealing, pimping and whoring in the cities or around the allied bases.
>
> Because of their agricultural life, the great mass of Vietnamese people have had a sentimental attachment to the land, which is a first step toward love of homeland and love of nation.
>
> Now that the ricefields are devastated, the homeland of the rice has become a very distant thing. Furthermore, the change in lifestyle and the ease of earning a living on the part of those "fortunate" peasants (having children who have American boyfriends, American husbands, or American jobs) has led them to no longer miss their ricefields and orchards.

Farming has become something tiresome and unrewarding; and it provides no TV, refrigerators, or varieties of canned meat.

This sort of thinking became common among urban intellectuals in the early 1970s. In the October 22, 1971, issue of *Trinh Bay*, Pham Cao Duong, a prominent social historian now living in Canada, presented an article entitled "Ten Years of Ecological Warfare in South Vietnam":

> Now ecological warfare, or warfare to destroy the means of subsistence, has taken place in Vietnam for exactly ten years.
>
> Beginning ten years ago with the experimental spraying of herbicides to the east of Saigon by American advisers, this war has continued strongly with all sorts of blue, white, red, and orange chemical agents.
>
> The application of these poisonous chemicals upon people, animals, crops, forest products, soil and climate . . . has been described in great detail in the pages of this journal.
>
> While another kind of warfare, according to some people, is gradually receding (?), the war of ecological destruction in South Vietnam, after ten long years, is still of a terrifying nature. The American authorities . . . still refuse actually to accept the barbaric and inhumane nature of ecological warfare. They stubbornly deny that the chemicals used in Vietnam are a form of chemical warfare. . . . Is it that they are afraid of losing face? . . . Or is it that they subscribe to and are pursuing the principle that "if you wish to break the fighting spirit of a people, you must destroy their subsistence base"?
>
> Ecological warfare continues, in one guise or another, with one type of weapon or another. For the past ten years, the American authorities have never had any intention of abandoning their war to exterminate the means of subsistence of the Vietnamese people.

Trinh Bay devoted an entire special issue to "The American Destruction in Indochina." It included translated statements from the U.S. *Congressional Record* and translated articles by American scientists discussing the damaging effects of herbicides. It is instructive to note the ironic extent to which even anti-Americanism in Saigon reflected a strong American influence. This is what the intellectuals were so agitated about in the first place.

The pervasive and deep-rooted nature of Vietnamese anxieties in regard to what might be called American "cultural imperialism" was vividly impressed upon me one Saturday morning early in 1970. Expecting to meet with a small group of writers and social scientists in a seminar room, I had accepted what seemed to be a casual invitation to give a talk on attitudes and values at the General Directorate for Psychological Warfare in Saigon. Not until I arrived at the Directorate that morning did I realize that I would be addressing a group of political officers, that there would be an audience of several hundred instead of half a dozen, and that I would have to go on stage and give a formal lecture in Vietnamese over a public address system. It had been my hope that the Vietnamese participants would do most of the talking and provide me with some insights into their own attitudes and values. But as it turned out, they would be asking all the questions and I would be alone at the podium.

I belatedly realized that these Saturday morning "guest lecture" sessions were thinly disguised scrimmage games in which the students exercised their newly taught skills to show off in front of their instructors. As I waited to begin I learned that several prominent and articulate Vietnamese whose names were familiar to me had sorely been put to the test on previous Saturdays on that very stage. While the army major who was to introduce me complimented me on my courage as the only foreigner ever to face one of these groups (was he genuinely sympathetic, I wondered, or was this part of the psychological assault?), I silently cursed the man who had been less than frank with me as to what his invitation had entailed. I managed to stumble through a forty-five-minute lecture before losing the initiative to the audience, with an hour and forty-five minutes remaining in the scheduled session. After a few polite questions about my pedantic and inappropriate talk, the "young tigers" in the audience set about their work. The first major theme to emerge from the questions concerned the relative material prosperity and spiritual and aesthetic poverty of the United States in comparison with other nations. "How would you respond," one man asked, "if someone said the United States was so preoccupied with constructing buildings and machines that despite the wealth and leisure enjoyed by many of its citizens, it has produced no art or philosophy worthy of a civilized nation?"

Questions flowed unremittingly, gradually becoming sharper and much more hostile. Some of the questioners seemed to be working up to real anger. The topics ranged from fiscal policy to relations between the sexes to alleged plots by the CIA. Herbicides, bombing, and refugees were of course included. But education was a major source of concern. A few men rattled off with impressive alacrity the facts and figures on how many classrooms had been built and how many million textbooks had been published under USAID programs. What they wanted to know was who decided which books got printed in such vast numbers and what criteria were used in making such decisions.

As I came to see the futility of satisfying these men by providing only American rationales for answers to their questions, I began to supplement my responses with a few parallels from Vietnamese history and culture. Finally a question came that I was able to. answer after a fashion by quoting a few apposite lines from *Kieu*, the widely known and loved Vietnamese epic poem. This marked a dramatic turning point in the nature of the inquisition. A few of the most hostile of my interrogators roared with laughter and the entire room burst into applause. No defense or explanation of the American point of view could have been so effective as this small gesture, which indicated that the Vietnamese point of view was being taken seriously.

The degree of hostility and suspicion in many of these questions was startling. These were men selected, indoctrinated, and trained to provide political education to their units in the army of the Republic of Vietnam. The United States had lavished billions of dollars worth of equipment and supplies on that army. American aid had purchased the uniforms these men were wearing, the chairs on which they sat, the weapons they bore. These young men were far above average in education and intelligence. They wanted to resist the Communists, and they wanted the United States to help them in that effort. Why should they of all people feel such resentment?

At last, exhausted by the ordeal and believing I had endured it for a reasonable length of time, I sought to achieve some closure in the session: "My friends, we have had a long and frank discussion. I didn't realize what I was getting into when I came here today, but it has been an experience I value. We have tried to be honest with each other; but I sense that there is an unspoken question behind the questions you have asked, and that you have been looking for some hidden answer behind the answers I have given you. I fear you have mistaken my naivete for cleverness. To tell the truth, I am not feeling very clever this morning. So before I go I would like one of you to try to articulate for me the big question behind the smaller ones. If there is an underlying question, can somebody please put it into words?" After a long silence, some members of the audience began to confer among themselves. Finally one young man stood up. Speaking slowly and carefully, he said:

"I believe, sir, that you are right in thinking there is something behind all these questions, something which troubles us but which no one has put into words. Let me try to put our real concerns into two questions. The first question, the one really big question, is this: 'Does the United States want to make Vietnam into a little America?' If the answer to that question is 'yes,' then the second question is 'Why should they want to do such a thing?' If the answer to the first question is 'no,' then our second question is 'Why do they consistently act the way they do?' We honestly cannot understand American behavior in Vietnam."

Needless to say, I could find no really satisfactory response to their questions. These political officers, the people who met at city hall to discuss cultural and moral depravity, those others who decried intermarriage between Vietnamese and foreigners, those who railed against the destructive effects of herbicide use and lashed out at USAID-produced textbooks in the public schools, all shared a common concern, more so, I think, than anyone realized. In the particular instance, their complaints were often out of proportion to the facts. USAID did not ruthlessly dictate school curricula in Vietnam. The ricefields of South Vietnam were not destroyed by herbicides. Not all that many Vietnamese girls were marrying or even dating Americans. In each of these areas there were certainly valid grounds for concern, even for legitimate criticism and complaint, to be sure; but the intensity of the protest arose not from the bare facts of herbicide damage or marriage rates or textbooks in use. The protestation over such matters became so intense and widespread because the particular issues symbolized a much larger and more generalized threat to Vietnamese identity.

The American presence in Vietnam, whatever the intentions of the individuals who constituted it and by whom it was directed, posed a severe and immediate threat to the dignity and integrity of the very people it was supposed to be assisting. Militarily, economically, politically, socially, culturally, the cumulative, combined impact of American actions in and directed toward Vietnam was of such a magnitude as to impair the process of self-determination in significant ways, to seriously disrupt the capability for autonomous learning and reorganization at a self-determined rate. Individually and collectively, the citizens of the Republic of Vietnam suffered from a keenly felt lack of dignity as they experienced a perceived loss of control over their own destiny. While they could not agree among themselves upon a preferred setting of the social thermostat, the more thoughtful among them could not avoid feeling anxious and resentful as it increasingly appeared that the thermostat was being set for them—neither wisely nor maliciously, but simply as the unplanned by-product of the functioning of a larger and much more powerful system.

Many Vietnamese with whom I was acquainted had begun by the early 1970s to speak in symbolic terms of self-reference that were extremely passive. They seemed increasingly to feel themselves to be objects being acted upon rather than as effective actors or initiators of action. Nha Ca's vignette about the little dog caught in midstream, being fired upon from both sides, forcefully expresses this attitude. Such a perception was widely shared. It extended from the men and women in the streets and ricefields to provincial administrative headquarters to the innermost chambers of the presidential palace.[22]

The one thing the Americans could not do, however, was anticipate or control the results of their actions, which surged through the smaller, complex, and precariously balanced sociocultural system of South Vietnam like bolts of lightning, overriding the weak and poorly integrated operating channels through which adaptation to previous change was still being formulated. Only one thing was certain: uncertainty. Only one thing was constant: change. After working with us and fighting with us for several years, even many of our friends began to doubt not just our efficacy but our motives.

A poem published in 1969 by an ARVN officer writing under a pseudonym was entitled "Letter to the People of the United States":

> I have sat with you in the same places
> I have gone with you down the same roads
> I have eaten with you from the same platter
> But I have not yet had a chance to speak of
> The things of which I wish to speak
> . . . .
> Though you, my friends, have molested the young girls of my
>   homeland

Though you, my friends, have inspired a number of vehicles to
    run down our laboring people
Though you, my friends, have senselessly destroyed some of
    our poor restaurants and cafes
Though you, my friends, have acted with a lack of politeness,
    with a deficiency of civilization
Have acted in a way that is not human
We are ready to be understanding
We are ready to forgive
You are soldiers far from home
Soldiers not fighting for your own nation
Soldiers gone off to defend a freedom of no commercial value
We have had to think of this
To understand this for a long time now
We want to find some words of praise for you
We want to find a gesture with which to express our gratitude
Don't be suspicious, my friends, don't jump to any false
    conclusions
We are people with hearts that are still hearts
We are people who know pain, who know shame
We are not puppets
Under the lenses of your cameras
We are not a troop of entertainers
Under your teasing eyes
You, my friends, have come to Vietnam
You, my friends, have drunk the water of this tiny nation
But you have not yet understood the soul of this people
You have not yet seen
Have not yet been willing to see the burning desire of this
    people
You are not deaf, my friends, nor are you blind
Why then do you keep on fighting
And at the same time barbecue, stunt and destroy these
    organisms created by heaven
Don't think that you have stood with us in the same line of
    defense
Though we have lain side by side in the battlefront opposing
    communism
Have sweat together and shed blood together
For the flesh and blood you have budgeted for my nation
Is not enough to prove that you are sincerely for freedom
That you are sincerely helping a weak nation without profit
Ah, it is extremely fortunate

That my people do not bear grudges
But are forgiving and tolerant
And even in misery are confidently optimistic
"After the rain the sun will come out."
O soldiers of the United States
O white friends and black friends who have fought with us
On the same battlefront
Not only have you shed your blood
But you have shed tears as well
We have seen you, my friends, very clearly
No matter how hard you tried
You could not kill the humanity in your hearts
Your tears have dropped upon the corpses of your comrades
Your tears have mingled with the ink in letters to your families
Oh, those tears
Those truly heroic and truly painful images
O my U.S. soldier friends
Have you never asked yourselves
With all the corpses of your comrades
With all the wealth of your nation
With all the modern weapons you use
Why you have not yet achieved victory
If we do not wish to say
If we do not wish to accept
That you are about to yield, about to retreat, about to be
    defeated
It is not that you lack the cruelty
Nor is it that you lack the courage
Rethink it, my friends
Figure it out again
Each person bearing arms in Vietnam
Each person sitting in the White House
Each person present at the Paris meetings
You must be able to say to yourselves
We are fighting for freedom
We are truly providing security and restoring peace
To a weak nation
We are not seeking profit
We are not seeking commerce
We are not seeking trade
Surely you know that we detest war
That we thirst for peace
Surely you know that we want to live in freedom

We do not need your rent for our land
We do not need your rent for our houses, your rent for our
  roads
We do not need your rent for our consciences nor for our
  corpses
Our nation is not so poor as you have thought it to be
So long as we have breath
We shall have the strength to fight
In search of freedom and in defense of peace
Go ahead and leave Vietnam, my friends
If you are exhausted
If you are ashamed
For not being honest with yourselves before you came
And take our thanks with you
To serve as a bit of victory
To inscribe upon the pages of your history
We pray that those pages do not make you troubled and
  bitter.[23]

The Vietnamese could not understand either our behavior or our
motives. In large part this was because they looked for a coherence
and a consistency that simply were not there. As protests against
the war mounted in the United States we began, shamefacedly, to
withdraw. And we departed as abruptly and as disruptively as we
had arrived.

THE DEMISE OF THE REPUBLIC OF VIETNAM   In 1960 the number
of U.S. military personnel stationed in Vietnam grew from 685 to
900. In June 1965 there had been 74,000 of us; in June 1967,
463,000. By June 1969 there were 541,000 American soldiers in
Vietnam, but by June 1972 only a residual force of about 60,000
remained. From a spending level that had exceeded ten billion
dollars a year on the war in Vietnam, the United States Congress
authorized one billion dollars and actually appropriated only 700
million dollars in military aid to the GVN in the last complete
fiscal year of its existence.[24]
    In deserted barrooms throughout Vietnam tens of thousands of
girls sat dolefully staring into space for hour after empty hour,
pathetic in their finery and their loneliness. The black market
shriveled to a fraction of its former size. Glittering new apartment
and office buildings sat half empty. Discharged maids and kitchen
helpers, chauffeurs and secretaries and elevator operators dejectedly
competed for scarce new jobs. The artificially inflated *yin* subsys-

tems in Saigon and Danang and Bien Hoa lurched toward collapse, sending shock waves throughout the society. Abruptly cast back largely upon its own resources, the GVN economy floundered. In 1971 it had exported less than 8 million dollars (US) worth of goods while imports totaled 373 million dollars. No longer were there half a million free-spending Americans on hand to make up the difference.

In a spring offensive of 1972 fresh PAVN divisions poured across the demilitarized zone with tanks and heavy artillery. With 1,100,000 men under arms, the Republic of Vietnam surprised many observers by withstanding this assault with little direct help from the withdrawing Americans. It was a good performance by an effective military organization.

In January 1973 the Paris peace accords were signed, and many GVN officials and supporters of the government concluded that the Americans had sold them out for some other consideration in global strategy through a secret quid pro quo deal struck with international communism.[25] Politically, militarily, and economically, the fabric of society began to unravel. Over the next two years it is estimated that the number of PAVN combat troops in the south climbed from 148,000 to 237,000 while ARVN's main force combat level fell from 250,000 to 104,000. Indeed the Communists seemed to be better armed and equipped than ARVN. The GVN was abruptly stuck with a military white elephant. At American insistence ARVN was designed and trained to be dependent on a level of technology and spending that the GVN could not maintain and that we would no longer even minimally support. When another major Communist offensive was launched in the spring of 1975, the cynical and disillusioned army of the Republic of Vietnam simply fell apart.[26] They believed that we had made them dependent on us, and that we had then abandoned them to larger American interests. Now, they felt sure, they were doomed by a destiny worked out behind closed doors of international diplomacy.

Experienced commanders made incredible errors of judgment. Men of proven bravery panicked. Terror spread through the population like a firestorm. Hundreds of thousands of people fled before the Communist advance. Catholics and northern families who had moved to the south twenty years earlier were conspicuously overrepresented among these refugees. Soldiers and civil servants joined the human wave as it swept past them. March and the early weeks of April became a nightmare. Nineteen of forty-three provincial capitals were overrun, and a final defense line was hastily formed to the north of Saigon. The American assistance that had been promised to gain acceptance of the 1973 "peace treaty" never materialized.[27] The tattered remnants of ARVN regrouped to fight their final battle, alone. Belatedly, with heart-rending gallantry, a few outnumbered and outgunned units made their last stand at Xuan Loc, just northeast of Saigon. It was bloody and futile, but with their backs to the wall these often maligned troops fought bravely and well. Those Americans who could bear to watch caught glimpses of it on television. But it was no longer our war.

Henry Kissinger and Le Duc Tho of the DRV had received the Nobel Peace Prize for producing the Paris agreement, and the United States was sighing with relief as we tried to convince ourselves that we had achieved "peace with honor." But within the Republic of Vietnam, mixed and overpowering emotions brought agony to millions of people. From the midst of the battle, *Chinh Luan's* distinguished war correspondent Nguyen Tu sent in an article, which appeared on March 31, 1975:

> This afternoon as the sun was setting slowly over a patch of jungle . . . I don't know why, but suddenly I thought of my friends. I thought of those soldiers who had fought heroically at the side of the soldiers of my nation in Vietnam for eight long years: the soldiers of Thailand, Korea, New Zealand, Australia, and the United States. . . . This year when visiting the ARVN 22nd Infantry Division . . . I was moved and overcome with emotion as I lowered my head before the monument to the Korean soldiers who had made heroic sacrifices to achieve victory at the battle of An Khe pass on Highway 19.
>
> And while lost in emotion before the monument to the Korean soldiers, I could not help remembering with the same deep feeling of emotion those soldiers of Thailand, New Zealand, Australia, and the United States who had fallen upon the soil of my country in order to mark with their very blood and bones a barrier to halt the fierce advance of the forces of communism, a barrier to protect those things which we all praise and revere: freedom, democracy. Their shattered bones, flowing blood, and torn flesh have entered the soil of all the battlefields of Vietnam, and along with the rivers of blood and mountains of bones of the soldiers of my country, and of my compatriots, merged into one great sacrifice, into one dream of Freedom and Democracy for all.

•   •   •

Those friends who have sacrificed their lives have now
been taken back to their homelands for somber burial services
before the stream of tears of their relatives and loved ones.
All the rest have boarded ships or airplanes to return to their
homeland and the love and warmth of their families. After
that, through the outstanding initiative and very strong leadership of the United States, the Paris Peace Agreement was
signed on the 27th of January 1973 to international applause
and to the applause of our friends, especially in the United
States, leading to "Peace With Honor" in accord with the desires of former President Nixon, the present Secretary of State
Henry Kissinger, Congress, and the entire American people.
The fact that these friends have been able to return to the
warmth of their families is something for which I personally,
with all my heart and soul, rejoice.

Now, after two years of "Peace With Honor" through the
reports of newspapers, wire services, radio, and television
all over the world, those friends are now observing the dis-
integration that is spreading daily across my homeland.
Thousands of my country's soldiers have continued to fall
throughout the two years of "Peace With Honor." Thousands
of my people, including many children, have continued to die
throughout these two years of "Peace With Honor." Hundreds of thousands of my people are homeless, hungry, cold;
and furthermore and even more important, without hope,
without even the dream of a life worth living for these two
years of "Peace With Honor," and for the coming days, the
coming months, and perhaps even the coming years. And
everyone in Vietnam, including me, my friends, we now ask
ourselves, how long will this "Peace With Honor" continue,
and where will it lead?

From the news reports of . . . all five continents, and especially from the United States, all of my country's soldiers, all
of my people, and I personally, have understood that our
friends, especially our American friends, the American Congress and the American people, of all factions and all social
classes, look upon the war in Vietnam from which they have
drawn so far away, as if it were a nightmare that must be
pushed completely away from their minds in order for them
to live peacefully and happily in the warmth of their families.
No one, in psychological terms or any other terms, can con-

tinue forever to retain the affection and assistance of the person next to them, be that a single person, a friendly country, or an ally in a desperate situation. The soldiers of my country, my people (please understand "people" here to mean the overwhelming majority, the poor, the war victims, and not the rich and fat minority in Saigon and a few other cities in Vietnam and in some foreign countries), and I myself, we understand all of this.

The graves stand in neat and orderly straight lines at each of the military cemeteries that are spread throughout Vietnam.

Twilight covers the mountainous jungles of Son Hoa. In the dim sunlight, it is as if it is the light in their eyes fading into death.

Out of a feeling of helplessness, because I cannot find any words of my own with which to express my deep gratitude and bid a respectful farewell to the allies, especially to the Americans in the United States Congress, in the United States government, to the American soldiers and the American people who cherish "Peace With Honor," let me with a heart that is completely sincere quote a line of poetry from Lord Byron to send to all these friends:

FARE THEE WELL! AND IF FOREVER,
STILL, FOR EVER FARE THEE WELL.

Exactly thirty days after this article appeared in *Chinh Luan*, the Republic of Vietnam ceased to exist as PAVN tanks drove into the city and proceeded to Independence Palace where they hoisted their red-starred banner in victory. The few thousand Americans who had remained to the end were evacuated by helicoper in the final days and hours, taking about 140,000 Vietnamese with them and abandoning to an uncertain fate millions of others who desperately wished to leave. On the final day as a group of Americans scurried to the safety of the helicopters while Vietnamese watched with tears and resentment, one man muttered to his companions: "Don't look in their eyes."[28] The advice was unnecessary. We left with our heads down, confused, frustrated, and ashamed, and thankful for the competence of the marines who plucked us to safety.

7 Another Cycle Unfolds

The alternating movement of *yin* and *yang* is what
is called the *Tao*. . . . Its culmination constitutes
the inherent characteristic of the world.
        "Great Appendix" to the *Tao Te Ching*

The Road to Victory

During the late 1960s, when relations between the Government of
Vietnam (GVN) and the United States were continuing to deteriorate and an antiwar protest movement flourished in the United
States and in Saigon and Hue, the Communist opposition showed
little evidence of faltering despite incredibly heavy losses, perhaps
three to four times the casualty rate of the Allied forces.[1] The huge
Tet offensive of 1968 had been a military failure that broke the back
of the insurgency in South Vietnam.[2] The National Liberation Front
(NLF) found its armed forces decimated and its political infrastructure seriously depleted. The "accelerated pacification campaign"
that followed Tet further eroded its strength throughout the
country.[3] Yet the offensive, despite being a military defeat, had
achieved a psychological victory in the United States and in urban
areas of South Vietnam, producing substantial political gains in the
sphere of public opinion. To capitalize on the new political opportunities offered while at a military disadvantage, in 1968 the NLF
organized a new front organization, the Alliance of National,
Democratic, and Peace Forces.

The Alliance's public program as well as its internal documents
called for an independent and sovereign state of South Vietnam, a
state that would be "truly democratic" and "neutral," with "free
trade," "freedom of speech," "freedom of the press," freedom of
travel, assembly, and other civil liberties. It also forcefully
espoused a policy of reconciliation, offering supporters of the GVN
full opportunity to participate in a postwar regime where "none

357

will be favored more than others." Beyond these liberal proposals for southern society, because of the fundamental political and cultural differences between the two halves of the country, the Alliance proposed that "the South and the North should hold talks on the basis of equality and respect for the characteristics of each zone."[4]

Subsequently, Nixon's policy of "Vietnamization" threatened to counter the public relations gains derived from the shock effect of the Tet offensive and the "national reconciliation" line successfully pursued by the Alliance. So in 1969 a Provisional Revolutionary Government (PRG) for South Vietnam was formed to further influence public opinion, not just in Vietnam, but internationally, and especially in the United States.[5]

In June 1969, as part of this process, the Congress of People's Representatives selected the NLF anthem, "Liberate South Vietnam," as the national anthem of South Vietnam:

Liberate the South.
We march forward with determination.
Eliminate imperialism, smash the gang of traitors.
With crushed bones and oozing blood,
Our hearts overflow with hatred.
Rivers and mountains separated for so many years.
Here the mighty Mekong River, there the majestic Truong Son
    Range.
We are spurred on to assault, to wipe out the foe.
Shoulder to shoulder beneath a common flag.
Rise up! Heroic people of the South!
Rise up! Dash forward through the storm.
Pledge yourselves to National Salvation! Pledge to sacrifice to
    the end.
Surge forward, grasping swords, clasping guns.
The nation's destiny is at hand.

Dawn shines everywhere.
Promise of building a bright future for our land for ever more.[6]

Madam Nguyen Thi Binh, a masterful choice for foreign affairs minister for the PRG, skillfully projected an air of moderation and reasonableness to the world press. The PRG pronouncements stressed a policy of "reconciliation and concord." The PRG publicized an "action program" that stressed "freedom" of thought, of speech, of business; and it avowed a prohibition of "any discriminatory treatment of those who have collaborated with this side or the other side living at home or abroad."[7] Hanoi proclaimed the PRG to be the sole legitimate representative of the people of South Vietnam.

Ho Chi Minh died on September 3, 1969, and hope sprang up in Washington and Saigon that his death was a serious loss that would hamper the Communist war effort. Little did they understand the paradigm opposing them. With his death Ho Chi Minh had merely moved up one step from being "father's older brother" to being "revered ancestor" within the supervillage/superfamily of the revolution. He was from this time on referred to in print as Ngai, a term reserved for a king or a tutelary spirit, and references to him (Him) were capitalized, as we in the West by convention capitalize any reference to God or the Christian Trinity.

By his death Ho Chi Minh provided the superfamily/supervillage of the Vietminh/DRV/NLF with a guardian spirit who linked them with the ancient tradition of "supernatural" succorance guaranteed by a special relationship with a powerful figure in the spirit world. As the Hung Kings invoked the assistance of the Dragon Lord of the Lac, great founder of their dynasty, and as the Trung Sisters invoked the blessing of the Hung kings before setting forth in their rebellion against the Chinese, so now could his followers call on the unsullied and larger-than-life memory of Ho Chi Minh, a mighty reservoir of solace and inspiration.

When in 1975 word reached Hanoi of the triumphant entry of North Vietnamese troops into Saigon, a spontaneous demonstration of unprecedented size erupted in the city streets. As crowds surged from all directions toward the center of Hanoi, cheering and literally dancing with joy, a huge portrait of Ho Chi Minh overlooked the downtown area, smiling benignly upon the happy throng of his followers and spiritual descendants. Beneath his picture a caption proclaimed in bold letters: "You Are Always Marching With Us, Uncle Ho!" What chant was taken up by this jubilant crowd? "Long Live Ho Chi Minh!" Six years after his death, he was still their real leader, the venerated ancestor, their guardian spirit. The final intense surge that brought ten bloodied but still enthusiastic divisions of the People's Army of Vietnam (PAVN) to the suburbs of Saigon had been code-named the Ho Chi Minh campaign, and one of the first actions of the victorious forces on capturing the city that had defied them for so long was to change its name to Ho Chi Minh City.[8]

The victorious forces were, however, PAVN, main force units of the North Vietnamese army, commanded from Hanoi. While officials of the south's PRG occupied the offices and carried the titles in Ho Chi Minh City, northern cadres took over the actual conduct of business. The Military Management Committee, taking its orders from the politburo in Hanoi, controlled all police and security functions, and thus controlled everything else. The bulk of the northern army was in the south, and it was they who were really in charge.

Resetting the Social Thermostat in the South

When the great victory parade was held on May 15, 1975, the northern PAVN troops presented an impressive sight. A few rag-tag companies of southern forces, the troops of the NLF under the nominal control of the PRG, brought up the rear. And they marched beneath the banner of the Democratic Republic of Vietnam, Hanoi's flag, not the banner under which they had fought for so many years. The two armies had been "unified."[9] There was no longer any need for pretense. There would be no pluralistic government in the south, no neutrality, no gradual evolution, and no reconciliation. And there would be no negotiations, because there was nothing left to negotiate. And, in fact, there was no one to negotiate with. Those leaders of the NLF, the PRG, and the Alliance who had actually believed that they would wield power were quickly disabused of their illusions.[10]

The politburo in Hanoi had decided to press ahead with rapid reunification and to achieve a quick transition to socialism in the south. A little over six months after the Communist victory Truong Chinh, the number two man in the politburo, representing the north, and Pham Hung, the number four man in the politburo, representing the south, met in Ho Chi Minh City to exchange views on the already settled question of reunification. The head of the PRG, Huynh Tan Phat (a covert Communist party member since 1940), raised no objections.[11]

The goal, Truong Chinh announced, was to "level" all differences between north and south.[12] To born-again Communists like Truong Chinh, the heterodoxy, the degree of individualism and freedom of thought and expression to which the people of South Vietnam had grown accustomed, was anathema. The "corrupted" culture of the south was an obstacle to progress. The aging Communist leaders believed they possessed a privileged insight into the future. They had power. Surely they would not lack the will to act upon their convictions. History, the Tao, the very structure of reality was on their side as they moved to achieve a new golden age.

Prime Minister Le Duan predicted that within ten years there would be plenty to eat and a refrigerator and a television set in every home. The party was now firmly in charge of the entire country. Guided by Marxism-Leninism, it expected to build a strong and prosperous society rather quickly. It was determined to fulfill Ho Chi Minh's final promise to his people: "Once the American invaders have been defeated, we will rebuild our land ten times more beautiful."

The Communist party embraced full responsibility for this rebuilding. A committee chaired by Truong Chinh was charged with drafting a constitution for the newly established Republic of Vietnam. This document, which was ratified by the National Assembly in 1979, unequivocally stated—and it was the first public document ever to do so—the hegemony of the party over everybody and everything in Vietnam: "The Communist Party of Vietnam . . . , armed with Marxism-Leninism, is the only force leading the state and society, and the main factor determining the success of the Vietnamese revolution" (Article 4).

An entirely different ambience was sought for the metropolis that now bore the name of the revered leader of the revolution.[13] The dozens of feisty newspapers and journals that had provided so animated and discordant a chorus of commentary upon social action for so many decades closed their doors and shut down their presses. The bars and brothels and nightclubs quickly went out of business. One by one, most of the popular shops and restaurants followed them into oblivion. Rock and roll music was no longer performed, and most of the leading singers and musicians of that *yin* world were on their way to the United States or Canada, New Zealand or Australia, or France. No more folksongs of protest were heard. Pham Duy had gone to sing in Canada and the United States. Trinh Cong Son remained behind, but his "voice," the popular singer Khanh Ly, was among those who left.

The Cercle Sportif, where the most fashionable elements of Vietnamese, French, and for a time American society in Saigon had lounged in the sun and gossiped while sipping excellent cocktails, became a People's Museum. The luxuriously appointed roof of the Caravelle Hotel became an official club frequented by Russian and Eastern European dignitaries. The hotel itself was now Independence Hotel. The famous Continental Hotel that stood across the square, where generations of soldiers and officials and business-men and reporters had gathered in the late afternoon to exchange information and rumors over gin and tonic, was renamed the Hotel of the General Uprising. Freedom (Tu Do) Street, the main thor-oughfare that ran beside these two noted hostelries, was now called General Uprising Street. Many unreconstructed Saigonese remarked to each other with wry smiles that the city had finally had its "general uprising," and now there was no more "freedom."

The works of Nguyen Tuong Tam and Khai Hung were carefully removed from library shelves along with those of many other au-thors whose works had dominated the literary scene over the past four decades. On August 20, 1975, the order went out to confiscate and to prohibit the circulation of "reactionary books and journals." The massive list of forbidden works appended to this document was expanded in subsequent documents issued in March 1976 and May 1977. The works of almost all of those writers and poets who had been most popular in the Republic of Vietnam—altogether some 129 authors—were banned outright, as were the works of many foreign authors, ranging from Mario Puzo to Françoise Sagan. In addition to banning the works of certain authors, another 932 specific books were banned. The stated goal was to "sweep away completely all remnants of the enslaving, reactionary culture of the enemy."[14] Many people, frightened by rumors, voluntarily burned all "inappropriate" or "decadent" reading mate-rial in their homes. The Westernized, individualistic, neo-*yin* dimension of modern Vietnamese society was neither dead nor for-gotten, but it was silent for the first time in many decades.

Yet there was no lack of communications activity in the city. All public channels of communication transmitted messages in support of the new *yang* ideology. Radio, television, newspapers, journals, poetry, songs, novels, motion pictures, all were transformed into high-volume, high-redundancy transmitters of selected themes, new values, and new role models. In a hundred different ways the new *yang* orthodoxy was inculcated, perfected, overdetermined, as multiple sources sang its praises, taught its virtues, explicated its values, rewarded conformity, and punished deviance.

Within twelve months more than 3,000,000 books were printed in Ho Chi Minh City, and some 170,000 books and 450,000 pictures (mostly of Ho Chi Minh) were sent down from Hanoi. The writings of Ho Chi Minh himself received the highest priority. Works by and about Marx, Lenin, and Engels were also featured, along with books presenting the achievements of the Vietnamese Communist party. Overnight To Huu, a devoted communist "Since Then" and now an important party official, became the most widely published poet in the south. Over 200 special Liberation Book Stores made these works readily available to the public.

Long lines had once formed outside theaters in Saigon to see movies such as *Love Story* or *The Exorcist*, and martial arts films from Hong Kong and Taiwan had enjoyed great popularity. But in Ho Chi Minh City a new film studio was organized to create motion pictures that exemplified and reinforced the new setting of the thermostat, that were designed to inculcate the new *yang* ideology. Such was the case for all mass media and public institutions. Formal adherence to the new dominant orthodoxy was required, not optional.

Schools were closed as educators were rushed to the south from Hanoi to remake them in conformity with the new *yang* ideology and worldview. School curricula were drastically revised, and textbooks were replaced by new ones shipped from Hanoi.[15] The Buddhist University of Van Hanh and the University of Saigon were incorporated into the massive new Ho Chi Minh University, administered from Hanoi by the national Ministry of Higher Education. The Hoa Hao University in Long Xuyen was dismantled.

But these changes, drastic and threatening as they appeared to millions of people in the south, were not enough to satisfy the devout Communists in Hanoi who felt compelled to impose their Marxist-Leninist version of *ly* upon the vigorous heterodoxy of the south. Flushed with victory that appeared to fulfill the dreams of fifty years of struggle and hardship, their ideological convictions seemed to be confirmed by reality. And so—like the Vietnamese Neo-Confucians they remained beneath their Marxist veneer, like the Nguyen emperors, and like Ngo Dinh Diem before them—they quickly set about to transform the alien reality of Saigon and the Mekong delta into conformity with the way, the Tao, the structure of reality as they conceived of it.

More than one million people in the Republic of Vietnam, out of a population of a little over twenty million, were ordered to report for "reeducation." According to the category to which they were assigned, they were instructed to bring along enough food and clothing to last for seven or thirty days. But there was little "education" awaiting these people, and very few would return home after thirty days. These were not "schools," as some tried to portray them, nor were they "prisons," as others claimed. They were psychological/spiritual "boot camps," places where human beings were to be literally "transformed" (*cai tao*), to be made over into "new people" (*nguoi moi*) whose beliefs and values and personalities would be better suited to the new socialist society being designed for them in Hanoi.

For hundreds of thousands of intellectuals, religious leaders, politicians, people who had worked with or for the Americans, soldiers, and civil servants, "reeducation" meant years of hard manual labor on starvation rations. Most who endured this would remember only an all-consuming and degrading hunger, maneuvering for a chance to drink the water their food had been cooked in, trying to catch birds and rats, scrambling to sneak a mouthful of wild berries on a work detail, wracking their brains for some means of obtaining any source of nourishment, however repulsive, to supplement their meager rations. Many died in these camps. Many more were broken there, either mentally or physically.

No group of people suffered more at the hands of the party than the writers and poets and journalists of the Republic of Vietnam. In April 1976 those literary artists who had not already fled the country or been arrested were rounded up in a series of swift raids, as if they were dangerous criminals, and trucked off to forced labor camps like a consignment of pigs to the market. A few examples taken from the lives of poets and writers already mentioned in this book can serve to illustrate the fate of hundreds of such people.

The noted journalist Nguyen Tu ("Fare Thee Well") was seized almost at once and incarcerated in prisons and labor camps for thirteen years. He now lives in France. The poet Thanh Tam Tuyen ("i need a secret place to kneel for my tiny little soul") spent five years in "reeducation" camps and now lives in Minnesota. Tran Da Tu ("I give you a gift of barbed wire, some creeping vine of this new age") and his wife, the illustrious poet and novelist Nha Ca (*Put on the Mourning Cloth for Hue*), were arrested at their home on April 3, 1976. She spent several years in reeducation camps and many more years as a political widow. He was kept in camps for nearly twelve years, until international protest led to his release and their subsequent resettlement to Sweden through official channels in 1988.[16]

One of the saddest fates was reserved for Thao Truong ("Color and Hue"), the gentle writer who had begged the ideologues on both sides not to teach the children to hate. His health broken by fifteen years in prison, he has been arrested, released, and rear-rested several times. Late in 1989 he was taken to the psychiatric ward of Cho Quan Hospital (the Vietnamese equivalent of Bedlam). As of 1990, according to relatives, he was back in prison.[17]

Everyone in the camps was there, in effect, indefinitely. There were no charges, no hearings, no sentences. No one knew when, if ever, they would be released. The power of their masters was total, and totally arbitrary. Most were released after two or three or four years, aged beyond their years, utterly cynical, concerned only with getting out of Vietnam or with the survival of themselves and their families in a society from which they were completely alienated. Tens of thousands, however, languished in these wretched camps for many more years, enduring not just the harsh physical conditions but the petty humiliations to which those deemed to be "unrepentant" or "stubbornly reactionary" were subjected.[18]

Meanwhile, other people were being moved around according to a master blueprint prepared in Hanoi that envisioned relocating ten million people within twenty years.[19] As a first step, about a million people were relocated, mainly from Ho Chi Minh City and other urban areas in the south, to "new economic zones," where they were expected to transform marginal ecological regions to productive farmland. There were a few successes, and many failures. And many people escaped back to the cities to lead an underground existence.

Another quarter of a million highland people were relocated by 1978. The tribal groups who lived "free in the forest" were supposed to "settle down to live in the valleys to grow food and industrial crops instead of continuing their unstable nomadic way of life on the mountaintops."[20] The highlanders would, it was hoped, become more "civilized," that is more like the Vietnamese. They were also to make room for an influx of industrious lowland Vietnamese, who were expected to exploit more effectively the upland ecosystems that seemed to lowland bureaucrats to be "empty" and "underutilized."

By 1987 the government had relocated approximately three million people. But by forcing tribal horticulturalists (whose way of life was neither unstable nor nomadic) to practice intensive fixed field agriculture in the valleys, and by trucking lowland Vietnamese into the mountains, the government experts had created maximum disjuncture between people's culture, their production techniques, and their environment. Traditional local cultures became a menace instead of a valuable resource when applied to unaccustomed tasks in unfamiliar environments. Environmental degradation, low productivity, and social stress have been inevitable.

By this time well over a million other people had fled the country in search of some more congenial social climate, unable or unwilling to adjust to the new setting of the thermostat. Some were caught and imprisoned. Countless thousands died at sea, victims of piracy, thirst and starvation, violent storms, unseaworthy vessels, and amateur navigators. Yet hundreds of thousands survived to become refugees in other lands while tens and eventually hundreds of thousands of others languished unwanted in bleak refugee camps in Thailand, Malaysia, the Philippines, Indonesia, and Hong Kong. Many are still in such camps, gamely pitting their fading hopes against growing despair.

This dangerous and illegal exodus continues. But meanwhile, since the establishment of an official Orderly Departure Program in 1980, over 130,000 Vietnamese have legally emigrated and another 670,000 applications for departure have been submitted. There are now over 750,000 Vietnamese living in the United States and about a million more living in other Western countries.[21]

The new rulers were especially disturbed by the vigor of small-scale capitalism in the south. The network of privately owned factories, small businesses, petty vendors, deal makers, and street hustlers who kept goods and money moving in Saigon was a disturbing anomaly in Ho Chi Minh City. From the perspective of the architects of the new society, over a million people in the south were "engaged in nonproductive commercial activity." So in March 1978 the government moved against "bourgeois trade." In Ho Chi Minh City alone about 30,000 businesses had their goods and assets frozen.[22] A smaller and more tightly controlled "socialist trade network" was supposed to replace this bewildering and undisciplined mass of diverse entrepreneurs who were in business simply to make a profit and who had no plan other than to improvise their operations as they went along, in response to a changing environment.

Not coincidentally, the ethnic Chinese were hit especially hard by these measures. Ethnic Chinese had fled in disproportionate numbers in the initial exodus of boat people in 1975 and 1976; by 1978 they began pouring out of the country in droves. By 1979 the

People's Republic of China had reportedly accepted 260,000 refugees from Vietnam, mostly Chinese.[23]

But Vietnam remained primarily an agricultural country, and the Mekong delta region south of Ho Chi Minh City contained over a third of the good farmland in all of the Socialist Republic of Vietnam. This was a very significant part of the national economy, too important to be left alone for very long. In July 1977 the party decided to push for the collectivization of agriculture in the south. They found few peasants, especially in the Mekong delta, who wished to participate; but this merely led to an effort to accelerate the creation of cooperatives.

Twenty years earlier collectivization of agriculture had been a difficult business in the north. Borrowing with only slight modification the Stalinist model with some Maoist touches, it had taken years of effort to get a modestly successful program of cooperatives functioning in the closed corporate communities of the' northern plains, those still much like the "traditional villages" described in earlier chapters. In such villages, so long as the new socialist collectivities remained coincident with the older and socially meaningful boundaries of neighborhood, hamlet, and village, the system worked, after a fashion. In many areas modest gains were achieved. The poorest of the poor gained better security against famine, and access to health care and education were greatly increased. And most people in the north were very poor to begin with. But the anticipated gains in productivity never materialized. Between 1958 and 1975, the production of food staples increased by only 10.9 percent while the population increased by 63.6 percent.[24] Even allowing for the inadequacy of the statistics, food production per capita declined.

But the villages of the Mekong delta had never been either closed or corporate in nature as those in the northern and central regions had been.[25] And the majority of delta farmers were relatively prosperous owner-operators. The south had already had a successful land reform program.[26] Perhaps more important, land had not been the trump card in the south that almost everyone had assumed it to be.[27] Technological innovations (like water pumps, high-yielding varieties of rice, chemical fertilizer) and improvements in transportation and communication had led to vigorous economic development in those areas not cut off by the war, and most people simply wanted to be left alone to earn a living.[28]

Although most of the inhabitants of the Mekong delta were farmers, they did not want their children to become farmers. Success for children was seen to lie outside of the village, and outside of agriculture.[29]

But the collectivization of agriculture in the Mekong delta was important to the new leaders for many reasons. Collectivization was a means to simultaneously extract "surplus" production from the most productive segment of the economy, stifle social differentiation and promote equality, and prevent the spontaneous generation of capitalism.[30] This model, neat and logical as it seemed, rested on the dubious assumption that the new leadership would be able to achieve a significant increase in production through so-called economies of scale and more "rational" division of labor and allocation of resources. Yet, tragically, although not (to some) unexpectedly, as the government seized land and accelerated the movement toward full collectivization, production dropped.

Lack of fuel and chemical fertilizers, bad weather, and bureaucratic bumbling combined with passive resistance by unhappy farmers to make a bad situation worse. As production fell, fearing that rising food prices would contribute to further unrest in urban areas (where people were already grumbling about shortages of consumer goods and scurrilously denouncing their new masters), the government tried to force peasants to sell their rice to the government at very low prices. This, of course, led to hoarding, a resurgence of black market activities, and a suspicious peasantry with very little motivation to produce more than they could eat. Some even fed any surplus rice to their livestock.[31]

These domestic crises were only half of the woe for Vietnam's leaders. Foreign policy debacles further exacerbated an already desperate situation. Relations with Pol Pot's new regime in Cambodia had been steadily deteriorating. The aggressive, xenophobic Khmer Rouge nurtured grievances against the Vietnamese that went back for centuries. And they began attacking border settlements. Finally, convinced that Pol Pot intended to conquer territory that had once been Cambodian but which had long been part of Vietnam, and perceiving that he was persecuting ethnic Vietnamese in Cambodia and along the border, the party leaders sent PAVN troops surging into Cambodia late in 1978 to put an end to the Pol Pot regime. By January 1979 Vietnamese troops occupied much of Cambodia, and a new government was installed in Phnom

Phen. But fighting continued, and to maintain the status quo Vietnam had to keep about 200,000 troops in Cambodia and conduct constant counterinsurgency operations.

Meanwhile, the People's Republic of China to the north had been a staunch supporter of the Pol Pot regime. The PRC resented the growing closeness of the Vietnamese to the Russians. And they perceived that the Vietnamese were persecuting ethnic Chinese to an unprecedented degree. So in February 1979, to teach the ungrateful Vietnamese a lesson, 100,000 Chinese Communist troops poured into Vietnam through the same mountain passes used by invaders from the north in the first, tenth, twelfth, thirteenth, fifteenth, and eighteenth centuries.

After seventeen days of fierce fighting, during which they suffered heavy losses, the Chinese withdrew. The Vietnamese had repulsed Chinese invaders one more time. But the economic costs were high. The Chinese inflicted considerable damage, destroying towns, roads, bridges, factories. And low-level conflict continued. Vietnam had to maintain a very large military force along the Chinese border while fighting a war of pacification in Cambodia.[32]

While not yet "at peace" after nearly fifty years of struggle, at one level the Communist party of Vietnam had finally achieved its goals. The country was free of foreign domination and was reunited. Arts and letters, science, industry, commerce, and even agriculture were once again in the service of and under the control of the state, and the state was firmly controlled by the party.

Despite radical differences in form and content, at an abstract level things were very much as they had been during the heavily *yang* regime of Le Thanh Tong in the second half of the fifteenth century. It should have been, by the values of the new leaders, a golden age. Literature and art in the broadest sense were again didactic rather than expressive, public rather than personal, social rather than individualistic. Once again a strong *yang* reaction was following a period of *yin* extremism.

In this new *yang* milieu the path of upward mobility rested upon demonstrated mastery of a new set of values, those of the new socialist person. To sit above and eat before others in the newly constituted world of Ho Chi Minh City, one had to be reliably immersed in a new social ethos in which individualism was anathema. A card indicating membership in the Communist party replaced the dragon hat of the successful examination candidate in an earlier age, and the canons of Marxism-Leninism replaced those of Neo-Confucianism as the ethical touchstone by which qualifications for elite status were evaluated.

This process of readjustment in the distribution of values in society entailed the simultaneous operation of diverse mechanisms. Not only was the bulk of the population subjected to intense resocialization in situ; certain key elements of the population in question were relocated: some forcibly, some through persuasion, and others by their own choice in reaction to changing circumstances. For millions of individual human beings this was, and for many it remains, a tragedy of unspeakable magnitude, but at a more abstract level it may be seen as a readjustment of the sociocultural system, a predictable and perhaps inevitable phase in resetting the social thermostat. The particular details and the specific people involved might, of course, have been quite different. But after a hundred years of controversy and thirty years of war, the shift to any new equilibrium was bound to be traumatic for some considerable proportion of the population. Vietnam provides us with a notable illustration of Bateson's observation that the most significant points in history are "the moments when attitudes were changed. These are the moments when people are hurt because of their former 'values.'"

There is nothing mystical or teleological about this process. It can be readily explicated in cybernetic terms. In the south in 1975 and immediately thereafter, as in the north in 1954–1955, the distribution of values in society was significantly altered by the departure of a high proportion of those individuals who deviated the most from the new normative patterns. Thus those "deviants" who remained were reduced to a size that could more effectively be convinced or coerced to conform by the new control group within their available resources. Vietnamese society quickly became very *yang*.

Under vigorous leadership spearheaded by the Communist party, Vietnam seemed destined to become an ever more active, group-oriented, disciplined, boundary-conscious, corporate, centralizing, redundant, and doctrinaire social system. Its decision makers and opinion leaders were resolute of purpose, firm in their beliefs, and sustained by a remarkably deep faith in the essential correctness of their doctrines and in the inevitability of success in achieving their goals. Millions of dedicated followers shared this faith and these beliefs. The social thermostat appeared to be fixed quite firmly for some time to come.

Yet the *Tao Te Ching* reminds all of us: "Nature is taciturn. Gales do not blow all morning; Rain does not pour all day."[33] Within this *yin-yang* framework, the particular form and content of ideology and government is irrelevant. And neither enthusiasm nor firm purpose can long serve as a safeguard against destiny. The workings of *yin* and *yang* play no favorites. They function through mechanisms that are above politics and prejudice of any kind. "Heaven and earth are without human feelings. To them every single thing is disposable."[34] The Tao operates in a thoroughly impartial manner; and, it would appear, inexorably. Any strong *yang* action will provoke a corresponding *yin* reaction. Too much of anything provokes its opposite, the ancient sages had taught; but twentieth-century Vietnam has always been ruled by people who subscribed to various nineteenth-century versions of lineal evolution.

A New Yin Reaction

Thus, by the early 1980s a new wave of *yin* reaction had arisen, within the party as well as outside it, in the north as well as in the south, forcing a relaxation, and in some cases even a reversal, of rigid and dogmatic policies that had made Vietnam one of the poorest countries in the world. After so many years of struggle, Vietnamese were dismayed to discover that they had moved no further up the status hierarchy of the world village, were no closer to the head of the table, than they had been when they began.

Many factors were involved in pushing Vietnam toward economic and ecological collapse, some beyond the control of any leadership, some caused by the debilitating effects of forty years of virtually uninterrupted war. But the rigid *yang* orthodoxy of the Vietnamese Communist leadership failed in its excess as surely as the excess of *yin* that had preceded it in the south. In both core areas of Vietnam there were problems of low productivity, land degradation, and a disenchanted peasantry. With agriculture stagnating, foreign exchange nearly exhausted, foreign aid low and shrinking, industrial capacity damaged by war, rebuilding stalled by a lack of capital, consumer goods in short supply, and per capita food consumption declining, the party began to sustain severe criticism and was forced to reverse its relentless pressure to transform Vietnam into its own vision of a utopian socialist paradise.

Criticism was coming not just from abroad, or from anticommunist elements in the south. Criticism was now coming from within the party, from southern revolutionaries, and even from people raised and educated in the Democratic Republic of Vietnam, and it cast a skeptical light into every corner of society. The north–dominated party had "managed" Vietnamese society into stagnant mediocrity. And with total control came total responsibility. If the party wished to tell people how to farm, how to write poetry, how to conduct business, they had also to explain why the results were so unsatisfactory.

More than forty years after seizing power in the August Revolution of 1945, the party presided over a Vietnam that had become one of the "least developed" nations in the entire world. The 1980s annual per capita income in the Socialist Republic was one of the lowest in the world.[35] For a variety of reasons, some the inevitable results of extended warfare, some a direct result of population growth increasing pressure upon limited resources, Vietnam was on the verge of economic, social, and ecological disaster.

Nor was a downward trend limited to economics and agriculture. Literature and art, education, commerce and industry, science and technology, journalism, entertainment and sports, scholarship and religion—all atrophied under the stultifying effects of heavy-handed guidance from an army of bureaucrats and officious party functionaries. With the stagnation of arts and letters under the stewardship of the party, writers and poets were asking the party to justify its control over these matters in light of the unsatisfactory results.

There had always been an underground literature in the north that pilloried the Communist establishment in the north. Nguyen Chi Thien, a remnant of the 1956 critical outpouring that brought Phan Khoi to grief (and Thien himself frequently to "reeducation camps" ever since), sneaked a hand-written manuscript of poems into the British embassy in Hanoi in 1980. No one knows what has happened to him since then. Decrying the "red lords" who "store away all dreams in jail," he had poured out his outrage into poems aptly called "Flowers from Hell."[36]

> More than ten years I've lived in jail,
> the very heart of their regime.
> . . . .
> If Uncle and the Party, let's suppose,
> allowed free movements in and out,
> Grandfather Marx's paradise
> would soon become the wilds where monkeys roam.
> . . . .

> On Uncle Ho's own soil
> life's sadder than a tomb.
>
> .   .   .   .
>
> The Party holds you down and you lie still.
> When all are equal—scholars, dunces, beasts—
> the paramount, hair-graying question is:
> two meals, oh for two meals.

People like Nguyen Chi Thien could be dismissed by the authorities as products of the old colonial regime, too selfish and too brainwashed to accept a wholesome socialist discipline for the common good. But beginning around 1980, there was a palpable "resurgence of criticism and independence" within the socialist-realist literary establishment itself.[37] Even the journal of the Association of Vietnamese Writers, *Arts and Letters*, began pointing out that not only was Vietnamese literature poor, it continued to get worse. Many writers and poets, especially younger ones, had come to believe that too much control by the party had sapped literary artists of the creativity and vitality essential to produce good literature.

While some liveliness has undoubtedly returned to Vietnamese literature in recent years, and some superior novels and films have appeared as a result, the relationship between the party and its writers remains ambiguous. While some party leaders encourage more openness, others still see it as an insidious process that will lead to ideological impurity. The editor of *Arts and Letters* who opened these issues to discussion has since lost his job, yet others speak out more forcefully than ever before.[38]

Against this background, numerous reforms have been initiated in recent years. Market incentives have been revived, and many management decisions have been returned to local farmers. Newspapers and journals, writers and poets, entrepreneurs and farmers have all been given more freedom to think for themselves. But the changes are uneven and tenuous, and the debate over the setting of the social thermostat in the Socialist Republic of Vietnam is intense.

In 1988 the first protest march in Saigon since the fall of the GVN in 1975 took place. Thousands of former southern revolutionaries, "Vietcong" leaders with impeccable war records and decades of service to the party, formed an organization called the Club of Resistance Fighters. Its members included General Tra, the former commander of forces in the Mekong delta, and many other former high-ranking officers and officials. They criticized government and party policies, and called for the resignation of some individuals. They called for more sweeping reforms in line with some of the old NLF/PRG/Alliance programmatic statements.

Disillusioned southern revolutionaries, southern farmers and northern farmers, intellectuals, writers and poets, businessmen, and housewives (not to mention those who espouse other ideologies) came together in the 1980s to form a fresh wind, another wave of *yin* reaction. Like the Buddhists and the Dai Viet, the students and the intellectuals and the young army officers who came together in opposition to the Diem regime in 1963, these people are unhappy for many different reasons. Their goals and values are not identical. But that is the essence of *yin*.

Powerful *yang* structures always arouse many different people for many different reasons. Then symbols can take on different meanings to different people (like the Buddhist protests or the suicide of Nguyen Tuong Tam), unifying disparate groups of people, temporarily, in the communitas of a common cause, the relaxation of pressure from the single *yang* core that they all see as the source of their discomfort. The debate over the setting of the social thermostat in Vietnam will not be over for a long time to come. Such debates never truly end; such is the nature of the Tao.

The age-old opposition between *yin* and *yang*, between the organization of diversity and the replication of uniformity, between freedom and order, will doubtless continue for some time. This is the human condition, but all Vietnamese, indeed everyone, may hope that the swings back and forth become less extreme. The outcome is unpredictable, but regardless of the specifics, a balance between *nhan* and *nghia*, history teaches us, will be beneficent.

The plurality of conditions and values and ways of life that constitute Vietnam will not disappear in the coming decades. To achieve the happy and prosperous Vietnam toward which Ho Chi Minh thought he was leading them, party leaders must adapt their policies to fit the people and their specific local conditions instead of trying to remake the people and the land itself to fit their policies. None of the factions need abandon their primary values to work together for the common good. And today, as poverty and environmental degradation and social unrest threaten to come together in a self-amplifying downward spiral, the Vietnamese face one of the gravest crises in their long history.

A Concluding Thought

Sociocultural systems seem to function best within a certain range in the ratio between entropy and redundancy, between public and private interest, between uniformity and diversity, between individual freedom and social control, between Eros and Arante, *nhan* and *nghia*. Metaphors such as *yin* and *yang*, or the Tao, are useful heuristic devices because they direct our attention to system characteristics such as these, which might otherwise be easily overlooked in analysis.

As we have seen, in twentieth-century Vietnam such considerations were overlooked, and such balance has not been maintained. The past sixty years of Vietnamese literature provides us with metaphorical insight into the nature of this imbalance. It illustrates how Vietnamese intellectuals became polarized into two distinct groups and how each threatened and frightened the other, how and why each rejected the other. Each group became deaf to the other's songs, perhaps because they had to reject all the more vehemently that which was repressed but still lurked within themselves.

Thus a generation of romantics became polarized and fanaticized as they sought to salvage identities shattered by the collision between the old and the new, producing two societies and two literatures, which have yet to be reconciled. This cultural schism and the pain and anger it has caused must be healed if the badly needed and long delayed reconstruction of Vietnam is to succeed.

The *yin-yang* paradigm that permeated traditional Vietnamese thought, in both its folk and its elite version, asserted that the health of the individual organism was intimately bound to a balance of *yin* and *yang* within the individual and between the individual and his or her environment. Society itself, from this time-honored but discarded perspective, was harmonious and prosperous precisely to the extent that a balance between *yin* and *yang* was maintained. Vietnam still requires what it has lacked for so long, a balance between *yin* and *yang*, between entropy and redundancy, between individual rights and the common welfare, between freedom and discipline, between *nhan* and *nghia*. Somehow, someday, Vietnamese culture must become reintegrated. The old balance is gone forever, but a new balance can and must be devised.

Both systems theory and the metaphor of *yin* and *yang* remind us to keep our attention firmly directed toward the emerging context and not be distracted by fixation upon ephemeral details of content and form except as they relate to and form a part of that context. Those of us concerned about patterns of continuity and change in human society in any of its myriad dimensions would do well to remember what both Lao Tse and Gregory Bateson have told us in provocatively different ways: *It is the context that evolves.* This is the deepest lesson of Vietnam, for Vietnamese and Americans alike. But it is not an easy one for any of us to learn, for it demands of us a fundamental revision of the way we perceive and strive to shape reality.

We must all seek, and attempt to understand, the larger pattern that connects Vietnamese across ideological divides and emotional biases. We must work toward enabling people who use different vocabularies and perceive reality through different models to "give a credible account of themselves to one another." We must recontextualize our own thoughts and feelings and actions, and those of a wide variety of other people, so as to make the shared tragedy more comprehensible to all concerned.

None of us, Americans or Vietnamese, can continue to marginalize all those who have opposed us or disappointed us. The human cost is simply too high. Americans and Vietnamese of all political persuasions and all generations and all walks of life must work to expand the sense of "we" and to diminish the sense of "they." If we cannot humanize those whose destinies have impinged upon our own, if we cannot increase empathy and vanquish self-righteousness, if we cannot expand our moral imaginations to discern and accept the pattern that connects us all in a common human condition, then we shall all continue to have lost the war in Vietnam, to perpetuate a struggle in which there are no winners.

Notes

Chapter 1

1. Rambo 1973 provides a detailed account of these ecological contrasts and their implications for differences in social organization.

2. This section is a greatly condensed and slightly modified version of Jamieson 1981a, 37–159. For a brief but scholarly summary of Vietnamese history, see Whitmore 1986.

3. Osborne 1984, 120; Pham Duc Duong 1982.

4. See Jamieson 1981c.

5. See Jeremy Davidson 1975; Nguyen Khac Vien (n.d.).

6. For a thorough scholarly treatment of early Vietnamese history, see Taylor 1983.

7. See Taylor 1988.

8. For examples of this poetry in translation, see Nguyen Ngoc Bich 1985, 80–83; Nguyen Ngoc Bich 1975, 4–10; Huynh Sanh Thong 1979, 18–20. Raffel 1968 also provides some relevant translations (pp. 21–23), but with serious errors in annotation.

9. See Whitmore 1985 for a detailed discussion of this period.

10. For examples of this literature, see Nguyen Ngoc Bich 1975, 92–116; Huynh Sanh Thong 1979, 105–15, 157–69.

11. See Woodside 1971 and 1973 for detailed and insightful discussions of late-eighteenth- and nineteenth-century Vietnam.

12. Ho Tai Hue Tam 1985, 25–26; Rambo 1982, 407; Nguyen Ngoc Bich 1975, 24; Hickey 1964, 55–56.

13. Some contemporary scholars might feel that this sentence overstates the case. Whitmore (1987, 16), a historian who responsibly represents the opposing point of view, has observed, "A large gap presently exists between premodern historians (like myself)

who follow the development of an initially shallow Confucianism in Vietnam and students of the twentieth century, especially anthropologists, who have found a deep-set Confucianism in modern Vietnamese society." He and I agree that "the major issue now existing is: How Confucian did the Vietnamese become? And when?" But that most educated Vietnamese living in the first half of the twentieth century saw their traditional heritage as strongly Neo-Confucian and equated this with the reign of Le Thanh Thong (1460–1497) is, I believe, not really debatable. I am interested, for the purposes of this book, in popular perceptions that were "true" (i.e., socially accepted) in the historical present of the 1920s, 1930s, and 1940s.

14. The phrase "root paradigm" comes from the work of Victor Turner, whose writings (1969, 1974) have influenced my thinking. Rappaport (1979, 97–144, especially 124, 127, 130) discusses systems of thought in which everything is an icon of everything else, probably inspiring this phrase.

15. Ngo Duc Thinh (1989) discusses folk views of diet and health in terms of *yin* and *yang*. Hickey (1964, 7) more generally discusses the concept of harmony in Vietnamese folk medicine.

16. See Jamieson 1981a, 18–29; Jamieson 1984, 322–28.

17. My understanding and use of cybernetic theory has been most heavily influenced by Bateson (1972, 1980) and Karl Deutsch (1966). Laszlo (1972), Buckley (1967), and Bertalanffy (1968) were also sources of stimulation. What I have done with their ideas, of course, does not gain legitimacy by invoking their names.

18. On this point see Bateson 1980, 47.

19. Bateson 1972, 470–71. See also Bateson and Bateson 1988, 37–42.

20. Bateson 1972, 476.

21. This is, in general, the view of Paul Mus, which greatly influenced many American scholars in the 1950s and 1960s and became popularized in simplified form by Frances Fitzgerald in *Fire in the Lake*.

22. This view had its origins in a legitimate effort to correct a one-sided view that had characterized much traditional Vietnamese historiography and the work of many French scholars, which played down the importance both of indigenous culture and of non-Confucian borrowed elements in Vietnamese culture. Especially during the past fifteen years, however, for reasons that have often been more political than scholarly, the pendulum has swung too far in the other direction.

23. For some recent discussions of the persistence of these logi-

cally contradictory but (I suggest) functionally complementary principles on the ground in recent decades, especially in the areas of kinship and family/household organization, see: Hy Van Luong 1984, 742–44; Hy Van Luong 1989, 742, 749, 752, 754; Haines 1984, 312–13; Haines 1986, 208; Nguyen Tu Chi, n.d., 36–37, 69–71, 80–89, 115–16, 118.

24. Le Thi Que 1976, 115.

25. Chaliand 1969, 60.

26. Le Thi Que 1976, 115; see also Vuong G. Thuy 1976, 29.

27. Huynh Sanh Thong 1979, 41. See also Ta Van Tai 1988, 147–48 on this point.

28. Steinberg 1971, 38; Jamieson 1981a, 84–87, 98–104.

29. For more detail on this model of the traditional family, with illustrative examples and further documentation, see Jamieson 1986b; 1981a, 206–68. See also Le Thi Que 1976, 1986; Jackson 1987.

30. Le Thi Que 1976, 59.

31. There was probably considerable variation in the relative freedom young Vietnamese had to choose, or influence the choice of, a marriage partner, according to time, region, social class, and family tradition. See Ta Van Tai 1988, 214–15; Hickey 1964, 100.

32. For more detail, illustrative examples, and further documentation, see Jamieson 1981a, 261–85; Jamieson 1985 and Jamieson 1986a are two shortened versions of this.

33. Dao Duy Anh 1951, 128.

34. Nguyen Khac Vien 1974, 39, 167.

35. Several works of early modern Vietnamese fiction depict this characteristic. See, for example, Khai Hung's 1936 short story, "Two Scenes of Decline" (Hai Canh Truy Lac) or Thach Lam's 1939 short story "The Family of Mother Le" (Nha Me Le).

36. Woodside 1971, 154.

37. See Gourou 1975, 217.

38. This section is based mainly on the work of Gourou. See especially Gourou 1955, 540–83; Gourou 1975, 127, 154.

39. The nature of the *giap* is complex and variable. See, for example, Toan Anh 1968, 142–47; Dao Duy Anh 1951, 128; and especially Nguyen Tu Chi, n.d., 44–59, 68–69, 71, 81, 97–119, for a somewhat different emphasis.

40. Based largely on field notes, 1967. See Jamieson 1981a, 237–38. See also Dao Duy Anh 1951, 218–21; Durand 1959; Simon and Simon-Barouh 1973; Nguyen Khac Kham 1983, 28; Coulet 1929, 19–21.

41. See Phan Ke Binh 1970, 178–80; Nguyen Tu Chi, n.d., 87.

42. Woodside 1971, 130–32.

43. McAlister and Mus 1970, 31–32.
44. Rambo 1982.
45. See, for example, Ta Van Tai 1988, 41, 93–94, 217–18.

Chapter 2

1. This chapter is a shortened version of Jamieson 1981a, 396–509. The period covered in this chapter, 1859–1930, has been treated in some detail elsewhere, from several other perspectives. In particular, see Marr 1971; Osborne 1969; Duiker 1976; Huynh Kim Khanh 1982, 1–188.
2. Buttinger 1961, 115; Ta Van Tai 1988, 140–41.
3. Ta Van Tai 1988, 110–20, 124–25.
4. Woodside 1971, 28; Ta Van Tai 1988, 154–57; Pham Van Son 1961, 301–2.
5. Pham Van Son 1961, 380–83; Hall 1964, 608–9, 611.
6. Ta Van Tai 1988, 168–73; Hall 1964, 608–11; Pham Van Son 1961, 380–83.
7. Steinberg 1971, 127–30; Pham Van Son 1962, 72–84.
8. Pham Van Son 1962, 125–44, 163–73.
9. Pham Van Son 1962, 42–43.
10. Marr 1971, 32; Pham Van Son 1962, 190.
11. Thanh Lang 1967, 65; Tran My Van 1976, 153.
12. Thanh Lang 1967, 66.
13. Ibid.; see also Tran My Van 1976, 142.
14. Marr 1971, 24–25; Pham Van Son 1962, 145–62.
15. Marr 1971, 35.
16. Tran My Van 1976, 23.
17. Ibid., 26–28.
18. Adapted from ibid.
19. From ibid., 29.
20. Pham Van Son 1962, 240.
21. Hickey 1988, 15–16; Hall 1964, 620–22; Pham Van Son 1962, 295–316.
22. Marr 1971, 40–41.
23. Hickey 1988, 17–18; Hall 1964, 624–25; Pham Van Son 1962, 381–87.
24. Hall 1964, 627; Pham Van Son 1962, 393–404.
25. Marr 1971, 55, 61.
26. Tran My Van 1976 provides a sensitive account of the lives and writings of these two men. For additional English-language translations of their poetry, see Nguyen Ngoc Bich 1975, 145–50; Huynh Sanh Thong 1979, 186–87, 202–10.
27. Xuan Dieu 1970, 64; Tran My Van 1976, 208.

28. Xuan Dieu et al., 1971, 9–10; Pham The Ngu 1965, 47; Thanh Lang 1967, 152–53; Tran My Van 1976, 161.

29. Xuan Dieu et al. 1971, 91; Tran My Van 1976, 164–65.

30. Xuan Dieu et al. 1971, 118.

31. Xuan Dieu et al. 1971, 92–93; see also Tran My Van 1976, 166–67; Nguyen Ngoc Bich 1975, 145.

32. Xuan Dieu et al. 1971, 131.

33. This section draws on Tran My Van 1976, 201–2; Doan Quoc Sy and Viet Tu 1959, 117–19; Xuan Dieu et al. 1971, 125.

34. Xuan Dieu et al. 1971, 75.

35. Ibid., 101.

36. Ibid., 200.

37. Ibid., 141.

38. Marr 1971, 55–86.

39. Mus 1952, 126–27; quoted in Buttinger 1967, 447.

40. Vu Duc Bang 1973, 85; Buttinger 1967, 33–34.

41. Vu Duc Bang 1973, 31; Marr 1971, 77; Buttinger 1967, 139–40.

42. Nguyen Hien Le 1968, 62.

43. Vinh Sinh 1988b, 108; Shiraishi Masaya 1988, 58; Steinberg 1987, 314–15; Duiker 1976, 35–37; Marr 1971, 98–100; Pham Van Son 1963, 358; Fairbank et al. 1965, 384–94.

44. Vu Duc Bang 1973, 33; Nguyen Hien Le 1968, 26–27; Vinh Sinh 1988b, 110–11.

45. Nguyen Hien Le 1968, 34; Marr 1971, 102, 109–13; Vu Duc Bang 1973, 53–90; Pham Van Son 1963, 362–64.

46. Duiker 1976, 52–53.

47. Conflicting estimates are given of the number of Vietnamese students in Japan. There were perhaps about one hundred who began in 1907, and two hundred altogether by summer 1908. See Buttinger 1967, 515; Marr 1971, 111, 141, 143; Vu Duc Bang 1973, 54; Nguyen Hien Le 1968, 37; Steinberg 1971, 304; Duiker 1976, 44–45; Pham Van Son 1963, 371.

48. Nguyen Hien Le 1968, 55–74.

49. Ibid., 82.

50. Nguyen Hien Le 1968, 82–83; Marr 1971, 169–70; Steinberg 1971, 305.

51. Vu Duc Bang 1973, 66–67.

52. Translation from Tran My Van 1976, 152.

53. Nguyen Hien Le 1968, 66.

54. Duiker 1976, 56–57; Marr 1971, 181.

55. Buttinger 1967, 55–62; Thompson 1937, 84; Pham Van Son 1963, 412–14.

56. Buttinger 1967, 464–65.

57. Ibid., 51–58, 61, 529–30; Thompson 1937, 186–87.

58. Buttinger 1967, 58.

59. Buttinger 1967, 56, 59–60; Thompson 1937, 188–91.

60. Thompson 1937, 162–64; Buttinger 1967, 72–73; Marr 1971, 187–93.

61. Marr 1971, 187–93; Thompson 1937, 80–81; Buttinger 1967, 45, 50, 55; Pham Van Son 1963, 414–19.

62. Nguyen Hien Le 1968, 117–24; Vu Duc Bang 1973, 70–71, 92; Marr 1971, 188–93; Pham Van Son 1963, 415–19.

63. Buttinger 1967, 457.

64. Fitzgerald 1972, 108.

65. Marr 1971, 146–49; Fairbank et al. 1965, 750; Duiker 1976, 66–68; Steinberg 1971, 119–304.

66. Quoted in Pham The Ngu 1965, 105; Huynh Van Tong 1973, 89. Original source was an interview in *Tan Van*, March 28, 1935.

67. Nguyen Hien Le 1968, 45.

68. Ibid., 55, 57, 79.

69. Thanh Lang 1967, 179; Duiker 1976, 112; Pham The Ngu 1965, 96; Hoang Ngoc Thanh 1973, 206–7; Vu Duc Ban 1973, 43, 88.

70. Huynh Van Tong 1973, 58–59, 69, 254; Duiker 1976, 112; Pham Van Son 1963, 83.

71. Huynh Van Tong 1973, 54–55.

72. Ibid., 55.

73. Quoted in Pham The Ngu 1965, 66.

74. Quoted in Ibid., 67.

75. The following paragraphs about these two men draw upon Pham The Ngu 1965, 68–85; Thanh Lang 1967, 27–38; Hoang Ngoc Thanh 1973, 194–96.

76. Marr 1971, 35–36; Pham Van Son 1962, 276–390.

77. Huynh Van Tong 1973, 65–66, 78, 88; Thanh Lang 1967, 183; Hoang Ngoc Thanh 1973, 212; Duiker 1976, 112–13.

78. The first public high school was opened in 1907 when the Dong Kinh Nghia Thuc movement was at its peak. The French selected a specialist from the mother country to undertake the difficult task of establishing the new public school system to compete with the shock waves of the Dong Kinh Nghia Thuc movement and the seductive appeal of Phan Boi Chau from Japan. The thirty-five-year-old educator who rushed to Vietnam and organized a high school in Hanoi to initiate modern public education in Vietnam was named Cyprian Mus. He brought his family with him, including his five-year-old son Paul, who would graduate from that very high school twelve years later and go on to become one of the foremost scholars of Southeast Asia in the Western academic community. See McAlister and Mus 1970, vii, 4, 7–8.

79. Hoang Ngoc Thanh 1973, 204, 235.

80. Vinh Sinh 1988b, 126–28; Marr 1971, 216–18; Duiker 1976, 70–71; Pham Van Son 1963, 446, 452.

81. Duiker 1976, 72.

82. Huynh Van Tong 1973, 88; Pham The Ngu 1965, 107; Hoang Ngoc Thanh 1973, 204–5.

83. Pham The Ngu 1965, 107; Duiker 1976, 114–15.

84. Quoted in Duiker 1976, 114.

85. Pham The Ngu 1965, 104–5.

86. *Indochina Journal* (Dong Duong Tap Chi), no. 22.

87. Pham The Ngu 1965, 112–13; Duiker 1976, 114.

88. In Pham The Ngu 1966, 22–23.

89. Pham The Ngu 1965, 114–15.

90. Nguyen Huyen Anh 1967, 355, 356, 482; Pham The Ngu 1965, 125, 282–84, 352; Huynh Van Tong 1973, 91; Thanh Lang 1967, 234–52.

91. Pham The Ngu 1965, 120; Thanh Lang 1967, 216–20.

92. Duiker 1976, 130.

93. Thompson 1937, 292.

94. Pham The Ngu 1965, 288–93.

95. Ibid., 286–87.

96. Ibid., 284.

97. Ibid., 284–85.

98. Ibid., 285.

99. *South Wind* (Nam Phong) 1 (2) (August 1917): 89–92.

100. *South Wind* 1 (4): 207–17.

101. *South Wind*, no. 25 (July 1919).

102. Pham The Ngu 1965, 151–67.

103. Ibid., 167–70.

104. Marr 1971, 214.

105. Robequaine 1944, 158–63; Frederick 1973, 98–99; Marr 1971, 261.

106. Isoart 1961, 184; Nguyen The Anh 1970, 212.

107. Nguyen The Anh 1970, 258; Buttinger 1967, vol. 1, 532.

108. Dao Duy Anh 1951, 339–40.

109. Nguyen The Anh 1970, 198; Marr 1971, 261; Buttinger 1967, vol. 1, 532.

110. Nguyen The Anh 1970, 240–42.

111. Fall 1967a, 32–33.

112. Truong Buu Lam 1973, 245–46.

113. Marr 1971, 263.

114. Nguyen The Anh 1970, 203–9.

115. Osborne 1973; Frederick 1973; Marr 1970, 262, 268–69.

116. Huynh Kim Khanh 1982, 57–63; Tran Van Giau 1973, 18–

22; Marr 1971, 262–63.

117. Lacouture 1966, 15–60; Marr 1971, 253–57; Bui Huu Khanh 1973, passim.

118. Huynh Kim Khanh 1982, 151–62; Buttinger 1967, vol. 1, 214–20.

Chapter 3

1. This chapter is a condensed and reorganized version of Jamieson 1981a, 510–644. For additional information and a different perspective on some of the issues discussed in this chapter, see Marr 1981; Duiker 1976; Woodside 1976.

2. Salleh 1977, 9–10, 81–82; Fairbank et al. 1965, 274–78, 730–31, 744, 762.

3. Woodside 1976, 77–89.

4. Quoted in Pham The Ngu 1965, 422.

5. Ibid.

6. Ibid., 433.

7. Thanh Lang 1967, 606.

8. Pham The Ngu 1965, 423–34.

9. Hoang Ngoc Thanh 1973, 204, 235; Thompson 1937, 292.

10. Le Thi Que 1976, 89.

11. Ibid., 66, 67, 127.

12. Thanh Lang 1967, 710.

13. See Cao Thi Nhu Quynh and John C. Schafer 1988a for more discussion of *To Tam* and its place in Vietnamese literary history. Their argument, developed elsewhere (1988b), that earlier novels had been written in the south, is undoubtedly correct. But these earlier works, while innovative in both content and style, were, as the authors note, more conservative in moral and psychological terms. *To Tam* best illustrates the psychological and cultural discontinuity I emphasize in this chapter. My discussion reflects what people expressed to me in conversations and what was being taught in the schools in Saigon during the 1960s. Earlier southern writers like Ho Bieu Chanh had little influence on the Hanoi literary scene in the 1920s and 1930s and were of minor importance in terms of the battle between the "old" and the "new," in large part because they straddled the two and emphasized story telling within a cultural context rather than efforts to effect (or resist) cultural change.

14. Schafer 1972, 109; Raffel 1968, 18.

15. Thanh Lang 1967, 665–67; Pham The Ngu 1965, 307–14; Marr 1981, 107–10.

16. *Phu Nu Tan Van* (Women's News), no. 122 (March 10, 1932).

17. Nguyen Tan Long and Nguyen Huu Trong 1968, vol. 1, 164–66.

18. Pham The Ngu 1965, 548–49.

19. Thanh Lang 1967, 789–90.

20. Dewey 1962, 76.

21. Ibid., 81.

22. Ibid., 168.

23. This story was published in *Nguoi Quay To* (The Silk Spinner) in 1927. See Nhat Thinh 1971, 50–52.

24. Nhat Thinh 1971, 37–40.

25. *Mores* (*Phong Hoa*), no. 87 (March 2, 1934).

26. Nguyen Tan Long and Nguyen Huu Trong 1968, vol. 1, 246–47.

27. Ibid., 260–61.

28. Nguyen Duy Dien n.d., 55–56.

29. Thanh Lang 1967, 655–63.

30. E.g., *Mores*, no. 180 (March 27, 1936).

31. Quoted in Nguyen Duy Dien and Bang Phong 1960, 55.

32. Quoted in Pham The Ngu 1965, 470–71.

33. Davidson 1988, 6–8; Patti 1980, 479–80, 381, passim; Huynh Kim Khanh 1982, 257–59.

34. On Vo Nguyen Giap, see Marr 1981, 327–29, passim; Patti 1980, 483–84 and passim; Davidson 1988, 3–26 and passim; Huynh Kim Khanh, 259; and of course Giap's own writings.

35. Pham The Ngu 1965, 442–43.

36. Nhat Thinh 1971, 110–21; Marr 1981, 179.

37. Pham The Ngu 1965, 488–89.

38. *Mores*, no. 135 (February 8, 1935); Nguyen Tan Long and Nguyen Huu Trong 1968, vol. 1, 245–46. See Nguyen Ngoc Bich 1975, 160–62, and Huynh Sanh Thong in the *Vietnam Forum*, no. 7 (Winter-Spring 1986): 8–11, for other translations.

39. Nguyen Tan Long and Nguyen Huu Trong 1968, vol. 1, 651.

40. Ibid., 653.

41. Ibid., 665–56.

42. Ibid., vol. 2, 416–17.

43. Ibid., 421.

44. Ibid., 415. (For English-language translations of other poems by Che Lan Vien, see Nguyen Ngoc Bich 1975, 166–69.)

45. Ibid., 535.

46. Ibid., 432–34.

47. Ibid., 434–35. (For another translation, see Nguyen Ngoc Bich 1975, 164–165.)

48. Ibid., vol. 1, 183.

49. Ibid., 175.

50. This and the following paragraphs are drawn from many sources, but I have relied heavily on a sympathetic account in Nguyen Vy 1970, 101–4.

51. Ibid., 101.

52. Pham The Ngu 1965, 425; Le Thi Que 1976, 12.

53. Ho Tai Hue Tam 1987, 74.

54. *Trang An*, March 13, 1935; quoted in Thanh Lang 1967, 633.

55. *Tao Dan*, no. 3 (April 1939); quoted in Thanh Lang 1967, 684–85.

56. *Mores*, October 20, 1932.

57. Berger and Luckman 1966, 22–23.

Chapter 4

1. Nhat Thinh 1971, 110–21, 135.

2. Fall 1967a, 97–98; Chen 1969, 46; Hammer 1966, 92–93.

3. Fall 1967a, 96–98; Fall 1967b, 76–81; Chen 1969, 26–30, 34–35; Lacouture 1968, 62–65, 69–70.

4. Vo Nguyen Giap 1980, 258–59; Davidson 1988, 7–8; Marr 1981, 327–29.

5. Chen 1969, 37–38, 45–48; Hammer 1966, 84.

6. Nhat Thinh 1971, 135–36. Writing under his pen name, Nhat Linh, Tam later wrote a fictional account of this experience, a trilogy entitled *Along the Thanh Thuy River* (Giong Song Thanh Thuy), published in Saigon in 1960–61.

7. Marr 1981, 415.

8. Fall 1967a, 98; Fall 1967b, 81–82; Chen 1969, 48–52; Lacouture 1968, 74–77; Marr 1981, 12, 183; Patti 1980, 132, 524–25.

9. Chen 1969, 55–67; Nhat Thinh 1971, 136; Hammer 1966, 96; Lacouture 1968, 78–84.

10. Chen 1969, 74–76; Truong Buu Lam 1973, 252–55, 258–59; Nhat Thinh 1971, 139; Lancaster 1961, 113–15.

11. Nhat Thinh 1971, 135–36; Truong Buu Lam 1973, 254–55.

12. Chen 1969, 68–70; Fall 1968a, 100; Hammer 1966, 96–97; Pike 1966, 26–27.

13. Chen 1969, 71–74, 77–85.

14. Chen 1969, 74–77, 85–89; Lacouture 1968, 88–90; Patti 1980, 56; Marr 1981, 246–47; Davidson 1988, 7–8.

15. Chen 1969, 93–97; Fall 1967a, 100; Patti 1980, 52–58.

16. Lacouture 1968, 88, 90; Patti 1980, 124–29.

17. Pham The Ngu 1965, 611–12.

18. Truong Buu Lam 1973, 247–48; Fall 1967a, 48–49; Lancaster 1961, 98–101; Pham The Ngu 1965, 611.

19. Pham The Ngu 1965, 632–35, 648–52.

20. This paragraph and those immediately following are based mainly on Tu Son 1988.

21. Hoai Thanh and Hoai Chan 1988, 52–54.

22. Pham The Ngu 1965, 610–14.

23. Bui Diem 1987, 17.

24. Ibid., 20–21.

25. Huynh Kim Khanh 1986, 273–74.

26. To Hoai 1978, 181–319; To Hoai 1990, 92–97, 222–23.

27. Huynh Kim Khanh 1986, 274.

28. Chen 1969, 99; Fall 1967a, 55–59; Lancaster 1961, 105–6; Buttinger 1967, vol. 1, 278–84.

29. Vu Ngu Chieu 1986; Huynh Kim Khanh 1971; Huynh Kim Khanh 1986, 294–302; Fall 1967a, 60–61; Chen 1969, 99–100; Lancaster 1961, 107–8; Hammer 1966, 99.

30. Nhat Thinh 1971, 140.

31. Chen 1969, 96, 100–1, 105; Lancaster 1961, 88.

32. Buttinger 1967, vol. 1, 581–82; Lancaster 1961, 108.

33. Patti 1980, 49–58, 104–15, 126, 490, 492; Fall 1967a, 67–68; Lacouture 1968, 95–99; Nhat Thinh 1971, 141.

34. Nhat Thinh 1971, 141.

35. Patti 1980, 58, 124–29, 134–36, 199–203; Fall 1967a, 61, 63, 66; Chen 1969, 102–9.

36. Patti 1980, 134–36; Huynh Kim Khanh 1986, 315–18.

37. Patti 1980, 141–46; Fall 1967a, 64–68, 70; Chen 1969, 106–10, 116; Lacouture 1968, 101–3.

38. Patti 1980, 141–57, 205–10; Fall 1967a, 68; Chen 1969, 110; Nhat Thinh 1971, 141; Buttinger 1967, vol. 1, 339–41.

39. Chen 1969, 110–11; Kim Nhat 1972, 14–15.

40. Nhat Thinh 1971, 141–42; Patti 1980, 234–36; Fall 1967a, 63–64; Chen 1969, 110–11.

41. Patti 1980, 248–55; Chen 1969, 111–13, 356; Lacouture 1968, 104–5, 107, 110–12; Lancaster 1961, 120.

42. Patti 1980, 64–65, 86, 101, 124, 129, 131–32, 268; Chen 1969, 97, 107–8; Fall 1967a, 56, 59, 68–69; Lacouture 1968, 95, 115, 267; Buttinger 1967, vol. 1, 340–44; Fall 1967b, 83; Harrison 1982, 91.

43. Chen 1969, 111–12; Kim Nhat 1972, 15.

44. Fall 1967a, 69; Fall 1967b, 135; Chen 1969, 90, 102, 105, 108; Lacouture 1968, 270–71; Lancaster 1961, 125.

45. Hammer 1966, 130, 137; Lancaster 1961, 127–28; Buttinger 1967, vol. 1, 349–53.

46. Hammer 1966, 106–8, 116; Lancaster 1961, 117–18, 129; Fall 1967a, 64–65.

47. Hammer 1966, 108–9, 115–17; Patti 1980, 309.

48. Patti 1980, 318–20; Lancaster 1961, 129–31; Hammer 1966,

113–19; Fall 1967, 71; Buttinger 1967, vol. 1, 319–23, 330–35.

49. Patti 1980, 322–25; Hammer 1966, 120–21; Lancaster 1961, 133–34; Buttinger 1967, vol. 1, 334–37.

50. Chen 1969, 123–29; Nhat Thinh 1971, 142.

51. Nhat Thinh 1971, 142; Lancaster 1961, 127; Buttinger 1967, vol. 1, 360–61; Chen 1969, 129–30.

52. Chen 1969, 140–43; Lancaster 1961, 127, 144–45; Buttinger 1967, vol. 1, 364–69; Hammer 1966, 151–53.

53. Buttinger 1967, vol. 1, 368–69; Fall 1967a, 72–73; Lancaster 1961, 146–47; Chen 1969, 143–45.

54. Nhat Thinh 1971, 143–44.

55. Hammer 1966, 150–51; Fall 1967a, 131.

56. Lancaster 1961, 154–55; Hammer 1966, 159–62; Buttinger 1967, vol. 1, 386–87; Nhat Thinh 1971, 145.

57. Lancaster 1961, 155–62; Hammer 1966, 165–72; Fall 1967a, 72–74; Buttinger 1967, vol. 1, 388–93.

58. Hammer 1966, 172–74; Lancaster 1961, 162–63; Fall 1967a, 74; Chen 1969, 150.

59. Hammer 1966, 176; Chen 1969, 151–52; Buttinger 1967, vol. 1, 401–3, 649–50; Lancaster 1961, 166–67; Fall 1967a, 130.

60. Buttinger 1967, vol. 1, 400–401, 648; Chen 1969, 151; Lancaster 1961, 165; Hammer 1966, 175.

61. Fall 1967a, 131; Chen 1969, 156–57; Hammer 1966, 178–81; Buttinger 1967, vol. 1, 405, 650.

62. Fall 1967a, 75–76; Buttinger 1967, vol. 1, 424–29, 657–58; Hammer 1966, 182–84; Chen 1969, 158.

63. The details of what actually happened in these few fateful days, marked by much intrigue and confusion on all sides, remain murky and surrounded by controversy. See Tonnesson 1988; Fall 1967a, 76; Fall 1967b, 86; Hammer 1966, 187–88.

64. Nguyen Vy 1970, 107.

65. Nguyen Tan Long and Nguyen Huu Trong 1968, vol. 1, 199–200.

66. Kim Nhat 1972, 93–94.

67. Ibid., 145–46, 215.

68. Tu Son 1988, 377.

69. Huynh Kim Khanh 1986, 276, 288–89, 302, 328–33.

70. Buttinger 1967, vol. 2, 690–97; Hammer 1966, 149, 175, 207–10; Lancaster 1961, 146, 149, 175, 179–82; Fall 1967a, 208–9.

71. Hammer 1966, 210–11; Fall 1967a, 210; Buttinger 1967, vol. 2, 703–7, 1020, 1241.

72. Hammer 1966, 206–7, 210; Fall 1967b, 88; Buttinger 1967, vol. 2, 690, 693.

73. Nhat Thinh 1971, 148, 150.

74. Ibid., 149–53.
75. Truong Chinh 1977, 296.
76. Ibid., 285.
77. Fall 1967a, 210.
78. Ibid., 204, 212, 216–23.
79. Ibid., 241–44; Hammer 1988, 51–54; Harrison 1982, 208–9.
80. See especially Turner 1969, from which much of this brief discussion has been abstracted. See also Ashley 1990, for extensions of this dimension of Turner's thought and for the discussion of Turner's career and publications by Frank Manning, from which I borrowed the felicitous phrase "intense, effervescent camaraderie."
81. Personal interviews; Buttinger 1967, vol. 2, 1021–22.
82. Field notes 1963; Lancaster 1961, 136–37, 182–83; Buttinger 1967, vol. 1, 252–55, 652; Hammer 1988, 66.
83. Lancaster 1961, 137, 183; Buttinger 1967, vol. 1, 255–57, 653.
84. Buttinger 1967, vol. 1, 410–11; Hammer 1988, 67–68, 78–79, 130–31.
85. Quoted in Fall 1967a, 134.
86. Quoted in Nguyen Khac Vien 1974, 48.
87. Vu Bang 1970, 48–49; Nhat Thinh 1971, 37–38.
88. Fall 1967a, 101; Hammer 1988, 66–67; Buttinger 1967, vol. 1, 407–12.
89. Fall 1967a, 216–20; Hammer 1966, 287–88.
90. Buttinger 1967, vol. 2, 731–33.
91. Hammer 1966, 248–50; Buttinger 1967, vol. 1, 400–401; vol. 2, 773–75; Fall 1967a, 179–80.
92. Hammer 1966, 250–51; Buttinger 1967, vol. 1, 230.
93. Fall 1967a, 179; Marr 1981, 415–17; Harrison 1982, 146–47.
94. Field notes; Buttinger 1967, vol. 2, 769.
95. This and the following songs were collected and transcribed by me in 1964.
96. Chen 1969, 60, 84–85, 229–48.
97. Ibid., 258–59; Fall 1967b, 54.
98. Kim Nhat 1972, 90–91, 98.
99. Ibid., 94–95.
100. Fall 1967a, 111; Davidson 1988, 83–92.
101. Fall 1967a, 122–25; Fall 1967b, 136–37; Chen 1969, 235, 237, 274–78.
102. Chen 1969, 297, 300, 304; Fall 1967b, 138; Lancaster 1961, 284–85, 294–97.
103. Chen 1969, 295–97; Fall 1967a, 127.
104. This song and the following one are from field notes (see n. 94).

105. Lancaster 1961, 333–36; Chen 1969, 309–19; Hammer 1966, 328–37; Fall 1967a, 231–33; Harrison 1982, 125–29; Lewy 1978, 9.

106. Lancaster 1961, 422; Buttinger 1967, vol. 2, 727–31.

107. Buttinger 1967, vol. 2, 730–35, 1034; Lancaster 1961, 430–31.

108. This and the following paragraph are from Toan Anh 1972, 85.

109. Fall 1967a, 244; Fall 1967b, 145; Hammer 1988, 57–58, 93–95; Lewy 1978, 7–10.

110. Pike 1966, 52–53; Buttinger 1967, vol. 2, 899–900, 1116–18.

Chapter 5

1. Fall 1967a, 235–38; Pike 1966, 58; Buttinger 1967, vol. 2, 858; Hammer 1988, 47–49.

2. Fall 1967a, 101, 237; Lacouture 1966, 19.

3. Le Thi Que 1976, 3.

4. Fall 1967a, 96, 157.

5. Field notes; Fall 1967a, 263–67.

6. Charlton and Moncrieff 1978, 42–47, 55–56; Fall 1967a, 245–46; Hammer 1988, 54–57, 67–75. The extent to which Greene had Lansdale in mind is debatable, but many readers certainly interpreted the book that way.

7. Spector 1983, 312–13; Karnow 1983, 237–39; Lewy 1980, 15–16; Hammer 1988, 98–99; Harrison 1982, 217–30. For a disillusioned noncommunist insider's perspective, see Truong Nhu Tang 1986, especially 68–69.

8. Field notes 1963, 1964; Spector 1983, 313–14; Karnow 1983, 223; Fall 1967a, 284; Fall 1967b, 104; Lacouture 1966, 53; Harrison 1982, 224; Truong Nhu Tang 1986, 64; Ho Tai Hue Tam 1985, 37–38.

9. This statement probably expresses a minority viewpoint. Many writers (e.g., Sansom 1970, Paige 1975) emphasize economic factors in the genesis of the insurgency. I believe they somewhat overestimate the extent and degree of economic problems and underestimate the impact of skilled Communist cadre, the extent of participation by disillusioned sect members, and the persistent influence of Vietminh networks from the 1945–1954 War of Resistance. Ideology, broadly conceived, and beliefs (some true, some false, and many exaggerated) about the extent to which American involvement constituted a continuation of French colonialism (i.e., perceived domination by foreigners) played a much larger role than most writers realize.

10. Fall 1967a, 243, 258–59; Lacouture 1966, 53; Nhat Thinh 1971, 190.

11. Nhat Thinh 1971, 192.

12. Ibid., 156–58.

13. Ibid., 156, 185, 207.

14. Ibid., 186–89, 194–95; field notes, 1963; Hammer 1988, 76–77.

15. Spector 1983, 329–43, 366–67; Harrison 1982, 225–26; Hammer 1988, 76.

16. These events, especially the causes and the meaning of Buddhist protests and the extent to which these activist urban monks represented something that might be called the "Buddhist majority," have been poorly understood and often presented in misleading terms. Catholics and anticommunists were indeed overrepresented in key posts, both military and civilian, but there was little if any persecution of anyone simply because they were Buddhist, and the majority of Vietnamese labeled as "Buddhists" did not identify themselves with these early acts of protest. There was no "supervillage" of mainstream Buddhism. See Hammer 1988, 111–19, 134–53 for a well-informed account sympathetic to the government. For versions by prominent members of the group of young anti-Diem journalists who played an important role in these events, see Browne 1968, 261–68; Halberstam 1989, 207–33; Sheehan 1988, 134–36. For a sound overview of the religious context in which these events took place, see Rambo 1982.

17. Nhat Thinh 1971, 186–89, 194–95, 207–9.

18. Ibid., 196; field notes 1963. For a different perspective on Tam's suicide, see Hammer 1988, 154–55.

19. Nhat Thinh 1971, 201, 203, 206, 210–15.

20. Ibid., 215–16.

21. Ibid., 216–17.

22. Ibid., 217–18.

23. Sheehan 1988, 354–56; Hammer 1988, 157–68.

24. Hammer 1988, 177–300.

25. Harrison 1982, 226–28; Lewy 1980, pp. 39–40.

26. Tran Tuan Kiet 1968, 864–65.

27. Nguyen Dinh Tuyen 1967, 297–98.

28. Ibid., 342–44.

29. Ibid., 340.

30. Ibid., 208–10.

31. Ibid., 243–44.

32. Tran Tuan Kiet 1968, 922.

33. Uyen Thao 1969, 482–83.

34. Tran Tuan Kiet 1968, 1000–1001.
35. Uyen Thao 1969, 510–11.
36. Tran Tuan Kiet 1968, 920.
37. Ibid., 961–62.
38. Cao The Dung 1969, 267.
39. This and the following songs were collected by me in 1964.
40. *Literary Selections (Giai Pham)*, September 1956; Hoang Van Chi 1958, 75.
41. Boudarel 1990, 171–72.
42. *Literary Selections*, September 1956; Hoang Van Chi 1958, 79.
43. Tran Tuan Kiet 1968, 659; Hoang Van Chi 1959, 105–8. For a full translation, see Nguyen Ngoc Bich 1975, 187–89.
44. Hoang Van Chi 1959, 115.
45. Tran Tuan Kiet 1968, 683–84; Hoang Van Chi 1959, 121.
46. Hoang Van Chi 1959, 24.
47. Ibid., 73–75.
48. Tran Tuan Kiet 1968, 22.
49. Hoang Van Chi 1964, 198.
50. Fall 1967a, 155–58; Buttinger 1967, vol. 2, 911–16, 964–65, 1123–24, 1159; Harrison 1982, 147–51.
51. Fall 1967a, 190.
52. Xuan Dieu 1958, 60.
53. Editeurs Français Réunis 1969, 135–36.
54. *Arts and Letters (Van Nghe)*, no. 9 (March 1958), p. 79.
55. *Arts and Letters*, no. 10 (March 1959): 77–78.
56. *Arts and Letters*, no. 12, 59.
57. *Literary Selections*, September 1956; Hoang Van Chi 1958, 77.
58. *Arts and Letters*, no. 12: 98–99.
59. *Arts and Letters*, no. 15: 7–8.
60. *Arts and Letters*, no. 18: 35–39.
61. *Arts and Letters*, no. 23: 21.
62. Fall 1967a, 184–85, 312–14.
63. Editeurs Français Réunis 1969, introduction.
64. *Arts and Letters*, no. 48: 67.
65. Ibid., 65.
66. Editeurs Français Réunis 1969.
67. Ibid., 88–93.
68. Kim Nhat 1972, 35, 37, 153.
69. *Come to the Fields, Buffalo*, 1958, 91–92.
70. Pham Duy 1968, 71–71.
71. Ibid., 91–92.
72. Field notes, 1967, 1969. Circulation figures are notoriously unreliable, for a variety of reasons, but this figure is based on numerous interviews and some cross-checking. The figures on

newspaper exposure are fairly reliable for the Mekong delta in the period 1967–69.

73. Editeurs Français Réunis 1969, 18; field notes, 1967.

74. Shaplen 1970, 433; Fall 1967b, 174, 181, 186, 399; Davidson 1988, 294, 301, 395, 426; Lewy 1980, 84, 455.

75. Field notes 1967, 1968, 1969, 1970; media estimates from JUSPAO, Saigon, 1970.

76. *Vietnam Statistical Yearbook 1971*, 313–19.

77. Fall 1967b, 175.

78. Hearing before United States Subcommittee on Refugees and Escapees, April 21, 1971, 1–18.

79. Field notes 1967, 1969; Rambo and Jamieson 1973, 39–49; Sternin et al., 1972, 76–77; Parsons et al. 1972, 71–72.

80. Rambo and Jamieson 1973, 39–44; Sternin et al. 1972, 70.

Chapter 6

1. *Vietnam Statistical Yearbook 1971*, 346–47, 353, 368.

2. Ibid., 102–7.

3. Browne 1968, 286–87, 295; Just 1968, 137–38; Rambo and Jamieson 1973, 57.

4. Le Thi Que 1976, 98.

5. See Just 1968, 67.

6. Mus 1964, xxi.

7. Ibid., xix.

8. See Eastman 1967, 19, on this phenomenon in China.

9. *Van Hoc*, no. 79 (February 1968): 70–72.

10. Shaplen 1970, 416–18; Fitzgerald 1972, 234–35; Lewy 1978, 274–75; Rambo and Jamieson 1973, 3; Braestrup 1978, 201–17.

11. Nha Ca 1969, 11–12.

12. *The Masses (Quan Chung)*, no. 16 (August 5, 1969).

13. Ta Ty 1970, 71.

14. See *Le Monde, Selection Hebdomadaire*, May 1970, 14–20, quoted in Fitzgerald 1972, 515, 624.

15. See Opinion Research Corporation, 1967.

16. Ton That Thien 1965, 600; Fishel 1968, 679–80.

17. Ton That Thien 1966, 345, 348, quoted in Fishel 1968, 677–78.

18. See Shaplen 1970, 423–24.

19. *Vietnam Statistical Yearbook 1971*, 387.

20. Toan Anh 1968, 71–72.

21. This excerpt and those in the following several pages are taken from a more detailed account in Murphy et al. 1974, chapter 9.

22. See, for example, Charlton and Moncrieff 1978, 216.

23. Cao The Dung 1969, 306–9.

24. Davidson 1988, 746.

25. Richard Nixon had visited both Moscow and Peking in 1972. The Communists in Hanoi felt "betrayed," but so did the anticommunists in the south when the "peace" accords were signed.

26. Davidson 1988, 736–37; Lewy 1978, 202–22.

27. Nguyen Tien Hung and J. Schecter 1989, 1–4, 240, 327, 363–437, 449–51.

28. Troute 1975.

Chapter 7

1. Davidson 1988, 627, 650; Williams et al., 1989, 300–302; Duiker 1985, 8.

2. Truong Nhu Tang 1986, 142, 191–92; Harrison 1982, 276–77; Davidson 1988, 609–11.

3. Davidson 1988, 590–91.

4. Truong Nhu Tang 1986, pp. 329–35.

5. See, for example, Truong Nhu Tang 1986, 146–47.

6. *Vietnam*, no. 143 (August 1969): 19. See also Truong Nhu Tang 1986, 146–47.

7. Truong Nhu Tang 1986, 329–35.

8. Davidson 1988, 787–91.

9. Truong Nhu Tang 1986, 264–65.

10. Read Truong Nhu Tang for a vivid account of this. See also Duiker 1985, 8.

11. Truong Nhu Tang 1986, 284–85, 68–69.

12. Ibid., 285.

13. The following account relies heavily on interviews and discussions with refugees, supplemented by many journalistic accounts and a few talks with Communist officials.

14. Tran Trong Dang Dan 1990, 618–72; Duiker 1985, 23–24.

15. Duiker 1985, 10.

16. Tran Da Tu 1990, 67–72.

17. Ibid., 45.

18. I had friends who spent years in these camps and subsequently escaped the country. I have spent many hours discussing the camps with them. Much has also been written about the camps by former inmates. See, for example, Huynh Sanh Thong, ed., 1988; Tran Tri Vu 1988; Tran Da Tu 1990; Doan Van Toai and D. Chanoff 1986.

19. Che Viet Tan 1977.

20. Broadcast from Hanoi, May 16, 1977; quoted in Hickey 1982, 287.

21. Brown 1989, 112–14; Greene 1989, 99.

22. See Hickey 1981, 139; Duiker 1985, 36–38.

23. See Chanda 1986, 240–47; Duiker 1985, 43–47, 49, for more detail on this complex phenomenon.

24. Vo Nhan Tri 1990, 21.

25. See Rambo 1973.

26. Hickey 1981, 9; Elliott 1985, 117.

27. See Rambo and Jamieson 1973, 60–62, for some documentation and discussion of this minority viewpoint. Most scholars and officials, American and Vietnamese, Communist and anticommunist, seem to have believed otherwise.

28. Field notes 1967, 1969, 1970, 1972. On the spontaneous diffusion and benefits of the water pump, see Sansom 1970, 164–79.

29. Rambo and Jamieson 1973, 73.

30. See Vickerman 1986, 2–11, for a discussion of the history of debates over these points by Communist theoreticians.

31. Vo Nhan Tri 1990, 77–81; Duiker 1985, 40–42.

32. On this conflict, see Chanda 1986. On a per capita basis, Vietnamese casualties in Cambodia were ultimately five times larger than those suffered by United States forces in Vietnam (Cima 1989, 68).

33. *Tao Te Ching*, chapter 23.

34. Ibid., chapter 5.

35. Vo Nhan Tri 1990, 105–6, 160–62, 178, 226–31.

36. Nguyen Chi Thien 1983, 151. See also Nguyen Chi Thien 1985; Nguyen Ngoc Bich 1989a, 167–97; Honolulu *Star Bulletin*, August 5, 1985, B1.

37. Nguyen Ngoc Bich 1989b, 7.

38. Ibid., 12–13.

Glossary

bac   Father's older brother; a form of address indicating great respect.

chi   Perseverance or willpower.

de   The proper relationship between brothers. *De* served as a model for all social roles: superiors to be treated as "older brothers," inferiors as "younger brothers," and so forth.

dieu   "Reasonable" in the sense of being moderate, of not being excessive. This word is used in compounds that refer to mixing colors, to harmonizing in music, to reconciling diverse opinions. *Dieu* always refers to interaction and dictates a willingness to adapt or modify one's position or actions to fit a concrete situation, to moderate one's stance in the interest of social harmony. *Dieu* serves as a counterbalance to the rigidity of *ly*, "the nature of things," which holds that there is one right answer, one right way of doing things, with harmony resulting from conformity to what was "right." The two form an example of the interplay of *yin* and *yang*; they are apparently contradictory, but complementary.

dinh   In each village the *dinh* was at once ritual center and town hall, where ritual life revolved around veneration of the guardian spirit of the village. The cult of the guardian spirit provided a focal point for village identity. The *dinh* was also a place for feasting, for public and private worship,

397

and for all public ceremonies, both secular and sacred.

dung   Courage.

giap   A common kind of mutual aid organization, organized on the basis of a lineage or a surname, membership in the same neighborhood or hamlet, worship of a particular spirit, or any other common bond.

hieu   Filial piety; *hieu* required children to obey, respect, and honor their parents, as a means of satisfying *on*, a moral debt.

le   Propriety.

le khao vong   "Celebration offerings," the name given to the feasts required of village members who had achieved an elevation of status. The higher the elevation, the more costly the feast was required to be, even to the point of hosting a party for the entire village membership at one's own expense.

ly   "The nature of things." Rationality, reason, consisted of conformity to the structural principles that governed the universe. *Ly* was an overarching principle, based on observation and experience, intended to provide harmony in the system by specifying the proper form of all relationships. The concept of *ly* rationalized and legitimated the hierarchical order of society and of nations, making hierarchy itself part of the intrinsic structure of the universe, a state of affairs that was both "natural" and unalterable.

nghia   Righteousness. *Nghia* implies duty, justice, and obligation; it demands calm rationality within the structure of *ly*, scrupulously living by an unbending set of rules. The concept was based entirely on behavior in key social roles, dictating, for example, how a son should behave to a father, younger brother to older brother, subject to king, and so on. It ignored relationships and behaviors that did not pertain to strategic social roles.

nhan   Benevolence, compassion, humaneness, love for one's fellow human beings; Confucian counterbalance to *nghia*.

nom   "Southern" writing; demotic script for transcribing vernacular Vietnamese. Flourished from the fifteenth to the nineteenth century and was replaced by *quoc ngu* early in the twentieth century.

on
: The moral debt incurred by children through their parents' giving them life. This debt was considered so immense as to be unpayable and was the basis for *hieu*, the filial piety owed to parents.

quoc ngu
: "National" writing; a romanized alphabet for phonetic transcription of Vietnamese.

ruoc dau
: A term used to refer to the ritualized transfer of the bride from her natal home to the household of the groom. *Ruoc* means "to welcome," "to greet," or "to escort." *Dau* has the double meaning of "bride" and "daughter-in-law."

Tao
: "The Way," the structure of reality. The *I Ching* says that "the alternating movements of the *yin* and the *yang* form what is called the Tao. The outcome of this process is beneficent. Its culmination constitutes the inherent characteristic of the world."

Tet
: The lunar new year, and the quintessential celebration of the family as a living entity. Tet for the Vietnamese was Christmas, Easter, New Year's Eve, Thanksgiving, and the Fourth of July all rolled into one celebration. Celebrating Tet with one's family was an essential part of what it meant to be Vietnamese, to be a complete human being.

tin
: Truthfulness.

tinh
: Used to refer to "love," but also used to signify passion, sentimentality, desire, or emotionalism—what might be called dictates of the heart.

tri
: Wisdom or learning.

trung
: Loyalty; an extension of *hieu* (filial piety) to the relationship of a subject to his lord.

truyen
: "Novel in verse," a distinctly Vietnamese literary form that flourished from the mid-eighteenth to the mid-nineteenth century.

yang and yin
: Two primordial forces from which everything else in the universe was created. Underlying the *I Ching* and the *Tao Te Ching*, the *yin-yang* concept is one of the oldest and most fundamental elements of Sinitic influence on Vietnam and became

a basic part of the way all Vietnamese viewed the world. *Yin* and *yang* elements tend to be functionally complementary based on their logical opposition. They not only coexist; they interlock. Their joint functioning forms a single, irreducible system, and one cannot exist without the other. When *yang* becomes unduly powerful, a *yin* reaction is provoked, and vice versa. In this work *yin* and *yang* are used as metaphors, with contrasts extended into domains and sometimes described in vocabularies that were not part of the traditional concept. *Yang* and *yin* characteristics can be viewed in pairs, as follows, with the *yang* characteristic preceding the slash and its contradictory but complementary *yin* characteristic following.

In general: predominantly male/more female; Sinitic in origin/indigenous; legal in basis/customary in basis; orthodox/heterodox; formal/informal; autocratic/consensual; culturally prescribed/culturally optional; rigid/flexible; active/passive, reactive; complex/simple; highly organized/loosely linked; prestigious/survival-subsistence oriented; more rational/more emotional; highly disciplined/succoring; nominally dominant/nominally subordinate; high degree of internal consistency/less internal consistency; tightly bounded (closed)/loosely bounded (open).

In relationships: role-based (part person)/spontaneous (whole person); highly differentiated, outward-looking/less differentiated; competitive, hierarchical/cooperative, egalitarian.

In social system—maintaining processes: highly centralizing/localizing; high ratio of positive (confirming or self-amplifying) feedback circuits/preponderance of negative (critical or error-correcting) feedback circuits; escalating/moderating; generates asymmetrical reciprocity/generates symmetrical reciprocity; low level of entropy/high level of entropy; high redundancy/low redundancy; centripetal force in society/often and in general centrifugal force in society.

Bibliography

Ashley, Kathleen M., ed. 1990. *Victor Turner and the Construction of Cultural Criticism*. Bloomington: University of Indiana Press.

Baritz, Loren. 1985. *Backfire*. New York: Ballantine.

Bateson, Gregory. 1972. *Steps to an Ecology of Mind*. New York: Ballantine.

———. 1980. *Mind and Nature: A Necessary Unity*. New York: Bantam Books.

Bateson, Gregory, and Mary Catherine Bateson. 1988. *Angels Fear: Towards an Epistemology of the Sacred*. New York: Bantam.

Berger, Peter L., and Thomas Luckman. 1966. *The Social Construction of Reality*. Garden City, N.Y.: Doubleday.

Bertalanffy, Ludwig von. 1968. *General Systems Theory*. New York: Braziller.

Bodde, Derk. 1967. "Harmony and Conflict in Chinese Philosophy." In *Studies in Chinese Thought*, ed. Arthur F. Wright, 19–80. Chicago: University of Chicago Press, Phoenix ed.

Boudarel, Georges. 1990. "Intellectual Dissidence in the 1950s: The Nhan Van-Giai Pham Affair." *Vietnam Forum* 13:154–174.

Braestrup, Peter. 1978. *Big Story*. Garden City, N.Y.: Doubleday.

Brown, Frederick Z. 1989. *Second Chance: The United States and Indochina in the 1990s*. New York: Council on Foreign Relations Press.

Browne, Malcolm. 1968. *The New Face of War*. Rev. ed. Indianapolis: Bobbs Merrill.

Buckley, Walter. 1967. *Sociology and Modern Systems Theory*. Englewood Cliffs, N.J.: Prentice-Hall.

Bui Diem, with David Chanoff. 1987. *In the Jaws of History*. Boston: Houghton Mifflin.

Bui Huu Khanh. 1973. "Tu con duong di tim chan ly cuu nuoc cua Ho Chu tich den viec thanh lap Dang cua giai cap cong nhan Viet-nam" ("Ho Chi Minh: From the National Salvation Path to the Founding of a Proletarian Party"), *Nghien Cuu Lich Su* (Historical Studies) 149:22–30 (March–April).

Buttinger, Joseph. 1961. *The Smaller Dragon: A Political History of Vietnam.* New York: Praeger.

———. 1967. *Vietnam: A Dragon Embattled.* 2 vols. New York: Praeger.

Cao The Dung. 1969. *Van Hoc Hien Dai: Thi Ca va Thi Nhan* (Contemporary Literature: Poetry and Poets). Saigon: Quan Chung.

Cao Thi Nhu Quynh and John C. Schafer. 1988a. "From Verse Narrative to Novel: The Development of Prose Fiction in Vietnam." *Journal of Asian Studies* 47(4): 756–77 (November).

———. 1988b. "Ho Bieu Chanh and the Early Development of the Vietnamese Novel." *Vietnam Forum* 12:100–11 (Summer-Fall).

Chaliand, Gerard. 1969. *The Peasants of North Vietnam.* Baltimore: Penguin.

Chambers, Robert. 1986. "Normal Professionalism, New Paradigms, and Development." Discussion Paper 227, Institute of Development Studies, University of Sussex, Brighton, England.

Chanda, Nayan. 1986. *Brother Enemy: The War After the War.* New York: Harcourt Brace Jovanovich.

Charlton, Michael, and Anthony Moncrieff. 1978. *Many Reasons Why: The American Involvement in Vietnam.* New York: Hill and Wang.

Che Viet Tan. 1977. "Why Vietnam Is Moving People Around." *Asiaweek,* June 17, 28–29.

Chen, King C. 1969. *Vietnam and China, 1938–1954.* Princeton: Princeton University Press.

Ch'u Chai, ed. 1969. *I Ching: Book of Changes.* New York: Bantam Books.

Cima, Ronald J. 1989. "Vietnam in 1988: The Brink of Renewal." *Asian Survey* 29(1): 64–72.

Come to the Fields, Buffalo. 1958. Hanoi: Foreign Languages Publishing House.

Coughlin, Richard J. 1950. *The Position of Women in Vietnam.* New Haven: Southeast Asia Studies, Yale University.

Coulet, Georges. 1929? *Cultes et Religions de l'Indochine Annamite.* Saigon: Impr. Commerciale C. Ardin.

Dao Duy Anh. 1951. *Viet Nam Van Hoa So Cuong* (An Outline of Vietnamese Culture). Hanoi: Bon Phuong. Originally published 1938.

Davidson, Jeremy H.C.S. 1975. "Recent Archeological Activity in Viet-Nam." *Journal of the Hong Kong Archeological Society* 6:80–99.

Davidson, Phillip P. 1988. *Vietnam at War: The History 1946–1975.* Novato, Calif.: Presidio Press.

Deutsch, Karl W. 1966. *The Nerves of Government: Models of Political Communication and Control.* New York: Macmillan. Free Press paperback edition with new introduction by author.

Dewey, John. 1962. *Individualism Old and New.* New York: Capricorn Books. First published 1929.

Doan Quoc Sy and Viet Tu. 1959. *Khao Luan Ve Tran Te Xuong* (A Discussion of Tran Te Xuong). Saigon: Hong Ha.

Doan Van Toai and David Chanoff. 1986. *The Vietnamese Gulag.* New York: Simon and Schuster.

Duiker, William J. 1976. *The Rise of Nationalism in Vietnam: 1900–41.* Ithaca, N.Y.: Cornell University Press.

————. 1983. *Vietnam: Nation in Revolution*. Boulder, Colo.: Westview Press.

————. 1985. *Vietnam Since the Fall of Saigon*. Rev. ed. Athens, Ohio: Ohio University Center for International Studies, Southeast Asia Series, no. 56.

Duong Quang Ham. 1968. *Viet-Nam van-Hoc Su Yeu* (An Outline History of Vietnamese Literature). Saigon: Bo Giao Duc, Trung Tam Hoc Lieu. Originally published 1941.

Durand, Maurice. 1959. *Technique et Panthéon des Médiums Vietnamiens (Dong)*. Paris: Publications de l'Ecole Française d'Extrême Orient, vol. 45.

Eastman, Lloyd E. 1967. *Throne and Mandarins: China's Search for a Policy During the Sino-French Controversy, 1880–1885*. Cambridge, Mass.: Harvard University Press.

Editeurs Français Réunis. 1969. *Anthologie de la Poésie Vietnamienne*. Paris: Editeurs Français Réunis.

Elliott, David W.P. 1985. "Waiting for the East Wind: Revolution and Social Change in Modern Vietnam." In *Vietnam: Essays on History, Culture, and Society*, 100–23. New York: Asia Society.

Fairbank, John K., Edwin O. Reischauer, and Albert M. Craig. 1965. *East Asia: The Modern Transformation*. Boston: Houghton Mifflin.

Fall, Bernard B. 1967a. *The Two Vietnams: A Political and Military Analysis*. 2nd rev. ed. New York: Doubleday.

————. 1967b. *Last Reflections on a War*. Garden City, N.Y.: Doubleday.

Fall, Bernard B., ed. 1967. *Ho Chi Minh on Revolution: Selected Writings, 1920–1966*. New York: Praeger.

Fishel, Wesley, ed. 1968. *Vietnam: Anatomy of a Conflict*. Itasca, Ill.: F.E. Peacock.

Fitzgerald, Frances. 1972. *Fire in the Lake: The Vietnamese and the Americans in Vietnam*. Boston: Little, Brown.

Frederick, W.H. 1973. "Alexander Varenne and Politics in Indochina, 1925–1926." In *Aspects of Vietnamese History*, ed. Walter F. Vella, 96–159. Honolulu: University Press of Hawaii.

Giles, Herbert A., ed. 1963. *San Tzu Ching*. 2d ed., rev. New York: Frederick Ungar.

Gourou, Pierre. 1955. *Peasants of the Tonkin Delta: A Study of Human Geography*. Translation of *Les Paysans du delta Tonkinois: Etude de geographique humaine*, Paris, 1936. New Haven: Human Relations Area Files.

————. 1975. *Man and Land in the Far East*. New York: Longman.

Greene, Fred. 1989. "The United States and Asia in 1988." *Asian Survey* 29(1): 89–100.

Haines, David W. 1984. "Reflections of Kinship and Society under Vietnam's Le Dynasty." *Journal of Southeast Asian Studies* 15(2): 307–14.

————. 1986. "Vietnamese Kinship, Gender Roles, and Societal Diversity: Some Lessons from Survey Research on Refugees." *Vietnam Forum* 8:204–17.

Halberstam, David. 1989. *The Making of a Quagmire*. New York: Ballantine. Originally published 1965.

Hall, D. G. E. 1964. *A History of South-East Asia*. 2nd ed. New York: Macmillan. 3d ed., 1968, New York: St. Martin's Press.

Hammer, Ellen J. 1966. *The Struggle for Indochina, 1940–1955*. Stanford: Stanford University Press.

———. 1988. *A Death in November*. New York: Oxford University Press.

Harrison, James Pinkney. 1982. *The Endless War: Vietnam's Struggle for Independence*. New York: McGraw-Hill Paperbacks.

Hendry, James B. 1964. *The Small World of Khanh Hau*. Chicago: Aldine.

Hickey, Gerald C. 1964. *Village in Vietnam*. New Haven: Yale University Press.

———. 1981. "Socialist Republic of Vietnam." *Encyclopaedia Brittanica*, Fifteenth Edition.

———. 1982. *Free In the Forest: Ethnohistory of the Vietnamese Central Highlands, 1954–1976*. New Haven: Yale University Press.

———. 1988. *Kingdom in the Morning Mist*. Philadelphia: University of Pennsylvania Press.

Ho Tai Hue Tam. 1985. "Religion in Vietnam: A World of Gods and Spirits." In *Vietnam: Essays on History, Culture, and Society*. New York: Asia Society.

———. 1987. "Literature for the People: From Soviet Policies to Vietnamese Polemics." In Truong Buu Lam, ed., *Borrowings and Adaptations in Vietnamese Culture*, pp. 63–83. Honolulu: University of Hawaii Press.

Hoai Thanh and Hoai Chan, eds. 1988. *Thi Nhan Viet Nam, 1932–1941* (Vietnamese Poets, 1932–1941). Hanoi: Nha Xuat Ban Van Hoc. Originally published 1942.

Hoang Ngoc Thanh. 1968. "The Social and Political Development of Vietnam as Seen Through the Modern Novel." Ph.D. diss., University of Hawaii.

———. 1973. "Quoc Ngu and the Development of Modern Vietnamese Literature." In *Aspects of Vietnamese History*, ed. Walter Vella, 191–236. Honolulu: University Press of Hawaii.

Hoang Van Chi, ed. 1958. *The New Class in North Vietnam*. Saigon: Cong Dan.

———. 1959. *Tram Hoa Dua No Tren Dat Bac* (A Hundred Flowers Bloom on Northern Soil). Saigon: Mat Tran Bao Ve Tu Do Van Hoa.

———. 1964. *From Colonialism to Communism: A Case History of North Vietnam*. New York: Praeger.

Huynh Kim Khanh. 1971. "The August Revolution Reinterpreted." *Journal of Asian Studies* 30(4): 761–82.

———. 1986. *Vietnamese Communism, 1925–1945*. Ithaca, N.Y.: Cornell University Press.

Huynh Sanh Thong, ed. 1973. *The Tale of Kieu*. New York: Random House.

———. 1979. *The Heritage of Vietnamese Poetry*. New Haven: Yale University Press.

———. 1988. *To Be Made Over: Tales of Socialist Reeducation in Vietnam*. New Haven: Yale Center for International and Area Studies Council on Southeast Asia Studies, The Lac Viet Series, no. 5.

Huynh Van Tong. 1973. *Lich Su Bao Chi Viet Nam* (The History of Vietnamese Newspapers). Saigon: Tri Dang.

Hy Van Luong. 1984. "'Brother' and 'Uncle': Rules, Structural Contradiction, and Meaning in Vietnamese Kinship." *American Anthropologist* 86:290–315, 705.

———. 1989. "Vietnamese Kinship: Structural Principles and the Socialist Transformation in Northern Vietnam." *Journal of Asian Studies* 48(4): 741–56.

Isoart, Paul. 1961. *Le Phénomène National Vietnamien, de l'Indépendance Unitaire à l'Indépendance Fractionnée.* Paris: Librairie Général de Droit et de Jurisprudence.

Jackson, H. Merrill. 1987. "Vietnamese Social Relationships: Hierarchy, Structure, Intimacy and Equality." *Interculture* 20(1) (Issue 94): 2–17.

Jamieson, Neil L. 1981a. "Vietnam: A Study of Continuity and Change in a Sociocultural System." Ph.D. diss., Honolulu: University of Hawaii.

———. 1981b. "Saigon (Ho Chi Minh City)," *Encyclopaedia Brittanica*, Fifteenth Edition.

———. 1981c. "A Perspective on Vietnamese Prehistory Based on the Relationship between Geological and Archeological Data: Summary of an Article by Nguyen Duc Tam." *Asian Perspectives* 24(2).

———. 1984. "Toward a Paradigm for Paradox: Observations on the Study of Social Organization in Southeast Asia." *Journal of Southeast Asian Studies* 15(2), September.

———. 1985. "The Traditional Vietnamese Village." *Interculture* 83, April–June.

———. 1986a. "The Traditional Family in Vietnam." *Vietnam Forum*, no. 8, Summer-Fall.

———. 1986b. "The Traditional Vietnamese Village." *Vietnam Forum*, no. 7, Winter-Spring.

———. 1987. "Relata, Relationships, and Context: A Perspective on Borrowed Elements in Vietnamese Culture." In *Borrowings and Adaptations in Vietnamese Culture*, ed. Truong Buu Lam. Honolulu: University of Hawaii Center for Asian and Pacific Studies. Southeast Asia Paper no. 25.

Just, Ward. 1968. *To What End: Report from Vietnam.* Boston: Houghton Mifflin.

Karnow, Stanley. 1983. *Vietnam: A History.* New York: Viking.

Kim Nhat. 1972. *Nhung Nha Van Tien Chien Hanoi Hom Nay* (Pre-War Hanoi Literary Figures Today). Saigon: Hoa Dang.

Kuhn, Thomas S. 1962. *The Structure of Scientific Revolutions.* Chicago: University of Chicago Press.

———. 1977. *The Essential Tension: Selected Studies in Scientific Tradition and Change.* Chicago: University of Chicago Press.

Lacouture, Jean. 1966. *Vietnam: Between Two Truces.* New York: Random House.

———. 1968. *Ho Chi Minh: A Political Biography.* New York: Random House.

Lancaster, Donald. 1961. *The Emancipation of French Indochina*. London: Oxford University Press.

Laszlo, Ervin. 1972. *The Systems View of the World: The Natural Philosophy of the New Developments in the Sciences*. New York: Braziller.

Le Thi Que. 1976. "Changing Structure of the Vietnamese Family from 1925 to 1975." Unpublished manuscript. Honolulu: Population Institute, East-West Center.

———. 1986. "The Vietnamese Family Yesterday and Today." *Interculture* 92 (Summer/July 1986): 1–38.

Legge, James, trans. 1969. *I Ching: Book of Changes*. New York: Bantam.

Leichty, Mary M. 1963. "Family Attitudes and Self-Concept in Vietnamese and United States Children." *American Journal of Orthopsychiatry* 33(1).

Lesser, Stephen O. 1986. "Images of the Vietnamese in American War Fiction." *Vietnam Forum* 7 (Winter-Spring): 202–23.

Lewy, Guenter. 1980. *America in Vietnam*. New York: Oxford University Press. First published 1978.

McAlister, John T., and Paul Mus. 1970. *The Vietnamese and Their Revolution*. New York: Harper and Row.

Marr, David G. 1971. *Vietnamese Anti-Colonialism: 1885–1925*. Berkeley: University of California Press.

———. 1981. *Vietnamese Tradition on Trial, 1920–1945*. Berkeley: University of California Press.

Masaya, Shiraishi. 1988. "Phan Boi Chau in Japan." In *Phan Boi Chau and the Dong-Du Movement*, ed. Vinh Sinh, 52–100.

Murphy, Jane, G.D. Murfin, N.L. Jamieson, A.T. Rambo, J.A. Glenn, L.P. Jones, and A.H. Leighton. 1974. *The Effects of Herbicides in South Vietnam; Part B: Working Paper, "Beliefs, Attitudes, and Behavior of Lowland Vietnamese."* Washington: National Academy of Sciences.

Mus, Paul. 1949. "The Role of the Village in Vietnamese Politics." *Pacific Affairs* 22:265–72.

———. 1952. *Vietnam, Sociologie d'une Guerre*. Paris: Editions du Seuil.

———. 1964. "Foreword," in G. Hickey, *Village in Vietnam*, xi–xxiii.

Ngo Duc Thinh. 1989. "Truyen Thong An Vong Viet Nam Voi Duong Sinh Va Tri Benh" (Traditional Vietnamese Eating Habits in Terms of Nutrition and Medication). In *Phong Vi Viet Nam* (Vietnamese Customary Tastes), ed. Dinh Gia Khanh, 181–85. Hanoi: Cong Ty Xuat Ban Doi Nguoi. Originally published in Tap Chi Van Hoa Dan Giau, no. 4, 1986, Hanoi.

Nguyen Chi Thien. 1983. "Flowers From Hell (Hoa Dia-Nguc): Forty-four Quatrains." Translations by Huynh Sanh Thong. *Vietnam Forum* 2:141–53.

———. 1985. *Flowers From Hell* (Hoa Dia-Nguc), trans. Huynh Sanh Thong. New Haven: Yale Center for International and Area Studies, Council on Southeast Asia Studies.

Nguyen Cong Hoan. 1963. *Impasse (Buoc Duong Cung)*. Hanoi: Foreign Languages Publishing House. Originally published 1939.

———. 1967a. *La Ngoc Canh Vang* (Golden Branches, Leaves of Jade). Saigon: Thieu Quang. Originally published 1934.

———. 1967b. *Co Giao Minh* (Miss Minh, The Schoolteacher). Saigon: Hop Luc. Originally published 1936.

Nguyen Dinh Tuyen. 1967. *Ngung Nha Tho Hom Nay* (Contemporary Poets). Saigon: Nha Van Viet Nam.

Nguyen Du. 1973. *The Tale of Kieu* (Truyen Kieu, early-nineteenth-century masterpiece of Vietnamese literature, translated and annotated by Huynh Sanh Thong, including essay "The Historical Background," by Alexander Woodside). New York: Random House, Vintage Books.

Nguyen Duy Dien. n.d. *Luan De Ve Tu Luc Van Doan* 3rd rev. ed. Saigon: Thang Long.

Nguyen Duy Dien and Bang Phong. 1960. *Luan De Ve Tran Te Xuong.* (A Study of Tran Te Xuong). Saigon: Khai Tri.

Nguyen Hien Le. 1968. *Dong Kinh Nghia Thuc* (Tonkin Free School). Saigon: La Boi.

Nguyen Huyen Anh. 1967. *Viet Nam Danh Nhan Tu Dien* (A Dictionary of Famous Vietnamese). Saigon: Khai Tri.

Nguyen Khac Kham. 1967. *An Introduction to Vietnamese Culture.* Saigon: Vietnam Council on Foreign Relations.

———. 1983. "Vietnamese Spirit Mediumship: A Tentative Reinterpretation of Its Basic Terminology." *Vietnam Forum*, no. 1:24–30.

Nguyen Khac Vien. 1974. *Tradition and Revolution in Vietnam.* Berkeley, Calif.: Indochina Resource Center.

———. (n.d.) *Traditional Vietnam: Some Historical Stages.* Vietnamese Studies [series]. Hanoi.

Nguyen Ngoc Bich, ed. 1975. *A Thousand Years of Vietnamese Poetry.* New York: Alfred A. Knopf.

———. 1985. "Vietnamese Poetry: The Classical Tradition." In *Vietnam: Essays on History, Culture, and Society*, 79–99. Asia Society.

———. 1989a. *War and Exile: A Vietnamese Anthology.* Springfield, Va.: Vietnamese PEN Abroad, East Coast U.S.A.

———. 1989b. "Socialist Literature in Reforming Vietnam." Paper presented at the 1989 Annual Meeting of the Association for Asian Studies, Washington, D.C.

Nguyen Tan Long and Nguyen Huu Trong, eds. 1968. *Viet-Nam Thi Nhan Tien Chien, Quyen Thuong* (Pre-war Vietnamese Poets, vol. 1). Saigon: Song Moi.

———. 1968. *Viet-Nam Thi Nhan Tien Chien, Quyen Trung* (Pre-War Vietnamese Poets, vol. 2). Saigon: Song Moi.

Nguyen The Anh. 1970. *Viet-Nam Duoi Thoi Phap Do-Ho* (Vietnam Under French Colonialism). Saigon: Lua Thieng.

Nguyen Tien Hung and Jerrold L. Schecter. 1989. *The Palace File: Vietnam Secret Documents.* New York: Harper and Row, Perennial Library.

Nguyen Tu Chi. n.d. "The Traditional Vietnamese Village in Bac Bo: Its Organizational Structure and Problems." In *The Traditional Vietnamese Village, Part 1.* Hanoi: *Vietnamese Studies*, no. 61.

Nguyen Vy. 1970. *Van Thi Si Tien Chien* (Pre-War Writers and Poets). Saigon: Khai Tri.

Nha Ca. 1969. *Giai Khan So Cho Hue* (Put on the Mourning Cloth for Hue). Saigon: Thuong Yeu.

Nhat Linh (Nguyen Tuong Tam). 1969. *Doan Tuyet* (Breaking the Ties). Saigon: Ngay Nay. Originally published 1935.

Nhat Thinh. 1971. *Chan Dung Nhat Linh* (A Biography of Nhat Linh [Nguyen Tuong Tam]). Saigon: Song Moi.

Opinion Research Corporation. 1967. *The People of South Vietnam: How They Feel About the War.* Princeton, N.J.: Opinion Research Corporation.

Osborne, Milton. 1969. *The French Presence in Cochinchina and Cambodia: Rule and Response (1859–1905).* Ithaca, N.Y.: Cornell University Press.

———. 1973. "The Faithful Few: The Politics of Collaboration in Cochinchina in the 1920s." In *Aspects of Vietnamese History,* ed. Walter Vella. Honolulu: University Press of Hawaii.

———. 1984. "History of Vietnam." *Encyclopaedia Britannica,* Fifteenth Edition, vol. 19, 120–31.

Paige, Jeffery M. 1975. *Agrarian Revolution.* New York: Free Press.

Parsons, John S., Dale K. Brown, and Nancy R. Kingsbury. 1972. *Americans and Vietnamese: A Comparison of Values in Two Cultures.* Arlington, Virginia: Advanced Research Projects Agency.

Patti, Archimedes. 1980. *Why Vietnam: Prelude to America's Albatross.* Berkeley: University of California Press.

Pham Duc Duong. 1982. "The Origin of Wet Rice Socio-Cultural Model of the Viets Through Linguistic Data." In *Environment and Human Life: Studies on History and Culture of Southeast Asia.* Hanoi: Department of Southeast Asian Studies, Social Sciences Committee of Vietnam.

Pham Duy. 1968. *Dan Ca Viet Nam, Vietnamese Folksongs* (in Vietnamese and English, English version by Steve Addiss). Saigon: Khai Tri.

Pham The Ngu. 1965. *Viet Nam Van Hoc Su Gian Uoc Tan Bien: Tap III, Van Hoc Hien Dai: 1862–1945* (A New Outline History of Vietnamese Literature: Contemporary Literature: 1862–1945). Saigon: Anh Phuong.

———. 1966. *Kim Van Tan Tuyen* (A New Selection of Modern Literature). Saigon: Anh Phuong.

Pham Van Dieu. 1960a. *Van Hoc Viet-Nam* (Vietnamese Literature). Saigon: Tan Viet.

———. 1960b. *Viet Nam Van Hoc Giang Binh* (Vietnamese Literature Explicated). Saigon: Tan Viet.

Pham Van Son. 1961. *Viet Su Tan Bien, Tap IV: Tu Tay Son Mat Diep Den Nguyen So* (A New History of Vietnam, Vol. IV: From the Late Tay Son to the Early Nguyen). Saigon: Pham Van Son.

———. 1962. *Viet Su Tan Bien, Tap V: Viet-Nam Khang Phap Su* (A New History of Vietnamese Resistance to the French). Saigon: Pham Van Son.

———. 1963. *Viet Su Tan Bien, Tap VI: Viet Nam Cach Mang Can Su, 1885–1914* (A New History of Vietnam, Vol. VI: The Recent History of Revolution in Vietnam, 1885–1914). Saigon: Khai Tri.

Phan Ke Binh. 1970. *Viet-Nam Phong Tuc* (Vietnamese Customs). Saigon: Phong Trao Van Hoa.

Phan Khoi. 1956. "Ong Binh Voi" (Mr. Limepot). In *Tram Hoa Dua No Tren Dat Bac,* ed. Hoang Van Chi (1959), 73–75.

Pike, Douglas. 1966. *Viet Cong: The Organization and Techniques of the National Liberation Front of South Vietnam.* Cambridge, Mass.: M.I.T. Press.

Raffel, Burton, ed. 1968. *From the Vietnamese Ten Centuries of Poetry.* New York: October House.

Rambo, A. Terry. 1973. *A Comparison of Peasant Social Systems of Northern and Southern Vietnam.* Carbondale: Southern Illinois University Center for Vietnamese Studies.

———. 1977. "Closed Corporate and Open Peasant Communities: Reopening a Hastily Shut Case." *Comparative Studies in Society and History* 19(2): 79–188.

———. 1982. "Vietnam: Searching for Integration." Chapter 12 in *Religion and Societies: Asia and the Middle East,* ed. Carlo Caldarola, 407–44. Berlin: Mouton.

———. 1987. "Black Flight Suits and White Ao-Dais: Borrowing and Adaptation of Symbols of Vietnamese Cultural Identity." In *Borrowings and Adaptations in Vietnamese Culture,* ed. Truong Buu Lam. Honolulu: University of Hawaii Center for Asian and Pacific Studies Southeast Asia Paper no. 25.

Rambo, A. Terry, and Neil L. Jamieson III. 1973. "Cultural Change in Rural Vietnam." New York: Asia Society, SEADAG Papers on Asia.

Rappaport, Roy. 1979. *Ecology, Meaning, and Religion.* Berkeley, Calif.: North Atlantic Books.

Robequaine, Charles. 1944. *The Economic Development of French Indochina.* London: Oxford University Press.

Salleh, Muhammad Haji. 1977. *Tradition and Change in Contemporary Malay-Indonesian Poetry.* Kuala Lumpur: Penerbit Universiti Kebangsaan Malaysia.

Sansom, Robert L. 1970. *The Economics of Insurgency in the Mekong Delta of Vietnam.* Cambridge, Mass.: M.I.T. Press.

Schafer, John C. 1972. "Thi Ca Doi Voi Nguoi Viet va Nguoi My" (Poetry in Regard to Vietnamese and Americans). *Dac San Van Khoa* 1972–1973, 109–113, Hue, Vien Dai Hoc Hue.

Shaplen, Robert. 1970. "The Challenge Ahead." *Columbia Journalism Review,* Winter 1970–71, 40–46.

Sheehan, Neil. 1988. *A Bright Shining Lie: John Paul Vann and America in Vietnam.* New York: Random House.

Simon, Pierre J., and Ida Simon-Barouh. 1973. *Hau Bong: Un Culte Vietnamien de Possession Transplante en France.* Paris: Mouton.

Smith, R.B. 1973. "The Cycle of Confucianism in Vietnam." In *Aspects of Vietnamese History,* ed. Walter Vella. Honolulu: University Press of Hawaii.

Spector, Ronald H. 1983. *United States Army in Vietnam. Advice and Support: The Early Years: 1941–1960.* Washington, D.C. Center of Military History, United States Army.

Steinberg, David Joel, ed. 1971. *In Search of Southeast Asia: A Modern History.* Kuala Lumpur: Oxford University Press.

———. 1987. *In Search of Southeast Asia: A Modern History,* rev. ed. Honolulu: University of Hawaii Press.

Sternin, M., R.J. Teare, and P.G. Nordlie. 1972. "A Study of Values, Communication Patterns, and Demography of Rural South Vietnamese." Arlington, Va.: Advanced Research Projects Agency.

Ta Ty. 1970. *Muoi Khuon Mat Van Nghe Hom Nay* (Ten Faces of Contemporary Literature). Saigon: La Boi.

Ta Van Tai. 1982. "Vietnam's Code of the Le Dynasty (1428–1788), *American Journal of Comparative Law* 30, no. 3 (Summer): 523–54. Reprint issued as Studies in East Asian Law, Vietnam: no. 2, Harvard Law School.

———. 1988. *The Vietnamese Tradition of Human Rights*. Berkeley: Institute of East Asian Studies, University of California. Indochina Research Monograph.

Taylor, Keith. 1983. *The Birth of Vietnam*. Berkeley: University of California Press.

———. 1988. "Authority and Legitimacy in Eleventh-Century Vietnam," *Vietnam Forum* 12:20–59. Originally published in *Southeast Asia in the 9th to 14th Centuries*, ed. David G. Marr and A.C. Milner.

Thanh Lang. 1967. *Bang Luoc Do Van Hoc Viet Nam. 3 Quyen* (An Overview of Vietnamese Literature. 3 vols.). Saigon: Trinh Bay.

Thompson, Virginia. 1937. *French Indochina*. London: Allen and Unwin.

To Hoai. 1978. *Tu Truyen* (Memoirs). Hanoi: Van Hoc.

———. 1990. *Chuyen Cu Hanoi* (Old Tales of Hanoi). Hanoi: Thong Tin.

Toan Anh. 1967. *Nep Cu: Tin Nguong Viet-Nam* (Old Ways: Vietnamese Beliefs). Saigon: Nam-Chi Tung Thu.

———. 1968. *Nep Cu: Lang Xom Viet-Nam* (Old Ways: The Vietnamese Village). Saigon: Nam Chi Tung Thu.

———. 1969. *Phong-Tuc Viet-Nam: Tu Ban Than Den Gia-Dinh* (Vietnamese Customs from the Individual to the Family). Saigon: Khai Tri.

———. 1970. *Nep Cu Con Nguoi Viet-Nam: Phong Tuc Co Truyen* (Old Ways of the Vietnamese: Ancient Customs). Saigon: Khai Tri.

———. 1972. "Hoanh, Truong" (Banners and Scrolls). *Dac San Van Khoa*, 1972–73, 81–87. Hue: Vien Dai Hoc Hue.

Toan Anh and Cuu Long Giang. 1969. *Mien Bac Khai Nguyen* (An Era in the Northern Region). Saigon: Tien Bo.

Ton That Thien. 1965. "Psychological Block." *Far Eastern Economic Review*, September 30. Quoted in Fishel, ed. (1968), 679–80.

———. 1966. "In Love and War." *Far Eastern Economic Review*, August 25. Quoted in Fishel, ed. (1968), 677–78.

Tonnesson, Stein. 1988. "A French Decision for War: French and Vietnamese Decision-Making before the Outbreak of War in Indochina, December 1946." *Vietnam Forum* 12:112–35.

Tran Da Tu. 1990. *Writers and Artists in Vietnamese Gulags*. Elkhart, Ind.: Century Publishing House.

Tran My Van. 1976. "Responses of Late Nineteenth Century Vietnamese Writers to the French Colonial Impact." Ph.D. diss., Australian National University.

Tran Tri Vu. 1988. *Lost Years: My 1,632 Days in Vietnamese Reeducation Camps*. Berkeley: Institute of East Asian studies, University of California.

Tran Trong Dang Dan. 1990. *Van Hoa, Van Nghe Phuc Vu Chu Nghia Thuc Dan Moi My Tai Nam Viet Nam, 1954–1975* (Culture and Literature in the Service of American Neo-imperialism in South Vietnam, 1954–1975). Long An, Vietnam: Nha Xuat Ban Thong Tin-Nha Xuat Ban Long An.

Tran Trong Kim. 1929–30. *Nho Giao* (Confucianism). 2 vols. Saigon: Tan Viet.

———. 1964. *Viet Nam Su Luoc* (An Outline History of Vietnam). Saigon: Tan Viet. First published 1920.

Tran Tuan Kiet. 1968. *Thi Ca Viet-Nam Hien Dai* (Contemporary Vietnamese Poetry). Saigon: Khai Tri.

Tran Van Giau. 1973. "Chu Nghia Dan Toc Cach Mang o Viet-Nam Va Su Bien Chuyen Cua No Trong Giai Doan Lich Su Giua Hai Cuoc Chien Tranh The Gidi" (Revolutionary Nationalism and Its Evolution between the Two World Wars). Hanoi: NCLS 151:6–26.

Troute, Dennis. 1975. "Last Days in Saigon." *Harper's*, July 1975.

Truong Buu Lam. 1967. "Patterns of Vietnamese Response to Foreign Intervention: 1858–1900." New Haven: Southeast Asian Studies, Yale University.

———. 1973. "Japan and the Disruption of the Vietnamese Nationalist Movement." In *Aspects of Vietnamese History*, ed. Walter Vella, 237–69. Honolulu: University Press of Hawaii.

Truong Buu Lam, ed. 1987. *Borrowings and Adaptations in Vietnamese Culture*. Honolulu: Southeast Asian Studies, Center for Asian and Pacific Studies. University of Hawaii at Manoa. Southeast Asia Paper no. 25.

Truong Chinh. 1977. *Selected Writings*. Hanoi: Foreign Languages Publishing House.

Truong Nhu Tang. 1986. *A Viet Cong Memoir: An Inside Account of the Vietnam War and Its Aftermath*. New York: Random House, Vintage.

Truong Vinh Ky. 1962. *Chuyen Doi Xua* (Tales from Long Ago). Saigon: Khai Tri. Originally published 1866.

Tu Son. 1988. "Loi Cuoi Sach" (Afterward). In *Thi Nhan Viet Nam, 1932–1941*, ed. Hoai Thanh and Hoai Chan, 377–99.

Turner, Victor. 1969. *The Ritual Process: Structure and Anti-Structure*. Chicago: Aldine.

———. 1974. *Dramas, Fields, and Metaphors*. Ithaca: Cornell University Press.

Uyen Thao. 1969. *Tho Viet Hien Dai* (Contemporary Vietnamese Poetry). Saigon: Hong Linh.

Vella, Walter, ed. 1973. *Aspects of Vietnamese History*. Honolulu: University Press of Hawaii.

Vickerman, Andrew. 1986. *The Fate of the Peasantry*. New Haven: Monograph Series Number 28, Yale University Southeast Asia Studies, Yale Center for International and Area Studies.

Vinh Sinh, ed. 1988a. *Phan Boi Chau and the Dong-Du Movement*. New Haven: Council on Southeast Asia Studies, the Lac-Viet Series, no. 8, Yale Center for International And Area Studies; co-published with the William Joiner Center, University of Massachusetts, Boston.

———. 1988b. "Phan Boi Chau and Fukusawa Yukichi: Perceptions of National Independence." In Vinh Sinh, ed., 1988a, 101–49.

Vo Nguyen Giap. 1980. "President Ho Chi Minh, Father of the Vietnam Revolutionary Army." In *Uncle Ho*. Hanoi: Foreign Languages Publishing House.

Vo Nhan Tri. 1990. *Vietnam's Economic Policy Since 1975*. Singapore: Institute of Southeast Asian Studies.

Vu Bang. 1970. "Nguyen Tuong Tam: Mot Nha Van Da Bat Man Hoai" (Nguyen Tuong Tam: A Very Dissatisfied Writer). *Van* 156 (June 15): 41–55.

Vu Duc Bang. 1973. "The Tonkin Free School Movement: 1907–1908." In *Aspects of Vietnamese History*, ed. Walter Vella, 30–95.

Vu Ngu Chieu. 1986. "The Other Side of the 1945 Vietnamese Revolution: The Empire of Viet Nam (March–August 1945)." *Journal of Asian Studies* 45(2): 293–328.

Vuong G. Thuy. 1976. *Getting to Know the Vietnamese and Their Culture*. New York: Unger.

Whitmore, John K. 1985. *Vietnam, Ho Quy Ly, and the Ming (1371–1421)*. New Haven: Yale Center for International and Area Studies, Council on Southeast Asia Studies, The Lac-Viet Series, no. 2.

———. 1986. "An Outline of Vietnamese History Before French Conquest." *Vietnam Forum* 8 (Summer-Fall): 1–9.

———. 1987. "Foreign Influences and the Vietnamese Cultural Core: A Discussion of the Premodern Period." In *Borrowings and Adaptations in Vietnamese Culture*, ed. Truong Buu Lam, 1–21.

Wilhelm, Hellmut. 1973. *Eight Lectures on the I Ching*. Princeton: Princeton University Press.

Williams, W.A., T. MCormick, L. Gardner, and W. LaFeber, eds. 1989. *America In Vietnam: A Documentary History*. New York: W.W. Norton.

Woodside, Alexander. 1971. *Vietnam and the Chinese Model: A Comparative Study of Nguyen and Ching Civil Government in the First Half of the Nineteenth Century*. Cambridge, Mass.: Harvard University Press.

———. 1973. "The Historical Background." In *The Tale of Kieu*, ed. Huynh Sanh Thong.

———. 1976. *Community and Revolution in Vietnam*. Boston: Houghton Mifflin.

Xuan Dieu. 1958. "Mot So Van De Dau Tranh Tu Tuong Trong Tho" (Some Issues of Struggle Regarding Thought in Poetry), *Van Nghe* 10:68–70.

Xuan Dieu, ed. 1970. *Tho Van Tran Te Xuong* (The Poetry of Tran Te Xuong). Hanoi: Van Hoc.

Xuan Dieu, ed. 1971. *Tho Van Nguyen Khuyen* (The Poetry of Nguyen Khuyen). Hanoi: Van Hoc.

Index

Compositor: Asco Trade Typesetting Ltd.
Text: 10/13 Palatino
Display: Palatino
Printer and Binder: Maple-Vail Book Manufacturing Group